The Psychology of Socialism

The Psychology of Socialism

Gustave Le Bon

With a New Introduction by
John L. Stanley

Transaction Books
New Brunswick (U.S.A.) and London (U.K.)

Library of Congress Catalog Number: 81-1973
ISBN: 0-87855-321-5 (cloth), 0-87855-703-2 (paper)
Printed in the United States of America

Library of Congress Cataloging in Publication Data

Le Bon, Gustave, 1841-1931.
  The psychology of socialism.

  (Social science classics series)
  Translation of: Psychōlogie du socialisme.
  Reprint. Originally published: New York: Macmillan, 1899.
Includes bibliographical references.
  1. Socialism. I. Title. II. Series.
HX266.L5   1981   335′.0019   81-1973
ISBN 0-87855-321-5

Introduction to the Transaction Edition

John L. Stanley

In many respects, the writings of Gustave Le Bon reflect the major political concerns and intellectual strategies of our times. The fundamental concern of the man who has been labeled the "father of social psychology" centers on the rise of what is popularly called "mass society." By this term is meant the dissolution in modernity of those traditions and habits that bind the individual to his community and the concurrent development of a highly volatile population devoid of the social roots, usages, and constraints that are essential to civilized man. It is in Le Bon's writings that we find a foreboding of the "era of crowds," of the epoch in which demagogues manipulate vast assemblies of fanatics imbued with jealousy, fear, and rage while introducing a force for vast social leveling, economic chaos, and wars inspired by ideological zealotry.

It is apparent from any perusal of his writing that Le Bon is hardly content merely to record the development of mass society, nor indeed does it appear that he is simply a detached scientist attempting to trace the causes of crowd behavior. On the contrary, it is obvious from the early chapters of *The Psychology of Socialism* that we are dealing with a highly committed writer who has set himself the task of showing that, for the immediate future, socialism is potentially the most dangerous of the modern ideologies. In Le Bon's view, it is socialism—with its religious frenzy, its jealousy of privilege, its pillaging of others' wealth, its flaunting of the natural laws of competition—that constitutes the greatest immediate danger for modern European civilization.

On the other hand, there is a pervasive mood in Le Bon's work to the effect that because certain cultures of modern Europe—especially Latin cultures—have reached such an advanced stage of decline, modern socialism will only be encouraged. The very failure of traditional Mediterranean societies to adapt to the exigencies of modern industrial life has served to foster socialist ideas. Le Bon is convinced that the conservatism of the old norms is almost as damaging to society as the extremism of the new ideologies because intransigence and stagnation beget violence and fanaticism. In his various works on social questions, Le Bon is attempting to develop a formula that balances social cohesion with social progress. His purpose is to express the nature of the "social cement" essential to civilized existence, while at the same time avoiding the hideous consequences of mass society and encouraging individual freedom and creativity.

Le Bon gives the impression at times that he is willing to sacrifice community for the sake of freedom; indeed, he embraces the radical liberalism characteristic of the English and American social Darwinists. For this reason alone, *The Psychology of Socialism* is an invaluable document because it touches on some of the central questions of this radical liberal tradition that today we would call "libertarianism": How does one distinguish between natural laws of competition and those which man has wrought? At what point does an alliance of the strong become a defense force for the weak? Does the principle of individual liberty so utterly shatter the ancient ties binding men in their community that it renders a population more vulnerable to the mass ideologies that run counter to liberty? Finally, how compatible are the optimistic and progressive views contained in Le Bon's individualist liberalism with his pessimistic science of social psychology which views most men as being hostile to individualism?

I

Le Bon published *The Psychology of Socialism* in 1899, a period of crisis in France. The Third Republic, founded in the aftermath of the Franco-Prussian war and the Paris Commune, was a grand compromise among many political traditions including liberalism, radicalism, and, due to a series of bizarre accidents, royalism. The consensus of liberal philosophy that Le Bon admired in the Anglo-Saxon countries was absent from the French scene. Though the republic had survived successfully the Panama affair and the aborted Bonapartist coup of 1888 led by General Boulanger, the Dreyfus affair succeeded, as no previous event in the republic had done, in opening the sores of social divisiveness—by recalling the recurrent political squabbles that had given France three republics, two empires, two monarchies, and three revolutions since 1789. When Le Bon was writing this book, the lines of political cleavage between those who supported Dreyfus (an army captain wrongly convicted of espionage) and those who opposed him had not yet been clearly drawn, but already the affair was a symbol. In June 1899, on the eve of publication of *The Psychology of Socialism*, the socialist Millerand, who orchestrated a coalition of pro-Dreyfus factions, was invited into the new government of Premier Waldeck-Rousseau. Millerand was the first socialist of any consequence to participate in a government of the Third Republic. Waldeck-Rousseau's government was the most leftist since the Paris Commune and Georges Sorel dubbed it "the Dreyfus Revolution."

For Le Bon, as for Sorel, the change constituted a worsening of the political climate in France. It was a victory for the Jacobin tradition, which Le Bon hated. In Le Bon's view, it was a further threat to the preeminence of the individual that had somehow become lost in the French democratic tradition; the Jacobin ideas of revolution, of which socialism was a variant, emphasized equality rather than liberty, sovereignty rather than pluralism. It was Alexis de Tocqueville, in his *Democracy in America* and more specifically in *The Old Regime and the French Revolution*, who had called Le Bon's attention to the notion that the Jacobin thirst for equality and its passionate defense of social leveling over other values would lead to the isolation of the individual, a fragmentation of society, the utter dissolution of initiative and the deliverance of society to a species of Caesarism. Tocqueville opposed the French equalitarian idea with a liberalism that placed social pluralism and liberty above equality. The Jacobin and the liberal ideas constitute, for Le Bon and for Tocqueville, two contrary tendencies in the history of democratic thought. In Tocqueville's words:

> As long as the democratic revolution was glowing with heat, the men who were bent upon the destruction of the old aristocratic powers hostile to that revolution displayed a strong spirit of independence; but as the victory of the principle of equality became more complete, they gradually surrendered themselves to the propensities natural to that condition of equality, and they strengthened and centralized their governments. They had sought to be free in order to make themselves equal; but in proportion as equality was more established by the aid of freedom, freedom itself was thereby rendered more difficult of attainment.[1]

Le Bon harkened back to Tocqueville for an explanation as to why the Jacobin idea had superseded conservative liberalism in France—reducing the school of Montesquieu and Tocqueville to a relatively small (although influential) group of notables. As Le Bon notes, Tocqueville portrayed the latter days of the old regime as having been run by a powerful royal administration. It was Louis XIV, jealous of rivalry and anxious to enhance the royal power, who had by various stratagems seriously weakened the intermediate powers of the feudal order. In place of the rich hierarchy of classes, bishops, universities, and townships, there stood only the immense and tutelary figure of the royal power bolstered by a highly centralized bureaucracy. The French Revolution did not do away with all the institutions of the old regime. The centralized bureaucracy was strengthened by the revolution, and local powers were only further weakened. Thus Tocqueville (and Le Bon followed him on this question) regarded the revolution as a social movement that was actually commenced by the royal power itself and only accelerated by the political movements of the new republic. A certain continuity was present in the revolutionary current from the start: "Superficial minds may still imagine that the revolution effected a kind of renovation of our institutions," Le Bon says. "In reality, as Tocqueville long ago pointed out, all that it did was to dash violently to the ground those elements of the old society that were already worm-eaten."[2] Thus the work of the revolution was far less revolutionary than generally believed. "By exaggerating the absorption and centralization of the state it only continued the Latin tradition deeply rooted through centuries of monarchy and followed by all [French] governments alike."[3] The paradox of strong bureaucratic stability or continuity on the one hand and great political volatility on the other developed as a consequence of the mentality that emerged from this revolutionary continuity. "It might be said of the French," he says, "that they are at once the most revolutionary and the most conservative people in the world. Their most bloody revolutions have never had any other object than to rechristen the most superannuated institutions."[4]

Le Bon thought the volatility of the Latin political temperament was rooted in an extremism that compensated for the stagnation produced by Mediterranean social institutions. Besides bureaucracy, Latin countries possessed a strong continuity in everyday life rooted in peasant-patrist societies. The resultant *immobilisme* of political and industrial life produced great frustration and eventually violence. "The peoples whose mind is most fixed and established," he argued, "often effect the most violent revolutions. Not having succeeded in evolving progressively, in adapting themselves to changes of environment, they are forced to adapt themselves violently when such adaptation becomes indispensable."[5] In France, Le Bon saw the old habits survive not only the political turbulence of the nineteenth century but, most importantly, the industrial revolution that accompanied it. Indeed this continuity, as Le Bon recognized, was due in part to the relatively meager achievements of that very revolution in France:

the tremendous industrial progress that had already been accomplished in his day by England and Germany had not been equalled in his own country, which remained one of the most economically underdeveloped of the great Western European powers.

In Le Bon's view, the advance of socialism becomes a natural consequence, indeed the *reductio ad absurdum*, of the long historical sequence commenced two centuries before, which developed into the Latin cult of the state. As with previous upheavals, the revolutionary consequences of socialism will be more apparent than real. It should only further the decadent qualities of Latin culture that are already so pronounced, and these qualities are embedded in the deepest recesses of the Latin mind. Nevertheless, the most important shortcoming of socialist theory is that it ignores the psychological aspects of Latin society as well as of society in general. "To create a revolution is a simple matter," he says, "to change the soul of a people is difficult indeed."[6] Violent revolution has little effect on the great stability of what Le Bon calls alternatively "the ancestral soul," the "national mind," or simply "race." It is very important not to confuse national mind, Le Bon's idea of race, with Nazi-like racialist ideologies. Although Le Bon argues that the "influences of race are greater than those of the environment," for the most part he asserts that race and environment are not mutually exclusive phenomena; that the term "race" does not have any anthropological meaning; that there are a few pure races as such; that race itself is a product of environment; that indeed by the term is meant a group of people of often varying origins that "has been subjected for centuries to similar conditions of environment, similar ways of life, common institutions and beliefs, and an identical education." That is to say, for Le Bon "race" really means culture.

For Le Bon, the conservatism of this national mind—culture if you will—is the basis of man's resistance to change. Critics will no doubt take great pleasure in indicting Le Bon for conflating the specific characteristics of the Latin mind with what he perceives to be general qualities of human nature. As any reader of the *Communist Manifesto* can testify, it is not only liberals like Le Bon who used French politics as a model for generalizing on the tendencies of other societies. Le Bon, however, derived vastly different generalizations about society and human nature from his observations on French politics than Marx did. Marx used French society as a sort of laboratory to predict the new socialist era; Le Bon sees French society as a particularly egregious demonstration of the ultimately ephemeral nature of normal politics. Ultimately (and with numerous qualifications), Marx understood mass movements as epiphenomena of productive relations and he viewed man as a productive animal. Le Bon insisted on reducing social relations to psychological relations that ultimately look upon man as a conservative animal. Revolutions disaggregate the normally staid psychological relations of society, but these occurrences, which might turn peaceful magistrates into bloodthirsty fanatics, are but brief interstices in an overwhelmingly normal pattern of events. Men invariably return to their conventional instincts and "clamor for the restoration of the very idols which they broke."[7]

It was principally in his works entitled *Opinions and Beliefs* and *The Crowd* that Le Bon elaborated his social psychology. In order to understand better Le Bon's view of socialism, it might be well to discuss briefly the ideas these two volumes share with *The Psychology of Socialism*.

II

Le Bon believed that the great ideological movements of history were the results of psychological dislocations that are largely nonrational, and that mankind for the most part is far from being the rational creature depicted in radical democratic ideologies. Belief and opinion arise from a highly complex and yet partly unfathomable array of impulses and wants based ultimately on a combination of a desire for pleasure and the will to attain it. Change occurs when the will to fulfill a new pleasure overcomes the regulator of individual life based on habit.

Le Bon thus represents a psychological state as being placed in a kind of balance between habit and innovation. Innovation occurs when a change takes place in the equilibrium of one or another component of our psychology. These components of a psychological system are based on five kinds of what Le Bon calls "forms of logic," though his use of the term "logic" differs markedly from what is usually meant by that term. What we normally view as an intellectual faculty par excellence Le Bon sees as only one of a number of "logical" patterns. Thus *intellectual logic*, to use Le Bon's term, constitutes only a small part of the human psyche. This logic is not a product of nature but a creation of man against nature. The more "natural" kinds of thought exist in *biological logic*, the natural laws ruling all organic life, and in *affective logic*, the logic of emotions in which one "feels before knowing."[8] These last two forms of "logic" are found in all animals and, taken together, are roughly equivalent to what one would call "instinct."

Mystical logic, along with *intellectual logic*, is exclusive to humans. It is not unconscious as are affective and biological logic; it corresponds to the mentality of primitive man who believes in magical powers independent of rational action. It is the logic which depends on superior beings or forces whose capricious will affects all our acts. "Indifferent to all criticism, mysticism engenders an unbounded credulity in its adepts . . . . No absurdity is too much for it."[9] Rational logic is powerless against it. It is *mystical logic* on which most of our modern ideologies—including socialism and Jacobinism—are based, but this logic cannot by itself constitute the basis of a mass movement. Yet another "logic," *collective logic*, socializes beliefs, provides a sort of fourth dimension to our psychology and makes crowds unique. *Collective logic* makes *mystical logic* public and thus transforms the very nature of mysticism itself from a private to a public experience.

In ordinary parlance, the idea of a nonrational logic is a contradiction in terms. By the word *logic*, Le Bon appears simply to mean an ordering principle or system. However, he admits that the various mechanisms by which these systems operate are "very little known."[10] Since any system should rely on known patterns, Le Bon asserts that these systems of logic can be judged only by their results, that is by their observed consequences. It is thus analogous to the theory of electricity in the physical world.

Now according to Le Bon, human psychology consists in a wide variety of these five modes of "logic." An equilibrium is established among these "logics" and, depending on the circumstances, a person's mentality is dominated by one or another of the permutations. Every one of these diverse psychological types is found in all adult civilized people in one form or another. According to Le Bon, that is why a laboratory scientist can be a fanatical political and religious zealot. The scientist may obey the commands of intellectual logic, but the whole man may be governed by mystical or affective logic like anyone else. Indeed, in Le Bon's view, mystical and affective logic are often mistaken for intellect; what are often thought to be intellectual battles are usually battles between competing sentiments or among various nonintellectual forms of logic. Le Bon says that a disequilibrium in these forms of logic is seen as providing the moving forces for social change, and that a grave imbalance of these forces, in which one or another of the logical forms becomes radically distended, portends a "world in revolt," a period of great upheaval, after which the normal stabilizing tendencies of human psychology reassert themselves.

Since Le Bon relies only on outward manifestations of behavior in deriving his various "logics," the concept of "cause" does not play a prominent role in his theory. Indeed, Le Bon appears confusing about the causal nature of these psychological constructions in their historical role as well as in their internal mechanisms. Thus he argues that history moves through a reconstitution of the personality generated by an imbalance of these logical expressions, while at the same time he asserts that "under the influence of the environment the old personality may give place to an entirely new one." But the modified environment often includes "a time of insurrection."[11] Le Bon never directly addresses the question of whether the psychology or the environment comes first. Instead he maintains that the crucial question for a future social science consists in determining the nature of the balance of logical forces; "the need for controlling those sentiments harmful to society by means of other sentiments fixed by education, morality and by codes constitutes the fundamental principle of collective life."[12] It is the idea of keeping the various psychological components in reciprocal check that becomes one of the norms guiding Le Bon's investigations of socialism.

In Le Bon's view, two components of human psychology become particularly important in socialist movements: mystical logic and collective logic. It is in mystical logic that we find sown the seeds of religious belief as well as all those ideas that "without bearing the name of religion, assume the same form of thought as religion—notably certain political beliefs."[13] The purpose of the present volume is to show that socialism—by which Le Bon means possession of all industries by a state which would distribute the products equally among citizens—is one of those beliefs; that which is often portrayed as the highest, most reasonable, and most human ideal in the history of social thought is in fact a repetition of the same religious and political ideas that, moved by extreme fanaticism, have disrupted societies for centuries. The French Revolution, for example, did not produce a regime governed by the reasoned deliberation of "enlightened men" but by the zealotry of people who were convinced that nothing could deter them from their goal. Like the invading hoards of Islam, the revolutionaries believed that "all those who contradicted their faith were worthy of death."

For Le Bon, the new religion of socialism is the descendent of the Jacobin democratic "religion" and has nearly all the powers of the older belief. Both ideas share the same statism, the hatred of superiority, a general leveling tendency, and praise of conformity. Although he argues that socialism will eventually cleave from its parent democratic doctrine, its religiosity will give it much the same strength in the foreseeable future: "The Jacobin religion—above all in its socialist form—has all the power of the ancient faith over feeble minds. Blinded by their faith, [Jacobins] believe that reason is their guide, but are really actuated solely by their passions and their dreams."[14]

In *The Crowd*, Le Bon discusses the fifth and final form of psychology, collective logic. It is through collective logic that mystical logic is transmitted to an entire crowd—to a civilization—and thus collective logic shares the religiosity of mystical logic. Only when the "soul of the masses" is mobilized can the upheavals resulting from mystical logic make their imprint on the history of humanity. In Le Bon's view, a crowd is defined by the existence of a certain biochemistry. It is a "provisional being formed of heterogeneous elements, which for a moment are combined, exactly as the cells which constitute a living body form by their reunion a new being which displays characteristics very different from those possessed by each of the cells singly."[15]

Perhaps another comparison from physical science (although it was developed after the formulation of Le Bon's theory of the crowd) would be the concept of critical mass drawn from nuclear physics. Le Bon appears to argue that the immense—one might say explosive—power of mystical ideas is gained only when a certain mass is reached. An individual who is part of a crowd, that is of a sociological mass, acquires by various qualities, including sheer force of numbers, "a sentiment of invincible power allowing him to yield to instincts which, had he been alone, he would perforce have kept under restraint."[16] Mass psychology erases not only a sense of physical limit but moral limits as well. Men feel that nothing can frustrate their wishes, that everything is possible, that their cause is certain to triumph.

In Le Bon's understanding, crowd sentiment—that is, mass psychology—develops from repeated affirmation, repetition, and contagion. With a constant repetition of certain themes, a "current of opinion" is formed in which ideas, sentiments, emotions, and beliefs possess in crowds "a contagious power as intense as that of microbes." Le Bon derives this theory from the early studies of hypnotic suggestion done by A.A. Liebeault as well as from the anti-intellectualistic school of Theodule Ribot and Nordeau. Le Bon portrays mass belief as a state bordering on hypnosis exerted by a kind of osmotic pressure on the subject by the sheer mass of public opinion itself. The self-generating effect of such opinions shows no respect for class or race. Crowd psychology is found equally in legislatures, juries, and mobs—even among isolated individuals sharing the same opinion sources. By ascribing collective logic to a natural tendency to imitation, Le Bon verges on describing the trends of public opinion in terms of fads. From Le Bon's depiction of the adolescent character of crowds as well as from the omnipresence of collective logic in any gathering, including juries, it would appear that no reasonable democratic politics, no collective intelligence, no rational decision-making by groups is possible.

III

Le Bon's skepticism about rational politics produces an ambivalent—one might say a two-valued—orientation in *The Psychology of Socialism*. On the one hand, as Sorel later noted, Le Bon proposed a historical hypothesis that attributes a certain beneficial role to collective logic in the course of world developments. On the other hand, the predominant tendency in Le Bon's writings is to reveal the inadequacies of the crowd mind by pointing out its affinities to the primitive mind of savages or as a legacy of the dark ages.

With regard to the positive role of one form of nonrational thought, religion, Le Bon recognizes that "a new society could not, any more than the societies of old, be built up without religious and moral beliefs." The historical importance which nonrational thinking plays in men's actions has transformed human history. "Were peoples only to be credited with the great actions performed in cold blood, the annals of the world would register but few of them."[17] At the bottom of great events "is always to be found the working soul of the masses and never the power of potentates." Indeed, collective logic produces a morality of self-sacrifice and heroism that would not be possible in individual, rational logic. This heroism makes possible the birth of great peoples. Islam transformed motley desert tribes into great nations.

On the other hand, Le Bon pays great heed to the intensely destructive aspects of nonrational thought. To be part of a great religious movement means to have apostles. For Le Bon, "it is a psychological law, almost universal in all ages, that one cannot be an apostle without experiencing an intense craving to massacre someone or smash something."[18]

Socialism shares with the old religions this same two-fold quality of creativity and destruction. As the heir of religious feelings it sums up our dreams and hopes. "However poor may be its value, however problematical its realization, it constitutes a new ideal which at least possesses the merit of bestowing on man a hope which the gods no longer give, and illusions that science has forbidden.''[19] Le Bon is aware that many French reformers were always endeavoring to recreate such beliefs in the minds of their followers. As a Frenchman, Le Bon is hardly introducing a startling innovation in associating socialism with religious belief. As he notes, St. Simon and more especially his follower Auguste Comte desired to reform society according to a new scientific philosophy supported by a positivist religion in which scientists were to constitute the new clergy. But it is at this point that Le Bon almost becomes a Comtean in reverse. The Comteans desired a religion of reason—of science—but "not one of them suspected the fact that no religious or moral belief ever had rational logic as its basis.''[20] Le Bon is not content merely to acknowledge the mystical and collective essence of religious thought. Unlike Comte, he refuses to accept reason as the basis for any religion, but in a vague harkening back to the French rationalist tradition, he appears to bring reason to bear in evaluating religious belief from a "scientific" point of view. As Sorel expressed it, Le Bon's writings strongly influenced the fanatical admirers of progress among the bourgeoisie who "regard religions as old rubbish destined to disappear under the influence of scientific development.'' At the same time the secular bourgeois who are adversaries of socialism "hope to rob it of all its mystique by maintaining that it is nothing but religious belief. The good people who show sympathy for socialism in hopes of passing themselves off as members of the avant-garde will scorn socialism when they see it as a legacy of the past.''[21]

There is a type of implied "higher positivism" in Le Bon's approach to religious feeling. Despite his professed acceptance of the nonrational aspects of human nature in general and thought processes in particular, there is a peculiar tendency to perform an unmasking or debunking process in this book. If the nonrational or mystical qualities of socialism can be demonstrated, the legitimacy of the ideology will be undermined. Such a procedure assumes the detachment and rationality of the scientist, who is at the same time a partisan of liberal individualism, a more "rational" theory. There is more than an implicit assumption in this work and in others by Le Bon that all ideologies (except Le Bon's own) can be explained away by dint of their mystical qualities. The corollary assumption is that despite the minor role played by intellectual logic, it is still the only logic by whose criteria all others are judged. To be less than intellectual, to be mystical, is to be somehow in the wrong.

Georges Sorel appeared to have perceived Le Bon in this way. In his view, Le Bon's insistence on the duality between knowledge and belief is correct, "but the question is of knowing if we are completely helpless in confronting this fatality; we are not compelled to dream of suppressing it by a more complete development of rationalism as the men of yesteryear believed. But perhaps in some way, we can submerge these baleful tendencies by harnessing the whole consciousness for the support of constructions that are satisfying for the mind and that also have strong roots in the heart." [22] In one sense, Sorel oversimplifies Le Bon for the latter did at times think the same thing. As we have seen, Le Bon, like Sorel, thought that religious forces "provoke an enthusiasm which makes us understand the nobility of life." [23] But the possibility of a redemptive quality to nonrational thought, later discussed in Georges Sorel's *Reflections on Violence* (and hinted at in the present work), is in fact explicitly denied in a later book by Le Bon. In his *La Psychologie politique et la défense sociale* (1910), Le Bon criticizes the use of instinctive, intuitive, and mystical logics in socialist and syndicalist writings. Without mentioning Sorel by name, Le Bon scorns the use of Bergsonian or pragmatic categories in social science. It is one thing to use nonrational logic to emancipate us from barbarism, it would appear, but it is quite another to use it in a civilization already established. He condemns pragmatism for disdaining reason and substituting instinct in its place. "It is only in freeing itself progressively from instinctive impulses that humanity can raise itself on the ladder of civilization. A civilization is the domination of

the instinctive by the rational. A revolution and the state of barbarism that accompanies it are the revenge of the instinctive
against the rational.''[24]

Le Bon is condemning the use of mystical logic as well as
instinctive and biological logic here. In any event, by equating
civilization with rationality, that is, with the domination of intellectual logic, Le Bon in his later works appears to have gone quite
a distance from his early opinion stated in this book, that intellectual logic plays a small part in any nonscientific enterprise. Instead he posits that in ''highly evolved races individual characteristics impose themselves on collective characteristics.''[25] But if
it follows that no rational collective decision-making is possible,
only individual action is rational; and if it is only civilized people
who are rational, then civilization is measured by the amount of
individual freedom men have. The final equation would appear to
be simple: socialism is religious and nonrational hence barbarous;
individual freedom is rational hence the highest expression of
civilization.

We arrive at a paradox in Le Bon's theory: no people can thrive
under the sway of a socialistic religion that denies the expression
of human excellence and individuality, but the doctrines of individualism and excellence cannot be cultivated without a collective
psychology which, by definition, transcends individualism.

No writer of Le Bon's calibre, who is so explicit about the
shortcomings of nonrational thought as well as the limited hori-
zons of rational thought, can leave off with this rather traditional
nineteenth-century view of human progress, despite the fact that
Le Bon obviously accepts this view in no little part. As a *politique*
sharing a liberal viewpoint he affirms human progress and rationality; as a psychologist sharing the dominant pessimism of nineteenth-century psychology he must question the very rationality of
these values. In *The Psychology of Socialism* and in his other
early works he attempts to bridge the gap between the rational and
the nonrational and between knowledge and belief by employing
nature rather than reason as a standard of evaluation. Or rather,
rationalism is mixed with a species of social Darwinism in such a

way as to make it appear that the brightest and cleverest are the most enterprising and the most enterprising are naturally the best.[26]

The role that nature plays in Le Bon's theory is demonstrated in his views on leadership. For Le Bon, if the crowd embodies mystical and nonrational elements of our character, the elite, secure in its power, is at least closer to rationality. But Le Bon's pessimism forbids him from arguing that the elite is necessarily more consciously rational than the crowd—for even small groups are obedient to mystical and collective logic. Instead he argues that the character of the elites allows them to conform more fully to the natural demands of social life; that they function more effectively as political leaders and more efficiently as economic beings than those beneath them even if they are not fully cognizant of the real reasons for their success.

Political leadership is not always discussed in terms of its rationality but often in terms of its strength or its Machiavellian *virtù*. If a mass takes on an autonomy of its own, such autonomy—though it may have world-shaking consequences—can only be temporary. It is the result of the decay of ruling elites who have become unsure of their rights and who lack "the firm and severe discipline" required of strong rulers. Weakened elites are inevitably replaced by other, stronger elites. Ironically, the same Le Bon who insists on the collective basis of great events argues herein that "social upheavals are commenced from above, never from below."[27] According to the suggestions of leaders, the crowd may be calm, furious, criminal, or heroic, but they will always be led. They are otherwise incapable of action. Le Bon is perhaps the first modern sociological thinker to propose what Roberto Michels, who acknowledged his debt to Le Bon, called "the iron law of oligarchy." By this both Michels and Le Bon mean that democracy in the purely Rousseauian sense is impossible; that the more democratic and equalitarian the claims of crowds become, the more dictatorial are the leaders of crowds; that indeed "no government is conceivable to popular democracy except in the form of an autocracy."[28] The inevitability of oligarchy does not contradict the crowd basis of history; it is rather a direct function of it.

But if Le Bon views a successful elite as possessing a certain *virtù*, that quality of boldness, virtue, and daring also has its rational element in both Machiavelli and Le Bon. Not only must the elite be lion-like in its boldness but fox-like in its canny ability to avoid traps. When Le Bon asks the elite to "act on the crowd," he implies that they must rely on more than instinct or intuition (which he condemned) to do so. It is implied that elites must master Le Bon's own science of mass psychology in order to know how to cultivate crowd sentiments. One must be familiar with the sentiments of the masses "in order to manipulate them." [29] Le Bon argues that it is in the province of education that the elite must reform itself. In France he says the university had been concerned primarily with intellectual development. Henceforth "it must follow the example of British and American universities: it must train the character or it must go." [30]

But, given his overall view of human nature, Le Bon must and does argue that leadership has only very limited opportunities. He admits that educational reform "would really imply a veritable miracle—the transformation of the national mind." Despite his law of oligarchy, he reverts to the fatalism of his theory that history is indeed made by crowds. Although oligarchies may dominate crowds in all times and in all places, ultimately the racial or cultural influences are determinant; in the present volume, in fact, Le Bon borders on a thoroughgoing determinism. Early on he argues that man cannot change through his own will those sentiments and beliefs that domimate his everyday existence. The influences of atavism always lurk "behind the vain struggles of the individual." He asserts that we can have very little influence on the present because it is the outcome of the past which we can do nothing to change; that the mysterious hereditary forces which survive us determine most of our actions. [31] Ultimately, in *The Psychology of Socialism* Le Bon juxtaposes one fatalistic view, one ironclad law of nature, with another: If one law says that men can do little to alter the basic circumstances and culture of their past, another law asserts they can do equally little to alter or abolish those "natural laws" of individuality and social competitiveness that would doom a culture, if by accident or design its people deign to contravene those laws.

It is fair to say that Le Bon employs two cultures, the Latin and the Anglo-Saxon, to exemplify the two types of laws. The laws of decay govern Latin societies because they have denied the laws of competition governing Anglo-Saxon cultures. Barring some miraculous transformation, French society will continue to be governed by laws impelling the national mind toward the traditional practices which have proved so harmful to industrial development. English traditions have, on the other hand, proved much more hospitable to the "laws" of classical economics emphasizing individual initiative, speculativeness, and respect for the rights and property of others. French society is therefore destined to fail in an industrial epoch while Anglo-Saxon civilization will triumph.

In Le Bon's eyes, Tocqueville's two types of democracy correspond to these divergent destinies. The Latin type of democracy stresses the importance of social equality at any price—a price that includes sacrificing freedom for the sake of equal justice. The English idea promises us only equality of opportunity, in this case opportunity to reveal our unequal talents. Both of these ideals call themselves democratic and it is the first or Latin type of which Le Bon is thinking when he argues that "natural laws do not agree with the aspirations of democracy."[32] Such a democracy flaunts nature's "absolute intolerance for weakness."[33] It is the second or Anglo-Saxon type that he has in mind when he says of democracy that "no other system gives the most capable such liberty of development"—in this case the development of "superiority of every kind."[34] It is the English idea, as Le Bon interprets it, that tells us that for nature "all that is weak is promptly doomed to perish. She respects only physical and intellectual strength. . . . Our ideas of justice are unknown to her."[35] For Le Bon, justice is in the interest of the stronger; "might and right are identical."[36] Sentimental ideas of charity, altruism, and pity only tend to obscure the real power relations governing mankind.

In asserting that Anglo-Saxon democracy, in favoring competition, conforms to the natural order of things, Le Bon appears to have both arbitrarily selected nature as a social standard as well as given us a rather narrow anthropology. Le Bon regards primitive society as savage society in which "the weak in body and mind are soon eliminated." Yet, as we have noted, he insists on assuming a stance that claims a scientific detachment. Rousseauianism and the socialist ideas that cater to the morality of the weak are not immoral; they are merely unnatural and hostile to the inevitable competition that rules the universe. Since it is the marketplace ethic that has triumphed in the modern world, the marketplace is the arena in which competition takes place in civilized society; it eliminates those who are weak willed and indolent and limits the rewards of the less gifted.

Yet there are those who would insist that Le Bon is hardly being a detached scientist here; that it is at this point that his anti-democratic ideology is most pronounced. It has been argued that the ideal of equality of opportunity is in fact the most highly oligarchic or aristocratic of all ideologies; that it is in fact hostile to the equalitarian impulses of democracy; that it is analogous to a starting line in a running race in which a group of inferior runners compete against a world record-holder. Under such "free" competition, equality becomes a mockery; the disparities of accomplishment will be so obvious that inequalities will become widened with the advance of civilization. As intellect becomes increasingly the standard of social achievement, the natural and political aristocracies become increasingly congruent.[37] In this Le Bon agrees: "Not only does nature not know equality, but since the beginning of the ages she has always realized progress by means of successive differentiation—that is to say, by increasing inequalities .... From the peasant to the feudal baron, the intellectual difference was not great, but from the working-man to the engineer, it is immense and is increasing daily."[38]

Le Bon insists that this increasing inequality is a natural law. But there is some question as to whether or not the differences between Einstein and the man on the street in our day are greater than those that prevailed between aristocracy and peasantry in medieval times.[39] Furthermore, even if it is true we may wonder how natural this development is. Intellectual differences may reflect natural differences among people. Le Bon has said elsewhere that intellectual logic is not a product of nature, that it is instead a creation of man against nature and that it is artificial. Le Bon has presented us with intellect as a natural phenomenon that has as its function the struggle against nature. Why then should we use nature as a standard? To put the question another way, is it "nature" or human artifice that determines that intellect should be used as a standard of personal evaluation? In other periods, as Le Bon notes, strength in war was the standard on which the hierarchy of human excellence was based. Le Bon seems to be arguing that the development of modern industrial society is the result of a "natural" historical evolution away from one standard toward another and that the intelligent capitalist is a more "highly evolved" person. In so doing, Le Bon would appear to be confusing nature and convention, evolution and historical development.

Le Bon was not the only writer to have confused natural selection with history, but his thinking seems to present a theory of history in which "natural man" reemerges periodically on the world's stage. In such a theory we find not only a cyclical notion of history, but a more "progressive" or linear idea that the more civilization develops the more complete will become the servitude of the incapable. But Le Bon must confront the question of justifying opposition to a victorious socialism if it should occur. If might and right are identical, would not collectivism be superior to individualism if socialism should prevail? In Le Bon's view, so pronounced is the tendency toward competition, and so historically inevitable, that Le Bon is constrained by the very logic of his position to assert that if socialism triumphs, its reign will be only temporary. Socialism will ultimately be swept away either by the new barbaric forces that would challenge the decayed civilization or by the epoch of capitalist competition. Socialism represents the union of the weak and sooner or later it is the weak who will be (and therefore should be) crushed.

IV

If Le Bon is somewhat selective in his scientific evidence for
the inevitable nature of competition, he is more forthrightly
evaluative in confronting the ethical consequences of the Dar-
winist struggle for superiority. He agrees that if we set no limits to
competition, the situation of the disinherited can only grow
worse, and he even foresees a process of increasing misery
whereby the future will show the lot of the ill-paid laborer "still
harder and still worse paid." To remedy this servitude is, Le Bon
admits, "perhaps the most difficult problem of modern times."[40]
Despite this slight squeamishness, Le Bon is equally cautious
about altering the "laws of nature," and his policy recommendations revolve mainly around ensuring that the competitors in the
daily struggle should compete fairly (though it might be objected
that fairness is not to be found in nature). He thus inclines toward
recommending highly progressive death taxes so as to render to
each generation an equal starting point in life. But, for Le Bon,
even fairness has its limits. His suggestion that landed property
should be divided is not made on the grounds of justice, but on the
simple expedient that it would promote a politically stable class of
petit bourgeois property holders who would remain hostile to
socialism.[41]

Such policy recommendations, however, bring to light certain
questions about the role the state plays in Le Bon's thought, and
how entities other than the individual should function in society.
Le Bon's apparently radical individualism must face up to questions posed by Tocqueville three generations before the publication of *The Psychology of Socialism*. While both theorists extolled
the rights of the individual and both drew distinctions between
equalitarian and libertarian democracy, Tocqueville was more un-
easy than Le Bon about what might happen if individualism were
taken to its logical conclusion. Thus for Tocqueville, the term
"individualism" appears to be a term of opprobrium. For Tocqueville, unrestricted individualism is a force that would shatter
the links that hold the individual to his community. It is these

links that preserve tradition and civilization itself. Individualism for Tocqueville was a condition of society. Isolating the subject from the community only makes him more vulnerable to mass manipulation. Individualism is self-negating. Tocqueville saw intermediate bodies and groups as powerful means for social control and for the promotion of civic virtue. Such groups along with strong local government and religion allowed the individual to look beyond himself; they enabled him to transcend narrow and destructive egotism. This viewpoint of corporate pluralism was endorsed by many of the apostles of modern positivistic sociology in France, especially by Emile Durkheim.

Echoing Tocqueville's nostalgia for medieval community, Le Bon recognizes that the old communes gave the individual a "cell in the social hive," but as he points out, it is the ethic of competition that has shattered these ancient ties and ushered in a period that has seen the "triumph of individualism freed from servitude but destitute of guidance." This need for "guidance" results in some interesting modifications of the ethic of dog-eat-dog competition extolled in *The Psychology of Socialism*. Le Bon argues that "solidarity" or group competition will replace the competition among individuals. "Association replaces the rampant egoism of the individual by a powerful collective egoism through which everyone profits.... This kind of solidarity is almost the only means remaining to the weak."[42] Thus cooperatives and profit-sharing plans are acceptable to Le Bon. Since the oppressed have no other weapon than association, the formation of groups is natural and inevitable. "Far from being contradicted by natural laws, it has the merit of being based on them."[43] But Le Bon also argues that this collective egoism is a function of the "abatement of individual will and initiative."[44] If this is so, then the ethic of competition receives a powerful check and unions of the weak over the strong are legitimized by Le Bon. On the other hand, Le Bon insists that group interest is different from altruism, charity, and pity. But this hardly solves the problem of determining when association becomes weakness.

An illustration will more clearly reveal this difficulty in Le

Bon's argument. While appearing to extol individual competition in the present volume, Le Bon elsewhere deplores the "narrow individualism" of French spinning mill owners who, concerned only with their own interests, ignore what he calls the "general requirements" of French industry: "They competed in the home markets, often practicing dumping outside their own territory on the national market. There is no real understanding among the employers," he laments. "They are unacquainted with the value of corporative grouping in order to defend their interests."[45] Why this industrial primitivism should disturb the apostle of market Darwinism is not entirely clear unless we note that Le Bon's response to the problem of cut-throat competition would appear to be the classic European device of cartelization. But is this not a sort of trade unionism of capitalists? Stated more broadly, Le Bon appears far more concerned with the survival of capitalists as a class than he does in taking the principles of individualism to their logical conclusion.

But if Le Bon is ambiguous about whether manufacturing associations are conforming to natural laws or frustrating them by killing initiative, he faces the problem more squarely with regard to trade unionism. While unreservedly hostile to socialism, Le Bon distinguishes it from trade unionism. The principal socialist dogmas—the leveling of wealth, statism, the suppression of private enterprise and competition—are different in Le Bon's view from nonrevolutionary trade unionism. The extension of the labor movement in all countries, he argues, is not, like socialism, hostile to economic laws but the result of economic necessities. It allows for the softening of the harshness of capitalism by allowing employees to stand up to rapacious employers. For similar reasons, he supports cooperatives against middlemen. Though hostile to any goal of unionism that would alter economic laws, Le Bon views unions in a positive way in their function as bargaining associations.

Le Bon remains quite ambiguous on how well workers have fared from unionism. On the one hand, he claims that unions have not only enabled workers to contend with capitalism and to "es-

cape its tyranny,''[46] he even goes so far as to assert that the
"progress of humanitarian ideas" and the enormous extension of
trade unions has brought about a great improvement in the lot of
the working class. "Taking into consideration the economic
necessities that rule the world, it is very probable that the workers
are passing through a golden age," he says. But what then of Le
Bon's prediction of increasing misery? This sanguine view hardly
accords with the dismal picture of the English sweating system
found 45 pages later.[47] Le Bon admits that the inexorable laws of
economics render this golden age temporary, such that workers
will never see this prosperity again.

If the laws of economics are as inexorable as Le Bon claims, he
is uncharacteristically optimistic about the future possibilities of
industrial psychology. Unlike his syndicalist acquaintance
Georges Sorel, Le Bon sees little hope in a self-assertive workers'
movement as a means of social renewal. In characteristic
Machiavellian fashion, Le Bon places his hopes in the manipula-
tive skill of the managerial classes. By mastering the principles of
social psychology, the same benefits of social peace, stability,
and industrial productivity would accrue to industrial leaders as
they would to the right political chieftains. For Le Bon, social
psychology is the key to industrial as well as political peace. Le
Bon regards certain trade unions in England and America as convenient instruments for containing class conflict and industrial
strife. By giving workers the illusion of power, such unions can
serve as vehicles for the promotion of the work ethic. By promot-
ing technical instruction and improving the technical capacity of
the workers, trade unions can become powerful instruments in the
development of industrial efficiency and competitiveness. The
Anglo-Saxon unionists have realized that the income of the
worker "depends solely on the health of the industry" and this
idea "is never admitted by Latin unionists."[48] Sorel also extolled
these productive virtues, but perhaps the great difference between
Sorel and Le Bon is that Le Bon distinguishes carefully between
the "pacific" trade unionism of English-speaking countries and
the "revolutionary trade unionism" or syndicalism of Latin
countries.[49] Sorel in his syndicalist period tended to see

similarities between the French General Confederation of Labor (CGT) and the American unions. For Sorel this federation together with its companion organizations, the *Bourses du Travail* or labor exchanges, possessed an almsot religious myth, a vision of the general strike that, by galvanizing the energies of the working class, would enable it to become the energizing force for social renewal. Le Bon never entertained such illusions. In later works he refers scornfully to the power of the CGT whose violence, in his view, revealed an extreme deficiency of genuine power, and he deprecates the "brave men" who believe that syndicalism heralds a new era.[50] On the contrary, Latin syndicalists, socialists, and anarchists, "although moved by entirely different conceptions, are . . . collaborating in the same eventual aim—the violent suppression of the ruling classes and the pillage of their wealth."[51]

V

The reception of *The Psychology of Socialism* varied with the political views of its readers. Sorel, who was still a socialist at the time, took it upon himself to defend socialism, although he was perhaps the leading social theorist who shared Le Bon's pessimistic psychology. Sorel insisted, contrary to Le Bon, that there was no proof that socialism was necessarily attached to "base ideals." Le Bon had failed to take account of the aspirations and conduct of members of workers' organizations, especially in English trade unions. Le Bon and Sorel agreed that these aspirations and dreams were primarily states of mind; what Le Bon called affective and mystical logic, Sorel called myths.[52] But Sorel insisted that precisely because socialism is rooted in our innermost feelings and impulses it is impossible to refute it as if it were some ordinary hypothesis.[53] Previously, in fact, Sorel had criticized Le Bon's inclination to treat mental phenomena positivistically, that is in a manner more suited to the physical sciences. In such a procedure, all branches of knowledge are united and "very dissimilar things are designated by the same term." Hence, in Sorel's view, Le Bon erroneously reduced the history of ideas to a reproduction of gestures, to mimicry, contagion, and above all race. These categories Sorel regards as pseudo-explanations that in fact "explain nothing at all."[54]

Liberals, such as Emile Faguet, were impressed with Le Bon's attack on the decline of Latin culture and its inability to cope with the demands of the industrial era. So impressed was Faguet with this theme that he said a more precise title for the work should have been "The Causes of the Decline in the Latin Peoples in General and the French People in Particular." But Faguet was more disposed to attribute the relative decline of French industry to divergent social interests rather than to crowd hysteria or to psychological leveling. "The workers are *a bit* socialistic," Faguet said. "This is because they have nothing and they find this condition disagreeable—not in itself because they have nothing at all, but (what is much more human) because someone else has something. The bourgeoisie and peasants are anti-socialist. This is not through lack of intelligence; it is quite intelligent from their point of view. Nothing is less passionate than French political and social opinion, and that is not such a bad thing."[55]

There is a certain irony to Faguet's criticism of Le Bon's failure to appreciate the calculating self-interested model of political man instead of the nonrational crowd mind. Half of Le Bon's own political philosophy, as we have intimated, inclined in this liberal direction; indeed it appears that he devoutly wished politics had been more rational. In failing to apply the rational self-interested model to socialism and syndicalism, Le Bon underestimated the change that was to take place in these theories in the ensuing decade. Sorel despaired of syndicalism after 1908, not because it had given in to rage and mob frenzy but because it tended to conform more to the self-interested model of acquisitive trade unionism. His own mythic vision of the general strike had given way to haggling over wages and hours.

Sorel and Faguet were not alone in criticizing Le Bon for paying too much heed to "racial" character as a factor in the industrial backwardness of Latin societies. One American reviewer doubted "whether it is advisable for Anglo-Saxondom to pride itself too much on individualism as a safeguard against what M. Le Bon describes."[56] It is well to recall, however, that Le Bon

defined race in largely cultural terms, and he was far more concerned with education than with genetic structure. The *Spectator*
of London criticized Le Bon for relying too much on the doctrine
of equality of opportunity: "For ourselves we believe in democracy and the open career; also believing in hereditary fitness and
the power of education, we would allow individuals to establish
handicaps in favor of their descendents . . . . It is not education but
Nature which made French pupils and French teachers what they
are."[57] Such criticisms only highlight Le Bon's comparatively
liberal and democratic point of view.

Anther English reviewer argued that, despite his scientific pre-
tentions, Le Bon "deals too much with abstractions and too little
with concrete facts." The critic asks us to "test Le Bon's theory
with regard to Germany. Here also we have a strong government
that leaves no department of the national life untouched. But we
have also no lack of individual energy and generally a natural
efficiency in all practical departments which is unsurpassed . . . .
When applied to Germany the theory falls to pieces."[58]

This judgment may have been too harsh. We have noted the
tension in Le Bon's theory between his professed individualism
and his call for social discipline. But Le Bon specifically argued
that Germany and German culture possessed the discipline that
produced a balance between "the instinctive impulses of human
nature" and social necessities. While by no means answering all
criticisms, Le Bon can still revert to his basic "racial" argument:
whatever institutions are imposed upon a people are soon transformed in accordance with the mentality of that people. Certainly
Le Bon was to have his worst fears realized when, as he noted in
1924, the real power of the Russian Soviets was abolished, thus
perpetuating a centuries-old tradition of autocracy now led by
"the Grand Bolshevist pontiff who reigns in Moscow."[59]

Le Bon's anti-communism prevented him from seeing that the
very laws of cultural continuity, of elites, and of crowds that he
had seen upheld in Russia might apply to fascist Italy as well.
There he saw fascism as a "brave" alternative to socialism, and
he praised it for "simplifying the administrative machinery"
while leaving "the maximum of liberty to private initiative."[60]

Yet if he mistook fascist "discipline" for liberty, Le Bon succeeds better than most writers as a prophet of the mass age. The most efficient and productive economies of our time have certainly been run with a combination of the "discipline" of social engineering and the profit motive. It is "collective egoism" bolstered by industrial relations psychology that has prevailed in the most efficient economic systems—not Marx's class struggle, not Sorel's myth of the general strike, and certainly not *Spectator's* inherited class privilege.

If Le Bon paid excessive heed to the precepts of classical economics, the most productive industrial powers of the twentieth century have avoided wholesale socialism in favor of mixed economies. Indeed the Japanese corporate state that has emerged as the prototype of industrial success in our time is not distant from Le Bon's corporate egotism; it is, in all events, aggressively capitalist.

In any case, if socialists complain about the "domination" of modern industrial capitalism and its technoscientific elites, Le Bon gave fair warning to those who ignored him: woebetide any would-be revolutionary who disdains the constant challenge of the productive system in the name of a soft and flabby humanism. It is this warning, however distasteful it is to modern liberals, that deserves a place on the bookshelf of every social scientist.

NOTES

1. Alexis de Tocqueville, *Democracy in America*, translated by Henry Reeve and revised by Francis Bowen (New York: Vintage Books, 1954), Volume II, p. 333.
2. Gustave Le Bon, *The Psychology of Socialism* (New Brunswick, N.J.: Transaction Books, 1981) pp. 145-46. The English translation appeared in 1899 and is from the first French edition of *Psychologie du socialisme* (Paris: Alcan, 1898).
3. Ibid., p. 26.
4. Ibid., p. 145.
5. Gustave Le Bon, *The French Revolution and the Psychology of Revolution* (New Brunswick, N.J.: Transaction Books, 1980), p. 61. Introduction by Robert A. Nye.(Hereafter cited as *The Psychology of Revolution*.)

6. Ibid., p. 59.
7. Gustave Le Bon, *Les opinions et les croyances* (Paris: Flammarion, 1911), p. 171.
8. Ibid., p. 86.
9. Ibid., p. 94.
10. Ibid., p. 74.
11. *The Psychology of Revolution*, p. 76.
12. *Les opinions et les croyances*, p. 114.
13. Ibid., p. 95.
14. *The Psychology of Revolution*, p. 304.
15. Gustave Le Bon, *The Crowd* (New York: Viking, 1960), p. 27.
16. Ibid., p. 30.
17. Ibid., p. 34.
18. *The Psychology of Socialism* (this edition), p. 94.
19. Ibid., p. 87.
20. *The Psychology of Revolution*, p. 291.
21. Georges Sorel, *Materiaux d'une théorie du prolétariat* (Paris: Marcel Rivière, 1919), p. 311.
22. Georges Sorel, "Sur la magie moderne," *L'Indépendance*, September 1911, p. 4.
23. Ibid., p. 5. For an excellent comparison of Le Bon and Sorel see Robert A. Nye, *The Origins of Crowd Psychology: Gustave Le Bon and the Crisis of Mass Democracy in the Third Republic* (London; Beverly Hills: Sage, 1975), Chapter 5. See footnote 52, below.
24. Le Bon, *La psychologie politique et la défense sociale* (Paris: Flammarion, 1910), p. 223. See footnote 52, below.
25. *Les opinions et les croyances*, p. 179.
26. In the first edition of the *Psychology of Socialism*, on which the present translation is based, Le Bon incorrectly identifies Spencer as a socialist on page 36 (below), but on page 405 (below), he notes that Spencer opposes socialism. In the third edition Le Bon removed the paragraph (on page 36 of the present edition) in which the former reference to Spencer is located.
27. *The Psychology of Socialism* (this edition), p. 400.
28. *The Psychology of Revolution*, p. 295. –
29. *The Psychology of Socialism*, p. 412.
30. Gustave Le Bon, *The World in Revolt: A Psychological Study of Our Times* (a translation of *Psychologie des Temps nouveaux*), translated by Bernard Miall (London: Unwin, 1921), p. 256.
31. *The Psychology of Socialism*, pp. 61, 391.
32. *The Psychology of Revolution*, p. 300.
33. *The Psychology of Socialism*, p, 325.
34. Ibid., p. 296.
35. Ibid., p. 325-26.

36. Ibid., p. 327.

37. For a cogent expression of this view see John Schaar, "Equality of Opportunity and Beyond," in *Legitimacy in the Modern State* (New Brunswick, N.J.: Transaction Books, 1981).

38. *The Psychology of Revolution*, p. 297-98.

39. Compare Schaar, op. cit., who says, "the disparity between the scientific knowledge of an Einstein and the scientific knowledge of the ordinary man of our day is greater than the disparity between a Newton and the ordinary man of his day" p. (232). I have criticized certain of Professor Schaar's ideas. See John Stanley, "Equality of Opportunity as Philosophy and Ideology," *Political Theory*, Vol. 5, No. 1, February 1977, p. 61.

40. *The Psychology of Socialism*, pp. 237, 297.

41. Ibid., p. 314.

42. Ibid., p. 344-45.

43. Ibid., pp. 352-53, 345.

44. Ibid., p. 344.

45. *The World in Revolt*, p. 49.

46. *The Psychology of Socialism*, p. 26.

47. Ibid., pp. 315, 361.

48. *La psychologie politique et la défense sociale*, p. 217.

49. Ibid., pp. 203-04.

50. Ibid., p. 212.

51. *The Psychology of Revolution*, p. 320.

52. There is no absolute identity in the two points of view, but there is enough similarity between the two thinkers to move Professor Nye to say: "The mutual bond linking Le Bon and Sorel presents itself in the form of a paradox: at those times they seem most politically opposed to one another, they are intellectually—by the canons of the social science they shared—most apposite" *The Origins of Crowd Psychology*, p. 102. Sorel's viewpoint is more subjectivistic than Le Bon's. Despite Sorel's frequent references to "social myth" and "mass sentiments," he invokes Bergson's doctrine of memory, which invokes "deep introspection" which fosters in turn "the individualist strength in the aroused masses." The myth of the general strike is an image of "an immense uprising which can be called individualistic." John L. Stanley, ed. *From Georges Sorel* (New York: Oxford University Press, 1976), pp. 204, 221-22. Sorel makes no mention of the *collective logic* that Le Bon viewed as essential to mass movements. In fact Sorel went further than Le Bon in condemning ordinary public opinion: "The masses are rather insensitive to elevated sentiments. They know only those social interests, public spirit or patriotism that the most vulgar agitators impart to them." Review of *Psychology of Socialism, Revue Internationale de sociologie* VII, February 1899, p. 154.

53. Sorel, Review of *Psychology of Socialism*, p. 153.

54. Georges Sorel, review of "La psychologie des foules," *Le Devenir Social*, I, November 1895, p. 767.

55. Emile Faguet, review of "Psychologie du socialisme," *La Revue Latine*, 25 January 1902, No. 6, pp. 327-28.

56. *Nation*, May 17, 1900, p. 385. A generation later Le Bon said that "English syndicalists would like to place the working classes under the Bolshevist Government in Moscow. Who would have foreseen that traditional and liberal-minded England would come to this?" *The World Unbalanced* (London: Unwin, 1924), p. 94.

57. *Spectator*, September 30, 1899, pp. 446-47.

58. T. Kirkup, *The Bookman* (London), October 1899, pp. 23-24.

59. *The World Unbalanced*, p. 72.

60. Ibid., pp. 95-96.

For Further Reading

Other Works by Le Bon in English:
The French Revolution and the Psychology of Revolution, ed. Robert Nye (New Brunswick, N.J.: Transaction Books, 1980).
The Crowd, ed. by Robert Merton (Hammondsworth: Penguin, 1960).
The World in Revolt, translated by Bernard Miall (London: Unwin, 1921).
The World Unbalanced, (London: Unwin, 1924).
The Psychology of Peoples: Its Influence on Their Evolution (New York: Macmillan, 1898).
The Psychology of the Great War (New York: Macmillan, 1916).
The Evolution of Forces (New York: Scribners, 1909).

Important Works as yet untranslated:
Les opinions et les croyances (Paris: Flammarion, 1911).
La psychologie politique et la défense sociale (Paris: Flammarion, 1910).
Psychologie de l'èducation (Paris: Flammarion, 1901).

Other works on Le Bon and Related Subjects:
Robert A. Nye, *The Origins of Crowd Psychology: Gustave LeBon and the Crisis of Mass Democracy in the Third Republic* (London; Beverly Hills: Sage, 1975).
Irving L. Horowitz, *Radicalism and the Revolt Against Reason* (New York: Humanities Press, 1961).
Jean Stoetzel, "Gustave Le Bon," *The International Encyclopedia of the*

Social Sciences, 9 (New York: Collier-Macmillan, 1968), p. 84.

William Kornhauser, The Politics of Mass Society (Glencoe, Ill.: The Free Press, 1959).

Murray Edelman, *Politics as Symbolic Action: Mass Arousal and Quiescence* (Chicago: 1971).

Mary Jo Nye, "Gustave Le Bon's Black Light: A Study in Physics and Philosophy in France at the Turn of the Century," *Historical Studies in the Physical Sciences*, 4.

Preface to the Third Edition

Translated by John L. Stanley

I do not think it necessary to respond to the criticisms that this work has inspired in France and in the countries where it has been translated. Hardly anyone changes his opinion regarding the domain of sentiment as opposed to that of reason. It is not through books that revolutions affect thought.[1]

Since I do not belong to any school and am not attempting to please one, I have tried to study social phenomena as I would any physical phenomenon, that is, by trying to make as few mistakes as possible.

Because of their necessary brevity, certain passages in this book seem a bit dogmatic, but that has not been my intention. One of the last chapters is devoted to showing that in such questions we can only know probabilities, never certainties.

---

1. I have no hope at all of changing the mind of any socialist, however I think that reading this work will not have been without some use to them. I make this judgment on the basis of certain articles published about it, notably from that of the most erudite pen of French socialism, M. Georges Sorel, a portion of which I quote: "Gustave Le Bon's book constitutes the most complete work on socialism published in France; it merits being studied with the greatest care because the author's ideas are always original and eminently suggestive" (*Revue Internationale de Sociologie*).

If I sometimes appear to stray from the subject, it is because it is impossible to understand the genesis of certain phenomena without first studying the circumstances encompassing them. In religious, moral, or political questions, the study of the text itself of a doctrine is not as important as people believe. What we should know above all are the milieux in which it develops, the sentiments on which it is based, and the state of the minds accepting it. In the period in which Buddhism and Christianity triumphed it would have been of little interest for a philosopher to discuss their dogmas and of great interest to know the causes that allowed them to be established, and, above all, the frame of mind which made them acceptable. However absurd a dogma may be in the eyes of reason, it always triumphs when it succeeds in producing certain mental transformations. In these transformations, the role of the dogma itself is at times quite secondary. It triumphs through the interaction of the environment and the time when it appears, through the passions that it arouses, and above all through the influence of apostles who are capable of speaking to crowds and engendering faith. It is not by acting on reason but only on feelings that the apostles bring about great popular movements from which new gods emerge.

Thus for these reasons I do not believe that I have strayed from my subject by writing certain chapters on the foundations of our beliefs, the role of traditions in the life of peoples, the formative concepts of the Latin soul, the economic evolution of the present age and others. They constitute perhaps the most essential parts of this study.

I have devoted only a rather small number of pages to the exposition of socialist doctrines. These doctrines are so malleable that they render all discussion useless. This changeability, moreover, constitutes a general law governing the birth of all new beliefs. Dogmas are truly constituted only when they have triumphed. Until the time of their victory, they remain uncertain and elusive. This imprecision is a condition of success because it allows the dogmas to adapt to the most diverse needs and thus to give satisfaction to the infinitely varied aspirations of the legions of malcontents who proliferate at certain historical moments.

As we shall try to show, socialism can be grouped in the family of religious beliefs and possesses this imprecise character of dogmas that do not yet rule. Its doctrines change from day to day and become increasingly uncertain and unstable. Putting the principles formulated by its founders in agreement with the new facts, which all too clearly contradict them, has been a task analogous to that of theologians trying to bring the Bible into accord with reason. The principles on which Marx, who was for so long the high priest of the new religion, had based socialism have been so contradicted by the facts that his most faithful followers have been driven to abandon them. Thus, it is, for example, that the essential theory of socialism forty years ago, according to which land and capital would be concentrated in an ever-smaller number of hands, has been absolutely belied by the statistics of various countries. These statistics make it clear indeed that capital and land, far from being ever more concentrated, are being rapidly diffused among an immense number of individuals. Therefore, in Germany, England, and Belgium we see the socialist leaders increasingly abandoning collectivism, which they now term a chimerical doctrine, good only for deceiving Latin peoples.

Furthermore, from the perspective of the advance of socialism, these discussions of the theoreticians are without any importance. The masses do not hear them. What they retain from socialism is solely the fundamental idea that the worker is the victim of a few exploiters, as a consequence of bad social organization, and that it would be enough to impose by revolution a few good decrees to change this organization. Theoreticians can evolve. The masses accept doctrines *en bloc* and never evolve. Their beliefs are always couched in very simple terms. Implanted forcefully in primitive minds, they remain secure there for a long time.

Outside of socialist reveries and usually in flagrant disagreement with them, the modern world is undergoing a deep and rapid revolution. It is the consequence of the change in the conditions of existence, in needs and ideas, brought about by the industrial and scientific discoveries made during the last fifty years. It is to these transformations that societies will adapt and not to fantasies of theoreticians who, not perceiving the working of necessity, think themselves capable of refashioning social organization to their liking. The problems raised by present-day world changes are serious in a different way from those which concern socialists. A good part of this work is devoted to studying them.

PREFACE

SOCIALISM consists of a synthesis of beliefs, aspirations, and ideas of reform which appeals profoundly to the mind. Governments fear it, legislators manipulate it, nations behold in it the dawn of happier destinies.

This book is devoted to the study of Socialism. In it will be found the application of those principles already set forth in my two last works—*The Psychology of Peoples* and *The Psychology of the Crowd*. Passing rapidly over the details of the doctrines in question, and retaining their essentials alone, I shall examine the causes which have given birth to Socialism, and those which favour or retard its propagation. I shall show the conflict of those ancient ideas, fixed by heredity, on which societies are still reposed, with the new ideas, born of the new conditions which have been created by the evolution of modern science and industry. Without contesting the lawfulness of the tendencies of the greater number to ameliorate their condition, I shall inquire whether it is possible for institutions to have a real influence in this amelioration, or whether our destinies are not decided by necessities entirely independent of the institutions which our wills may create.

Socialism has not wanted apologists to write its history, economists to discuss its dogmas, and apostles to propagate its faith. Hitherto psychologists have disdained to study it, perceiving in it only one of those elusive and indefinite subjects, like theology and politics, which can lead only to such impassioned and futile discussions as are hateful to the scientific mind. It would seem, however, that nothing but an intent psychology can exhibit the genesis of the new doctrines, or explain the influence exerted by them over the vulgar mind as well as over a certain number of cultivated understandings. We must dive to the deepest roots of the events whose evolution we are considering if we would attain a comprehension of the blossom.

No apostle has ever doubted of the future of his faith, and the Socialists are persuaded of the approaching triumph of theirs. Such a victory implies of necessity the destruction of the present society, and its reconstruction on other bases. To the disciples of the new dogmas nothing appears more simple. It is evident that a society may be disorganised by violence, just as a building, laboriously constructed, may be destroyed in an hour by fire. But does our modern knowledge of the evolution of things allow us to admit that man is able to re-fashion, according to his liking, a society that has so been destroyed? So soon as we penetrate a little into the mechanism of civilisations we quickly discover that a society, with its institutions, its beliefs, and its arts, represents a tissue of ideas, sentiments, customs, and modes of thought determined by heredity, the cohesion of which constitutes its strength. No society is firmly held together unless this moral heritage is solidly established, and established not in codes but in the natures of men; the one declines when the other crumbles, and when this moral heritage is finally disintegrated the society is doomed to disappear.

Such a conception has never influenced the writers and the peoples of the Latin States. Persuaded as they are that the necessities of nature will efface themselves before their ideal of levelment, regularity, and justice, they believe it sufficient to imagine enlightened constitutions, and laws founded on reason, in order to re-fashion the world. They are still possessed by the illusions of the heroic epoch of the Revolution, when philosophers and legislators held it certain that a society was an artificial thing, which benevolent dictators could rebuild in entirety.

Such theories do not appear tenable to-day. We must not, however, disdain them, for they constitute the motives of action of a destructive influence which is greatly to be feared, because very considerable. The power of creation waits upon time and place ; it is beyond the immediate reach of our desires ; but the destructive faculty is always at hand. The destruction of a society may be very rapid, but its reconstruction is always very slow. Sometimes man requires centuries of effort to rebuild, painfully, that which he destroyed in a day.

If we would comprehend the profound influence of modern Socialism we need only to examine its doctrines. When we come to investigate the causes of its success we find that this success is altogether alien to the theories proposed, and the negations imposed by these doctrines. Like religions (and Socialism is tending more and more to put on the guise of a religion) it propagates itself in any manner rather than by reason. Feeble in the extreme when it attempts to reason, and to support itself by economic arguments, it becomes on the contrary extremely powerful when it remains in the region of dreams, affirmations, and chimerical promises, and if it were never to issue thence it would become even more redoubtable.

Thanks to its promises of regeneration, thanks to the hope it flashes before all the disinherited of life, Socialism is becoming a belief of a religious character rather than a doctrine. Now the great power of beliefs, when they tend to assume this religious form, of whose mechanism I have elsewhere treated, lies in the fact that their propagation is independent of the proportion of truth or error that they may contain, for as soon as a belief has gained a lodging in the minds of men its absurdity no longer appears ; reason cannot reach it, and only time can impair it. The most profound thinkers of humanity—Leibnitz, Descartes, Newton—have bowed themselves without a murmur before religious doctrines whose weaknesses reason would quickly have discovered, had they been able to submit them to the ordeal of criticism. What has once entered the region of sentiment can no longer be touched by discussion. Religions, acting as they do only on the sentiments, cannot be destroyed by arguments, and it is for this reason that their power over the mind has always been so absolute.

The present age is one of those periods of transition in which the old beliefs have lost their empire, while those which must replace the old are not yet established. Hitherto man has been unable to live without divinities. They fall often from their throne, but that throne has never remained empty ; new phantoms are rising always from the dust of the dead gods.

Science, which has wrestled with the gods, has never been able to dispute their prodigious empire. No civilisation has ever yet succeeded in establishing and extending itself without them. The most flourishing civilisations have always been propped up by religious dogmas which, from the rational point of view, possessed not an atom of logic, not a spice of truth, nor even of simple good sense. Reason and logic have never been the true guides of nations. The irrational has always been one of the most powerful motives of action known to humanity.

It is not by the faint light of reason that the world has been transformed. While religions, founded on chimeras, have marked their indelible imprint on all the elements of civilisations, and continue to retain the immense majority of men under their laws, the systems of philosophy built on reason have played only an insignificant part in the life of nations, and have had none but an ephemeral existence. They indeed offer the crowd nothing but arguments, while the human soul demands nothing but hopes.

These hopes are those that religions have always given, and they have given also an ideal capable of seducing and stirring the mind. It is under their magic wand that the most powerful empires have been created, and the marvels of literature and art, which form the common treasure of civilisation, have risen out of chaos.

Socialism, whose dream is to substitute itself for the ancient faiths, proposes but a very low ideal, and to establish it appeals but to sentiments lower still. What, in effect, does it promise, more than merely our daily bread, and that at the price of hard labour ? With what lever does it seek to raise the soul ? With the sentiments of envy and hatred which it creates in the hearts of multitudes ? To the crowd, no longer satisfied with political and civic equality, it proposes equality of condition, without dreaming that social inequalities are born of those natural inequalities that man has always been powerless to change.

It would seem that beliefs founded on so feeble an ideal, on sentiments so little elevated, could have but few chances of propagating themselves. However, they do propagate themselves, for man possesses the marvellous faculty of transforming things to the liking of his desires, of regarding them only through that magical prism of the thoughts and sentiments which shows us the world as we wish it to be. Each, at the bidding of his dreams, his ambitions, his hopes, perceives in Socialism what the founders of the new faith never dreamed of putting into it. In Socialism the priest perceives the universal extension of charity, and dreams of charity while he forgets the altar. The slave, bowed in his painful labour, catches a confused glimpse of the shining paradise where he, in his turn, will be loaded with good things. The enormous legion of the discontented—and who is not of it to-day ? —hopes, through the triumph of Socialism, for the amelioration of its destiny. It is the sum of all these dreams, all these discontents, all these hopes, that endows the new faith with its incontestable power.

In order that the Socialism of the present day might assume so quickly that religious form which constitutes the secret of its power, it was necessary that it should appear at one of those rare moments of history when the old religions lose their might (men being weary of their gods), and exist only on sufferance, while awaiting the new faith that is to succeed them. Socialism, coming as it came, at the precise instant when the power of the old divinities had considerably waned, is naturally tending to possess itself of their place. There is nothing to show that it will not succeed in taking it. There is everything to show that it will not succeed in keeping it long.

CONTENTS

——◦◦◦——

BOOK I

THE SOCIALISTIC THEORIES AND THEIR DISCIPLES

BOOK II

SOCIALISM AS A BELIEF

xlvii

CONTENTS

BOOK III

SOCIALISM AS AFFECTED BY RACE

BOOK IV

THE CONFLICT BETWEEN ECONOMIC NECESSITIES AND THE ASPIRATIONS OF THE SOCIALISTS

BOOK V

THE CONFLICT BETWEEN THE LAWS OF EVOLUTION, THE DEMOCRATIC IDEAL, AND THE ASPIRATIONS OF THE SOCIALISTS

CONTENTS

BOOK VI

THE DESTINIES OF SOCIALISM

BOOK I

THE SOCIALISTIC THEORIES AND THEIR DISCIPLES

CHAPTER I

THE VARIOUS ASPECTS OF SOCIALISM

1. *The factors of social evolution* :—Factors which direct the modern evolution of societies—In what manner they differ from the ancient factors—Economic factors—Psychological factors—Political factors. 2. *The various aspects of Socialism* : — The necessity of studying Socialism as a political conception, as an economic conception, as a philosophic conception, and as a belief—Conflict between these various conceptions—Philosophical definition of Socialism—The Collective Being and the Individual Being.

1. The Factors of Social Evolution.

CIVILISATIONS have always had, as their basis, a certain small number of directing or controlling ideas. When these ideas, after gradually waning, have entirely lost their force, the civilisations which rest on them are doomed to change.

We are to-day in the midst of one of those phases of transition so rare in the history of the world. In the course of the ages it has not been given to many philosophers to live at the precise moment at which a new idea shapes itself, and to be able to study, as we can study to-day, the successive degrees of its crystallisation.

In the present condition of things the evolution of

1

societies is subject to factors of three orders : political, economic, and psychological.   These have existed in every period, but the respective importance of each has varied with the age of the nation.

The political factors comprise the laws and institutions. Theorists of every kind, and above all the modern Socialists, generally accord to these a very great importance. They are persuaded that the happiness of a people depends on its institutions, and that to change these is at the same stroke to change its destinies.   Some thinkers hold, on the contrary, that institutions exercise but a very feeble influence ; that the destiny of a nation is decreed by its character ; that is to say, by the soul of the race. This would explain why peoples possessing similar institutions, and living in identical environments, occupy very different places in the scale of civilisation.

To-day the economic factors have an immense importance.   Very feeble at a period when the nations lived in isolation, when the divers industries hardly varied from century to century, these factors have ended by acquiring a pre-eminent influence.   Scientific and industrial discoveries have transformed all our conditions of existence. A simple chemical reaction, discovered in a laboratory, ruins one country and enriches another.   The culture of a cereal in the heart of Asia compels whole provinces of Europe to renounce agriculture.   The developments of machinery revolutionise the life of a large proportion of the civilised nations.

The factors of the psychological order, such as race, beliefs, and opinions, have also a considerable importance.   Till quite lately their influence was preponderant, but to-day the economic factors are tending to prevail.

It is especially in these changes of relation between the directing factors to which they are subject that the societies of to-day differ from those of the past.

Dominated of old above all by faiths, they have since become more and more obedient to economic necessities.

The psychological factors are nevertheless far from having lost their influence. The degree in which man escapes the tyranny of economic factors depends on his mental constitution ; that is to say, on his race ; and this is why we see certain nations subject these economic factors to their needs, while others allow themselves to become more and more enslaved by them, and seek to react on them only by laws of protection, which are incapable of defending them against the formidable necessities which rule them.

Such are the principal motive forces of social evolution. Their action is simultaneous, but often contradictory. To ignore them, or to misconceive them, does not hinder their action. The laws of nature operate with the blind punctuality of clockwork, and he that offends them is broken by their march.

2. THE VARIOUS ASPECTS OF SOCIALISM.

This brief presentment already allows us to foresee that Socialism offers to the view different facets, which we must examine in succession. We must investigate Socialism as a political conception, as an economic conception, as a philosophic conception, and as a belief. We must also consider the inevitable conflict between these various concepts and the social realities ; that is, between the yet abstract idea and the inexorable laws of nature which the cunning of man cannot change.

The economic side of Socialism is that which best lends itself to analysis. We find ourselves in the presence of very clearly defined problems. How is wealth to be produced and divided ? What are the respective *rôles* of labour, capital, and intelligence ? What is the influence of economic facts, and to what extent can they be adapted to the requirements of social evolution?

If we consider Socialism as a belief, if we inquire into the moral impression which it produces, the conviction and the devotion which it inspires, the point of view is very different, and the aspect of the problem is entirely changed. We now no longer have to occupy ourselves with the theoretic value of Socialism as a doctrine, nor with the economic impossibilities with which it may clash. We have only to consider the new faith in its genesis, its moral progress, and its possible psychological consequences. Then only does the fatuity of discussion with its defenders become apparent. If the economists marvel that demonstrations based on impeccable evidence have absolutely no influence over those who hear and understand them, we have only to refer them to the history of all dogmas, and to the study of the psychology of crowds. We have not triumphed over a doctrine when we have shown its chimerical nature. We do not attack dreams with argument; nothing but recurring experience can show that they are dreams.

In order to comprehend the present force of Socialism it must be considered above all as a belief, and we then discover it to be founded on a very secure psychologic basis. It matters very little to its immediate success that it may be contrary to social and economic necessities. The history of all beliefs, and especially of religious beliefs, sufficiently proves that their success has most often been entirely independent of the proportion of truth that they might contain.

Having considered Socialism as a belief we must examine it as a philosophic conception. This new facet is the one its adepts have most neglected, and yet the very one they might the best defend. They consider the realisation of their doctrines as the necessary consequence of economic evolution, whereas it is precisely this evolution that forms the most real obstacle. From the point of view of pure philosophy—that is to say, putting psychologic and economic necessities aside — many of their theories are highly defensible.

What in effect is Socialism, speaking philosophically : or, at least, what is its best-known form, Collectivism ? Simply a reaction of the collective being against the encroachments of the individual being. Now if we put aside the interests of intelligence, and the possibly immense utility of husbanding these interests for the progress of civilisation, it is undeniable that collectivity —if only by that law of the greater number which has become the great *credo* of modern democracies—may be considered as invented to subject to itself the individual sprung from its loins, and who would be nothing without it. For centuries, that is to say during the succession of the ages which have preceded our own, collectivity has always been all-powerful, at least among the Latin peoples. The individual outside it was nothing. Perhaps the French Revolution, the culmination of all the doctrines of the eighteenth-century writers, represents the first serious attempt at reaction of Individualism, but in enfranchising the individual (at least theoretically), it has also isolated him. In isolating him from his caste, from his family, from the social or religious groups of which he was a unit, it has left him delivered over to himself, and has thus transformed society into a mass of individuals, without cohesion and without ties.

Such a work cannot have very lasting results. Only the strong can support isolation, and rely only on themselves ; the weak are unable to do so. To isolation, and the absence of support, they prefer servitude ; even painful servitude. The castes and corporations destroyed by the Revolution formed, of old, the fabric which served to

support the individual in life ; and it is evident that they
corresponded to a psychologic necessity, since they are
reviving on every hand under various names to-day, and
notably under that of trades-unions. These associations
permit the individual to reduce his efforts to a minimum,
while Individualism obliges him to increase his efforts to
the maximum. Isolated, the proletariat is nothing, and
can do nothing ; incorporated he becomes a redoubtable
force. If incorporation is unable to give him capacity
and intelligence it does at least give him strength, and
forbids him nothing but a liberty with which he would
not know what to do.

From the philosophic point of view, then, Socialism is
certainly a reaction of the collectivity against the individual : a return to the past. Individualism and Collectivism are, in their general essentials, two opposing
forces, which tend, if not to annihilate, at least to paralyse
one another. In this struggle between the generally
conflicting interests of the individual and those of the
aggregate lies the true philosophic problem of Socialism.
The individual who is sufficiently strong to count only
on his own intelligence and initiative, and is therefore
highly capable of making headway, finds himself face to
face with the masses, feeble in initiative and intelligence,
but to whom their number gives might, the only upholder
of right. The interests of the two opposing parties are
conflicting. The problem is to discover whether they
can maintain without destroying themselves, at the price
of reciprocal concessions. Hitherto religion has succeeded in persuading the individual to sacrifice his
personal interests to those of his fellows only to replace
individual egoism by the collective egoism. But the old
religions are in sight of death, and those that must replace
them are yet unborn. In investigating the evolution
of the social solidarity we have to consider how far

conciliation between the two contradictory principles is allowed by economic necessities. As M. Léon Bourgeois justly remarked in one of his speeches : " We can attempt nothing against the laws of nature ; that goes without saying ; but we must incessantly study them and avail ourselves of them so as to diminish the chances of inequality and injustice between man and man."

To complete our examination of the various aspects of Socialism we must consider its variations in respect of race. If those principles are true that I have set forth in a previous work on the profound transformations under-gone by all the elements of civilisation — institutions, religions, arts, beliefs, etc.—in passing from one people to another, we can already prophesy that, under the often similar words which serve to denote the conceptions formed by the various nations of the proper *rôle* of the State, we shall find very different realities. We shall see that this is so.

Among vigorous and energetic races which have arrived at the culminating point of their development we observe a considerable extension of what is confided to personal initiative, and a progressive reduction of all that is left to the State to perform ; and this is true of republics equally with monarchies. We find a precisely opposite part given to the State by those peoples among whom the individual has arrived at such a degree of mental exhaustion as no longer permits him to rely on his own forces. For such peoples, whatever may be the names of their institutions, the Government is always a power absorbing everything, manufacturing everything, and controlling the least details of the citizen's life. Socialism is only the extension of this concept. It would be a dictatorship ; impersonal, but absolute.

We see now the complexity of the problems we must encounter, but we see also how they resolve themselves into simpler forms when their data are separately investigated.

CHAPTER II

THE ORIGIN OF SOCIALISM AND THE CAUSES OF ITS PRESENT DEVELOPMENT

1. *The antiquity of Socialism:*—The social struggles engendered by the inequality of conditions go back to the earliest historical ages—Collectivist doctrines among the Greeks—How Socialism caused the destruction of the Greek Independence—Socialism among the Romans and the Jews—Primitive Christianity represents a period of triumph for Socialism—How it was quickly obliged to renounce the Socialistic doctrines—The Socialistic illusions of fifty years ago. 2. *The causes of the present development of Socialism :*—The modern exaggeration of sensibility—The upheavals and instability due to the progress of industry—Needs have developed more quickly than the means of satisfying them—The appetites of modern youth—University ideas— The part played by financiers—The pessimism of thinkers—The present state of societies compared to their state in the past. 3. *The percentage method in the appreciation of social phenomena :*—Necessity of establishing an exact relation between the useful and hurtful elements entering into the composition of a society—Insufficiency of the method of averages—Social phenomena are governed by percentages, not by averages.

1. THE ANTIQUITY OF SOCIALISM.

SOCIALISM has not made its first appearance in the world to-day. To use an expression dear to ancient historians, we may say that its origins are lost in the night of time ; for its prime cause is the inequality of conditions, and this inequality was the law of the ancient world, as it is that of the modern. Unless some all-powerful deity takes it upon himself to re-fashion the nature of man, this inequality is undoubtedly destined to subsist until the final sterilisation of our planet. It would seem that the struggle between rich and poor must be eternal.

Without harking back to primitive Communism, a form of inferior development from which all societies have sprung, we may say that antiquity has experimented with all the forms of Socialism that are proposed to us to-day. Greece, notably, put them all into practice, and ended by dying of her dangerous experiments. The Collectivist doctrines were exposed long ago in the *Republic* of Plato. Aristotle contests them, and as M. Guirand remarks, reviewing their writings in his book on *Landed Property among the Greeks :* " All the contemporary doctrines are represented here, from Christian Socialism to the most advanced Collectivism."

These doctrines were many times put into practice. All the political revolutions in Greece were at the same time social revolutions, or revolutions with the object of changing the inequalities of conditions by despoiling the rich and oppressing the aristocracy. They often succeeded, but their triumph was always ephemeral. The final result was the Hellenic decadence, and the loss of national independence. The Socialists of those days agreed no better than the Socialists of these, or, at least, agreed only to destroy : until Rome put an end to their perpetual dissensions by reducing Greece to servitude.

The Romans themselves did not escape from the attempts of the Socialists. They suffered the experimental agrarian Socialism of the Gracchi, which limited the territorial property of each citizen, distributed the surplus among the poor, and obliged the State to nourish necessitous citizens. Thence resulted the struggles which gave rise to Marius, Sylla, the civil wars, and finally to the ruin of the Republic and the domination of the Emperors.

The Jews also were familiar with the demands of the Socialists. The imprecations of their prophets, the true anarchists of their times, were above all imprecations against riches. Jesus, the most illustrious of them, asserted the right of the poor before everything. His maledictions and menaces are addressed only to the rich; the Kingdom of God is reserved for the poor alone. " It is easier for a camel to go through the eye of a needle than for a rich man to enter into the kingdom of God."

During the first two or three centuries of our era the Christian religion was the Socialism of the poor, the disinherited, and the discontented ; and, like modern Socialism, it was in perpetual conflict with the established institutions. Nevertheless, Christian Socialism ended by triumphing ; it was the first time that the Socialistic ideas obtained a lasting success.

But although it possessed one immense advantage— that of promising happiness only for a future life, and therefore of certainty that it could never see its promises disproved—Christian Socialism could maintain itself only by renouncing its principles after victory. It was obliged to lean on the rich and powerful, and so to become the defender of the fortune and property it had formerly cursed. Like all triumphant revolutionaries, it became conservative in its turn, and the social ideal of Catholic Rome was not very far removed from that of Imperial Rome. Once more had the poor to content themselves with resignation, labour, and obedience ; with a prospect of heaven if they were quiet, and a threat of hell and the devil if they harassed their masters. What a marvellous story is this of this two thousand years' dream ! When our descendants, freed from the heritages that oppress our thoughts, are able to consider it from a purely philosophical point of view, they will never tire of admiring the formidable might of this gigantic Minerva by which our civilisations are still propped up. How thin do the most brilliant systems of philosophy show before the genesis and growth of this belief, so puerile from a rational point of view, and yet so powerful ! Its enduring empire shows us well to what extent it is the unreal that governs the world, and not the real. The founders of religion have created nothing but hopes ; yet they are their works that have lasted the longest. What Socialist outlook can ever equal the paradises of Jesus and Mahomet ? How miserable in comparison are the perspectives of earthly happiness that the apostle of Socialism promises us to-day !

They seem very ancient, all these historical events which take us back to the Greeks, the Romans, and the Jews ; but in reality they are always young, for always they betray the laws of human nature,—that human nature that as yet the course of ages has not changed. Humanity has aged much since then, but she always pursues the same dreams and suffers the same experiences without learning anything from them. Let any one read the declarations, full of hope and enthusiasm, issued by our Socialists of fifty years ago, at the moment of the revolution of 1848, of which they were the most valiant partisans. The new age was born, and, thanks to them, the face of the world was about to be changed. Thanks to them, their country sank into a despotism ; and, a few years later, into a formidable war and invasion. Scarcely half a century has passed since this phase of Socialism, and already forgetful of this latest lesson we are preparing ourselves to repeat the same round.

2. The Causes of the Present Development of Socialism.

To-day, then, we are merely repeating once more the plaint that our fathers have uttered so often, and if our cry is louder, it is because the progress of civilisation has rendered our sensibility keener. Our conditions of existence are far better than of old ; yet we are less and less satisfied. Despoiled of beliefs, and having no perspective other than that of austere duty and dismal solidarity, disquieted by the upheavals and instability caused by the transformations of industry, seeing all social institutions crumble one by one, seeing family and property menaced with extinction, the modern man attaches himself eagerly to the present, the only reality he can seize. Interested only in himself, he wishes at all costs to rejoice in the present hour, of whose brevity he is so sensible. In default of his lost illusions he must enjoy well-being, and consequently riches. Wealth is all the more necessary to him in that the progress of industry and the sciences have created a host of luxuries which were formerly unknown, but have to-day become necessaries. The thirst for riches becomes more and more general, while at the same time the number of those amongst whom wealth is to be divided increases.

The needs of the modern man, therefore, have become very great, and have increased far more rapidly than the means of satisfying them. Statisticians prove that comfort and convenience have never been so highly developed as to-day, but they show also that requirements have never been so imperious. Now the equality of the two terms in an equation only subsists when these two terms progress equally. The ratio of requirements and the means of satisfying them represents the equation of happiness. When these two terms are equal, however small they may be, the man is satisfied. He is also satisfied when, the two terms being unequal by reason of the insufficiency of the means of satisfaction, he is able to re-establish equality by the reduction of his requirements. Such a solution was discovered long ago

by the Orientals, and this is why we see them always
contented with their lot. In modern Europe, on the
other hand, requirements have increased enormously,
while the means of satisfying them have not kept up
with that increase. In consequence, the two terms of
the equation have become very unequal, and the greater
number of civilised men to-day are accustomed to curse
their lot. From top to bottom the discontent is the same,
because from top to bottom the requirements and means
of satisfying them are out of proportion. Every one
is drawn into the same tumultuous chase after Fortune,
and dreams of breaking through all the obstacles that
separate him from her. Individual egoism has increased
without a check on a basis of pessimistic indifference for
all doctrines and general interests. Wealth has become
the end that each desires, and this goal has obscured all
others.

Such tendencies are certainly not new to history, but
it would appear that of old they presented themselves in
a less general and less exclusive form. " The men of
the eighteenth century," says Tocqueville, "scarcely knew
this passion for well-being, which is, as it were, the
mother of servitude. In the higher classes men were
concerned far more to embellish their lives than to render
them comfortable, to become illustrious rather than
wealthy."

This universal pursuit of wealth has had as its inevitable corollary a general lowering of morality, and all the
ensuing consequences of this abatement. The most
clearly visible result has been an enormous decrease of
the prestige enjoyed by the middle classes in the eyes of
their social inferiors. Bourgeois society has aged as
much in a century as the aristocracy in a thousand
years. It becomes exhausted in less than three generations, and only renews itself by constant recruiting from

the classes below it.   It may endow its sons with wealth,
but how can it endow them with the accidental qualities
that only centuries can implant ?   Great fortunes are
substituted for great hereditary qualities, but these great
fortunes fall too often into lamentable hands.

Modern youth has shaken off all precedent, all prejudices.   To it the ideas of duty, patriotism, and honour
seem too often ridiculous fetters, mere vain prejudices.
Educated exclusively in the cult of success, it exhibits
the most furious appetites and covetousness.   When
speculation, intrigue, rich marriages, or inheritances put
fortunes into its hands, it consecrates them only to the
most vulgar delights.

The youth of our universities does not present a more
consoling spectacle.   It is the melancholy product of our
classical education.   Completely steeped in Latin rationalism, possessed of an education entirely theoretical and
bookish, it is incapable of understanding anything of the
realities of life, of the necessities which uphold the fabric
of society.   The idea of the fatherland, without which no
nation can exist, seems to it, as an eminent critic, M.
Jules Lemaître, wrote but recently, the conception "of
imbecile Jingoes completely devoid of philosophy."   He
continues :—

"What are we to say to them ?   They are great
reasoners, and expert in dialectic.   Besides, it is not so
imperative to convince them by reasoning as to induce in
them a sentiment which they have always ignored.

"Some (I have heard them) declare that it is a matter
of indifference to them whether our political capital be at
Berlin or Paris, and that they would accept the just administration of a German prefect with perfectly equal
minds.   And I do not see what I can reply to them,
except that our hearts, our brains, are not fashioned alike.

"Others are patriots in a feeble way ; they detest war

on humanitarian principles, as one used to say fifty years ago, and also because they dream of international Socialism." [1] (*La France extérieure*, May 1, 1898.)

This demoralisation of all the strata of the *bourgeoisie*, the too often dubious means they employ to obtain wealth, and the scandals they provoke every day, are the factors that have perhaps chiefly contributed to sow hatred in the middle and lower classes of society. This demoralisation has given a serious justification to the diatribes of the modern Socialists against the unequal partition of wealth. It has been only too easy for the latter to show that the great fortunes of the present day are too often based upon a gigantic rapine levied on the modest resources of thousands of unhappy creatures. How else are we to qualify such financial operations as the foreign loans launched by great banking houses

[1] The very long-established antipathy entertained by many of our university professors for the army and the fatherland obtains often from the causes mentioned by M. Lemaître, more often from the incapacity of theorists to understand the necessities of the organisation and defence of societies, and very frequently from causes on which it would be useless to insist here. This hatred of the army is often dissimulated, but it bursts forth sometimes with a violence to which witness is borne by the following lines, which were written by one of our best-known university professors, and have recently been quoted by numerous journals :—

"When we no longer see thousands of gabies at every military review; when, instead of admiring titles and epaulettes, you have accustomed your child to say to itself : 'The uniform is a livery, and all liveries are ignominious : that of the priest and that of the soldier, that of the magistrate and that of the lackey;' then you will have taken a step towards reason."

In an interesting article recently published by the *Bibliothèque universelle*, M. Abel Veuglaire has very clearly shown how the outburst of passion let loose recently in France by a certain number of university men was due to their hatred of the army. "It is against the officers that the 'intellectuals' have risen; it is against them that the movement has been directed." Let such sentiments propagate themselves a little, and the societies in which they spread will submit without resistance to Socialism, invasion, and slavery. It is the last pillar of society that is being sapped to-day.

perfectly informed of the affairs of the borrowers, perfectly sure that their too confident subscribers will be
ruined, but ruining them without hesitation in order to
touch commissions which sometimes, as in the case of the
Honduras loan, amount to more than 50 per cent. of the
total sum ?   Is not the poor devil who, goaded by hunger,
steals your watch in the corner of the park, infinitely less
culpable in reality than these pirates of finance ?   Again,
what are we to say of the "rings" of great capitalists,
who band themselves together to buy up all over the
world the whole products of some particular branch of
commerce—copper, for example, or petroleum—the result
of which operation is to double or treble the price of an
indispensable article, and to throw thousands of workmen
into idleness and misery ?   What shall we say of speculations like that of the young American millionaire who, at
the time of the Spanish-American war, bought at one
stroke all the corn obtainable in almost all the markets
of the world, to re-sell it only when the commencement
of the scarcity he had provoked had greatly increased the
price ?   The affair should have brought him in four
million pounds ; but it provoked a crisis in Europe,
famine and riots in Spain and Italy, and plenty of poor
devils died of hunger.   Are Socialists really in the wrong
when they compare the authors of such speculations to
common pirates, and declare that they deserve the hang-
man's rope ?

The demoralisation of the upper strata of society, the
unequal and often very inequitable partition of wealth,
the increasing irritation of the masses, requirements
always greater than enjoyment, the waning of old hierarchies and old faiths—there are in all these circumstances
plenty of reasons for discontent which go to justify the
rapid extension of Socialism.

The most distinguished spirits suffer from a malady not

less pronounced, although of a different nature. This malady does not always transform them into partisans of the new doctrines, but it prevents them from greatly interesting themselves in the defence of the present· social State. The successive disintegration of all religious beliefs, and of the institutions founded upon them ; the total failure of science to throw any light on the mysteries which surround us, and which only deepen when we seek to sound them ; the only too evident proof that all our systems of philosophy represent merely an empty and useless farrago ; the universal triumph of brute force, and the discouragement provoked by that triumph, have ended by throwing even the elect into a gloomy pessimism.

The pessimistic tendencies of modern minds are incontestable ; it would be easy to compose a volume of the phrases in which our writers express them. The following extracts will suffice to illustrate this general disorder of the mind :—

" As for the picture of the sufferings of humanity," says one of our most distinguished contemporary philosophers, M. Renouvier, "without speaking of the ills that appertain to the general laws of the animal kingdom, it is enough to make Schopenhauer pass as mild to-day, rather than excessively gloomy, if we think of the social phenomena which characterise our epoch, the war of nations, the war of classes, the universal extension of militarism, the increase of extreme misery, parallel with the development of great wealth and the refinements of the life of pleasure, the forward march of criminality, often hereditary as much as professional, the increase of suicide, the relaxation of family ties and the abandonment of supramundane beliefs which are being gradually replaced by the sterile materialistic cult of the dead. All these signs of a visible retrogression of civilisation towards barbarism, which the contact of Americans and Europeans with the stationary or decadent populations of the old world cannot fail to augment—all these signs had not yet made their appearance at the time when Schopenhauer gave the signal for the return of the mind to pessimistic judgment of the world's merits."

"The strongest trample on the rights of the weakest without shame," writes another philosopher, M. Boilley ; "the Americans exterminate the Redskins, the English oppress the Hindoos. Under the pretext of civilisation the European nations are dividing Africa amongst themselves, but in reality are only concerning themselves to open new markets. The jealousy between Power and Power has assumed unheard-of proportions. The Triple Alliance threatens us by fear and by covetousness. Russia comes to us through interest."

The abuse of the right of the strongest is incontestable, as are also the iniquities of society. To these iniquities we must add all the social lies to which we are forced to submit, and which are well reviewed by M. de Vogüé in the following lines :—

"Lies of faces, lies of hearts ; lies of thoughts, lies of words ; lies of false glory, false talent, false money, false names, false opinions, false loves ; lies in all things, and even in the best ; in art, in thought, in sentiment, in the public welfare, because to-day these things no longer have their end in themselves, because they are nothing but the means of obtaining fame and lucre."

Without question our civilisations are founded upon lies enough, but if we wish to extirpate these lies we must at the same blow destroy all the elements they support, and notably religion, diplomacy, commerce, and love. What would become of the relations between individuals and between peoples if the lies of faces and words did not dissemble the real sentiments of our hearts ? He who hates falsehood must live solitary and ignored. As for the young man who wishes to make his way in the world, as we understand the matter to-day, the most important advice one can give him is that he should studiously cultivate the art of lying skilfully.

Hatred and envy in the lower classes, intense egoism and the exclusive cult of wealth in the directing classes, pessimism among thinkers : such are the general modern tendencies. A society must be very solidly established to resist such causes of dissolution. It is doubtful if it can resist them long. Some philosophers console themselves for this state of general discontent by arguing that it constitutes a factor of progress, and that peoples too well satisfied with their lot, such as the Orientals, progress no further.

Easy as it may be to raise up these hopes and demands against the actual state of things, it must be conceded that all these social iniquities seem inevitable, since they have always existed. They seem to be the inevitable results of human nature, and no experience gives us leave to think that by changing our institutions, and substituting one kind for another, we should be able to abolish, or even lessen, the iniquities of which we complain so greatly The army of virtuous men has always numbered but few soldiers, and far fewer officers, and we have scarcely discovered the means of augmenting the number. We must therefore rank social iniquities with those natural iniquities, such as age and death, to whose yoke we must submit, and against which all recriminations are vain.

In short, if we resent our misfortunes more keenly than of old, it would nevertheless seem that they have never been lighter. Without going back to the ages when man, taking refuge in the depths of caverns, painfully contested with the beasts for his meagre fare, and often served them as food, let us recall that our fathers knew slavery, invasion, famine, war of all kinds, murderous epidemics, the

Inquisition, the Terror, and many another misery still. Do not let us forget that, thanks to the progress of science and industry, to higher rates of wage and increased cheapness of articles of luxury, the most humble individual lives to-day with more comfort than a feudal gentleman of old in his manor, always menaced as he was with pillage and destruction by his neighbours. Thanks to steam, electricity, and all the other modern discoveries, the poorest of peasants is possessed of a host of commodities that Louis Quatorze in all his pomp never knew.

3. The Percentage Method in the Appreciation of Social Phenomena.

To form just and equitable judgments on a given social environment we must consider not only those evils which touch ourselves, or those injustices which clash with our own sentiments. Every society contains a certain proportion of good and bad, a certain number of virtuous men and of scoundrels, of men of genius and of mediocre or imbecile men. To compare, across the ages, one society with another, we must not only consider their component elements separately, but also their respective proportions one to another ; that is to say, the percentage of these elements. We must put aside the particular cases which strike us and deceive us, and the averages of the statisticians, which deceive us yet more. *Social phenomena are determined by percentages, and not by particular cases or by averages.*

The greater part of our errors of judgment, and the hasty generalisations resulting therefrom, spring from an insufficient knowledge of the *percentage* of the elements observed. The habitual tendency, a characteristic one in partially developed minds, is to generalise from particular cases without considering in what proportion they exist.

We are like the traveller, who, being attacked by thieves while passing through a forest, affirmed that this forest was habitually infested with brigands, without ever dreaming of inquiring how many other travellers, and in how many years, had previously been attacked.

A strict application of the method of percentages will teach us to avoid these hasty generalisations. The judgments we pronounce upon a people or a society are only of value when they deal with a number of individuals so large as to allow of our knowing in what proportions the qualities or faults in question exist. Only from such data are generalisations possible. For instance, if we state that a certain people is characterised by enterprise and energy, we do not by any means say that there may not be among this people individuals completely destitute of such qualities, but simply that the percentage of individuals so gifted is considerable. If it were possible to substitute figures for this clear, yet vague, "considerable," the value of our judgment would be greatly enhanced ; but in evaluations of this kind we must, in default of sufficiently sensible reagents, content ourselves with approximations. Sensible reagents are not altogether wanting, but they require very delicate handling.

This idea of percentages is important. It was after introducing this method into anthropology that I was able to show the profound cerebral differences that separate the various human races—differences which the method of averages could never have established. What until then did we find in comparing the average cranial capacity of the divers races ? Differences which were really insignificant, and which tended to make one believe, as indeed the majority of anatomists did believe, that the cranial volume of all the races was almost identical. By means of certain curves, giving the exact percentage of different capacities, I was able, by taking data from a considerable number of skulls, to demonstrate unquestionably that, on the contrary, cranial capacity varies enormously according to race, and that the fact which clearly distinguishes the superior from the inferior races is that the former possess a certain number of large skulls and the latter do not. By reason of their small number these large skulls do not affect averages. This anatomical demonstration also confirms the psychological notion that the intellectual level of a nation is determined by the greater or less number of the eminent minds it contains.

The methods of investigation employed in the observation of sociological facts are as yet too imperfect to permit the application of such methods of exact evaluation as allow us to translate phenomena into geometric curves. Unable as we are to see all the aspects of a question, we must none the less bear in mind that these facets are very diverse, and that there are many which we do not suspect or comprehend. But it is often the case that these less visible elements are precisely the more important. In order to form not too erroneous judgments upon complex problems—and all sociological problems are complex—we must revise our judgments unceasingly, by a series of verifications and successive approximations, while endeavouring absolutely to put aside our own interests and preferences. We must consider long before concluding, and more often than not we must confine ourselves to considering. These are not the principles which have been applied heretofore by writers who have treated of Socialism, and this doubtless is the reason why the influence of their work has been equally feeble and ephemeral.

CHAPTER III

THE THEORIES OF SOCIALISM

1. *The Fundamental principles of the Socialist theories :*—The theories of
Socialism revert to Collectivism and Individualism—These opposing
principles have always been in conflict. 2. *Individualism :*—The
part played by it in the evolution of civilisations—Its development is
possible only among peoples endowed with certain qualities—
Individualism and the Revolution. 3. *Collectivism :*—All the contemporary forms of Socialism demand the intervention of the State—
The *rôle* which Collectivism reserves for the State—The absolute
dictatorship of the State or the community in Collectivism—The
antipathy of Socialists for liberty—How the Collectivists hope to
arrive at the suppression of inequalities—The common factor of all the
programmes of the various Socialistic sects—Anarchism and its
doctrine—The programmes of the modern Socialists are very old.
4. *The Socialistic ideas of nations, like the various institutions of
nations, are the consequence of their race :*—Importance of the idea
of race—The great difference of the social and political concepts
harboured by the same words—Nations cannot change their institutions of their own free will, and can only modify the terms by
which they denote them—The differences between the Socialistic
concepts of writers belonging to different races.

1. THE FUNDAMENTAL PRINCIPLES OF THE SOCIALIST THEORIES.

TO investigate the political and social concepts of the
theorists of Socialism would be a proceeding of
very little interest, if by so doing we did not often arrive
at those conceptions which are in sympathy with the
spirit of a period, and for this reason produce a certain
impression on the general mind. If, as I have so often

maintained, and as I propose to show once more, the institutions of a people are the consequences of its inherited mental organisation, and not the product of the philosophical theories created on every hand, the small importance of Utopias and speculative constitutions can readily be conceived. But that which the philosophers and orators effect in their imaginings is often nothing other than to invest with a tangible form the unconscious aspirations of their time and race. The few writers who have really influenced the world by their books, such as Adam Smith in England, and Rousseau in France, have merely condensed, into clear and intelligible form, the ideas which were already spreading on every hand. They did not create what they expressed. Only the remoteness of their time can delude us on this point.

If we limit the diverse concepts of the Socialists to the fundamental principles on which they repose the investigation will be very brief.

The modern theories of social organisation, under all their apparent diversity, lead back to two different and opposing fundamental principles—Individualism and Collectivism. By Individualism man is abandoned to himself ; his initiative is carried to a maximum, and that of the State to a minimum. By Collectivism a man's least actions are directed by the State, that is to say, by the aggregate ; the individual possesses no initiative ; all the acts of his life are mapped out. The two principles have always been more or less in conflict, and the development of modern civilisation has rendered this conflict more keen than ever. Neither has any intrinsic or absolute value of itself, but each must be judged according to the time, and above all the race, in which it manifests itself ; and this we shall see in the course of this book.

2. INDIVIDUALISM.

All that has gone to make the greatness of civilisations : sciences, arts, philosophies, religions, military power, etc., has been the work of individuals and not of aggregates. It is by favoured individuals, the rare and supreme fruits of a few superior races, that the most important discoveries and advances, by which all humanity profits, have been realised. The peoples among whom Individualism is most highly developed are by this fact alone at the head of civilisation, and to-day dominate the world.

It is only in our days, and above all since the Revolution, that Individualism, at least under certain forms, has at all developed among the Latin races. These peoples are unfortunately but little adapted, by their ancestral qualities, their institutions, and their education, to rely upon themselves or to govern themselves. Extremely eager for equality, they have always shown themselves very little anxious for liberty. Liberty is competition and incessant conflict, the mother of all progress, in which only the most capable can triumph, and the weakest, as in nature, are condemned to annihilation.

The Revolution has been reproached with having developed Individualism of an exaggerated kind ; but this reproach does not seem just. It is a far cry from the form of Individualism which the Revolution has made prevalent to the Individualism practised by the Anglo-Saxons, for example, amongst other nations. The revolutionary ideal was to shatter the classes and corporations, to reduce every individual to a common type, and to absorb all these individuals, thus dissociated from their categories, into the guardianship of a strongly centralised State. Nothing could be more strongly opposed to the Anglo-Saxon Individualism, which favours the banding together of individuals, obtains everything by it, and confines the action of the State within narrow limits. The work of the Revolution was far less revolutionary than is generally believed. By exaggerating the absorption and centralisation of the State it only continued in a Latin tradition deeply rooted through centuries of monarchy, and followed by all governments alike. By dissolving the industrial, political, religious, and other corporations, it has made this absorption and centralisation still more complete, and, moreover, by so doing, has obeyed the inspirations of all the philosophers of the period.

The development of Individualism, as its necessary consequence, leaves the individual isolated amidst the competition of eager appetites. Young and vigorous races, such as the Anglo-Saxon, in which the mental inequalities between individuals are not too great, accommodate themselves very well to such a state of things. The Anglo-Saxon and American workers are perfectly able, by means of trades-unions, to contend with the demands of capitalism, and to escape its tyranny. Every interest has thus been able to establish itself. But among older races, whose initiative has been exhausted by their systems of education and the march of time, the consequences of individualism have ended by becoming severe in the extreme.

The philosophers of the last century, and the Revolution, in breaking or trying to break up all the religious and social ties which served as a support to man, and which were established on a solid basis, whether that basis were the Church, family, caste, guild, or corporation, certainly thought to effect a thoroughly democratic work. What they really favoured, without foreseeing it, was the birth of an aristocracy of financiers of formidable power, reigning over a mob of individuals possessing neither cohesion nor defence. The feudal seigneur did not use his serfs more hardly than the modern industrial seigneur, the king of a workshop, sometimes uses his mercenaries. Theoretically the latter enjoy every liberty ; theoretically, again, they are the equals of their master. Practically they feel weighing on them the heavy chains of misery and dependence, in menace if not in fact.

The idea of remedying the unforeseen consequences of the Revolution was bound to germinate, and the adversaries of Individualism have had no lack of sound pretexts for attacking it. It was easy for them to maintain that the social organism was of greater importance than the individual organism, and most often strongly opposed to it, and that the latter must give way before the former ; that the weak and incapable have a right to be protected, and that the inequalities created by nature must be çorrected by a new partition of wealth made by society itself. Thus was born the Socialism of the present day, the offspring of the ancient Socialism, and which, like the old, wishes to change the division of wealth by depriving the rich for the benefit of the poor.

Theoretically, the means of annihilating social inequalities are very simple. The State has only to intervene and proceed to the distribution of wealth, and to establish in perpetuity the equilibrium destroyed for the profit of the few. From this idea, so little novel and yet so seductive, have issued the Socialistic concepts of which we are about to treat.

3. COLLECTIVISM.

Modern Socialism presents itself in a number of forms greatly differing in detail. By their general characteristics they rank themselves under the head of Collectivism. All would invariably have recourse to the State to repair the injustice of destiny, and to proceed to the re-distribution of wealth. Their fundamental propositions have at least the merit of extreme simplicity : confiscation by the State of capital, mines, and property, and the administration and re-distribution of the public wealth by an immense army of functionaries. The State, or the community, if you will—for the Collectivists now no longer use the word State—would manufacture everything, and permit no competition. The least signs of initiative, individual liberty, or competition, would be suppressed. The country would be nothing else than an immense monastery subjected to a strict discipline. The inheritance of property being abolished, no accumulation of fortune would be possible.

As for the needs of the individual, Collectivism scarcely regards anything else than his alimentary necessities, and only occupies itself with satisfying them. M. Rouanet, cited by M. Boilley, writes as follows :—

" According to the Marxist explanation the necessities of nutrition are at the summit as well as at the base of human development. Humanity would be at the end, as at the beginning, *a stomach*. Nothing but an enormous stomach, whose physical necessities would constitute the sole motive of all mental activities. The stomach would be the prime cause and the end of humanity. As a Marxist has maintained, Socialism is in effect nothing but the religion of the stomach."

It is evident that such a *régime* implies the absolute dictatorship of the State, or, what comes to exactly the same thing, of the community, with regard to the distribution of wealth, and a no less absolute servitude on the part of the workers. But the latter are not affected by this argument. They are not at all eager for liberty, as is proved by the enthusiasm with which they have acclaimed all the Cæsars when a Cæsar has arisen ; and they care as little for all that goes to make the greatness of a civilisation : for arts, sciences, literature, and so forth, which would disappear at once in such a society ; so that the Collectivist doctrine has nothing in it that could seem antipathetic to them.

In exchange for their rations, which the theorists of Socialism promise him, " the worker would perform his work under the surveillance of State functionaries, like so many convicts under the eye and hand of the warder. All individual motive would be stifled, and each worker would rest, sleep, and eat at the bidding of headmen put in authority over matters of food, work, recreation, and the perfect equality of all."

All stimulus being destroyed, no one would make an effort to ameliorate or to escape from his position. It would be slavery of the gloomiest kind, without a hope of enfranchisement. Under the domination of the capitalist the worker can at least dream of becoming, and some-times does become, a capitalist in his turn. What dream could he indulge in under the anonymous and brutally despotic tyranny of a levelling State which should foresee all his needs and direct his will ? M. Bourdeau has remarked that the Collectivist organisation would be very like that of the Jesuits of Paraguay. Would it not resemble rather the organisation of the negroes on the old slave-plantations ?

Blinded as they are by their dreams, and convinced though they be of the superiority of institutions over economic laws, the more intelligent of the Socialists have been obliged to understand that the great objections to their system are those terrible natural equalities against which no amount of recrimination has ever been able to prevail. Except there were each generation a systematic massacre of all individuals surpassing by however little the lowest imaginable average, social inequality, the child of mental inequality, would quickly re-establish itself.

The theorists meet this objection by assuring us that, in the new social environment thus artificially created, individual capacity would quickly equalise itself, and that the stimulant of personal interest, which has hitherto been the great motive of human nature and the source of all progress, would become useless, and would be replaced by the sudden formation of altruistic instincts which would lead the individual to devote himself to the Collective interest. It cannot be denied that religions, at least during the short periods of ardent belief ensuing on their birth, have obtained some analogous result ; but they had Heaven to offer to their believers, with an eternal life of rewards, while the Socialists propose to their disciples, in exchange for the sacrifice of their liberty, only a hell of servitude and hopeless baseness.

To suppress the effects of natural inequality is theoretically an easy thing, but to suppress these inequalities themselves will always be impossible. They, with death and age, form a part of these eternal fatalities to which a man must submit himself.

But so long as we keep within the frontiers of dreamland it is easy to promise all ; easy, like the Prometheus of Æschylus, "to make blind hopes inhabit mortal souls." So man will change to adapt himself to the new society created by the Socialists. The differences that divide individual from individual will disappear, and we shall have only the average type so well described by the mathematician Bertrand : "Without passions or vices, neither mad nor wise, with average ideas, average opinions, he will die at an average age, of an average malady invented by the statisticians."

The methods of realisation proposed by the various Socialist sects differ in form, though all tending to a common end. They aim finally at obtaining an immediate State monopoly of the soil, and of wealth in general, either by simple decree or by enormously increasing the death duties, so as to lead to the suppression of family property in a few generations.

The enumeration of the programmes and theories of these various sects would be without interest, for at present Collectivism prevails over them all, and alone exerts any influence. Most of them have dropped into oblivion ; "in this manner Christian Socialism, which was pre-eminent in 1848, now marches in the rear," as Léon Say justly remarks. As for State Socialism, only its name has changed ; it is nothing else than the Collectivism of to-day.

It has with reason been said of Christian Socialism that it meets the modern doctrines at many points. " Like Socialism," writes M. Bourdeau, "the Church allows no merit to anything that partakes of genius, talent, grace, originality, or personal gift. *Individualism*, for the Church, is the synonym of *egoism ;* and that which it has always sought to impose on the world is precisely the end of Socialism : *fraternity* under *authority*. The same international organisation, the same reprobation of war, the same sentiments as to suffering and social necessities. According to Bebel it is the Pope who, from the heights of the Vatican, sees most clearly the gathering storm which is upheaving itself upon the horizon. The Papacy might even be in danger of becoming a dangerous competitor with revolutionary Socialism if it were resolutely to place itself in the van of the universal democracy."

To-day the programme of the Christian Socialists differs very little from that of the Collectivists. But the other Socialists repudiate them in their hatred of all religious ideas, and if revolutionary Socialism were to triumph the Christian Socialists would assuredly be its first victims.

Assuredly also they would find no one to take pity on their fate.

Among the various sects that are born and die every day Anarchism deserves to be mentioned. Theoretically the Anarchists appear to come under the heading of Individualists, since they desire to allow the individual an unlimited liberty ; but in practice we must consider them as merely the Extreme Left of the Socialist party, for they are equally intent on the destruction of the present social system. Their theories are characterised by that extreme simplicity which is the keynote of all Socialist Utopias : " Society is worthless ; let us destroy it by steel and fire ! " Thanks to the natural instincts of man they will form a new society, of course perfect. By what train of astonishing miracles would the new society differ from those that have preceded it ? That is what no Anarchist has ever told us. It is evident, on the contrary, that if the present civilisations were to be completely destroyed, humanity would once again pass through all the forms it has, perforce, successively outgrown : savagery, slavery, barbarism, etc. One does not very well see what the Anarchists would gain by this. Admit the immediate realisation of all their dreams ; that is to say, the execution of all the bourgeois *en bloc*, the reunion of all capital in one immense heap, to which every man can resort as he wills : how will this heap renew itself when it has become exhausted, and all the Anarchists have become momentary capitalists in their turn ?

Be it as it may, the Anarchists and the Collectivists are the only sects possessing any influence to-day. The Collectivists imagine their theories were created by the German Karl Marx. As a matter of fact, we find them in detail in the writers of antiquity. Without going back so far, we may remark with Tocqueville, who wrote more than fifty years ago, that all the Socialist theories are exposed at length in the *Code de la Nature*, published by Morelly in 1755.

" You will there find, together with all the doctrines asserting the omnipotence of the State and its unlimited rights, several of the political theories by which France has been most frightened of late, and whose birth we flatter ourselves to have witnessed : the community of goods, the right to work, absolute equality, uniformity in everything, mechanical regularity in all the movements of the individual, regulated tyranny, and the complete absorption of the personality of the citizen into the body of society :

" ' In this society nothing will belong to any person as his personal property,' says Article 1 of the *Code*. ' Every citizen will be fed, maintained, and occupied at the expense of the public,' says Article 2. ' All products will be amassed in the public magazines, thence to be distributed to all citizens and to supply their vital need. At five years of age every child will be taken from his family and educated in common, at the expense of the State, in a uniform manner,' etc."

4. THE SOCIALISTIC IDEAS OF NATIONS, LIKE THE VARIOUS INSTITUTIONS OF NATIONS, ARE THE CONSEQUENCE OF THEIR RACE.

The Racial idea, so little understood a few years ago, is becoming more and more widely spread, and is tending to dominate all our historical, political, and social concepts.[1]

[1] The significance of race, which to-day one might have thought to be an axiom of the most elementary kind, is nevertheless still perfectly incomprehensible to numbers of persons. Thus we find M. Novikoff uphold in a recent work " the small importance of race

I dedicated my penultimate work[1] to showing how the various peoples, mingled and united by the hazard of migration or conquest, came to form the nations known to history, the only ones existing to-day : for pure races, anthropologically speaking, are scarcely to be found except among savages. This idea being thoroughly established, I indicated the limits of variation of character among these races ; that is to say, how variable and mobile characteristics become superimposed upon a fixed substratum. I then demonstrated that all the elements of a civilisation—language, arts, customs, institutions, beliefs—were the consequences of a certain mental constitution, and therefore could not pass from one nation to another without undergoing profound transformations.

It is the same with Socialism ; this law of transformation being general, Socialism also must be subject to it. Despite the deceptive labels which in politics, as in religion and morals, often cover very dissimilar things, there are often hidden behind identical words very different social or political concepts, just as the same concept is often sheltered by very different words. Some Latin nations live under monarchies, some under republics, but under these constitutions, so nominally opposed, the political *rôle* of the State and the individual remains the same,

in human affairs." He believes the negro can easily become the equal of the white man, &c.

Such assertions only show us how, in the author's own words, "in the domain of sociology people still content themselves with declamatory phrases instead of making a careful study of facts." All that M. Novikoff does not understand he qualifies by contradiction, and the authors who do not think with him are classed as pessimists. This kind of psychology is easy, to be sure, but it is equally elementary. To admit "the small importance of race in human affairs" we must absolutely ignore the history of San Domingo, of Hayti, of the twenty-two Spanish-American republics, and of the United States. To misunderstand the part played by race is to condemn oneself forever to misunderstand history.

[1] *The Psychology of Peoples.*

and represents the invariable ideal of the race. Be the nominal government of a Latin people what it may, the action of the State will always be preponderant, and that of the private person very small. Among the Anglo-Saxons the same constitution, republic or monarchy, realises absolutely the opposite of the Latin ideal. Instead of being carried to a maximum, the *rôle* of the State is with them reduced to a minimum, while the political or social part reserved for private initiative reaches, on the contrary, a maximum.

From the preceding facts it results that the nature of institutions plays a very small part in the life of nations. It will probably be several centuries before such a notion can penetrate the popular imagination ; but only when it has done so will the futility of constitutions and revolutions clearly appear. Of all the errors that history has given birth, the most disastrous, that which has uselessly shed the most blood, and heaped up the greatest ruin, is this idea that a people, that any people, can change its institutions as it pleases. All that it can do is to change the names of its institutions, to clothe with new words old conceptions, which represent the natural outcome of a long past.

The foregoing assertions can be justified only by examples, and I have furnished several in my preceding works ; but the study of Socialism among the various races, to which part of the ensuing chapters will be dedicated, will present us with many others. I shall show, first of all, by taking a given nation, how the advent of Socialism has been prepared in that nation by the mental constitution and history of its race. We shall then see how it is that Socialistic doctrines have been unable to succeed among other peoples of different race.

In order to discover to what extent our social conceptions are truly the resultants of race one might even confine oneself to comparing the works of the Socialist writers of various races. The most eminent of English Socialist writers (Herbert Spencer, for example), are partisans of the liberty of the citizen and the limitation of the *rôle* of the State. The Socialist writers of Latin race profess, on the contrary, a perfect disdain of liberty, and invariably clamour for extended action on the part of the State, and the utmost State regulation. One must run through the works of all the theorists of Latin race—those of Auguste Comte, for example—in order to see to what extent the disdain of liberty and the desire to be governed may be carried. " The energetic preponderance of a central power" appeared indispensable to the latter. The State must intervene in all questions economic, industrial, and moral. The people have no rights, but only duties. It must be directed by a dictatorial Government composed of scientists, having at their head an absolute Positivist Pope. Stuart Mill said with reason of these conceptions that they formed the most complete system of spiritual and temporal despotism that had ever issued from the brain of man, except perhaps from that of Ignatius Loyola. Of all modern conquests the most precious was liberty. How much longer shall we keep it ?

CHAPTER IV

THE DISCIPLES OF SOCIALISM AND THEIR MENTAL STATE

1. THE CLASSIFICATION OF THE DISCIPLES OF SOCIALISM.

SOCIALISM comprises many strongly differing and sometimes strongly contradictory theories. The army of its disciples have scarcely anything in common, save an intense antipathy for the present state of things, and vague aspirations towards a new ideal, which is destined to procure them better conditions, and to replace the old ideals. Although all the soldiers of this army appear to be marching together towards the destruction

37

of the inheritance of the past, they are animated by strongly differing sentiments. It is only by examining separately their principal sects that we can attain to at all a clear idea of their psychology, and hence of their receptivity towards the new doctrines.

At first sight Socialism would appear to draw the greater number of its recruits from the popular classes, and more especially from the working classes. The new ideal presents itself to them in this very elementary, and, therefore, very comprehensible shape : less work and more pleasure. In place of an uncertain salary, an often miserable old age, and the slavery of the workshop or factory, often very hard, they are promised a regenerated society in which, thanks to a re-distribution of riches by the omnipotence of the State, work will be thoroughly distributed, and very light.

It would seem as though the popular classes could not hesitate in the face of promises so enticing, and so often repeated : above all, when they hold all the reins in their hands, thanks to universal suffrage and the right to choose their legislators. Yet they do hesitate. The most astonishing thing to-day is not the rapidity, but the slowness with which the new doctrines propagate themselves. To understand the unequal influence of these doctrines in different environments it is imperative to study the various categories of Socialists as we are now about to do.

We shall examine, from this point of view, the following classes in turn : the working classes, the directing classes, the *demi-savants*, and the *doctrinaires*.

2. THE WORKING CLASSES.

The psychology of the working classes differs too greatly in respect of their particular trades, provinces, and surroundings, to be exposed in detail. It would demand, moreover, a very long and laborious study, to which great faculties of observation would be necessary, and for these reasons probably it has never been attempted.

In this chapter, therefore, I shall concern myself only with one class of workers, the only one I have been able to study at all closely : the class of Parisian workmen. The subject is one of peculiar interest in that our revolutions always take place in Paris, and are possible or impossible as their leaders have or have not at their backs the working classes of Paris.

This interesting class evidently contains many varieties : but, in the manner of a naturalist who describes the general characteristics of a genera proper to all the species comprised in that genera, shall deal only with the general characteristics common to the greater number of the observed varieties.

But there is one division which we must clearly define at the outset, that we may not unite elements too dissimilar. We find in the working classes two well-defined subdivisions, each with a different psychology—the labourers and the artisans.

The class of labourers is the inferior as regards intelligence, but also the more numerous. It is the direct product of machinery, and is growing every day. The perfecting of machinery tends to render work more and more automatic, and consequently reduces, more and more, the quantum of intelligence necessary to perform it. The duty of a factory or workshop hand comprises hardly anything more than superintending the running of a thread, or feeding machines with sheets of metal that are bent, stamped, and sheared automatically. Certain everyday articles—for example, the cheap lanterns which are sold for twopence-halfpenny, and serve to light up the ditches—are made up of fifty pieces, each made by its special workman, who does nothing else all his life. As he performs an easy work he is inevitably ill paid, the more so as he is competing with women and children equally capable of performing the same task. . As he does not know how to do anything but this one task, he is necessarily completely dependent on the manufacturer who employs him.

The class of labourers is the class that Socialism can most surely count on ; firstly, because it is the least intelligent, and secondly because it is the least happy, and is inevitably enamoured of all the doctrines that promise to better its condition. It will never take the initiative in a revolution, but it will follow all revolutions with docility.

At the side of, or rather very far above this class of workers, we have that of the artisans. It comprises the workers occupied in the building and engineering trades, in the industrial arts and minor industries— carpenters, cabinet-makers, fitters, electro-platers, foundry hands, electricians, painters, decorators, masons, &c. These have every day to undertake a new task, to over-come difficulties which oblige them to reflect and develop their intelligence.

This class of workers is the most familiar in Paris ; and this class, above all, I have in mind in the following pages. Its psychology is the more interesting because the characteristics of this particular class are very clearly defined, which is very far from being the case with many of the other social categories.

The Parisian artisan constitutes a caste, from which he rarely essays to issue. The son of a working man, he likes his sons to remain working men, while the dream of the peasant, on the contrary, and of the small clerk or shop-hand, is to make "gentlemen" of his sons.

The clerk or shop-hand [1] despises the artisan, but the artisan despises the clerk far more, and thinks him an idle and incapable person. He knows he is less well dressed, less refined in his manners, but he thinks himself by far the superior in energy, activity, and intelligence ; and more often than not he is. The artisan advances only by merit, the *employé* by seniority. The *employé* is only of significance through the whole of which he is a part. The artisan represents a unit having a value by itself. If the artisan knows his trade thoroughly he is always sure of finding work wherever he goes ; the *employé* is not, and is always trembling before the principals who may make him lose his employment. The artisan has far more dignity and independence. The *employé* is incapable of moving outside of the narrow limits of regulations the observance of which constitutes his entire function. The artisan, on the contrary, encounters fresh difficulties every day, which stimulate his enterprise and intelligence. Finally, an artisan, being generally paid better than a clerk, and not being subjected to the same necessities of external decorum, is able to live a much fuller life. At twenty-five a fairly capable artisan is earning without difficulty a sum that a commercial or civil service clerk will scarcely receive till after twenty years of service.

The psychological characteristics I am about to treat of in detail are sufficiently general to allow of their being attributed to the majority of Parisian artisans of the same race. This ceases to be with regard to artisans of difference race, so true is it that the influences of race are greater than those of environment. I shall show in another part of this book in what manner English and Irish workers differ, though working in the same shop—that is to say, subjected to identical

[1] *Employé.*

conditions of trade. Again, we in Paris have only
to compare the Parisian workman with Italians or Germans working under the same conditions—that is to
say, subjected to the same surrounding influences. We
will not undertake to study the subject, but will confine
ourselves to noticing that these racial influences are
clearly to be seen in Parisian workmen who have come
from certain provinces—for example, from Limousins.
Several of the psychological characteristics enumerated
further on by no means apply to the latter. The workman from Limousins is quiet, sober, and patient, and
neither noise nor luxury are necessary to him. He
frequents neither the wine-shop nor the theatre; he
keeps to the costume of his native province in the city,
and his only dream is to save money and return to
his village. He confines himself to a few difficult,
but well-remunerated callings; that of mason, for
instance, in which his punctuality and sobriety make him
much sought after.

These general principles and divisions being defined,
we will now consider the psychology of the Parisian
workmen, having more especially in view the class of
artisans. Here are the more striking elements of their
mental state :

The Parisian workman approaches the savage in his
impulsive nature, his lack of foresight, his want of self-
control, and his habit of having no guide but the instinct
of the moment; but he possesses an artistic and sometimes critical sense extremely refined for his environment. Apart from the matters of his trade, which he
performs excellently, though with more taste than finish,
he reasons little or ill, and is hardly accessible to any
argument but that of his sentiments.

He likes to commiserate himself, and is given to railing,
but his complaints are more passive than active. He

is at heart a true conversative and stay-at-home, and has little stomach for change. Indifferent in the extreme to political doctrines, he has always submitted readily to all *régimes*, provided always that they had at their head individuals possessed of prestige. A general's *panache* always produces in him a species of respectful emotion that he can scarcely resist. With words and prestige one can easily manipulate him ; with reasons not at all.

He is very sociable, and fond of the company of his comrades; hence his custom of haunting the wine-shop, the true club and salon of the people. It is not the taste for alcohol that takes him there, as is often supposed. Drink is a pretext that may become a habit ; but it is not the craving for alcohol that takes him to the *cabaret*.

If he escapes his home by means of the public-house, as the *bourgeois* escapes his by means of his club, it is because his home has nothing very attractive about it. His wife, his housekeeper, as he calls her, has undeniable qualities of economy and foresight, but she takes no interest in anything beyond her children, the prices of things, and bargaining. Totally refractory to general conceptions and to discussions, she enters into the latter only when the purse and the cupboard are empty. She, at least, is not one to choose the gallows merely to uphold a principle.

The practice of frequenting the wine-shops, theatres, and public meeting-places is for the Parisian workman the consequence of his craving for excitement, expansion, and emotion ; for uproarious discussion and the intoxication of words. Doubtless he would do better to please the moralists by soberly keeping to his room. But in order to do that he must have, in the place of the mental constitution of a workman, the brain of a moralist.

Political ideas do sometimes lead the workman, but

they hardly ever absorb him. He will readily become a rebel, a fanatic, for an instant, but he never remains a sectarian. He is so impulsive that no idea whatever can permanently impress itself on him. His hatred of the *bourgeois* is as often as not a convention, a wholly superficial sentiment.

One must know very little indeed of the workman to suppose him capable of pursuing seriously the realisation of any ideal whatever, Socialistic or otherwise. The ideal of the workman, when by chance he has one, is everything that is not revolutionary, not Socialistic, and everything that is middle-class. His ideal is always the little house in the country ; a little house that must not be too far from the wine-seller's shop.

He possesses a great stock of generosity and confidence. He will most readily and cordially lodge a comrade in distress, often at great inconvenience to himself, and will every instant render him a host of little services which men of the world would never perform under the same circumstances. He has no egotism, and in this respect shows himself greatly the superior of the *bourgeois*, whose egotism is on the contrary very highly developed. From this point of view he deserves a sympathy of which the *bourgeoisie* are not always worthy. Besides, it is evident that this development of egotism in the superior classes is the necessary consequence of their wealth and culture, and proportional to the degree of their wealth and culture. Only the poor man is really humane, because only he really knows what misery is.

This absence of egotism, together with the readiness with which he becomes filled with enthusiasm for the individuals that charm him, render the Parisian workman liable to devote himself, if not to the triumph of an idea, at least to the leaders who have seduced his mind. The recent Boulangist adventure affords us an instructive example.

The Parisian workman willingly derides all matters of religion. At heart he has an unconscious respect for them ; his derision is directed never against religion as such, but against the clergy, whom he considers rather as a sort of branch of the Government. Marriages and burials without the rites of the Church are rare among the working classes of Paris. Married only at the *mairie* the workman would always feel himself badly married. His religious instincts—that is, his tendency to allow himself to be dominated by any creed whatever, political, social, or religious—are very tenacious. Instincts like these will one day constitute one of the elements of suc- cess of Socialism, which is in reality only a new creed. If Socialism does succeed in propagating itself among the workers, it will be not at all as the theorists hold, by the satisfactions it promises them, but by the disinterested devotion which its apostles will be able to awaken.

The political conceptions of the working man are very rudimentary and of an extreme simplicity. The Govern- ment represents for him a mysterious absolute power, able to decree at will the increase or decrease of salaries, but, as a general thing, hostile to the workers and favour- able to the employers. Anything disagreeable happening to the working man is necessarily the fault of the Government ; this is why he so easily accepts the pro- position to change it. For the rest, he cares little for the nature of the Government which directs him, and is only certain that there must be one. The good Government is that which protects the workers, raises wages, and molests the employer. Having little occasion to make use of his political liberties he cares little for them. If he has a sympathy for Socialism, it is that he beholds in it a system of government which will increase wages

while reducing the hours of work. If he could realise
to what a system of regimentation and surveillance the
Socialists propose to subject themselves in their ideal
society, he would at once become the implacable enemy
of the new doctrines.

The theorists of Socialism think they know the mind
of the working classes well ; they really know very little
about the matter. They imagine the elements of persuasion are found in discussion and argument ; in reality
they have very different sources. What remains of all
their speeches in the vulgar mind ? Very little indeed.
When we freely question a workman who calls himself a
Socialist, if we ignore the shreds of ready-made humanitarian phrases and the stale imprecations against capital
which he repeats mechanically, we find that his Socialistic concept is a vague reverie, very like that of the
early Christians. In a very distant future, too distant
greatly to impress him, he perceives the advent of the
kingdom of the poor, the poor in fortune and the poor
in spirit ; the kingdom from which the rich will be
jealously expelled, the rich in money and the rich in
mind.

As for the means of realising this remote ideal, the
workman scarcely dreams of them. The theorists, who
know very little of his real nature, have no suspicion that
it is precisely in the plebeian that Socialism will one
day meet its most formidable enemy ; on the day when
it shall seek to pass from theory to practice. The working classes, and still more the peasants, have the instinct
of property at least as highly developed as the middle
classes. They are anxious enough to increase their
possessions, but they will elect to dispose of the fruits of
their labour in their own fashion, rather than abandon
them to a collectivity, although this collectivity may
pretend to satisfy all their desires. Such a sentiment has

secular origins, and it will always uprear itself as an inviolable wall against every attempt of Collectivism.

Although he is headstrong, turbulent, and always ready to side with the promoters of revolution, the working man is strongly attached to the old order of things ; he is extremely arbitrary, a thorough conservative, and a firm believer in authority. He has always acclaimed those who have shattered altars and thrones, but he has acclaimed with far greater fervour those who have re-established them. When by chance he becomes employer in his turn he behaves like an absolute monarch, and is far harder on his former comrades than the employer of the middle. class. General du Barrail describes in the following words the psychology of the workman who has emigrated to Algeria to become a colonist—a profession which consists simply in making the natives work by hitting them with a stick : " A democrat in soul, he entertained all the instincts of the feudal age ; escaped from the workshops of the manufacturing towns, he spoke and reasoned like the vassals of Pepin the Short or Charlemagne, or like the knights of William the Conqueror, who carved out vast domains from the territories of vanquished peoples."

Always a jester, often sprightly, he is an expert in seizing the comic side of things, and appreciates, above all, the humorous or rowdy side of political events. The arraignment of a minister by a deputy or a journalist amuses him immensely, but the opinions defended by the minister and his opponents interest him but little. A discussion carried on by exchange of invective excites him as much as a scene at the Ambigu, [1] while debate by exchange of arguments leaves him totally indifferent.

This characteristic turn of mind is naturally exemplified in his manner of conducting debates, as far as one

[1] A theatre corresponding to our Adelphi.—*Trans.*

is able to observe it at political meetings of the people. He never discusses the worth of an opinion ; only that of the person expressing it.   He is seduced by the personal prestige of an orator, not by his reasoning.   He does not attack the opinions of a speaker who displeases him, but only his person.   The probity of his adversary is immediately called into question, and that adversary may consider himself lucky if he is treated simply as a poor fool, and has nothing harder than words about his head. As we know, the debates at public meetings consist invariably of an exchange of savage invective and promiscuous blows.   This, however, is a racial vice which is by no means peculiar to the working man.   To numbers of people it is impossible to hear any person give expression to an opinion widely differing from their own without becoming intimately persuaded that this individual is a complete imbecile or an infamous scoundrel.   The comprehension of the ideas of others has always been inaccessible to the Latins.

The careless, impulsive, changeful, and turbulent character of the Parisian working classes has always prevented them from associating themselves to undertake important enterprises, as do the English workers.   This incorrigible incapacity makes it impossible for them to dispense with direction, and condemns them by this alone to remain in perpetual tutelage.   They feel an incurable need of having some one over them to govern them, to whom they can resort with regard to everything that may befall them.   Here again we find a racial characteristic.

The only well-defined result of the Socialist propaganda among the working classes has been to sow the opinion that they are exploited by their employers, and that by changing the Government they would receive higher wages and far less work.   But their conservative instincts withhold the majority of them from rallying to this idea. At the elections of 1893, out of ten million electors only 556,000 gave their votes to Socialist deputies, and the latter numbered only 49. This low percentage, which showed hardly any increase at the elections of 1898, proves how tenacious are the conservative interests of the working classes.

There is another fundamental reason which singularly hinders the propagation of Socialistic ideas. The number of workmen who are small proprietors and small stockholders is increasing on all hands. The little house, the smallest one can imagine, the small share, though it be only a fraction of a share, suddenly transforms its possessor into a calculating capitalist, and develops his instincts of property to an astonishing extent. As soon as he has a family, a house, and a few savings, the workman becomes immediately a stubborn Conservative. The Socialist, above all the Anarchist-Socialist, is usually a bachelor, without home, means, or family ; that is to say, a nomad, and in all ages the nomad has been a refractory and a barbarian. When the evolution of economics has made the workman the proprietor of a part, as small as one chooses to suppose, of the factory he works in, his conceptions of the relations between labour and capital will undergo a complete change. The proof is furnished by the few workshops in which such transformations have already been realised, and also by the mental state of the peasant. The latter, as a general thing, leads a far harder life than the urban workman, but he usually has a field to cultivate, and for that simple reason is scarcely ever a Socialist, unless the idea germinates in his primitive brain that it might be possible to take possession of his neighbour's field, without, of course, abandoning his own.

We may sum up the preceding remarks by observing

that the class most refractory to Socialism will be pre
cisely the working class on which the Socialists count
so much.   The propaganda of the Socialists have given
rise to covetousness and hatred, but the new doctrines
have not seriously affected the mind of the people.   It is
quite possible that the Socialists may recruit from the
people the soldiers of a revolution, after one of those
events—such as a long turn of idleness or a fall in wages
as the result of some economic competition—which the
working classes always attribute to the Government ; but
it will be precisely these soldiers who will rally with all
celerity round the plume of the Cæsar who shall arise to
suppress this revolution.

3. THE DIRECTING CLASSES.

"A fact that largely aids the progress of Socialism,"
writes M. de Laveleye, "is its gradual invasion of the
upper and educated classes."

The factors of this invasion, to my mind, are of several
orders : the contagion of fashionable beliefs, fear, and
indifference.

"A large proportion of the middle classes," writes
Signor Garofalo, "while regarding the Socialist movement with a certain trepidation, are convinced to-day
that it is irresistible and inevitable.   Among this number
are those candid souls who are ingenuously enamoured
of the Socialist ideal, and see in it the aspiration towards
the reign of justice and universal felicity."

There we have simply the expression of a superficial
and unreasoning sentiment, accepted through contagion.
To adopt a political or social opinion only when, after
mature reflection, it appears to respond to the reality of
things, is a process apparently impossible to the average
Latin mind.   If in the adoption of an opinion—political,
social, or religious—we were to employ a fractional part

of the lucidity and reflection which the pettiest of grocers employs in a matter of business, we should not be, as we are in political or religious questions, at the mercy of our circumstances, of sentiments, of an hour's fashion ; we should not be floating, as we are, at the mercy of the events and opinions of the moment.

Socialistic tendencies to-day are far more prevalent among the middle classes than among the populace. They spread by simple contagion, and with remarkable rapidity.   Philosophers, *littérateurs*, and artists follow the movement with docility, and contribute actively to spread it.   The theatre, books, pictures even, are becoming more and more steeped in this tearful and sentimental Socialism, which is entirely reminiscent of the humanitarianism of the controlling classes at the time of the Revolution.   The guillotine promptly taught them that in the struggle for life one cannot renounce self-defence without at the same stroke renouncing life.   Considering with what complaisance the upper classes are to-day allowing themselves to be progressively disarmed, the historian of the future will feel only contempt for their lamentable want of foresight, and will not lament their fate.

Fear is another of the factors which favour the propagation of Socialism among the *bourgeoisie*.   "The *bourgeoisie*," writes the author I quoted but now, "are afraid.   They grope about irresolutely, and hope to save themselves by concessions, forgetting that this is the most insensate policy imaginable, and that indecision, parleyings, and the desire to content everybody, are faults of character which, by an eternal injustice, the world has always cruelly punished, more cruelly than if they had been crimes."

The last of the factors which I cited, the factor of indifference, if it does not directly favour the propagation of Socialism, at least facilitates it by restraining people from fighting it. Sceptical indifference, "*je m'enfichisme*," as the current saying goes, is the great malady of the modern *bourgeoisie*. When, to the declamations and assaults of an increasing minority, which is pursuing with fervour the realisation of an ideal, nothing is opposed but indifference, one may be sure that the triumph of that minority is very near at hand. Are the worst enemies of society those that attack it, or those who do not even give themselves the trouble of defending it ?

4. DEMI-SAVANTS AND DOCTRINAIRES.

I apply the term *demi-savant* to those who have no other knowledge than that contained in books, and who consequently know absolutely nothing of the realities of life. They are the product of our schools and universities, those lamentable factories of degeneration whose disastrous effects have been exposed by Taine, Paul Bourget, and many others. A professor, a scholar, or a graduate of one of our great colleges is always for years, and often all his life, nothing but a *demi-savant*.

It is from the ranks of the *demi-savant*, and notably from the ranks of unemployed licentiates and bachelors of the universities, outcasts from society whom the State has been unable to place, ushers discontented with their lot, university professors who find their merits overlooked, that the most dangerous disciples of Socialism are recruited, and even the worst Anarchists. The last Anarchist executed in Paris was an unsuccessful candidate from the *École Polytechnique;* a man unable to find any employment for his useless and superficial science, and consequently the enemy of a society which was not wise enough to appreciate his merits, and naturally anxious to replace it it by a new world in which the vast capacities he supposed himself to possess would have found an outlet. The discontented *demi-savant* is the worst of malcontents. It is this discontent that explains the frequency of Socialism among certain bodies of individuals—schoolmasters, for example, who always consider themselves ill-used and unappreciated.

The learned Italian criminologist, Signor Garofalo, recounts a remark made by one of his compatriots : " All the masters in Piedmont, where I spent some time last year, are ardent Socialists. You should hear them talk to their pupils ! "

It is the same in France, and it is perhaps from among our university instructors and professors that Socialism draws most recruits. The chief leader of the French Socialists is an ex-professor of the university. A judicious critic, M. Maurice Talmeyr, has recently drawn attention, in a leading journal, to the stupefying fact, that this Socialist having applied for authorisation to deliver a course on collectivism at the Sorbonne, 16 professors out of 37 supported his request.

To show what the opinions of the candidate for this chair of Socialism are like, M. Talmeyr gives the following extract from one of his lectures :—

" When we have *destroyed everything,* we shall construct from top to bottom the social republic on *the blood-stained and smoking ruins* of what was once reactionary France ! . . ."

Then he adds :

" What is the general spirit of the University to-day ? The majority of the professors are sane, but they are side by side with a minority who are afflicted with gangrene, and a singularly virulent gangrene. Is it not an unheard-of thing, and one full of incalculable promises, this manifestation of the sixteen of the Sorbonne at the present hour ? Are there really to be found there, instituted, maintained, and consecrated by the

State, sixteen professors of history, rhetoric, poetry, and what not, who are perfectly ready to suppress individual property, to abolish the army, and to continue on its ruins, from the sentry-boxes of the Prussian soldiers, the lessons they have delivered to us up to the present from their chairs ? Our university instructors make over-much noise for their number, but their number, however, does not appear negligible, and all these muddy con-sciences of pedants, [1] who call themselves 'troubled consciences,' show us of what rancid pride and blustering hypocrisy they are made. The actual condition of certain university functionaries denotes more than the fondness of 'being in advance.' A cynical scepticism, an ardent habit of ranting, and a vague delirium of destruction are strangely combined in the impotent ' spirit of the day,' and plenty of our professors, to-day, are only too much of their time. They push too far the puerility of believing in nothing, and run too instinctively to anything that seems to represent a science, or to corrosive manifestations of any kind. They are too fond of dangerous courses and evil doctrines because they are dangerous courses and evil doctrines, and they give vent on too many occasions to too much fermented pretension and malevolence. Consider carefully the university professor and his un-solicited intervention in recent affairs, and you will see it exclusively under two aspects ; he was there to destroy and to exhibit himself. He puts himself forward without motive, in an attitude without frankness, sobbing without tears, and degrades, corrupts, and demolishes without reason. He has the appearance of a pedant ; he is an Anarchist."

[1] "*Et toutes ces consciences troubles de pédants, qui se disent des 'consciences troublées.'*" There is here an untranslatable play of words ; *trouble* means dull, muddy, dim, cloudy ; *troublée* means afflicted.—*Trans.*

The part played to-day by university functionaries in the Latin countries is altogether threatening to the societies in which they live. " All these theorists of the absolute," as a penetrating thinker, M. Maurice Barrès, justly remarks, "always impede public affairs." They may be distinguished in their specialities,[1] but they are total strangers to the realities of the world, and by that reason are even incapable of understanding the artificial but necessary conditions which render the existence of a society possible. A society directed by an areopagus of scientists, such as Auguste Comte dreamed of, would not last six months. In questions of general interest the opinions of specialists in letters or science are of no greater value than that of ignorant people, and very often are of much less value, if these ignorant people be peasants or workmen whose profession has brought them into contact with the realities of life. I have elsewhere insisted on this point, which constitutes the most solid argument in favour of universal suffrage. It is among the crowd that we often find the political spirit, patriotism, and the sentiment of the value of social interests, but rarely found among the specialists.

By the crowd, in fact, is most often manifested the soul of a race and the comprehension of its interests. They are doubtless guided by instinct, not by reason ; but are not the acts determined by instinct, often enough, superior to those of reason ?

Instinct, which directs all the acts of our inorganic life,

---

[1] They belong to that order of scientists of which M. René Sand has recently given an excellent analysis in the *Revue Scientifique* : " Confined in their speciality, incapable of intellectual co-ordination, they know nothing of general ideas, and leave their method and principles behind when they sally from their narrow domain ; they are anti-scientific in their relations with men and things in their social, literary, and artistic ideas, in all the relations of life. . . . They are not thinkers, they are monks."

and the immense majority of the acts of intellectual life, is to the conscious life of the mind what the profound waters of the ocean are to the waves that ruffle their surface. If the incessant action of instinct were to cease, man could not live a day. Renan, who was far more a poet than a philosopher, has, nevertheless, well defined the part played by this powerful factor in the following passage, which becomes extremely just if we substitute for the words "spontaneous," "hidden God," and "universal force," the simple word "instinct." The latter term represents simply the inheritance of all the adaptations acquired by our long series of ancestors, dating back to the monad of the first geological ages :—

"The mechanism of intelligence is difficult to analyse ; yet, without knowing its analysis, the simplest man knows how to touch its every spring. Applied to the spontaneous, the words *easy* and *difficult* have no meaning. The child learning his language, or humanity building up a science, meets with no more difficulties than a plant in growing, than an organic body in reaching its complete development. Everywhere is the hidden God, the universal force; which, acting in sleep, in the absence of the individual soul, produces these marvellous effects, as far above human artifice, as the Infinite Power surpasses finite powers."

It is because the half-science of the *demi-savant* obscures the instinctive intuitions, that its intervention in social affairs is so often harmful.

Social failures, misunderstood geniuses, lawyers without clients, writers without readers, doctors without patients, professors ill-paid, graduates without employment, clerks whose employers disdain them for their insufficiency, puffed-up university instructors—these are the natural adepts of Socialism. In reality they care very little for doctrines. Their dream is to create by violent means a society in which they will be the masters. Their cry of equality does not prevent them from having an intense scorn of the rabble who have not, as they have, learned out of books. They believe themselves greatly the superiors of the working man, and are really greatly his inferiors in their lack of practical sense and their exaggerated egotism. If they became masters their despotism would be no less than that of Marat, Saint-Just, or Robespierre, those excellent types of the unappreciated *demi-savant*. The hope of tyrannising in one's turn, when one has always been ignored, humiliated, thrust into the shade, must have created many disciples of Socialism. Their mental state may be compared to that of those Kaffirs whose rudimentary psychology was recently depicted in one of the journals in the following terms : " Attracted by the promise of gain, they enlist themselves *en masse* in the mines, where they work at very low wages, with the sole ambition of saving some fifty or sixty pounds, with which they return to their village, not without having first acquired a fashionable silk hat, a red umbrella, and a pair of boots. In this remarkable attire they install themselves at the doors of their huts, while making women and children work for them under pain of the lash."

To this category of *demi-savants* belong most often the *doctrinaires* who formulate, in poisonous publications, the theories their ingenuous disciples at once begin to propagate. These are the generals who appear to direct the soldiers, but who really confine themselves to following them. They form a small majority whose influence is far more apparent than real. In reality they do little else than transform aspirations which they have not created into noisy invective, and give them that dogmatic form which permits the leaders to appear in print. Their books are often a sort of evangels, which no one ever reads, but from which one may cite in argument the title, or a few fragmentary phrases reproduced by special papers. There is not a Socialist who does not constantly invoke the work of Karl Marx on Capital, but I very much doubt if one in ten thousand has even turned over the leaves of this indigestible volume. The obscurity of such works is, however, a fundamental condition of their success. Like the Bible for the Protestant clergy, they constitute a sort of prophetic conjuring book, which one has only to open at random to find—provided that one possesses faith — the solution of any question in the world.

The *doctrinaire*, then, may be highly educated ; that in no way saves him from being always obtuse and ingenuous, and most often an envious malcontent as well. Struck only by one side of a question, he remains in ignorance of the march of events and their recurrence. He is incapable of understanding anything of the complexity of social phenomena, of economic necessities, of atavistic influences, of the passions which really rule men. Having no guide but a bookish and rudimentary logic he readily believes that his ideas are about to transform the evolution of humanity and overcome destiny.

The lucubrations of all these noisy *doctrinaires* are sufficiently vague, and their ideal of the future society sufficiently chimerical ; but one thing is not at all chimerical, and that is their furious hatred of the actual state of society, and their burning desire to destroy it.

If the revolutionaries of all ages have always shown themselves powerless to construct anything whatever, they have never found much difficulty in destroying. The hand of a child may set fire to all the treasures of art that centuries have hoarded together in a museum. Their influence may go so far as to provoke a successful and ruinous revolution, but it will not be able to go further. The incorrigible need of being governed which has always been manifested by a crowd would quickly bring these innovators under the sabre of a despot, no matter who, and whom they would be the first to acclaim, as our history proves. Revolutions cannot modify the minds of peoples ; revolutions have never effected more than ironical changes of words and super-ficial transformations. Nevertheless, it is for the sake of insignificant changes that the world has been so often overturned, and will doubtless continue to be.

If one were to review the parts played by the various classes in the dissolution of society among the Latin peoples, one would say that the *doctrinaires* and mal-contents manufactured by the universities act above all by attacking ideals, and are, by reason of the intellectual anarchy they give rise to, one of the most corrosive factors of destruction ; the middle classes help the downfall by their indifference, their egotism, their feeble will, and their absence of initiative or political perception ; the lower classes act in a revolutionary manner by seeking to destroy, so soon as it shall be sufficiently undermined, the edifice which is tottering on its foundations.

BOOK II

SOCIALISM AS A BELIEF

CHAPTER I

THE FOUNDATIONS OF OUR BELIEFS

1. *The ancestral origins of our beliefs :*—To understand Socialism it is necessary to examine how our beliefs are formed—Ancestral, or sentimental concepts—Acquired, or intellectual concepts—The influence of these two categories of concepts—Beliefs that appear now are always the offspring of older beliefs—Slowness with which beliefs change—Utility of common beliefs—Their establishment marks the culminating period of a civilisation—The great civilisations represent the efflorescence of a small number of beliefs—No civilisation has been able to maintain itself without basing itself on common beliefs. 2. *The part played by beliefs with regard to our ideas and sentiments. Psychology of incomprehension :*—How our knowledge of the world is obscured by our hereditary beliefs—They affect not only our conduct, but the senses we attach to words—Individuals of different race and different class in reality speak different languages — Incomprehension separates them quite as much as the divergence of their interests—Why persuasion has never depended on reason—The overwhelming influence of the dead in discussions between the living—The consequence of incomprehension—Impossibility of colonisation for peoples among whom incomprehension is too pronounced—Why histories are so far removed from the reality. 3. *The ancestral formation of the moral idea :*—The real motives of conduct are most often hereditary instincts—The Moral Idea only exists when it has become instinctive and hereditary—The slight value of precept in morals.

1. THE ANCESTRAL ORIGINS OF OUR BELIEFS.

ALL the civilisations that have succeeded one another in the course of ages have reposed on a certain number of beliefs, which beliefs have always played a fundamental part in the lives of the nations.

How are these beliefs born, and how do they develop ?
We have already treated this matter, in a summary fashion,
in the *Psychology of Peoples*. It may be useful to return
to the question. Socialism is a faith far more than a
doctrine. Only by making ourselves perfectly familiar
with the mechanism of the genesis of beliefs can we
perceive what a part Socialism may perhaps be called
upon to play.

Man cannot change, of his own will, the sentiments
and beliefs which dominate him. Behind the vain
struggles of the individual lurk always the influences
of atavism. These are they that give to the crowd that
narrow conservatism which their momentary revolts
obscure. The thing that men are least able to support is
a thing they never do support for long—change in their
hereditary thoughts and habits.

These very ancestral influences are the influences which
still protect civilisations that are already too old, of which
we are the possessors, which we keep alive, and which
many elements of destruction are threatening at the
present day.

This slowness of the evolution of beliefs constitutes
one of the most essential facts of history, and at the same
time one of the facts the least explained by historians.
Psychology alone permits us to determine its causes.

In addition to the exterior and variable conditions to
which he is perforce subject, man is especially guided in
life by conceptions of two kinds—*ancestral or sentimental
concepts* and *acquired or intellectual concepts*.

Ancestral concepts are the heritage of the race, the legacy
of ancestors immediate or far removed, an unconscious
legacy bestowed at birth, and which determines the
principal motives of conduct.

Acquired or intellectual concepts are those which man
acquires under the influence of his environment and

education. They aid him to reason, to explain, to dis
course, but are very rarely the cause of his conduct.
Their influence over his actions remains practically nil,
until, by repeated hereditary accumulations, they have
penetrated his sub-consciousness and have become sentiments. If the acquired concepts do sometimes succeed
in contending with the ancestral concepts it is that the
latter have been neutralised or annulled by contrary
heritages, as happens, for example, in crosses between
members of different races. The individual then becomes
a sort of *tabula rasa*. He has lost his ancestral concepts;
he is nothing but a hybrid without morals or character,
at the mercy of every impulse.

One reason of the so heavy weight of secular heredity
is that amongst the so numerous beliefs and opinions
which are born every day we find so few, in the course
of the ages, that become preponderant and universal.
One might even say that, in a humanity already aged,
no new general belief could form itself if this belief did
not attach itself intimately to anterior beliefs. The nations
have scarcely known such a thing as a totally new belief.
Religions which seem original — such as Buddhism,
Christianity, Islamism — when we consider only an
advanced stage of their evolution, are in reality
the simple efflorescence of former beliefs. They have
only been able to develop when the beliefs replaced by
them had lost their empire through the passage of time.
They vary according to the various races which practise
them, and are in nothing universal but in the letter of
their dogmas. We have already seen, in another work,
that in passing from nation to nation they become funda-
mentally transformed in order to graft themselves on the
previous religions of those nations. A new faith becomes
thus nothing but the rejuvenescence of a preceding faith.
There are not only Jewish elements in Christianity; it has

its sources in the most ancient religions of the peoples of
Europe and Asia. The thread of water that trickled from
the Sea of Galilee became an impetuous river only because
all Pagan antiquity thither turned its waters. "The con-
tributions of the Jews to Christian mythology," says M.
Louis Ménard very truly, " are scarcely equal to those of
the Egyptians and the Persians."

Simple and slight though these changes of faith may
be, yet ages and ages are required to fix them in the soul
of a people. A faith is quite other than an opinion
which one debates ; it exists as a factor of conduct, and
consequently is really possessed of power only when it
has been handed down in the sub-consciousness, and
has there formed the solid concretion called a sentiment.
Then faith possesses the character which is essential if it
is to be imperative, and keeps aloof from the influences
of discussion and analysis.[1] Only in its beginnings,
when it is still floating in the air, can a faith be rooted
at all in the intelligence ; but to assure its triumph it is
necessary, I repeat, that it should sink into the region

[1] We need not go back to heroic times for an example of faith
immune against all discussion. We need only look about us to
discover a host of people possessing, like sprouts of an hereditary
stock of mysticism, faith upon faith derived from this mystic stock,
and which no argument can shake. All the little religious sects
which have sprung up during the last twenty-five years, as they
sprung up at the close of Paganism — Spiritualism, Theosophy,
Esoterism, &c.—can boast of numerous disciples who present this
mental state in which faith can no longer be destroyed by any
argument whatever. The celebrated affair of the spirit-photographs
is full of instruction on this point. The photographer B. publicly
declared that all the photographs of phantoms supplied to his
ingenuous clients were obtained by photographing dummies. The
argument would seem conclusive. But in spite of the avowals
of the factitious photographer, despite the production in public of
the dummies which had served as models, the spiritualist clients
maintained with energy that they recognised perfectly in the photographs the features of their defunct relatives. This marvellous
obstinacy of faith is extremely instructive, and helps us thoroughly
to understand the power of a belief.

of the sentiments, and so pass from the conscious into the unconscious or instinctive.

I must insist on this influence of the past in the elaboration of faiths, and on the fact that a new faith can only establish itself by attaching itself to an anterior faith. This establishment of beliefs is perhaps the most important phase of the evolution of civilisations. One of the greatest benefits of an established belief is to give a people common sentiments, to create common thoughts, and by consequence common words ; that is to say, to cause identity of ideas. The established faith finally creates a common state of mind, and this is why it sets its mark on all the elements of a civilisation. A common faith constitutes perhaps the most powerful factor of the creation of a national soul, a national mind, and consequently the identical orientation of national sentiments and ideas. The great civilisations have always been the logical efflorescence of a small number of beliefs, and the decadence of a nation is always near when the common beliefs are becoming dissociated.

A collective belief has the immense advantage of uniting in a single bundle all the manifold individual desires, of making a nation act as a single individual would act. It is with reason that people have said that the great periods of history have been precisely those at which a universal belief has established itself.

The part played in the life of nations by universal beliefs is so fundamental that its importance can hardly be exaggerated. History does not furnish an example of a civilisation establishing and maintaining itself without having at its base the common beliefs of all the individuals of a nation, or at the very least of a city. This community of beliefs gives the nation which possesses it a formidable strength, even when the belief is transitory. We have seen how the French at the time of the Revolution, animated by a new faith, which could not last because it could not perform its promises, struggled victoriously against all Europe in arms.

2. THE PART PLAYED BY BELIEFS WITH REGARD TO OUR IDEAS AND SENTIMENTS—THE PSYCHOLOGY OF INCOMPREHENSION.

As soon as a belief is securely established in the understanding it becomes the regulator of life, the touchstone of judgment, the director of intelligence. The mind can receive nothing new that does not conform to the new faith. Like Christianity in the Middle Ages and Islam among the Arabs, the prevailing faith sets its imprint on all the elements of civilisation, and notably on philosophy, literature, and the arts. It is the supreme criterion; it explains everything. The *rationale* of all our knowledge, for the sage as well as for the fool, consists in nothing else than in carrying the unknown to the known; that is to say, to what we think we know. Comprehension supposes the observation of a fact, and then its co-ordination with the small number of ideas already possessed by the individual. We thus relate unknown facts to facts we believe ourselves to understand, and each brain accomplishes this relation according to the sub-conscious concepts which rule it. From the most inferior mind to the highest the mechanism of explanation is always the same, and consists invariably of introducing a new idea in the midst of already acquired conceptions.

And it is precisely because we co-relate our perceptions of the world to particular ancestral conceptions that the individuals of the different races have such different judgments. We perceive things only by deforming them, and we deform them according to our beliefs.

Beliefs that have become transformed into sentiments act not only upon our conduct in life, they influence also the sense we attach to words. The causes of the dissensions and the struggles which divide humanity are engendered for the most part by the same phenomena, but according to diverse mental constitutions and strongly differing ideas. Follow from century to century, from race to race, and from one sex to the other, the ideas evoked by the *same words*. Consider, for example, what are represented, to minds of differing origin, by the following words—religion, liberty, republic, *bourgeoisie*, property, capital, labour—and you will see how profound are the abysses which separate these mental representations.[1] The different classes of the same society, individuals of different sex, seem to speak the same language, but it is only in appearance. The *nuances* of signification of this language are as numerous as the social and mental categories that employ it. Sometimes these *nuances* escape them reciprocally to the extent of leading them to absolute incomprehension.

The different classes of society, and still more the different nations, are as widely separated by divergence of conception as by divergence of interests ; this is why the conflict of classes and races, and not their chimerical concord, has always constituted a dominant fact of

---

[1] The refraction of ideas, that is to say, the deformation of concepts according to race, age, sex, education, is one of the least explored questions of psychology. I have touched on it in one of my latter works, in showing how institutions, religions, languages, and arts become transformed in passing from one people to another. I have recently sketched the programme of this study for a young and intelligent psychologist, M. E. Renoult, living on account of his profession among the lower classes, who furnished me with some interesting documents for the above work, and notably on the psychology of the working man. If he succeeds in bringing this task to a successful end he will have rendered a great service to psychology and sociology.

history. This discordance can only increase in the future. Far from tending to equalise men, civilisation tends to differentiate them more and more. Between a powerful feudal baron and the least of his retainers there was infinitely less mental difference than there is to-day between an engineer and the labourer he directs.

Between different races, different classes, different sexes, agreement is only possible on technical subjects into which the instinctive sentiments do not enter. In morals, in religion, in politics, on the contrary, agreement is impossible, or is only possible when the individuals in question have the same origin ; and then they agree, not by reasoning, but by the identity of their conceptions. Persuasion is never rooted in reason. When people are gathered together to consider a question of politics, religions, or morals, they are the dead, not the living, who discuss. They are the souls of their ancestors that speak from their mouths, and their words are the echoes of the eternal voices of the dead, to which the living are always obedient.

Words, then, have senses very different according to our beliefs, and for this reason they evoke in our minds very different sentiments and ideas. Perhaps the most arduous effort of thought is to succeed in penetrating to the minds of individuals who constitute types differing from our own. We succeed in so doing with difficulty enough in the case of compatriots who differ from us only in age, sex, or in education ; how shall we succeed in the case of men of different race, above all when centuries separate us ? To make another person understand one must speak in his own tongue, with the *nuances* of his own personal conceptions. One may live for years beside another being without ever understanding him, as parents do by their children. All our usual psychology is based on the hypothesis that all men experience identical sentiments under similar exciting influences, and nothing is more erroneous.

We can never hope to see things as they really are, since we are aware only of states of consciousness created by our senses. We can no more hope that the deformation undergone may be identical for all men, for this deformation varies according to their various inherited or acquired conceptions; that is to say, according to race, sex, environment, and so forth; and for this reason one may say that an almost total incomprehension most often qualifies the relations between individuals of different race, sex, or environment. They may employ the same words; they never speak the same language.

Our vision of things, therefore, is always a deformed vision, but we have no suspicion of this deformation. We are even generally persuaded that it cannot exist; it is almost impossible for us to admit that other men can think and act otherwise than exactly as we ourselves think and act. This incomprehension has for its final result an absolute intolerance, above all in respect of beliefs and opinions which repose entirely on the sentiments.

All those who profess different opinions to our own in religion, morals, art, or politics immediately become, in our eyes, persons of dubious character, or, at least, lamentable imbeciles. We also consider it our strict duty, as soon as we possess the power, rigorously to persecute such dangerous monsters. If we no longer burn them and guillotine them, it is because the decadence of manners and the regrettable mildness of the laws oppose such proceedings.

As for individuals of very different race: we freely admit, at least in theory, that they cannot think exactly as we do, but not without commiserating their lamen-

table blindness. We also consider it a benefit to them
to convert them to our manners and customs and laws
by the most energetic means, when by chance we become
their masters. Arabs, negroes, Annamese, Malagasy, and
so forth, on whom we aspire to impress our manners,
laws, and customs—whom, as the politicians say, we desire
to assimilate, have learned by experience what it costs to
think otherwise than their conquerors. They continue
certainly to retain their ancestral conceptions, but they
have learned to hide their thoughts, and have acquired
at the same time an implacable hatred for their new
masters.

Incomprehension presents itself in different degrees
among the different peoples. Among those who travel
little or not at all—for example, the Latins—it is absolute, and their intolerance is accordingly complete. Our
incapacity to understand the ideas of other peoples,
civilised or not, is amazing. It is also the principal
cause of the lamentable state of our colonies. The
most eminent Latins, and even men of genius such as
Napoleon, do not differ from the common run of men
in this particular. Napoleon never had the vaguest
notion of the psychology of a Spaniard or an Englishman. His judgments upon them were about as valuable
as that one read, recently, in one of our great political
journals, as to the conduct of England with regard to
the African savages. " She intervenes always," said the
worthy editor, with indignation, "to prevent the tribes
from getting rid of their kings, and setting up republics."
Nothing could be more incomprehensible and ingenuous.

The works of our historians teem with similar ap-
preciations, and it is partly because their works are full
of such that I have arrived at this conclusion, for which
I have been reproached by the illustrious philologist

Max Müller : that historical works are nothing but pure romances, absolutely removed from all reality. That which we learn from them is never the soul of history, but only that of the historian.

And again, because the concepts of the nations have no common denominator, and because the same words evoke such different ideas in different minds, I have come to yet another conclusion, apparently paradoxical : that written works are absolutely untranslatable from one language to another. This is true even of modern languages, and how much more of languages representing the ideas of extinct peoples ? There are hosts of examples ; I will confine myself, in passing, to citing one.

When the translations of Ibsen's plays were represented in Paris, the critics immediately discovered in them profound and mysterious symbols, until one day a Scandinavian critic demonstrated to them that these profound and mysterious symbols were of their own fabrication, that Ibsen was a very simple and straightforward dramatist for people who lived in Scandanavian society, and that his personages meant to say only what they said. When, for example, in one of his plays, certain of his characters are advised to hunt the wolves in which Scandanavia abounds, what is meant is merely that they had best live the life of hunters, and this very ordinary remark had by no means the Socialistic meaning which was ascribed to it by the equally subtle and incomprehensive critics.

It is only, I repeat, between individuals of the same race, long subjected to the same conditions of life and the same environment, that a little comprehension may exist in reciprocal relations. Thanks to the hereditary mould of their ideas, the words they exchange are then able to evoke ideas almost similar.

3. THE ANCESTRAL FORMATION OF THE MORAL SENSE.

The part played by certain moral qualities in the destiny of peoples is altogether preponderant. I shall have occasion to show this presently, in studying the comparative psychology of the different nations. For the moment I would only indicate the fact that the moral qualities, like beliefs, are bequeathed by heredity, and form, consequently, part of the ancestral soul. It is in this soil, that our forefathers have bequeathed to us, that the motives of our actions germinate, and our conscious activity serves us only to perceive their fruits. The general rules of our conduct have for their habitual guides the sentiments acquired by heredity, and are rarely influenced by reason.

These sentiments are very slowly acquired. The moral sense has but little stability until, being fixed by heredity, it has become unconscious, and consequently escapes from influences of reason, always egotistical, and most often contrary to the interests of the race. The principles of morality which education instils have a very slight influence ; I would say none at all if it were not necessary to take into account those beings of neutral character, whom Professor Ribot calls "amorphous subjects," and who are on that vague border-line from which the least factor may incline them towards good or evil. It is, above all, with regard to these neutral characters that codes of law and policemen are of use. They refrain from doing what the law and the police forbid, but they do not attain to a more elevated morality. An intelligent education—that is, an education altogether neglecting the discussions and dissertations of philosophy—may show them that it is entirely to their interest not to enter the policeman's sphere of action. Such a demonstration will strike them far more than vague generalisations and the fatiguing dissertations on which moral instruction is nowadays based.

The doctrine of Kant, which is to-day the basis of all the courses of philosophy in our educational establishments, and which one finds even in the manuals intended for children, may seem sufficiently elevated ; but it is not, as M. Maurice Barrès justly observes, of the least practical value, for it addresses itself to an abstract and ideal person, always and everywhere identical with himself, whereas the real man, the only man we have to live with, varies according to time and race.

So long as our reason does not intervene our moral sense remains instinctive, and our motives of action do not differ from those of the most unthinking crowds. These motives are unreasoned, in the sense that they are instinctive, and not the product of reflection. They are not irrational, in the sense that they are the result of slow adaptations, induced by anterior necessities. It is in the popular mind that they are manifested in all their force, and this is why the instinct of the crowds is so profoundly conservative, and so ready to defend the collective interests of a race as long as the theorists and orators do not trouble it.

CHAPTER II

TRADITION AS A FACTOR OF CIVILISATION—THE LIMITS OF VARIABILITY OF THE ANCESTRAL SOUL

1. *The Influence of tradition in the life of nations :*—Difficulty of shaking off the yoke of tradition—The rarity of true freethinkers—Difficulty of establishing the clearest truths—Origins of our everyday opinions —Slight influence of reason—Influence of traditions in institutions, beliefs, and arts—Artists unable to shake off the influences of the past. 2. *The Limits of variability of the ancestral soul :*—The various elements of which the soul bequeathed us by our ancestors is composed—Its heterogeneous elements—How such arise. 3. *The conflict between traditional beliefs and modern necessities—The modern instability of opinion :*—How the nations are enabled to shake off the yoke of tradition—The impossibility of doing so suddenly— The tendency of the Latin races to reject the influence of the past entirely, and categorically to rebuild their institutions and laws— The struggle between their traditions and the needs of the present moment — Transitory and momentary beliefs are substituted for permanent beliefs—Fickleness, violence, and influence of opinions— Various examples—Public opinion dictates their decrees to judges, and wars and alliances to governments—The influence of the press and the secret power of financiers—The necessity of a universally accepted belief—Socialism is impotent to play this part.

1. THE INFLUENCE OF TRADITION IN THE LIFE OF NATIONS.

WE may abjure the fetters of tradition that bind us ; but how few, at any period, is the number of those — artists, thinkers, or philosophers—capable of shaking off the yoke ! It is given to very few to dis-engage themselves in any degree from the ties of the past. The persons who call themselves freethinkers may be counted perhaps by millions ; in reality, there are scarcely a few dozen to an epoch.   The clearest scientific truths often establish themselves only with the greatest difficulty, and even when they are so established it is by the reputations of those that uphold them,[1] rather than by demonstration.   The doctors for a whole century denied the phenomena of magnetism, although they might observe them everywhere, until a scientist of great prestige affirmed that these phenomena were real.

In everyday parlance the word "freethinker" is merely a synonym for "anti-clerical." The provincial apothecary, who passes for a freethinker because he does not go to mass, and persecutes the parish priest by laughing at his dogmas, is, at the bottom, as little of a freethinker as the priest.   They belong to the same psychological family, and are equally guided by the thoughts of the dead.

We must be able to study, in detail, the everyday opinions which we form on everything, to see how true is the preceding theory.

These opinions, which we suppose to be so free, are imposed on us by our surroundings, by books, by journals ; and according to our hereditary traditions we accept or reject them *en bloc,* and most often reason plays no part whatever in this acceptance or refusal.

---

[1] There is no error that prestige cannot palm off as a truth. Thirty years ago the Academy of Sciences—in which one would suppose the critical spirit to be found in its highest degree— published, as authentic, several hundreds of letters supposed to be written by Newton, Pascal, Galileo, Cassini, &c., which, as a matter of fact, were one and all fabricated by an almost illiterate forger. They teemed with vulgarities and errors, but the prestige of their supposed authors, and of the illustrious scientist who brought them to light, made everybody accept them.   The majority of the academicians, including the permanent secretary, had no doubts of the authenticity of these documents until the day when the forger admitted his guilt.   When once their prestige had vanished the style of the letters, which at first was considered marvellous, and fully worthy of their supposed authors, was declared by every- body to be wretched in the extreme.

Reason is invoked often enough, but in reality it plays as small a part in the formation of our opinions as in the determination of our actions. To discover the principal sources of our ideas we must go to heredity for our fundamental opinions, and to suggestion for our secondary opinions, and it is for this reason that individuals of the same profession in the different social classes are so much alike. Living in the same environment, incessantly mouthing the same words, the same phrases, the same ideas, they finally end by possessing ideas as banal as identical.

In matters of institutions, beliefs, arts, or of any elements whatever of civilisation, we are always heavily weighed upon by our surroundings, and above all by the past. If we do not as a rule perceive this to be so it is because our facility in giving new names to old things deludes us into believing that in changing these words we have also changed the things they represent.

To make the weight of ancestral influences clearly sensible, we must take some well-defined element of civilisation—for instance, the arts. The weight of the past appears clearly in these, and also the struggle between tradition and the modern ideas. When an artist imagines he is shaking off the burden of the past, he is in reality only returning to more ancient forms, or altering the most necessary elements of his art ; replacing, for example, one colour by another, the pink of the face by green, or abandoning himself to all those fantasies, the spectacle of which we have been afforded by our recent annual exhibitions. But even in his incoherent ramblings the artist is only confirming his impotence to throw off the yoke of tradition. A penetrating writer, Daniel Lesueur, has written a page on these atavistic influences, which I reproduce here, because it very clearly develops the preceding remarks :—

" Powerlessness to create outside the limits of every-day things. . . . Tyranny of the memory, which deceives the artist in every attempt, and sends him straying back to the ancient altars, to the forms that bygone generations adored.

" The less audacious resign themselves to this servitude of inspiration, the prisoner of ancient dreams. With a humble and fervent brush, with a chisel that has never trembled with the mystic fear of an unknown ideal, they represent the visions and the symbols, they eternise the legends, they set up the gods that no longer have worship, that no longer give oracles, and that every new incarnation brings a little closer to the earth.

" Again, by a plainly inevitable aberration, certain minds, impatient of the yoke, exasperated by the haunting of this past without which all becomes petrified—in art more than in any other branch of human evolution—certain artists, finally exasperated, have sought to re-act by denying this too rigid reign of the traditions of splendour, by insulting the conventional beauty, the classic perfection, and the ideals of the academies and schools.

" How shall we describe the work of our modern artists, masters of technique, but destitute of inspiration, who imagine themselves to produce original work by calmly parodying the sincere awkwardness and the anguished uncertainties of sublime initiators ?

" They, too, are copyists, but they are going in the wrong direction. These revolutionaries have no more true independence than those who have submitted to the traditional. On them, as on the latter, weighs the formidable yoke of the past.

" Symbolists by intention, in literature as in painting, they symbolise nothing but vanished dreams and dead emotions.

"This malady of exasperated impotence reaches a crisis only in the case of poets, painters, and sculptors. The architects have up to the present escaped the fever. They do not appear to suffer in any way from their frightful incapacity to conceive of anything outside of the forms which the centuries have established. Theirs is a placid impotence, a serene nullity. They raise up their neo-Grecian palaces, their Renaissance railway stations, and their pseudo-Gothic villas with the most touching unconsciousness."

2. THE LIMITS OF VARIABILITY OF THE ANCESTRAL SOUL.

Such is the influence of the past ; and we must bear it always in mind, if we would understand the evolution of all the elements of a civilisation : how our institutions, our beliefs, and our arts form and develop themselves, and the enormous influence which the bygone centuries exert over their growth. The modern man has made the most conscientious efforts to escape from the Past. Our great Revolution thought to cast it off for ever. But how vain are such attempts ! A people may be con-quered, enslaved, annihilated ; but where is the power shall change its soul ?

But this hereditary soul, from whose influence it is so difficult to escape, has taken centuries to form itself. Many different elements have found place in it, and under the influence of certain exciting causes the most hidden of these elements may come to the surface. A complete change of environment may develop in us germs that are at present dormant. Hence those possibilities of character of which I have spoken in another work, and which certain circumstances may bring to light. Thus it is that the peaceable nature of a *chef de bureau*, a magistrate, or a shopkeeper, may contain a Robespierre, a Marat, a Fouquier-Tinville, and certain exciting elements will bring these latent personalities to the front. Then we see Government clerks shooting hostages, artists ordering the destruction of monuments, and after the crisis, having come to themselves again, asking themselves of what aberration they have been the victims. The *bourgeois* of the Convention, having returned, after the Terror, to their peaceful occupation as notary, professor, magistrate, or advocate, more than once asked themselves, in stupefaction, how they could have followed such bloody instincts, and immolated so many victims. It is not without danger that one disturbs the sediment deposited by our ancestors in the depths of our beings. We do not know what will arise from it : whether the soul of a hero or the soul of a bandit.

3. THE CONFLICT BETWEEN TRADITIONAL BELIEFS AND MODERN NECESSITIES—THE MODERN INSTABILITY OF OPINION.

Thanks to those few original minds to which every period gives birth, every civilisation escapes, little by little, from the fetters of tradition ; very slowly, it is true, because such minds are rare. This double necessity of fixity and variability is the fundamental condition of the birth and development of societies. A civilisation only becomes established when it creates a tradition, and it progresses only when it succeeds in modifying this tradition a little in each generation. If it does not so modify tradition it does not progress ; like China, it remains stationary. If it attempts to modify it too quickly it loses all fixity ; it becomes disintegrated, and is quickly doomed to disappear. The strength of the Anglo-Saxons consists in this : that while accepting the influence of the past they understand how to escape its tyranny in the necessary degree. The weakness of the Latins, on the contrary, is that they desire entirely to reject the influence of the past, and entirely to rebuild, without ceasing, all their institutions, beliefs, and laws. For this sole reason they have been living for a century in a state of revolution and incessant upheavals, from which they do not appear to be emerging.

The great danger of the present is that we have scarcely any common beliefs. Collective and identical interests are becoming further and further supplanted by dissimilar and particular interests. Our institutions, our laws, our arts, our education, have been established on beliefs which are crumbling every day, and which science and philosophy cannot replace ; and of old it was never their part to do so.

We certainly have not escaped from the influence of the past, since man cannot avoid that influence ; but we no longer believe in the principles on which our entire social edifice is built. There is a perpetual discord between our hereditary sentiments and the ideas of the present day. In morals, in religion, in politics, there is no recognised authority as there used to be of old, and no one can hope nowadays to enforce any one aim on these essential things. It follows that the Governments, instead of directing opinion, are obliged to submit to it, and to obey its incessant fluctuations.

The modern man, and above all he of Latin race, is bound by his unconscious desires to the past, although his reason incessantly seeks to escape from its yoke. While awaiting the appearance of fixed beliefs, he possesses only those beliefs which, by the sole fact that they are not hereditary, are transient and momentary. They are generated spontaneously by the events of the day, like waves raised by the tempest. They are often

vehement, but they are also ephemeral. Whatever circumstances may give rise to them, they are propagated
by contagion and imitation. By reason of the neurotic
condition of certain peoples to-day, the slightest cause
provokes excessive sentiments. Explosions of hate, fury,
indignation, enthusiasm, thunder forth at the most trivial
event. A few soldiers are surprised by the Chinese in
Langson ; an explosion of fury overthrows the Government in a few hours. A village, hidden away in a corner
of Europe, is destroyed by floods ; there follows an
explosion of national sympathy, which displays itself in
subscriptions, charity bazaars, and what not, and makes
us send to a distance sums of money which we need
only too much to alleviate our own misery. Public
opinion no longer knows anything but extreme sentiment or profound indifference. It is terribly feminine,
and, like woman, has no control over its reflex movements. It veers without ceasing to every wind of
external circumstance.

This extreme mobility of sentiments which are no
longer directed by any fundamental belief renders them
highly dangerous. In default of authority deceased,
public opinion becomes more and more the master of
all things, and, as it has at its service an all-powerful
press to excite it or follow it, the *rôle* of the Government
becomes day by day more difficult, and the policy of
statesmen more vacillating. We may discover many
useful qualities in the popular mind, but never the
thought of a Richelieu, nor even the lucid views of
a modest diplomatist having some consistency in his
ideas and conduct.

This power of public opinion, so great, and so
fluctuating, extends not only to politics, but to all the
elements of civilisation. It dictates to artists their works,
to judges their decrees, to governments their conduct.

One of the most curious examples of its invasion of the courts, formerly presided over by the firmest characters, is afforded by the very instructive case of Dr. Laporte. It will remain an example to be cited in all the treatises of psychology.

He was called out at night to an extremely difficult accouchement. Not having any of the necessary instruments at hand, and seeing that the patient was at the point of death, the doctor made use of an instrument of iron borrowed from a workman in the neighbourhood, which differed from the classic instrument only in insignificant details. But as the makeshift instrument did not come out of a surgeon's case (a mysterious thing, enjoying a certain prestige) the gossips of the neighbourhood immediately declared that the surgeon was an ignorant fool and a butcher. They stirred up all the neighbours by their clamouring; the rumour spread, the papers recorded the matter; public opinion waxed indignant; a magistrate was found to commit the unfortunate doctor to prison; then a tribunal, to condemn him to a new imprisonment, after a long remand. But in the meantime the affair was taken in hand by eminent specialists, who entirely reversed the opinion of the public, and in a few weeks the murderer had become a martyr. The case was carried to the Court of Appeal, and the magistrates, continuing to follow the opinion of the public, this time acquitted the accused.

The dangerous character of this influence of the tides of popular opinion consists in the fact that they act unconsciously on our ideas, and modify them without our suspecting it. The magistrates who condemned Laporte, as well as those who acquitted him, certainly obeyed public opinion without realising the fact. Their subconsciousness became transformed in order to follow it, and their reason only served them to find justifications for the reversal of judgment, which really took place, unknown to themselves, in their own minds.

These popular movements, so characteristic of the present hour, deprive all governments of all stability in their conduct. Public opinion decrees alliances : the Franco-Russian, for example, which arose from an explosion of national enthusiasm. It also declares war : for example, the Spanish-American war, which arose from a movement created by journalists and financiers.

An American writer, Mr. Godkin, in his recent book, *Unforeseen Tendencies of Democracy*, denounces the lamentable part which the American papers play in respect of public opinion, most of them being in the pay of advertisers and speculators. A prospective war, he says, will always be favoured by the journals, simply because the new soldiers, victorious or defeated, will enormously increase their sales. The book was written before the war in Cuba, which event has shown how just were the author's previsions. The journals direct the opinion of United States, but a few financiers direct the journals from their office chairs. Their power is more evil than that of the worst tyrants, for it is anonymous, and it is guided by their sole personal interest, and not that of their country. One of the great problems of the future will be to find the means of escaping from the sovereign and demoralising power of the cosmopolitan financiers, who in many countries are tending more and more to become, indirectly, the masters of public opinion, and consequently of governments. An American paper, the *Evening Post*, recently remarked that although all other influences have little or no effect on popular movements, the power of the daily press has grown immeasurably ; a power the more to be feared because it is without limit, without responsibility, without control, and is exercised by anonymous and absolute individuals. The two most influential " public organs " of the United States, those that obliged the public authorities to declare war, are directed the one by an ex-cab-driver, and the other by a very young man who has inherited millions. Their opinion, observes the American critic, has more influence over the manner in which the nation employs its army, its navy, its credit, and its traditions, than have all the statesmen, philosophers, and professors of the country.

Here again we discover one of the great desiderata of the present hour ; we see the necessity of discovering some belief, universally accepted, which shall replace those that have hitherto ruled the world.

We may sum up this and the preceding chapter by saying that civilisations have always reposed on a certain small number of beliefs, very slow to establish themselves and very slow to disappear ; that a belief does not become accepted, or at least does not sufficiently penetrate the nature to become a factor of conduct, until it has more or less attached itself to previous beliefs ; that modern man possesses by inheritance the beliefs on which his institutions and his moral ideas are still based, but that these beliefs are to-day in perpetual conflict with his reason. From this he is reduced to seeking for elaborate new dogmas which shall be sufficiently attached to the old beliefs, and shall yet conform with his present ideas. In this conflict between the past and the present, that is, between our sub-conscious nature and our self-conscious reason, are to be found the causes of the present anarchy of minds.

Will Socialism be the new religion which shall come to substitute itself for the old beliefs ? It lacks one factor of success ; the magic power of creating a future life, hitherto the principal strength of the great religions which have conquered the world and have endured. All the promises of happiness given by Socialism must be realised here on earth. Now the realisation of such promises will clash fatally with the economic and psychologic necessities over which man has no power, and therefore the hour of the advent of Socialism will undoubtedly be the hour of its decline. Socialism may triumph for an instant, as the humanitarian ideas of the Revolution triumphed, but it will quickly perish in bloody cataclysms, for the soul of a nation is not stirred up in vain. It will constitute one of those ephemeral religions of which the same century sees the birth and the death, and which are only of use in preparing or renewing other religions better adapted to human nature and to the manifold necessities to whose laws all societies are doomed to submit. It is in considering Socialism as an agent of dissolution, destined to prepare the advent of new dogmas, that the future will perhaps judge the part played by Socialism to have been not absolutely baneful.

CHAPTER III

THE EVOLUTION OF SOCIALISM TOWARDS A RELIGIOUS FORM

1. *The present tendency of Socialism to substitute itself for the old beliefs :*—The religious evolution of Socialism—The elements of success in Socialistic concepts considered as religious beliefs able to attach themselves to anterior beliefs—The sentiment of religion is an ineradicable instinct—Man aspires not to liberty of thought but to slavery of thought—The new doctrine responds to needs and hopes of the present hour—The powerlessness of those who defend the old dogmas—The small scientific value of the dogmas of Socialism cannot hinder their propagation—The great religious beliefs which have swayed humanity were never born of reason. 2. *The propagation of the belief. Its apostles :*—The part of apostles in establishing beliefs—Their means of persuasion—The important part played in the world by visionaries—The religious spirit of the apostles of Socialism—Inaccessible to all reasoning, they experience an imperious need to propagate their faith—Their exaltation, their devotion, their simplicism, and their passion for destruction—Their psychology is that of the apostles of all times—Bossuet and the Dragonnades, Torquemada and Robespierre—The baneful influence of philanthropists—Why the apostles of Socialism must not be confounded with ordinary madmen and criminals—How the apostles of Socialism receive additional recruits from the various classes of degenerates. 3. *The propagation of beliefs among the masses :*—All political, social, or religious concepts finally establish their roots in the masses—The nature of the masses or of the crowd—It is never directed by personal interest—The collective interests of the race are manifested by the crowd—By the crowd are accomplished such works of general interest as demand a blind devotion—The apparent violence and real conservatism of crowds—They are the slaves of fixity, and of mobility—Why Socialism will not attract them for long.

I. THE PRESENT TENDENCY OF SOCIALISM TO SUBSTITUTE ITSELF FOR THE OLD BELIEFS.

HAVING considered the part played by our beliefs, and the distant foundations of those beliefs, we are prepared to understand the religious form of evolution to which the Socialism of the present day is subject, and which will doubtless constitute its most considerable element of success.   I have already shown, in *The Crowd*, that the convictions of the masses always tend to assume a religious form.   The masses are devoid equally of scepticism and of the critical spirit.   The political, social, or religious creed accepted by them is always adopted without discussion, and fervently venerated.

In this chapter we have to consider, not the philosophic or economic value of the new doctrines, but only the impression which they produce on the mind.   We have often repeated that the success of a belief depends not at all on the proportion of truth or error it may contain, but only on the sentiments it evokes and the devotion it inspires.   The history of all beliefs is a manifest proof of this.

Considering their future as religious beliefs, the concepts of Socialism possess incontestable elements of success.   In the first place, there can be no great conflict between them and the old beliefs, because the latter are on the way to disappear.   In the second place, they present themselves under extremely simple forms, and are thus accessible to every mind.   In the third place, they cohere readily with the beliefs which preceded them, and are consequently able to replace them without difficulty. We have already shown, in fact, that the doctrines of the Christian Socialists are almost identical with those of the other sects of Socialists.

The first point is of prime importance.   Hitherto, humanity has not been able to exist without beliefs. When an old belief is on the point of death a new one immediately comes to replace it.   The sentiment of religion, that is to say, the need of submitting oneself to a faith of some kind, whether divine, political, or social, is one of our most imperious instincts.   Man requires a belief so that he may direct his life mechanically, and escape all efforts of reason. It is not to liberty of thought that man aspires, but to slavery of thought. He sometimes shakes off the yoke of the tyrants who oppress him, but how can he deliver himself from the far more imperious domination of his beliefs? At first the expression of his cravings, and above all of his hopes, his beliefs end by modifying them, and by controlling the instinctive region of his aspirations. .

The new doctrine fits to perfection the desires and hopes of the present hour. It appeared at the precise moment of the final disappearance of the social and religious beliefs by which our fathers lived, and it is ready to renew their promises. Its mere name is a magic word, which, like the Paradise of the past ages, sums up our dreams and our hopes. However poor may be its value, however problematical its realisation, it constitutes a new ideal which at least possesses the merit of bestowing on man a hope which the gods no longer give, and illusions that science has forbidden. If it is true that the happiness of man must, for a long time yet, reside in the marvellous faculty of creating, and believing in, divinities, we cannot misconceive the importance of the new faith.

It increases every day, and its power becomes more and more imperious. The ancient faiths have lost their might, the altars of the old gods are deserted, the family becomes disunited, institutions crumble, hierarchies disappear; only the mirage of Socialism hovers over the heaped-up ruins. It spreads without encountering very serious detractors. While its disciples are ardent apostles, persuaded, as were formerly the disciples of Jesus, that they are the possessors of a new ideal, destined to regenerate the world, the timid defenders of the old state of things are but slightly persuaded of the worth of

the cause they uphold. Almost their only method of
defence is painfully to mumble ancient economic or theological formulæ, which were decrepit long ago, and have
now lost all their virtue. They are like so many mummies
trying to struggle in spite of their windings. In a notice
of a meeting of the Academy, M. Léon Say called attention to the astonishing mediocrity of the works destined
to oppose Socialism, despite the importance of the recompense offered. Not even the defenders of paganism
showed themselves more powerless when a new god
came out of the plains of Galilee, struck the last blows at
the old tottering divinities, and gathered their heritage.

Certainly the new beliefs are not based on logic, but
what beliefs have, since the beginning of the world, ever
been so based ? Nevertheless the greater number have
presided over the blossoming of brilliant civilisations.
The irrational that endures becomes the rational, and man
ends always by accommodating himself to it. Societies
are founded on desires, beliefs, and wants ; that is to say,
on sentiments, and never on reasons or even on probabilities. These sentiments are no doubt evolved according to some hidden logic, but no thinker has ever yet
discovered its laws.

Not one of the great beliefs that have ruled humanity
was ever born of reason ; and although each has bowed
before the common law, which forces gods and empires,
one by one, to decline and die, it was never reason that
compassed their end. There is one quality that beliefs [1]

[1] The advance of science showed at first how slight are the foundations of all religious beliefs, but in advancing further it has also
demonstrated that they have been of immense utility, quite apart
from the part they have played in history. In the time of Voltaire
the pilgrimages to miraculous relics and waters might be regarded
as utterly ridiculous. But since the modern investigations of the
effects of suggestion we know that the curative action of miraculous
waters, relics, and Madonnas, is at least equal and often superior to
that of the most potent remedies. From the point of view of pure

possess in a high degree, while reason has never possessed it ; the splendid power to bind together things that have no relation to one another, to transform the most glaring errors into glittering truths ; absolutely to enslave the soul, to seduce the heart, and finally to transform civilisations and empires.   Beliefs are not the slaves of logic ; they are the queens of history.

Given the seductive side of these new dogmas ; their extreme simplicity, which renders them accessible to every mind ; the present hatred of the populace for the wrongful possessors of wealth and power ; the absolute power of changing their political institutions which the populace enjoy, thanks to universal suffrage ; given, I say, such remarkably favourable conditions of propagation, we may well inquire why the progress of the new doctrines is relatively so slow, and what are the mysterious forces that control their advance.   The explanation we have given of the origins of our beliefs and of the slowness of their transformations will give us the answer to this question.

2. The Propagation of the Belief. Its Apostles.

The present hour affords us the spectacle of the elaboration of the Socialist religion.   We are able to study the actions of its apostles and of all the important factors

reason it may seem altogether absurd to implore the aid of gods and saints who exist only in our imagination.   Science, however, has shown us that these prayers are not vain.   The auto-suggestion produced by sufficiently fervent prayer has comforted innumerable minds, and has given them the necessary strength to bear up against the cruelest trials.   It is prayer, again, that strengthens faith, the most powerful lever humanity has ever wielded.   Far from despising the error, we must recognise that the part it has played in the history of humanity has always been preponderant, and that it has constituted a motive of action that has never yet been equalled.

whose parts I have elsewhere shown—illusions, words and formulæ, affirmation, repetition, prestige, and contagion.

Perhaps it is above all through its apostles that Socialism may be able to triumph for a moment. Only these enthusiasts possess the zeal indispensable to create a faith, the magic power which has at several periods transformed the world. They are skilled in the art of persuasion ; an art simple at once and subtle, whose actual laws no book has ever taught. They know that the crowd has a horror of doubt ; that they know none but extreme sentiments ; energetic affirmation, energetic denial, intense love, or violent hatred ; and they know how to evoke these sentiments, and how to develop them.

They need not, necessarily, be very numerous in order to accomplish their task. Witness the small number of zealots who sufficed to provoke an event so colossal as the Crusades ; an event perhaps more marvellous than the founding of a religion, since many millions of men were moved to leave all behind and to fling themselves upon the East, and to recommence their task over and over again, in spite of all reverses and terrible privations.

Whatever beliefs have once reigned in the world— whether Christianity, Buddhism, or Islam, or merely some political theory, such as was predominant at the time of the Revolution—they have only been propagated by the efforts of that particular class of converts we call apostles. Hypnotised by the belief that has conquered them, they are ready for every sacrifice that may propagate it, and finally have no object in life but to establish its empire. They are *demi-hallucinés*, and their study is the especial province of mental pathology, but they have always played a stupendous part in the history of the world.

They are recruited, for the most part, from those who

possess the instinct of religion ; an instinct of which the chief characteristic is the craving to be ruled by no matter what being or creed, and to sacrifice all to secure the triumph of the adored object.

The religious instinct, being a sub-conscious sentiment, naturally survives the disappearance of the belief which first maintained it. The apostles of Socialism, who anathematise or deny the old dogmas of Christianity, are none the less eminently religious persons. The nature of their faith has changed, but they are still under the sway of all the ancestral instincts of their race. The paradisial society of their dreams is very like the celestial paradise of our fathers. In these ingenuous minds, entirely at the mercy of atavism, the old deism is objectified under the earthly form of a providential State, repairing all injustice, and possessing the illimitable power of the ancient gods. Man does sometimes change his idols, but how shall he shatter the hereditary matrices of thought that give them birth ?

The apostle, then, is always a religious person, desirous of propagating his faith ; but he is also, and above all, a simplician, totally refractory to the influences of reason. His logic is rudimentary. Necessities and the relations of things are quite beyond his understanding. We may form a very clear idea of his perceptions by perusing the interesting extracts from one hundred and seventy auto-biographies of militant Socialists which were recently published by M. Hamon, a writer of their persuasion. Among this number are many who profess very different doctrines ; for Anarchism is really only an exaggeration of Individualism, since it wishes to suppress all government and leave the individual to himself, while Collectivism implies a rigid subjection of the individual to the State. But in practice these differences, which are scarcely perceived by the apostles, entirely disappear.

The members of the various sects of Socialism manifest the same hatred of society, capital, and the *bourgeoisie*, and propose identical means to suppress them. The more pacific would simply deprive the rich of their possessions ; the more belligerent would absolutely insist on completing this spoliation by exterminating the vanquished.

Their declamations betray before all things the simplicity of their minds. They are embarrassed by no difficulty. To them nothing is easier than to reconstruct a society. " We have only to expel the Government by revolution, expropriate the wrongful possessors of social wealth, and place it at the disposition of all. . . . In a society in which the difference between capitalists and workers had disappeared there would be no need of Government."

M. de Vogüé has given the following interesting account of an interview with one of these apostles :—

" He had one of those narrow, stubborn skulls, in which the cerebral convolutions only seize hold of two or three ideas, of which they never let go ; a wonderful microcosm for one desirous of investigating the distillation which remains of the general thought of a period after the popular alembic has deposited the essence of it in these little retorts. Here we find the great systems of philosophy concentrated into a few Liebig's tabloids. My man had only two tabloids at his service ; they represented two centuries of effort of the human mind. He explained his Utopia : a society without laws, without ties, without hierarchies, in which each individual, absolutely free, would be paid by the collectivity according to his capacity and his needs. To all the objections one could devise he opposed his first axiom : ' Man is naturally good ; it is society that depraves him. Suppress the social State, and there will no longer be any need of laws and mutual protection.' This is not exactly novel ; you recognise the Rousseau tabloid, the residue of all the dreams of the eighteenth century. But as I insisted on the difficulty of producing in sufficient quantity the necessaries of life, and of distributing them in proportion to requirements, given the little taste that a large number of citizens exhibit for voluntary work when their well-being is otherwise assured, I ran up against the second axiom : ' Thanks to the indefinite progress of science and machinery man will obtain abundance of all he requires, with little labour. Science will better his condition, and will resolve the difficulties you raise.' "

Hypnotised more and more completely by the two or three formulæ he incessantly repeats, the apostle experiences a burning desire to propagate the faith that is in him, and publish to the world the gospel which shall raise humanity from the error in which it has hitherto stagnated. Is not the torch he carries plain to see, and must not all, save hypocrites and sinners, be converted ?

" Prompted by their proselytising zeal," writes M. Hamon, "they spread their faith without fear of suffering for it. For it they break the ties of family and friendship ; for it they lose their place, their very means of existence. In their enthusiasm they run the risks of imprisonment and death ; they are determined to enforce their ideal, to effect the salvation of the populace despite itself. They are like the Terrorists of 1793, who slaughtered human beings for the love of humanity."

Their instinct of destruction is a phenomena found in the apostles of all cults. One of those mentioned by M. Hamon was anxious to destroy all monuments, and especially churches, convinced that their destruction " would effect the destruction of all the spiritualistic religions." This ingenuous soul was only following illustrious examples. Not otherwise did the Christian

Emperor Theodosius reason when in the year 389 he destroyed all the religious monuments that had been erected by the Egyptians on the banks of the Nile during six thousand years, leaving upright only the walls and columns too solid to be broken.

It would seem, then, that it is a psychological law, almost universal in all ages, that one cannot be an apostle without experiencing an intense craving to massacre some one or smash something.

The apostle who is concerned only with monuments belongs to a variety relatively inoffensive, but evidently a little lukewarm. The perfect apostle is not satisfied with these half-measures. He understands that when you have destroyed the temples of the false gods you must proceed to suppress their worshippers. What are hecatombs, what are massacres, when it is a question of regenerating humanity, establishing truth, and destroying error ? Is it not plain that the best means of suppressing infidels is to kill all you may meet, and leave none standing but the apostles and their disciples ? This is the programme for purists, for those who disdain the compromises of hypocritical and cowardly transactions with heresy.

Unhappily the heretics are still refractory, and while awaiting the possibility of exterminating them one must content oneself with isolated murders and with threats. The latter, by the way, are perfectly explicit, and leave the future victims no illusions. One of the vanguard of the Italian Socialists, quoted by Signor Garofalo, sums up his programme thus : " We shall slit the throats of all we find with arms in their hands ; the old men, women, and children we shall pitch over the balconies or throw into the sea."

These proceedings of the new sectaries have nothing very novel about them ; they recur in the same form at various historical periods. All the apostles have thundered at the impiety of their adversaries in the same terms, and as soon as they have obtained the power to do so they have employed the same tactics of swift and energetic destruction. Mohammed converted by the sabre, the men of the Inquisition by faggots, the men of the Convention by the guillotine, and our modern Socialists by dynamite. Only the implements have a little changed.

The most lamentable thing about these explosions of fanaticism, which societies must, periodically, suffer, is that among the converts the highest intelligence is powerless against the ferocious seductiveness of their faith. Our modern Socialists act and speak just as did Bossuet with regard to the heretics, when he began the campaign which was to end in their massacre and expulsion. In what sulphurous terms does the illustrious prelate thunder against the enemies of his faith ! "who love better to rot in their ignorance than to avow it, and to nourish in their stubborn souls the liberty to think all that it pleases them to think, rather than to bow to the Divine authority." One should read, in the writings of the time, the savage joy with which the clergy welcomed the Dragonnades and the Revocation of the Edict of Nantes. The bishops and pious Bossuet were delirious with enthusiasm. "You have exterminated the heretics,'' said the latter to Louis Quatorze. " It is the great work of your reign ; it is your crown."

The extermination was really sufficiently thorough. This " great work" had as its consequence the emigration of 400,000 French, the elect of the nation, to say nothing of a considerable number of recalcitrant persons who were burned at the stake, hung, drawn, and quartered, or sent to the King's galleys. Not less did the Inquisition decimate Spain ; and the Convention, France. The Convention too possessed the absolute truth, and was

anxious to extirpate error. It had always far more the
air of an ecclesiastical council than of a political assembly.

We can easily account for the ravages committed by
these terrible destroyers of men when we know how to
read their souls. Torquemada, Bossuet, Marat, Robespierre considered themselves to be gentle philanthropists,
dreaming of nothing but the happiness of humanity.
Philanthropists, whether social, religious, or political, all
belong to the same family. They regard themselves in
all good faith as the friends of humanity, and have always
been its most pernicious enemies. They are more
dangerous than wild beasts.

Mental pathologists of the present day are generally of
opinion that the sectaries of the vanguard of Socialism
belong to a criminal type, to the type they call criminal-
born. But this qualification is far too summary, and
more often than not very inexact, for it embraces
individuals belonging to very different classes, for the
most part without any kinship to the true criminal. That
there are a certain number of criminals among the propagandists of the new faith is indubitable ; but the
greater number of the criminals who qualify as Socialist
Anarchists only do so to give a political gloss to crimes
against the common law. The true apostle may commit
acts which are justly qualified as crimes by the Code, but
which have nothing criminal about them from a psychological point of view. Far from being the result of
personal interest, which is the characteristic of true crime,
their acts are most often contrary to their most obvious
interests. They are ingenuous mystics, absolutely incapable of reasoning, and possessed by a religious
sentiment which invades every corner of their understanding. They are certainly dangerous enough, and a
society which does not desire to be destroyed by them
must eliminate them carefully from its midst ; but their

mental state is a matter for the pathologist, not for the criminologist.

History is full of their exploits ; for they constitute a psychologic species which has existed in every age.

" Insane persons and fanatics with altruistic tendencies have arisen in all ages," writes Lombroso, "even in savage times, but then they draw their aliment from religions.   Later, they throw themselves into the political factions and anti-monarchical conspiracies of the period. First crusaders ; then rebels ; then knights-errant ; then martyrs of faith or atheism.

" In our days, and more especially among the Latin races, when one of these altruist fanatics arises he can only find food for his passions in the social and economic regions.

" They are almost always the least certain and most debated ideas that give a free rein to the enthusiasm of fanatics.   You will find a hundred fanatics for a problem in theology or metaphysics ; you will find none for a theorem in geometry. The more strange and absurd an idea is the more it will drag after it the alienated and the hysterical ; above all, in the political world, in which every private triumph is a failure, or a public triumph ; and this idea will often sustain these fanatics in death, and will serve as a compensation for the life they lose or the torments they endure."

Besides the class of apostles we have described, the propagandists necessary to all religions, there are other less important varieties whose state of hypnosis is limited to a single point of the understanding.   We constantly meet, in everyday life, people who are highly intelligent, and even eminent, yet become absolutely incapable of reasoning on approaching certain subjects, when they are dominated by their political or religious passion, and show a surprising intolerance or incomprehension. These are the occasional fanatics whose fanaticism grows dangerous as soon as it is sufficiently excited. They reason with clearness and moderation on all questions excepting those in which their ruling passion is their only guide. On this narrow ground they array themselves with all the persecuting fury of the true apostles, who find in them, at the hour of a crisis, auxiliaries full of blind zeal.

There is, finally, another category of Socialists, who are not attracted by ideas alone, and whose beliefs even are feeble. They belong to the great family of the degenerates. Maintained by their hereditary taints, their physical or mental deficiencies, in inferior positions, from which they cannot escape, they are the natural enemies of a society to which they are prevented from adapting themselves by their incurable incapacity, by the morbid heredities of which they are the victims. They are the spontaneous defenders of doctrines which promise them, together with a happier future, a kind of regeneration. These outcasts form an immense addition to the crowd of apostles. The part of our civilisations is precisely to create, and, by a sort of fantastic humanitarian irony, to conserve and protect, with the most short-sighted solicitude, an ever-increasing stock of social failures, under whose weight they will necessarily end by foundering.

The new religion of Socialism is now entering on the phase in which its propagation is undertaken by its apostles. To these apostles may already be added a few martyrs ; they constitute a new element of success. After the last executions of Anarchists in Paris the intervention of the police was necessary to prevent pious pilgrimages to the tombs of the victims, and the sale of their images surrounded with all kinds of religious attributes. Fetichism is the most ancient of cults, and will be perhaps the last. A people must always have a few fetiches to embody their dreams, desires, and hates.

Thus do these dogmas disseminate themselves, and no reasoning can struggle against them. Their might is invincible, for it is based on the material inferiority of the masses, and on the external illusion of happiness, whose mirage is always alluring men, and preventing them from seeing the barriers which separate realities from dreams.

3. THE PROPAGATION OF BELIEFS AMONG THE MASSES.

Having explained at length in my two last works the mechanism of the propagation of beliefs, I can only refer the reader to them. He will there see how every civilisation is based on a small number of fundamental beliefs, which, after a whole series of transformations, finally appear, in the form of religions, in the popular mind. This process of fixation is of great importance, for ideas do not play their part in society, whether for good or ill, until they have descended into the mind of the crowd. Then, and only then, they become general opinions, and then invulnerable beliefs; that is to say, the essential factors of religions, revolutions, and changes of civilisation.

It is into this deepest soil, the soul of the crowd, that all our metaphysical, political, social, and religious conceptions finally thrust their roots. It is of importance to understand this, and for this reason a study of the mechanism of the mental evolution of nations and of the psychology of the crowd appeared to be a necessary preface to a work on Socialism. This study was the more indispensable in that these important subjects, and the latter especially, were very little known. The few

writers who have studied the subject of the crowd have
arrived at conclusions which present, with sufficient
precision, either the exact reverse of the reality,[1] or at
least one facet of a question which comprises many.
They have hardly perceived in the crowd anything but
" an insatiable wild beast, thirsting for blood and rapine."
When we sound the subject a little we find, on the
contrary, that the worst excesses of crowds have often
arisen from extremely generous and disinterested ideas,
and that the crowd is as often victim as murderer. A
book entitled *The Virtuous Masses* would be as justifiable
as a book entitled *The Criminal Masses*. I have elsewhere
insisted at length on this point. But one of the fundamental characteristics which most profoundly divide the

[1] I may cite, as an example of the total incomprehension of this
subject, the compilation of an Italian writer, Signor Sighele, entitled
The Criminal Masses. The book contains scarcely a trace of personal
thought, and is almost entirely composed of quotations intended to
prop up the old theory that the masses must be considered as
ferocious beasts, always ready for the most atrocious crimes. In
order to make his book known to his compatriots, the author for
several months inundated the small Italian papers with letters in
which a number of French writers were accused, with all manners
of invective, of having stolen his ideas from him. One must be
indulgent towards the meridional exaggerations of a beginner ; but
this indulgence must have its limits. I have been well accustomed
these twenty years to see my books regarded as a kind of public
mine where any one may dig without scruple, and I do not complain, considering that an author must hold himself rewarded if his
ideas make headway—even if they are hardly ever quoted. I am
happy, therefore, to see Signor Sighele profit from the perusal of my
books, and will confine myself to asking him to observe that before
complaining so loudly of French writers who, for the greater part,
do not know his name, he should have refrained from availing himself of so many loans, and above all of such dissimulated loans such
as that which figures on page 38, lines 12 *et seq.*, of his little work on
The Psychology of Sects, in which, after a quotation between inverted
commas, taken from one of my books, the author gives as being his
own, changing only a few words, a passage copied directly out of
my *Psychology of Crowds*, page 8, lines 4 *et seq.* (3rd edition). Otherwise I can say with pleasure that Signor Sighele's last work is not
nearly so mediocre as his preceding one.

isolated individual from the crowd is the fact that the first is almost always guided by his personal interest, while the masses are rarely swayed by egoistical motives, but most often by collective and disinterested interests.[1] Heroism and self-forgetfulness are more frequently found in crowds than in individuals. Behind all collective cruelty there is more often than not a belief, an idea of justice, a desire for moral satisfaction, a complete forgetfulness of personal interest, or readiness to sacrifice to the general interest, which is precisely the opposite of egoism.

The crowd may become cruel, but it is above all altruistic, and is as easily led away to sacrifice itself as to destroy others. Dominated by the sub-consciousness, it has a morality and a generosity which are always tending towards activity, whilst those of the individual generally remain contemplative, and most frequently are limited to his speeches. Reflection and reasoning most frequently lead to egoism ; and egoism, so deeply rooted in the isolated individual, is a sentiment unknown to the crowd, simply because the crowd cannot reason and reflect. No religions, no empires could ever have been founded had the armies of their disciples been able to reason and reflect. Very few soldiers of such armies would have sacrificed their lives for the triumph of any cause.

History can only be clearly understood if we bear always in mind that the *morale* and the conduct of the isolated man are very different to those of the same man when he has become part of a collectivity. The collective interests of a race, interests which always imply greater or less forgetfulness of personal interest, are

---

[1] This fundamental point does not appear to have been clearly seized by the critics of my book on *The Psychology of Crowds*. I must, however, make exception of M. Pillon, who, in the *Anneé Philosophique*, has very clearly shown that it is by this demonstration that I stand entirely apart from other writers on the same subject.

maintained by the crowd. Profound altruism, the altruism of acts, and not of words, is a collective virtue. All work of general import, demanding for its accomplishment a minimum of egoism and a maximum of blind devotion, self-abnegation, and sacrifice, can scarcely be accomplished but by crowds.

Despite their momentary outbursts of violence, the masses have always shown themselves ready to suffer all things. The tyrants and fanatics of all ages have never had any difficulty in finding crowds ready to immolate themselves to defend whatever cause. To religious and political tyranny—the tyranny of the living and the dead—they have never shown themselves rebellious. To become their master a man must make himself loved or feared, and by prestige rather than by force.

A distinguished thinker, M. Mazel, in his recent work, *La Synergie sociale*, remarks, of the hecatombs of the Terror, massacres which affected all the classes of society, not excluding the most humble, that " nothing is more astonishing than to see the Jacobin staff come and go, without danger, in a city peopled with the relations or friends of their victims, or of their countless future victims." One cannot but perceive, in the bloody ferocity of the men of the Terror on the one, and the submission of the victims on the other hand, those two so contrary qualities of the crowd, already mentioned : violence and resignation equally unlimited. The Jacobin crowd believed all things permitted, and committed deeds from which an isolated tyrant had recoiled. The victims formed another crowd, which proved itself capable of suffering all things, even death.

Occasional ephemeral violence, and more frequent blind submission, are two opposing characteristics, but two that we must not separate if we wish to understand the mind of the crowd. Their bursts of violence are like the tumultuous waves which the tempest raises on the surface of the ocean, but without troubling the serenity of its profounder waters. The agitations of the crowd have their being above immutable depths that the movements of the surface do not reach ; and this depth consists of those hereditary instincts whose sum is the soul of a nation. This substratum is solid in proportion as the race is ancient, and in consequence possesses a greater fixity. To these hereditary instincts the crowd always returns. Such is the solid woof on which every civilisation has hitherto reposed.

The Socialists imagine that they will easily carry the masses with them. They are wrong ; they will very quickly discover that they will find among the masses, not their allies, but their most implacable enemies. The crowd may, doubtless, in its anger of a day, shatter, furiously, the social edifice ; but, on the morrow, it will acclaim the first-come Cæsar of whose plume it shall catch a glimpse, and who shall promise to restore to it what it has broken. The actual dominating principle of crowds, among nations having a long past, is not mobility, not fickleness, but fixity. Their destructive and revolutionary instincts are ephemeral ; their conservative instincts are of an extreme tenacity. Their destructive instincts may, for a moment, suffer the triumph of Socialism, but their conservative instincts will not permit of its duration ; at least, in its present form. In its triumph, as in its fall, the heavy arguments of theorists will play no part. The hour is yet to sound when logic and reason shall be called to guide the current of History.

BOOK III

SOCIALISM AS AFFECTED BY RACE

CHAPTER I

SOCIALISM IN GERMANY

I. *The theoretical bases of Socialism in Germany :*—The scientific forms of German Socialism—Difference between the fundamental principles of German and Latin Socialism—Latin rationalism, and the evolutionist conception of the world—Starting from different fundamental principles, German and Latin Socialism arrive at practically identical conclusions. 2. *The modern evolution of Socialism in Germany :*—The artificial means by which Germany has arrived at a Socialist concept identical with that of the Latin races—Transformations produced in the German mind by the universal military *régime*—The progressive absorption by the State in Germany—The present transformation of Socialism in Germany—The old theories abandoned—German Socialism tends to assume an anodyne form.

1. THE THEORETICAL BASES OF SOCIALISM IN GERMANY.

IT is in Germany that Socialism has to-day made the greatest strides, above all among the middle and upper classes. The history of Socialism in Germany is altogether beyond the scope of this volume, and if I devote a few pages to it, I do so only because the evolution of Socialism in Germany might, at the first view, seem to contradict my theory of the strict relation which exists between the social conceptions of a nation and the mind of that nation. Between the minds of France and of Germany there are assuredly profound differences, and yet the Socialists of the two countries arrive at identical conceptions.

Before inquiring why the theorists of two so different races should arrive at conclusions so similar, let us first observe in what manner the German methods of reasoning differ from those of the Latin theorists.

The Germans, after having been for a long time inspired by French ideas, are now inspiring these ideas in their turn. Their provisional pontiff, for they change him often, is to-day Karl Marx. His task has principally consisted in attempting to give a scientific shape to very old and common ideas, borrowed, as a brilliant economist, M. Paul Deschanel, has very well shown, from French and English writers. This leaning towards a scientific spirit is a characteristic quality of the German Socialists, and entirely significant of the national mind. Far from regarding Socialism, as do their Latin equivalents, as an arbitrary organisation, able to establish and enforce itself here, there, and everywhere, they see in it only the inevitable development of economic evolution, and they profess an utter disdain of the geometrical constructions of our revolutionary rationalism. They teach that there are no more permanent economic laws than permanent natural laws, but only transitory forms. " Economic ideas are by no means logical ideas, but historical ideas." The value of social institutions is entirely relative, never absolute. Collectivism is a phase of evolution into which all societies, by the mere fact of modern economic evolution, must of necessity enter.

This evolutionist conception of the world is certainly as far removed as possible from the rationalism of the Latins, which, after the fashion of our fathers of the Revolution, wishes to destroy absolutely and absolutely to reconstruct society.

Although they have set out from different principles, in which may be found the fundamental characteristics of the two races, both German Socialists and Latin Socialists arrive exactly at the same conclusions—*reconstruct society by making the State absorb it.* The first desire to effect this reconstruction in the name of evolution, of which, they maintain, it is the consequence. The second wish to effect a demolition, in the name of reason. But the societies of the future appear to them in identical forms. Both profess the same hatred of private enterprise and capital, the same indifference towards liberty, the same craving for forming people into brigades, and for ruling them with an iron discipline. Both demand the destruction of the modern State ; but both would reconstruct it, immediately, under another name, with an administration which would differ from the modern State only in its possession of more extensive powers.

2. The Modern Evolution of Socialism in Germany.

State Socialism is, among the Latin peoples, as I shall presently show, a consequence of their past ; of century on century of centralisation, and the progressive development of the central power. Among the Germans it is not precisely this ; they have been led to a conception of the duty of the State identical with that entertained by the Latin peoples by certain artificial factors. With them, this conception is the result of the transformation of character and conditions of life which has been effected during a century by the extension of the universal military *régime.* This, by the more enlightened of the German writers, notably by Ziegler, has been perfectly recognised. The only means by which the mind, or at least the customs

and the conduct of a nation, can be modified, is a rigid
military discipline. It is the only means against which
the individual is powerless to struggle. It makes him
part of an hierarchy, and prohibits all sentiments of
enterprise and independence. He may severely criticise
its dogmas, but how can he dispute the orders of a chief
who has the right of life and death over his subalterns,
and can reply to the most humble observation by
imprisonment ?

So long as it has not been universal, the military *régime*
has constituted an admirable means of tyranny and conquest. It has been the strength of all the nations who
have succeeded in developing it ; none could have
subsisted without it. But the present age has introduced
universal military service. Instead of acting, as formerly,
on a very small portion of the nation, it acts on the entire
mind of the nation. One may study best its effects in
countries where, as in Germany, it has reached its highest
development. No discipline, not even of the convent,
more completely sacrifices the individual to the community; none more nearly approaches the social type
dreamed of by the Socialists. Prussian martinetry, in
one century, has transformed Germany, and adapted her
admirably to submit to State Socialism. I recommend
those of our young professors who are in search of
subjects a little less commonplace than those which too
often content them to a study of the transformations
effected, during the nineteenth century, in the social and
political ideals of Germany, by the application of compulsory and universal military service.

Modern Germany, ruled by the Prussian monarchy, is
not the product of the slow evolution of history ; its
present unity was effected only by force of arms, after the
Prussian victories over France and Austria. A large
number of small kingdoms, formerly very prosperous,

were suddenly united by Prussia, under a power practically absolute. It established, on the ruins of local and provincial life, a powerful centralisation, recalling that in France under Louis Quatorze and Napoleon. Such *régime* of centralisation must infallibly produce, before long, the effects which it everywhere has produced ; the destruction of local life, above all of intellectual life ; the destruction of private enterprise ; the progressive absorption of all functions by the State. History shows us that these great military monarchies prosper only when they have eminent men at their heads, and as these eminent men are rare they never prosper for very long.

The absorption of functions by the State has been the more easy in Germany, in that the Prussian monarchy, having acquired a great prestige by its successful wars, is able to exercise a power almost absolute, which is not the case in those countries whose Governments, destroyed by frequent revolutions, find many obstacles to the exercise of power. Germany to-day is the great centre of authoritativeness, and will not much longer be the home of any liberty whatever.

One readily understands how Socialism, which demands the wider and wider extension of the intervention of the State, should have found in Germany a soil excellently prepared. Its development could not have been displeasing to the government of a nation so hierarchical, so enregimented, as modern Germany. For a long time, accordingly, the Socialists were regarded with a very benevolent eye. They were *protégés* of Bismarck at first, and might have continued so, had they not finally become troublesome to the Government by a very maladroit opposition.

Since then they have not been considered ; and as the German Empire is a military monarchy, very well able, despite its constitutional form, to become an absolute monarchy, the Socialists have been treated in an energetic and summary manner. In two years only, from 1894 to 1896, according to the *Worwartz*, the courts have inflicted on the Socialists, in press or political cases, penalties to the total sum of 226 years of imprisonment, and £112,000 in fines.

Whether it be that such radical proceedings have made the Socialists reflect, or simply that the gradual enslavement of the mind produced by a severe and universal military rule has made its imprint on the already very practical and highly disciplined mind of the German people, it is certain that to-day Socialism among the Germans is beginning to assume a very mild form. It is becoming opportunist, is establishing itself on an exclusively parliamentary footing, and renounces the immediate triumph of its principles.

The extinction of the capitalist classes and the suppression of monopoly no longer appears more than a theoretic ideal, whose realisation must be very distant. German Socialism teaches to-day that " as *bourgeois* society was not created in a day, it cannot be destroyed in a day." More and more it is tending towards union with the democratic movement in favour of the amelioration of the working classes, of which the most practical and surely the most useful result has been the development of co-operative associations of workmen.

I fear, therefore, that we must renounce the hope I have elsewhere expressed—the hope that the Germans might be the first to undergo the instructive experience of Socialism. Evidently they prefer to leave this task to the Latin races.

Moreover, it is not only in practice that the German Socialists are becoming more docile. Their theorists, formerly so absolute, so unbridled, are gradually abandoning the essential points of their doctrines. Collectivism

itself, so powerful for so long, is now regarded as a somewhat frail and played-out Utopia, without real interest,
though good enough perhaps for the thick-headed public.
The German mind was undoubtedly too scientific and
too practical not to see, finally, the singular poverty of the
doctrine for which our French Socialists still preserve
such a religious respect.

It is interesting to note the easy and rapid evolution of
German Socialism, not only in the details of its theories,
but in their most fundamental parts. For example :
Schultze Delitsch, who at one time possessed much
influence, used to attach a great importance to the co-
operative movement, which he thought of value " to
habituate the people to rely on their own initiative for
the bettering of their condition." Lasalle and all his
followers have always upheld, on the contrary, that
" what the people required above all was a more extensive
recourse to the assistance of the State."

The doctrine of Schultze Delitsch represents the very
negation of Socialism, unless we give the word the very
vague and very general sense of the amelioration of the
conditions of existence of the greater number. This
doctrine is by no means honoured in Germany to-day.
The appeal to individual initiative, on the contrary, is a
characteristic of the peoples we are now going to consider.

CHAPTER II

SOCIALISM IN ENGLAND AND AMERICA

1. *The Anglo-Saxon conceptions of the State, and of education* :—A nation is affected, not by the political system it may adopt, but by the conception it holds of the respective duties of the State and the individual—The Anglo-Saxon social ideal—This ideal remains the same under the most various political systems—The mental characteristics of the Anglo-Saxon—Differences between his private and collective morality —Solidarity and energy—Anglo-Saxon diplomatists—How the qualities of the race are preserved by education—Characteristics of the Anglo Saxon education—The results. 2. *The social ideals of the Anglo-Saxon workers* :—Education of the workers—How they become employers— Rarity of social failures—Why manual work is not despised among the Anglo-Saxons — Administrative capacities of the Anglo-Saxon workers—How acquired—Working men are often made justices of the peace in England—How the Anglo-Saxon worker defends his interests against his employer—Aversion of the English working man for State intervention—The American working man— Industry and private enterprise in America—Collectivism and anarchy in England and America—Their disciples are gathered only from inferior trades exercised by the less capable workers—The army of Socialists in the United States—It will be necessary to fight against it.

1. The Anglo-Saxon Conceptions of the State, and of Education.

IT is above all in comparing the conceptions of the State held respectively by the English and the Latins that we perceive clearly that institutions are the outcome of race, and also to what an extent similar names may conceal profoundly dissimilar things. We may, as did Montesquieu, and many another, discourse upon the advantages, as far as we can perceive them, which a republic offers over a monarchy, or the reverse ; but if, under such dissimilar systems, we find nations possessing identical social conceptions, and very similar institutions, we must conclude that these political systems, nominally so different, have no real influence over the minds of the nations they are supposed to rule.

I have already insisted on this absolutely fundamental thesis in my preceding volumes. In my volume on the psychologic laws of the evolution of nations I have shown, with regard to neighbouring peoples, the English of the United States and the Latins of the Spanish American republics, that their evolution has not been the same, although their political institutions are very similar, those of the latter being in general copied from those of the former. Yet, while the great Anglo-Saxon republic is in the heyday of prosperity, the Spanish-American republics, notwithstanding an admirable soil and inexhaustible natural wealth, are in the lowest slough of decadence. Without arts, without commerce, without industries, they have one and all fallen into decay, bankruptcy, and anarchy. They have had so very many men at the head of affairs that a few of them must have been capable ; but none have been able to alter the course of their destinies.

The political system which a nation adopts is not a matter of great importance. This vain exterior costume is, like all costumes, without real influence on the mind of those it covers. The thing important to know, in order to comprehend the evolution of a nation, is the conception it holds of the respective duties of the State and the individual. The name, be it of monarchy or republic, inscribed on the pediment of the social edifice, has no virtue of itself.

What I am about to say concerning the conception of the State in England and America will justify the foregoing assertions. Having already presented, in the above-mentioned volume, the characteristics of the Anglo-Saxon mind, I shall confine myself at present to briefly summing them up.

Its most essential qualities may be stated in a few words—enterprise, energy, strength of will, and, above all, self-control; that is to say, that internal discipline which makes it needless for the individual to seek other guides than himself.

The social ideal of the Anglo-Saxons is very clearly defined, whether under the English monarchy or the republic of the United States. It consists in reducing the functions of the State to a minimum, and increasing the functions of the individual to a maximum, precisely the contrary of the Latin ideal. Railways, seaports, universities, schools, &c., are created solely by private enterprise, and the State—above all in America—has never any voice in such matters.

A fact that prevents other peoples from properly understanding the English character is that they forget to draw a very distinct line of demarcation between the individual conduct of the Englishman and his collective conduct. His individual morality is, as a general thing, very strict. The Englishman acting in the character of a private person is extremely conscientious, extremely honest, and respects his engagements in general; but English statesmen, acting in the name of the collective interests of England, are of quite another complexion. They are often completely without scruple. A man who should point out to an English minister an opportunity of enriching himself without danger by having an elderly millionaire lady strangled, might be sure of being immediately sent to prison; but let any adventurer, Dr. Jameson, for example, propose to an English statesman—I suppose to Mr. Chamberlain—that he should gather together a band of brigands; should invade, under arms, the ill-defended territory of a little republic in the south of Africa, massacre part of its inhabitants, take possession of the country, and thus augment the wealth of England—the adventurer is certain to receive a cordial welcome, and to see his proposition immediately accepted. If he succeeds, public opinion will be in his favour. It is by proceedings analogous to these that English statesmen have succeeded in conquering the greater number of the small kingdoms of India. It is true that other nations employ the same tactics in matters of colonisation; if they are more prominent in English affairs, it is that the English, being abler and more audacious, more often see their enterprises crowned with success. The wretched lucubrations which the makers of books call the laws of nations, international laws, &c., &c., merely represent a kind of code of theoretical politeness, fit only to distract the leisure of such elderly juriconsults as are too worn out to busy themselves in a useful occupation. In practice they mean precisely as much as do the formulæ of protestation, consideration, and friendship at the end of diplomatic despatches.

The Englishman entertains, with regard to the individuals of his race—other races do not exist for him—sentiments of fellowship which no other peoples possess in the same degree. These sentiments amount to a community of thoughts; the English national mind is very solidly constituted. An Englishman isolated in no matter what quarter of the world regards himself as a representative of England, and considers it his strict duty to act in the interests of his country. England for him is the first power in the universe, the only power, in fact, of any account.

"In the countries where he is already preponderant,

and above all in those where he wishes to be so, the Englishman," writes the Transvaal correspondent of the *Temps*, " begins by stating, as an axiom, his superiority over all the other peoples of the world. By his perseverance and tenacity, by his clannishness and force of will, he introduces his manners, his pleasures, his language, his newspapers, and even succeeds in transplanting his cookery ! The other nations he regards with sovereign disdain ; even with hostility, when their representatives show themselves inclined, or bold enough, to dispute with him the right of a little portion of colonial soil. In the Transvaal we have the daily proof of this. England is not only the paramount power, she is the first, the one and only nation of the world."

A French deputy, M. de Mahy, has cited in Parliament a good example of British solidarity. Uganda, as every one knows, is the finest province of Equatorial Africa. At one time we could have obtained it ; we hesitated. A simple English missionary who happened to be on the spot took it upon himself, seeing the importance of the country, to sign a protectorate treaty with the native chiefs ; he then set out for London, and naturally obtained the most cordial reception from the English Government. All his clauses were ratified, and England became possessed of Uganda without expense. To complete her conquest she only had to shoot down a few thousand natives who had been converted by our missionaries, and who, for this reason, were suspected of favouring France.

This national unity, so rare among the Latin races, gives England an irresistible strength. This it is that makes their diplomacy everywhere so powerful. As the national mind has been a fixed quantity for a long period, their diplomatists all think in the same fashion on essential subjects. They receive perhaps less instructions than the agents of any other nation, and yet they have more unity of action and more sense of consequences than any others. They may be regarded as interchangeable pieces. Any English diplomatist succeeding any other English diplomatist will act exactly as his predecessor acted.[1] Among the Latins absolutely the reverse is true. In Tonkin, in Madagascar, and in our other colonies we have had precisely as many different political systems as governors, and we know whether the latter are often changed ! The French diplomatist creates a political system, but is incapable of possessing a policy.

The English system of education, though summary in appearance, does not prevent the English from producing a class of thinkers and scientists equal to those of the nations possessing the most cultured schools. These thinkers, recruited outside of the universities and societies, are characterised above all by an originality which only self-made minds can possess, and which is never found among those who have been poured into identical moulds on college benches ?

This originality of thought and style is found even in scientific works where one would least expect it to show itself. Let us, for instance, compare the scientific works of Tyndall, Kelvin, Tait, &c., with the analogous works written by our professors. On every page we find originality, on every page expressive and striking demonstrations, while the cold and correct works of our professors

[1] I used to think this theory evident to every one who had travelled and looked about him, until the day when I expressed it at a gathering in which several French diplomatists were present. Except from an admiral, who was entirely of my opinion, I met with unanimous protest. "Interchangeable diplomatists ! was not this the negation of diplomacy ? What then was the use of intelligence ?" &c., &c. Once more I was able to measure the width of the gulf which separates the concepts of the Latins from those of the Anglo-Saxons, and to judge how irremediable is our colonial weakness.

are all written on the same model. When we have read one we have read all. Their end is by no means science for its own sake ; they are mere preludes to examination. This, by the way, is always carefully stated on the cover.

To resume : the Englishman seeks to make of his son a man armed for life, able to rely on himself, and to grow out of that perpetual tutelage which the Latins cannot shake off. This education gives, above all, and before all, self-control, which is the national virtue of England, and which would have sufficed almost of itself to assure her prosperity and greatness.

The above-mentioned principles resulting from those sentiments whose aggregate constitute the English national mind, we should naturally look to find them in all the countries inhabited by the same race, and notably in America ; and we do actually find them there. A judicious observer, M. de Chasseloup-Laubat, expresses himself as follows :—

"The manner in which the Americans understand the functions of education in society is yet another cause of the stability of their institutions. They hold that general education, and not instruction, should be the aim of the pedagogue ; excepting, of course, a minimum of facts which they teach their children in the primary schools. In their eyes physical, intellectual, and moral education, that is to say, the development of the energy and endurance whether of body, mind, or character, constitutes, for every individual, the principal factor of success. Certain it is that the power to work, the will to succeed, and the habit of repeated effort towards a determined point are inestimable things, for they may be applied in every career at every moment ; while instruction, on the contrary, must vary according to the pupil's condition, and the functions to which he is destined."

The ideal of the Americans is to prepare men to live,

not to gain diplomas. Encouragement of initiative, development of will, the habit of thinking for oneself—these are the results obtained. From these ideals to the ideals of the Latin races is a far cry. In the course of this investigation we shall see the differences between the two grow more and more accentuated.

2. The Social Ideals of the Anglo-Saxon Workers.

But in England the Socialists are recruited above all from the working classes, not from the leisured classes. We must therefore abandon the preceding generalities, and inquire as to the sources of instruction and education of the Anglo-Saxon working man, and as to how his ideas are formed.

His instruction and education differ very little from those of the lower middle classes, being equally effected by contact with things themselves, and not at all by the influence of books. For this very reason there could not exist in England that profound gulf created between the different classes by the competitions and diplomas of the Latin nations. You may often find in France a factory hand or a miner who has become an employer ; you will never find one who has become an official engineer, since in order to do so he would have first of all to pass through the schools that grant diplomas, and grant them only to those who enter the schools before twenty. The English working man, if he has sufficient capacity, becomes first foreman and then engineer, and cannot become an engineer in any other way. Nothing could be more democratic, and with such a system there should be neither wasted abilities nor social failures. No one would entertain the idea of despising manual labour, so disdained and ignored by our bachelors and licentiates, since manual labour constitutes a necessary period of transition.

We have seen what are the English workman's sources of technical instruction ; we will now inquire into the sources of his theoretical instruction, of that kind of instruction which is so necessary when it follows or accompanies practice, instead of preceding it. The primary school having furnished him with the rudiments only of instruction, he himself feels the need of completing the process, and to this complementary study, of whose utility he is sensible, he carries all the energy of his race. This necessary complement he acquires easily by means of evening classes, which have been founded everywhere by private enterprise, the subjects of which always bear on what the students learn practically in the mine and workshop. Thus they always have the means of verifying the utility of what they learn.

To this source of instruction we must add the free libraries, which are founded all over the country, and also the newspapers and journals. No comparison can be made between the futile French journals, which have not a reader across the Channel, and the English journals, so rich in precise information of every kind. Journals dealing with mechanical inventions, such as *Engineering*, are read above all by workmen. The small popular provincial papers are full of instruction with regard to industrial and economic questions in all parts of the globe. M. des Rouziers speaks of his conversations with workshop hands, whose remarks showed him that they are "far better informed of the affairs of the world than the great majority of Frenchmen who have received what is conventionally called a liberal education." He quotes a discussion which he had with two of them on the question of bi-metallism, the effects of the McKinley tariff, and so forth ; no elegant phrases, but just and practical observations.

So much for theoretical instruction. But how does the working man acquire those general economic ideas which exercise his judgment and help him to manage his affairs ? Simply by taking part in the direction of the undertakings in which he is interested, instead of getting them attended to by the State or by an employer. The smallest labour centres possess co-operative, friendly, insurance, and other societies, directed solely by working men. Thus the Anglo-Saxon workers find themselves daily confronted with realities, and soon learn not to meddle with impossibilities and dreams. "Great Britain," writes M. des Rouziers, "by means of this multitude of autonomous societies—co-operative societies, temperance associations, mutual aid societies, trades-unions, &c.—is preparing generations of capable citizens, and at the same time prepares herself to suffer, without violent revolution, the political transformations which may take place." As a proof of the practical ability which the English working man thus acquires, M. des Rouziers mentions that in one year seventy working men were made justices of the peace, while there were twelve in Parliament, in the last Liberal Administration of 1892, amongst them an Under-Secretary of State. The sums deposited by working men in trades-unions, private societies, and savings banks, are valued at £320,000,000.

It is easy to perceive that these results are purely the consequence of racial characteristics, and not of environment, from the fact that workers of different race, placed beside English working men, and subjected to conditions absolutely identical, present none of the qualities I have just described. Such, for example, are the Irish hands in the English shops. M. des Rouziers, with many others, has noted their inferiority, which persists equally in America. "They show no desire to better themselves ; they are satisfied as soon as they have enough to eat." In

America, the Irish, like the Italians elsewhere, scarcely ever exercise any other trades than those of beggar, politician, bricklayer, servant, or rag-picker.

Thoroughly impressed with the necessities of economics, the English working man is perfectly able to discuss his interests with his employer, and at need to force his demands by a strike ; but he is not jealous of him, and does not hate him, precisely because he does not consider him to be made of different clay. He knows exactly what his employer gains, and consequently what he can give. He will only risk a strike if, after due deliberation, he decides that the disproportion between the respective remuneration of capital and labour is too great. " He does not seriously abuse his employer for two reasons : if he abuses him he ruins him, and if he ruins him he is no longer an employer." The idea of forcing State intervention between worker and master, so dear to our Socialists, is altogether antipathetic to the English workman. To demand strike pay of the State would appear at once immoral and absurd. Taine, in his *Notes sur l'Angleterre*, had already noticed this aversion of the English working man for Government protection, and opposed this characteristic aversion to the constant appeal of the French working man to the State.

Otherwise than on the Continent, the English working man is the victim of economic fluctuations, and of the industrial disasters thereby occasioned ; but he has too much of the sense of necessities and the knowledge of affairs to hold his employer responsible for such accidents. He will have nothing to do with the dithyrambics on the exploiters of labour, and infamous capital, so dear to our Latin demagogues. He is well aware that the labour question is not limited to the conflict between labour and capital, but that both are subject to an equally important factor — demand. He accordingly submits when he judges a reduction of salary or a term of enforced idleness to be inevitable.   Thanks to his enterprise and his education he can even change his calling at need.   M. des Rouziers makes mention of English masons spending six months of the year in the United States in order to find work there, and of other workers who, finding themselves ruined by the importation of Australian wool, sent out delegates to study the question on the spot.   They bought Colonial wool on the spot, and very soon, by opening a new branch of trade, transformed the conditions of life in their district.   Such energy, enterprise, and ability among workmen would seem very extraordinary in a Latin country.   We have only to cross the Atlantic in order to find these qualities yet further developed among the Anglo-Saxons of America, in which country, above all others, no one ever counts on the State.   It would never enter an American's mind to require the State to establish railways, ports, universities, &c.   Private enterprise alone suffices for all such matters, and is shown above all, and to a most remarkable degree, in the construction of the immense railroads which enmesh the great Republic. Nothing could better show the gulf which separates the Latin from the Anglo-Saxon mind in matters of enterprise and independence.

The railroad industry is regarded, in the United States, as any other industry.   Undertaken by associated individuals, it is only maintained if it be productive.   The thought would never occur to any one that the shareholders might, as in France, be requited by the Government.   The largest lines at present running were in every case begun on a small scale, in order to limit risk.   A line is extended only if its commencement be successful. By this simple means the American lines have reached a development unequalled in any European nation, despite the protection of their Governments. Yet nothing

could be more simple than the administrative machinery
of these enormous concerns; a very small number of
interested and responsible officials suffices to conduct
them.

"Let us examine," writes M. L. P. Dubois, "the
simple, precise, and rapid working of the administrative
machinery. No bureaux, no irresponsible clerks, preparing reports which their chiefs sign without reading.
The motto is 'each for himself.' The work, necessarily
divided, is at the same time decentralised; from top to
bottom of the scale each has his own functions and his
own responsibilities, and does all by himself; it is the
best of all systems for discovering individual qualities.
Errand-boys and type-writer girls for writing letters to
dictation are the only personal auxiliaries. Nothing
drags: *every matter must be settled within twenty-four
hours.* Every one is as busy as he can be, and from the
president to the simple clerk every one works nine hours
a day. Consequently the headquarters of a great railroad
require only a small staff, and occupy only a small space;
the Chicago, Burlington, and Quincy Railway, which
has more than six thousand miles of lines in the Western
States, occupies only one story of its building in Adams
Street, Chicago; the St. Paul Railway does the same.

"The president personally directs the entire business;
he is the commander-in-chief. He is a universal person;
all important questions of every branch of the service are
submitted to him; he is by turns engineer, economist,
and financier; an advocate in the courts of justice, a
diplomatist in his relations with the Legislature. He is
always in the breach. Often a president will have passed
through all the stages, active or sedentary, of the service;
one began as machinist in the service of the company
he now directs. All are men of the high worth entirely
characteristic of the best type of the American business

man, formed by practice, and through practice led to general ideas."

The preceding remarks enable us easily to foresee what small chance of success our ideas of State Socialism, so natural to the Latin peoples, can have among the Anglo-Saxons. It is, therefore, not astonishing that the completest discord should immediately occur when the delegates of Anglo-Saxon and Latin workers respectively encounter one another at a Socialist congress. The English race owes its power to the development of private enterprise, and the limitation of the attributes of the State. Its progress is therefore the reverse of Socialism, and it only prospers by the fact.

Yet both England and America also have heard the worst forms of collectivism and even anarchy preached. For several years we have seen the progress of Socialism in England, but we see also that it gathers its recruits almost exclusively from among the trades which are badly paid, and which are consequently exercised by the less capable workers, that is, by those " unfit," to whom I shall subsequently devote a chapter. These alone demand, and these alone are interested in demanding, the nationalisation of the soil and of capital, and the protection of Government intervention.

But it is more especially in the United States that the Socialists possess an immense army of disciples ; an army which grows every day more numerous and more menacing, recruited from the increasing flood of immigrants of foreign blood, without resources, without energy, and without adaptability to the conditions of existence in their new country, who to-day form an immense social drain. The United States already foresee the day when it will be necessary to plunge into bloody warfare to defend themselves against these multitudes. It will be a merciless war of extermination, which will recall, but on a far larger scale, the destruction of the barbarian hordes to which Marius was forced, that he might save Roman civilisation from their invasion. Knowing the qualities of the two combatants, the issue of the conflict is certain ; but it will undoubtedly be one of the most frightful struggles that have ever been recorded by history. Yet only, perhaps, at the price of such holocausts can the holy cause of the independence of man and the progress of civilisation be saved ; that cause which more than one nation seems ready to-day to abandon.

CHAPTER III

LATIN SOCIALISM AND THE PSYCHOLOGY OF THE LATIN PEOPLES

1. *How the actual political system of a nation is determined :*—We must go back to the roots of institutions to understand their genesis—How we may discover a nation's principles of government behind its visible institutions—Theoretical institutions are only borrowed clothes. 2. *The mental state of the Latin peoples :*—What one understands by the Latin peoples—Their characteristics—Quickness of intelligence—Weakness of initiative and will—Love of equality and indifference for liberty—Need of guidance—The cult of words and of logic—Opposition between the Anglo-Saxon and Latin mind as regards logic—The consequences—Development of sociability among the Latins, and weakness of solidarity—The qualities which formerly gave the Latins superiority are to-day becoming useless—The parts of character and intelligence in the development of civilisations.

1. HOW THE ACTUAL POLITICAL SYSTEM OF A NATION IS DETERMINED.

THE study of Socialism among the Anglo-Saxons has shown us that among these peoples all Socialistic theories must clash with racial characteristics which will render their development impossible. We are about to show that among the Latin peoples, on the contrary, Socialism is the result of previous evolution, of a system of government to which they have, unconsciously, for a long time submitted, and whose development they call for more and more loudly.

On account of the importance of the subject it will be

necessary to devote to it several chapters. We can only measure the progress of certain institutions by going back to their roots. When an institution of any kind is seen to prosper in any nation, we may be very certain that it is the culmination of a whole previous process of evolution.

This evolutionary process is not always visible, because —above all in modern times—an institution is often merely a borrowed garment for which the theorist is responsible, and which, not being moulded on realities, possesses no significance. To study institutions and constitutions from the outside, to state that such a nation is under a monarchy, and such under a republic, will teach us absolutely nothing, and can only confuse the mind. There are more countries than one—for example, the Spanish-American republics—possessing constitutions which are admirable on paper, and perfect institutions, which yet are plunged into the completest anarchy, under the absolute despotism of petty tyrants whose fantasies know no limits. In other parts of the world, on the other hand, we find countries like England, living under a monarchical and aristocratic government, having the most obscure and imperfect constitutions that a theorist could imagine, but in which the personal liberty, prerogatives, and functions of the citizens are more highly developed than they have ever been elsewhere.

The best means of discovering, behind meaningless exterior forms, the actual political system of a people is to study, in the details of public affairs, the respective limits of the functions of the Government and the unit ; that is, to determine the conception which the nation entertains of the State. As soon as we enter on this study the borrowed garments disappear, and the realities stand out. We then very quickly see how futile are all theoretical discussions on the value of the exterior forms

of governments and institutions, and we clearly perceive
that a nation can no more choose the institutions that
really govern it, than a man can choose his age.   Theoretical institutions are about as valuable as the artifices
by means of which man seeks to dissimulate his years.
The reality is not apparent to the inattentive observer, but
it none the less exists.

2. THE MENTAL STATE OF THE LATIN PEOPLES.

My reader knows what I mean by the phrases " Latin
peoples," " Latin races."   I do not intend the term
to have an anthropological meaning, since pure races,
except among the savage peoples, have long ago all but
vanished.   Among civilised peoples there are now only
what I have elsewhere called historic races ; races entirely created by the events of history.   Such races are
established when a people, often comprising elements
of very different origin, has been subjected for centuries
to similar conditions of environment, similar ways of
life, common institutions and beliefs, and an identical
education.   Unless the populations in juxtaposition are
of too different origin—as, for example, the Irish under
the English rule, and the heterogeneous races under the
domination of Austria—they become fused, and acquire
a national spirit ; that is to say, they acquire similar
sentiments, interests, and manners of thought.
Such a work is not accomplished in a day, but a people
is formed, a civilisation is established, a historical race
comes into existence, only when the creation of a national
spirit is consummated.
Accordingly, when I speak of the Latin peoples, I
speak of the peoples which may, perhaps, have no Latin
elements in their blood, and which greatly differ from
one another, but which for centuries and centuries have

been subjected to the yoke of the Latin ideals. They are Latin by sentiment, in their institutions, their literature, their beliefs, and their arts, and their education continues to maintain the Latin ideals among them. "After the Renascence," writes M. Hanotaux, "the image of Rome inscribed itself in ineffaceable characters on the face of France. . . . For three centuries French civilisation appeared nothing but a patchwork of Roman civilisation." Is it not so still?

In a recent essay published *apropos* of a new edition of Michelet's *Histoire romaine*, M. Gaston Boissier upholds the same idea. He justly remarks that "from Rome we draw the greater part of what we are; when we analyse ourselves we find a deposit of sentiments and ideas that Rome has bequeathed to us, which nothing has been able to take from us, and on which everything else has its foundation."

If we wished to define in a few words the present psychology of the Latin peoples, we might say that they are characterised by feebleness of will, energy, and enterprise alike.

They, and notably the Celts, exhibit the fundamental peculiarity of possessing at once a very lively intelligence and very little enterprise or stability of will. Incapable of protracted efforts, they love to be guided, and for their failures they hold their governors, and never themselves, responsible. Ready, as Cæsar even in his time observed, to undertake wars without motive, they are downcast at the first reverse. They have a feminine fickleness, which was already noted by the great conqueror as a Gallic infirmity. This fickleness makes them the slaves of every impulse. Perhaps their most definite characteristic is the lack of self-control, which, enabling a man to rule himself, prevents him from seeking to be ruled.

Much in love with equality, extremely jealous of all

superiority, they have always shown themselves indifferent to liberty. So soon as they possess it they seek to place it in the hands of a master, in order to enjoy that control and government without which they cannot live. They have played an important part in history only when they have had great men at their head ; and for this reason, by a long-established and secret instinct, they are always seeking them out.

In all times they have been great speakers, lovers of logic and of words. Very little concerned with facts, they greatly love an idea, so long as it be simple, general, and presented in elegant language.[1]

Words and dialectic have always been the most terrible enemies of the Latin peoples. "The French," said von Moltke, "always take words for facts." This is equally true of the other Latin peoples. It was justly remarked that, while the Americans were attacking the Philippines, the Spanish Cortes contented themselves merely with delivering pompous speeches and provoking crises in which the different parties struggled for power, instead of attempting to take the measures necessary to defend the last remnants of their national inheritance. An immense pyramid, higher than the highest of Egypt, might be

[1] This admiration of elegant language is carefully fostered by our lamentable classical education. The "prix d'honneur" of our great *concours* is always given to a dissertation in which urchins of sixteen hold forth in the style of gods, heroes, and kings. The idea of suggesting the narration, in a correct style, of the things they have seen for themselves about themselves, in a mere stroll, for example, has never entered the heads of their professors. To them it seems far better to make their scholars learn to recite from books than to make them learn to observe. What astonishing ignorance on the part of our pedagogues ! When the dust of ages lies heavy on the Latin peoples the philosophers of the future will be able to reconstruct their psychology merely by perusing—if they find it—the list of the subjects of composition which are given in our great *concours*. [The *concours* is the competition which takes place annually between the best pupils of the various classes of the schools and colleges of Paris and Versailles.]

built with the skulls of the victims to words and logic
among the Latin races. An Anglo-Saxon complies with
facts and necessities, never throws the responsibility for
what happens to him on the Government, and cares very
little for the obvious indications of logic. He believes in
experience, and knows that men are not conducted by
reason. A Latin always deduces all from logic, and
reconstructs societies from bottom to top on plans traced
by the light of reason. Such was the dream of Rousseau,
and of all the writers of his century. The Revolution
merely applied their doctrines, and so far no amount of
deception has shaken the power of such illusions. This
is what Taine called the classic spirit : " To isolate a few
very simple and very general ideas ; then, leaving experience behind, to compare and combine them ; then,
from the artificial compound thus obtained, to deduce, by
a little reasoning, all the consequences it implies." The
great writer has admirably seized on the effects of this
mental disposition on the speeches of our revolutionary
assemblies :—

"Glance through the harangues of senate and club,
the newspaper reports, the law cases, the pamphlets, all
the writings inspired by present and pressing events :
there is no conception of the human creature as one has
him before one's eyes, in the fields or in the street ; he is
figured always as a simple automaton, whose mechanism
is known. For the writer, he was but of late a musical-
box producing phrases ; for the politician, he is to-day a
musical-box producing votes, and he needs only a touch
of the finger in the proper place to make him give the
proper answer. Never a fact ; nothing but abstractions ;
strings of sentences on Nature, reason, the people, tyrants,
liberty ; like so many air-balloons idly jostling one
another in space. If we did not ·know that all this has
practical and terrible effect, we should think it a game of

logic, or so many school exercises, so much academic fencing, so many combinations of the science of ideas."

The sociability of the Latins, and especially of the French, is very great, but their feelings of solidarity are very feeble. The Englishman, on the other hand, is unsociable, but he coheres strongly with all the individuals of his race. We have seen that this cohesion is one of the great causes of his strength. The Latins are guided above all by individual egoism ; the Anglo-Saxons by collective egoism.

This complete lack of solidarity, which is met with in all the Latin peoples, is one of their most hurtful defects. It is a racial vice, but it is very largely developed by their education. By their perpetual examinations and competitions they set the individual always in competition with his fellows, and develop individual egoism at the expense of collective egoism.

The absence of solidarity is visible in the least circumstances of life among the Latins. For a long time it has been remarked that in the football matches against English teams the French are always losers, simply because the English player, preoccupied not with his personal success, but with that of his team, passes the ball when he is unable to stick to it, while the French player holds it obstinately, preferring that his side should lose, rather than he should see the ball gained by a comrade. The success of his team is indifferent to him ; he is concerned only with his individual success. This egoism will naturally follow him through life, and, if he become a general, he will even allow the enemy to crush a colleague whom he might have succoured, in order to avoid procuring him a success. We had lamentable examples of this in our last war.

This lack of solidarity among the Latins has especially

struck those travellers who have visited our colonies. I have often been enabled to verify the justice of the following remarks of M. A. Maillet :—

" When two Frenchmen are neighbours in the colonies it is an exceptional thing if they are not enemies. The first sensation of the traveller who sets foot in a colony is one of stupefaction. Every colonist, every official, every officer even, expresses himself with regard to the others with so much acrimony, that the traveller demands how it is these people do not draw their revolvers."

Only by totally suppressing competition and examination in our educational system—as was done long ago in England—can we remedy a little this dangerous defect of egoism.

The Latin peoples have always exhibited great courage. But their indecision, their want of foresight, their lack of solidarity, their absence of *sang-froid*, their fear of responsibilities, render their bravery useless so soon as they are not thoroughly well commanded.

In modern warfare the part played by the officers becomes more and more restricted, on account of the size of the field of battle. The qualities that count are coolness of head, foresight, solidarity, and a methodical spirit, and therefore the Latin peoples will hardly see their ancient successes renewed.

At one period, not yet very remote, wit, elegant speech, chivalrous qualities, and literary and artistic aptitude, constituted the principal factors of civilisation. Thanks to these qualities, which they possessed in a high degree, the Latin peoples were long at the head of all the nations. With the industrial, geographic, and economic evolution of the modern period the conditions of national superiority called for very different abilities. The factors of superiority to-day are the qualities of enduring energy, of enterprise, and of method. These the Latin nations hardly possess, and therefore they have had to give place progressively to those that do possess them.

The system of education imposed on the young of the Latin nations is gradually destroying what remains of these qualities. Persistent will-power, perseverance, and enterprise are vanishing one by one, and, above all, that self-control is vanishing which allows a man to dispense with a master.

Many events have contributed to decimate, by an often-repeated negative selection, those individuals whose energy, activity, and independence of mind were most highly developed. The Latin peoples are to-day paying for the errors of their past. In Spain the Inquisition steadily decimated, during many centuries, all the best elements of the country. In France the Revocation of the Edict of Nantes, the Revolution, the Empire, and the civil wars destroyed her most energetic and enterprising sons. The insignificant increase of population observed among most of the Latin peoples contributes to these causes of decadence. Nevertheless, if only they were the best elements of the population that reproduce themselves this smallness of increase would by no means be a disadvantage, for the strength of a country consists not in the number but the quality of its inhabitants. Unhappily they are the most incapable, the weakest, and the most imprudent who maintain the numerical level of the population. M. Fouillée very justly writes as follows :—

"France is practising Darwinism the wrong way about. She is relying, for the recruiting of her population, on the selection of inferior types. The more wealthy classes, who by means of work and intelligence have arrived at a certain degree of ease, and by this very fact exhibit a certain intellectual superiority, are precisely those who are eliminating themselves by a voluntary sterility. On the other hand, imprudence, unintelligence, idleness, insanity, and misery intellectual and material, are prolific, and are responsible for a great proportion of the national population. It has been remarked, and with reason, that if a stock-breeder were to proceed on these lines he would soon procure the degeneration of his horses and cattle."

This observation is extremely just. It is indisputable, and it is a point on which I have elsewhere insisted at length, that the worth of a nation is caused by the number of remarkable men of all kinds which it produces. Its decadence arises from the diminution and disappearance of its superior elements. In an essay which recently appeared in the *Revue scientifique* M. Lapouge arrives at analogous conclusions with regard to the Romans.

" If, for example, we consider the great Roman families, at an interval of two hundred years, we find that the most illustrious of the old families no longer exist, and that in their place have risen other families, of inferior worth, and recruited from all classes, even from the freedmen. When Cicero lamented the decay of the Roman virtues he forgot that in the city, and even in the Senate, Romans of pure descent were rare ; that for one scion of the Quirites there were ten mongrel Latins and ten Etruscans. He forgot that the Roman city began to be endangered as soon as it was thrown open to all, and that if the title of citizen was incessantly diminishing in lustre, it was because it was borne by more sons of the vanquished than of the conquerors. When, by naturalisation after naturalisation, the city of Rome was laid open to every nation ; when Bretons, Syrians, Thracians, and Africans were muffled up in the livery of the Roman citizen, too heavy for their hearts, the Romans of pure blood had disappeared."

The rapid progress of certain races, the Anglo-Saxon for example, has been determined by the fact that selection, instead of operating in a reverse sense, as in Latin Europe, has operated in the direction of progress. The United States were populated for a long time by all the most independent and energetic persons of the various European countries, and notably of England. It was necessary for a man to possess the most emphatically virile character to dare to emigrate with his family to a distant country, inhabited by hostile and warlike nations, and there create a civilisation.

It is important to note here a fact that I have already emphasised in my later books—that nations are effaced from the page of history not by the diminution of intelligence, but by weakening of character. This law was verified of old by the Greeks and Romans, and it is tending to verify itself again to-day.

This is a fundamental notion, still much disputed, but tending, however, to extend itself more and more. I find it very well expressed in a recent work by an English writer, Mr. Benjamin Kidd, and I cannot better support my argument than by borrowing from him a few passages in which he shows, with great justice and impartiality, what are the differences of character that divide the Anglo-Saxon from the Frenchman, and the historical consequences of these differences :—

" If we take France, which of the three leading countries of Western Europe probably possesses the largest leaven of Celtic blood, any impartial person, who had fairly considered the evidence, would probably find himself compelled to admit that a very strong if not a conclusive case could be made out for placing the French people a degree higher as regards certain intellectual characteristics than any other of the Western peoples. . . . The influence of the French intellect is, in fact, felt throughout the whole fabric of our Western civilisation ; in the entire region of politics, in nearly every branch of art, and in every department of higher thought. . . .

"The Teutonic peoples tend, as a rule, to obtain the most striking intellectual results where profound research, painstaking, conscientious endeavour, and the laborious piecing together and building up of the fabric of knowledge go to produce the highest effects. But the idealism of the French mind is largely wanting. . . . Any conscientious observer, when first brought into close contact with the French mind, must feel that there is something in it of a distinctly high intellectual order which is not native either to the German or the English peoples. It is felt in the current literature and the current art of the time no less than in the highest products of the national genius of the past."

Having recognised this mental superiority of the French, the English author insists on the greater social importance of character over intelligence, and shows to what extent intelligence has been able to serve those nations who have possessed it. Taking the history of the colonial struggle between France and England which occupied the latter half of the eighteenth century, he says :—

"By the middle of the eighteenth century England and France had closed in what—when all the issues dependent on the struggle are taken into account—is undoubtedly one of the most stupendous duels that history records. Before it came to a close the shock had been felt through the whole civilised world. The contest was waged in Europe, in India, in Africa, over the North American continent, and on the high seas. Judged by all those appearances which impress the imagination, everything was in favour of the more brilliant race. In armaments, in resources, in population, they were the superior people. In 1789 the population of Great Britain was only 9,600,000, the population of France was 26,000,000. The annual revenue of France was £24,000,000, that of Great Britain was only £15,650,000. At the beginning of the nineteenth century the French people numbered some 27,000,000, while the whole English-speaking peoples, including the Irish and the population of the North American states and colonies, did not exceed 20,000,000.

" By the beginning of the last decade of the nineteenth century the English-speaking peoples, not including subject peoples, aboriginal races, or the coloured population of the United States, had, however, expanded to the enormous total of 101,000,000, while the French people scarcely numbered 40,000,000. Looking back it will be seen that the former peoples have been successful at almost every point throughout the world at which the conflict has been waged. In nearly the whole of the North American and Australian continents, and in those parts of Southern Africa most suitable for European races, the English-speaking races are in possession. No other peoples have so firmly and permanently established their position. No limits can be set to the expansion they are likely to undergo even in the next century, and it would seem almost inevitable that they must in future exercise a preponderating influence in the world."

Then, examining the qualities which have allowed the English to accomplish their tremendous progress, to administer their gigantic colonial empire with so great success, to transform Egypt to the extent of establishing, in a few years, the credit of a nation which was on the brink of bankruptcy, in the highest degree of prosperity, the author expresses himself as follows :—

" All these results were attained by simple means ; by the exercise of qualities which are not usually counted either brilliant or intellectual. . . . These qualities are not as a rule of the brilliant order, nor such as strike the imagination. Occupying a high place among them, are such characteristics as strength and energy of character, humanity, probity and integrity, and simple-minded devotion to conceptions of duty in such circumstances as may arise. Those who incline to attribute the very wide influence which the English-speaking peoples have come to exercise in the world to the Machiavelian schemes of their rulers are often very wide of the truth. This influence is, to a large extent, due to qualities of not at all a showy character."

We are now prepared to understand how those nations that are strong as to intelligence but weak as to energy and character have always been led naturally to replace their destinies in the hands of their governments. A rapid survey of their past history will show us that this form of State Socialism known as Collectivism, which is proposed to us to-day, is, so far from being a novelty, the natural outcome of the past institutions and hereditary needs of the races in which it is to-day developing itself. Reducing to a minimum the source of energy and initiative which the individual must possess to conduct his life, and freeing him from all responsibility, Collectivism seems for these reasons well adapted to the needs of nations whose will, energy, and initiative have progressively decayed.

CHAPTER IV

THE LATIN CONCEPTION OF THE STATE

1. *How the concepts of a people become fixed :*—A nation must submit to its traditions, and at the same time must afterwards be able to free itself from their yoke—Few nations have possessed the plasticity necessary to realise the double condition of variability and fixity—Impossibility of escaping the yoke of tradition when too firmly fixed—Power of the principles of authority among the Latins—Political and religious authority—Why the Latin peoples have not suffered from their submission to the traditional dogmas of authority until modern times, and why they are suffering from it to-day—The inevitable instability of their governments—The conception of the State is the same in every part of France. 2. *The Latin conception of the State :*—The *ancien régime*—The Revolution introduced only very slight changes —Details of administration under the old system—Constant intervention of the State in the most trifling matters under the old system —Various examples—The present development of Socialism among the Latins is the outcome of their past institutions and their conception of the State.

1. HOW THE CONCEPTS OF A PEOPLE BECOME FIXED.

WE have just seen, in our study of the psychology of the Latin peoples, that their character has favoured the development of certain institutions among them. We have now to discover how these institutions became fixed, and how, having become causes in their turn, they have finally produced certain effects.

We have already seen that a civilisation can be born only on condition that a people submits itself for a long time to the yoke of a tradition. At the period of a people's formation, when the elements gathered together are dissimilar, and have different and fluctuating interests, those institutions and beliefs which are stable have a considerable importance.[1] It is important that these beliefs and institutions should be in agreement with the needs and mental characteristics of the people they are required to rule, and also that they should be sufficiently rigid. This latter point is of fundamental importance, and I have already insisted on it. But, after showing that all nations must for a long time be subjected to the yoke of tradition, I have also pointed out the fact that they progress only on condition of their ability to free themselves slowly from this yoke.

They never free themselves by violent revolutions. Revolutions are always ephemeral. Societies, like animal species, are transformed only by the hereditary addition of small successive changes.

Few peoples have possessed the plasticity of nature necessary to realise this double condition of fixity and variability. Without a sufficient fixity no civilisation can establish itself ; without a sufficient variability no civilisation can progress.

We must always consider the institutions of a nation as effects, which in their turn become causes. After they have been maintained for a certain number of generations they render completely fixed those psychologic

---

[1] The reader might find an apparent contradiction between this proposition and that elsewhere formulated : that institutions play no part in the life of nations. But we were then considering nations which had reached maturity, and in which the elements of civilisation have become fixed by inheritance. Such nations cannot be modified by new institutions, and can adopt them even only in appearance. It is quite otherwise with new, that is to say, more or less barbarous nations, among whom none of the elements of civilisation have yet become fixed. The reader desirous of entering into this subject more deeply should refer to my book *The Psychology of Peoples*.

characters which at first were a little uncertain and fluctuating. A lump of clay, at first plastic, quickly becomes less so, and ends by acquiring the hardness of stone, when it will break rather than change its form. It is often difficult enough for a people to acquire a stable and coherent mass of sentiments and thoughts, but it is far more difficult for it to modify this mass afterwards.

When, by heredity, the yoke of tradition has been too long imposed on the national mind, a nation can free itself from this yoke only by great efforts, and most often it cannot free itself at all. We know what violent convulsions agitated the Western world at the time of the Reformation, when the northern nations strove to set themselves free from the religious centralisation and the dogmatic authority which forbade them all independence, and against which their reason revolted more and more.

The Latin peoples, they also, wished to set themselves free from the yoke of the Past. Our great Revolution had no other end in view. But it was too late. After a few years of convulsions the ties of the past resumed their empire. These bonds were indeed too powerful, and had left too profound an imprint on the mind, to be broken in a day.

Imbued with the necessity of the principle of authority, the governments of the Latin peoples had for centuries prevented them from thinking, willing, and acting, and all education had as its aim the maintenance of this triple interdiction. Why should the men of the Latin races have thought and reasoned ?—religion forbade them. Why should they have willed and acted ?—the heads of the State willed and acted for them. In the long run the Latin mind has bent itself to these necessities ; men have acquired the habit of submitting themselves without discussion to the dogmas of a Church supposed to be infallible, and of kings by Divine right, and equally infallible. They have left the entire direction of their thoughts and actions to their political and religious chiefs. This submission was the necessary condition of their unity. At certain periods it has endowed them with great strength. When the Latins have had men of genius at their head they have been extremely brilliant, but they have been brilliant only at such times.

The Latin peoples had not so very much to suffer from this absolute submission to authority before the economic evolution of the world came to overturn the old conditions of existence. So long as the means of communication were very imperfect, and the progress of industry almost imperceptible, the nations remained isolated from one another, and, in consequence, entirely in the hands of their governments, which then were able completely to control the acts of the life of nations. By means of such regulations as those of Colbert they were able to direct the least details of industry as easily as they regulated the beliefs and institutions of their country.

The scientific and industrial discoveries which have so profoundly modified the conditions of national existence have also to an equal degree transformed the action of governments, and have further and further reduced the possible limits of this action. Industrial and economic questions have become preponderant; steam and the telegraph, by suppressing distances, have made the whole world a single market, impossible of control. The Governments, accordingly, have been obliged to renounce totally their old ambition to regulate industry and commerce.

In those countries in which individual initiative had been long developed, and in which the action of the Government had become more and more restrained, the consequences of the present state of economic evolution have been easily supported. Those countries, on the other hand, in which the initiative of the citizen did not exist, found themselves disarmed, and were forced to implore the aid of those masters who for so many centuries had thought and acted for them. It is for this reason that some Governments are obliged, in continuance of their traditional *rôle*, to conduct so many industrial enterprises. But as, for many reasons, which we shall very soon perceive, those products of which the production is directed by the State are obtained slowly and expensively, those nations which have left to the State the execution of those enterprises which they should have undertaken themselves are now in a position inferior to that of the other nations.

Far from seeking, as in the past, to direct one and all things, it is plain that the Latin Governments are anxious to direct as few things as possible, but it is also evident that it is now the people who demand imperiously to be governed. In examining the evolution of Socialism among the Latins we shall see how their craving for control increases day by day. The State has accordingly continued to control, protect, and rule, simply because it could not do otherwise. It is a task which is always becoming heavier and more difficult, which calls for very superior, and, therefore, very rare abilities. To-day the least error of Governments has infinite reverberations. Hence the great instability of Governments and the perpetual revolutions to which the Latin peoples have devoted themselves for the last century.

But we do not find in reality any instability of *régime* corresponding with this instability of government. At first sight France would seem divided into many parties ; but all these parties, whether republican, monarchical, or Socialist, have the same conception of the State. All clamour for the extension of its functions. Under all these different labels, then, there is only one party, the

Latin party, and this is the reason why all these changes of Government labels have never produced any real change of *régime*.

2. THE LATIN CONCEPTION OF THE STATE. HOW THE PROGRESS OF SOCIALISM IS THE NATURAL OUT-COME OF THE EVOLUTION OF THIS CONCEPTION.

In determining the manner in which the fundamental concepts of the Latin peoples become fixed I sufficiently indicated the nature of their conception of the State. We shall now perceive that the advance of Socialism is the natural consequence of the evolution of the Latin conception of the State.

To the characteristics of the Latin peoples, and of the French especially, which are investigated in the foregoing pages, might be added this : that there are perhaps no peoples who have raised more revolutions, and yet none that are more obstinately attached to their past institutions. It might be said of the French that they are at once the most revolutionary and the most conservative nation in the world. Their most bloody revolutions have never had any other object than to rechristen the most superannuated institutions.

The gist of the matter is this : it is easy to unroll theories, to make speeches, to excite revolutions, but it is not possible to change the established mind of a nation. New institutions certainly can be imposed on it, momentarily, and by force, but it quickly reverts to those of the past, because those alone are in agreement with the necessities of its mental constitution.

Superficial minds may still imagine that the Revolution effected a kind of renovation of our institutions, that it created, on every hand, new principles, and a new society. In reality, as Tocqueville long ago pointed out, all that it did was to dash violently to the ground those elements of the old society which were already worm-eaten, and must have fallen a few years later by sheer old age.   But the institutions which had not yet grown old, which were in agreement with the sentiments of the race, were touched not at all by the Revolution, or at most but for a moment. A few years later the very men who had sought to abolish them re-established them under other names.   It is no easy thing to change the inheritance of twelve centuries.

Above all, the Revolution did not change and could not have changed the conception of the State ; it could not affect the perpetual increase of its functions, nor the perpetual straitening of the limits of the citizen's power of initiative : that increasing limitation which is the very foundation of modern Socialism.   And if we would comprehend how deeply this tendency to place everything in the hands of the Government, and consequently to multiply the public functions, is rooted in the soul of the race, we have only to go back to a few years before the Revolution.   The action of the central Government was then almost as comprehensive as to-day.

"The cities," writes Tocqueville, " can neither establish an octroi, nor levy a tax, nor hypothecate, nor sell, nor sue, nor farm their possessions, nor administrate them, nor make use of their surplus receipts, without the intervention of a decree of the Council, following the report of the Intendant.   All their works are carried out according to the plans and estimates approved by decree of the Council, which are adjudicated before the Intendant or his subordinates, and are usually executed by the State engineer or architect.   This will greatly surprise those who imagine that all they see in France is new. . . . It was necessary to obtain a decree of the Council to repair the damage caused by the wind to a church roof, or to prop up a rickety vicarage wall.   The country parish furthest from Paris was subjected to this rule as well as the nearest. I have seen parishes demand of the Council the right to expend twenty-five pounds."

Then, as to-day, the local life of the provinces had long been extinguished by the progressive centralisation arising not from the autocratic power of the sovereign, but from the indifference of the citizen. Tocqueville says further :—

"One is astonished at the surprising ease with which the Constituent Assembly was able to destroy, at one blow, all the ancient provinces of France, many of which were older than the monarchy; and methodically to divide the kingdom into eighty-three distinct portions, as though the virgin soil of the New World were in question. Nothing more surprised, and even terrified, the rest of Europe, which was not prepared for such a spectacle. It was, said Burke, the first time one had beheld men cut their native land into morsels in such a barbarous manner. It seemed, indeed, as if they were rending living bodies ; they were only dismembering the dead."

It was this disappearance of provincial life that facilitated the progressive centralisation of the *ancien régime*.

"Let us no longer marvel," says Tocqueville, "at seeing with what astonishing facility centralisation was re-established in France at the beginning of this century. The men of '89 had overthrown the edifice, but its foundations remained, even in the minds of its destroyers, and on these foundations they were able to build it anew, of a sudden, and more solidly than it was ever built before."

Under the *ancien régime* the progressive absorbing powers of the State necessitated, as to-day, an increasing number of functionaries, and the zeal of the citizen in getting himself nominated as such was unequalled.

"In 1750, in a provincial town of medium size, 129 persons were employed in administrating justice, and 126 were charged with executing the decrees of the former, all of these being townsfolk. The zeal of the citizens in filling these situations was really unequalled. As soon as one of them became possessed of a little capital, instead of employing it in commerce he at once expended it in buying a place. This wretched ambition did more to hinder the progress of agriculture and commerce in France even than monopolies and taxation."

We are not living to-day, as is so often repeated, according to the principles of 1789. We are living according to the principles set up by the *ancien régime*, and the development of Socialism is only the final blossoming of these principles, the ultimate consequence of an ideal which has been pursued for centuries. Formerly, no doubt, this ideal was of great utility in a country so divided as ours, and which could be unified only by strenuous centralisation. But, unhappily, when once this unity was effected the mental habits thus established could not change. When once the local life of the provinces and the initiative of the citizen were destroyed the latter could not spring up again. The mental constitution of a people is slow to establish itself, but it is also very slow to change when once established.

For the rest, everything, institutions as well as education, has contributed to this absorption of functions by the State, of which we shall presently show the lamentable effects. Our system of education alone would be enough utterly to annihilate the most perdurable of nations.

CHAPTER V

THE LATIN CONCEPTS OF EDUCATION AND RELIGION

1. *The Latin concepts of education and instruction :*—The conception of education prevalent among the Latins arises from their conception of the State—The basis of our university system—How it causes banality of thought and weakness of character in entire classes of individuals—The normal school—Why the university is a stronghold of levelling State Socialism—Modern attacks on the noxious effects of our system of classical education—Comparison of the principles of education and instruction found among the Anglo-Saxons and the Latins respectively—The general misunderstanding on this subject— It is not what is taught that signifies, but the manner of teaching— Various examples of the results of our methods of teaching. 2. *The Latin concept of religion :*—The religious concept of the Latins, after having played, for a long time, a very useful part, has now become hurtful to them—How the Anglo-Saxons have succeeded in putting their religious beliefs in agreement with modern necessities—Indocility of the religious dogmas of the Latins, and its results—General consequences of the Latin ideas from a Socialist point of view.

1. THE LATIN CONCEPTS OF EDUCATION AND INSTRUCTION.

THE Latin concept of education is the consequence of the Latin concept of the State. Since the State ought to direct everything it ought also to direct education, and since the State ought to think and act for the citizen it must take care to imbue his mind with the sentiment of obedience, respect for all the hierarchies, and severely repress all signs of initiative and independence. The pupil should limit himself to learning by heart the manuals informing him of the decisions of political, religious, philosophic, and scientific authority on all imaginable questions. This was the old ideal of the Jesuits, and it was skilfully completed by Napoleon. The University, as it was created by this great despot, is a most excellent example of the methods to be employed in order to enslave the intelligence, weaken the character, and transform the Latin youth into slaves or rebels.

The times have progressed, but our University has hardly changed. On her, above all, lies the imperious yoke of the dead. The State, the exclusive director of instruction, has preserved a system of education which might be called fair in the Middle Ages, when professorial chairs were filled by theologians. This system leaves its corroding imprint on every Latin mind. It no longer actually proposes to itself, as it did of old, to enslave the intelligence, to silence reason, to destroy initiative and independence ; but as its methods have not changed the effects produced by it are the same as ever. We possess institutions which, regarded solely with regard to their psychologic action, might be qualified as admirable, when we perceive with what ingenuity they turn out whole batches of individuals, perfect in their banality of thought and ineptness of character. What, for example, could be more astonishing than our *École normale supérieure*, with its prodigious system of examinations ? Where but in the depths of China could we find anything comparable to it ? The greater number of the young men who leave it have identical ideas on every subject, and a not less identical fashion of expressing them. A page begun by one of them might be continued by another indifferently, without any change of idea or of style. Only the Jesuits have succeeded in inventing an equally perfect order of discipline. As the professors who come from this college possess almost exclusively the right of giving superior instruction to the youth of France, we may be perfectly certain that they will everywhere spread identical ideas, ideas as fatuous as they are official. As a certain Minister of Instruction remarked, taking his watch in his hand, we know exactly, at any given moment, the exercise or translation on which all budding Frenchmen, lashed to their Procrustean beds, are employed.

Accustomed, by minute regulation, to forecast, to a minute almost, the manner in which their time is employed, these pupils are suitably prepared, for the rest of their lives, for the uniformity of thought and action necessitated by State Socialism. They will always have an intense horror of originality, of all personal effort, a profound suspicion of all that is not specialised and catalogued, and a somewhat envious but always reverent admiration of hierarchies and of gold braid. All tendencies to initiative or to individual effort will in them be utterly extinguished. They may succeed in rebelling now and again, just as they rebelled at college when their preceptors were too severe, but they will never, as rebels, be either disquieting or persistent. The *École normale*, the *lycées*, and other analogous institutions are thus the most admirable schools of State Socialism of the equalising and levelling kind.[1] It is thanks to such a system that we are tending more and more towards this form of government.

It is only by studying our Latin system of education that we can well understand the present success of Socialism among the Latins, and for this reason we are obliged to enter into details which might seem, at first sight, to be outside the scope of this volume.

[1] One of the most interesting examples to be discovered of the effects of the Latin education is that which I give apropos of the modern Greeks in the chapter devoted to the present condition of the Latin peoples.

This great problem of education and instruction I cannot, assuredly, treat briefly. I will permit myself to refer the reader to the long chapter which I devoted to the subject, eighteen years ago, in the second volume of my *l'Homme et les Sociétés*. There he will find exposed at length all the projects of reform which are to-day put forward as novelties. Even before that time many illustrious spirits had pointed out the dangers of our educational system, but their voices were heard as little as mine. Of our primary instruction it was then said by Michel Bréal: "The half-knowledge given by these schools recruits soldiers for disorder as surely as ignorance." Far more surely, one should say; the increase of criminality, alcoholism, and anarchy among the young men turned out by these colleges is a proof in point. As for our University education, it was then qualified by Renan in the following words: "The University of France is too reminiscent of the orators of the Decadence. The French disease of peroration, the tendency to let everything degenerate into declamation—why, one party of the University actually fosters it by its obstinacy in disdaining the fountain-heads of knowledge, and esteeming nothing but style and talent." "I have no hesitation in saying," wrote Paul Bert, "that the fundamental ignorance of our *bourgeoisie*, which leaves our colleges all petrified with impotent presumption, is as injurious to the progress of the public spirit, and to the future of our country, as the ignorance of the children of the people who have never crossed the threshold of a school.

Nothing has changed since then; the same complaints are still heard, couched in almost identical terms.

"Our education," wrote M. C. Lauth recently, "has taken a wrong path; the Abstract has invaded everything, and has stifled the sense of application. . . . It is the spirit of our professors, the tendency of our education, the very root of our methods that must be transformed. . . . This education is bad from top to bottom ; it consists entirely of the worst methods of mediæval scholasticism, and seems established for no other purpose than to produce failures, rhetoricians, and shuttlecocks."

We must, however, point out, as a happy symptom, that a small number of University functionaries—so far, a very small number—are beginning to see the absurdity of our classical education. One of the most eminent, M. Jules Lemaître, expressed himself recently as follows :

"Despite the groping, contradictory modifications introduced, these twenty-five years, into our programmes, despite the additions and renovations, our secondary classical instruction remains at root what it was under the *ancien régime*. It is given more badly ; that is all.

"What does this mean ? Everything is altered ; the discoveries of applied science have profoundly modified the conditions of life, both for the individual and the nation ; have altered even the face of the earth. The universal reign of industry and commerce has begun ; we form a democratic and industrial society, already menaced, or rather half undermined, by the competition of powerful nations, and the children of our *petite bourgeoisie*, and many children of the lower classes, spend eight years in learning—very badly—the very things that were formerly taught—very well—by the Jesuit fathers, in a monarchical society, in a France whose supremacy was recognised by Europe, at a period when Latin was an international language, to the sons of the nobles, the magistrates, and the privileged classes.

"Is this not a shameless anachronism ? And is not this belief in the present utility of such an education a monstrous prejudice ?

"One is stupefied at the poverty of the arguments

employed by the partisans of Greek and Latin, which invariably amount to the assertion that an apprenticeship to these languages constitutes an admirable intellectual gymnastic ; notwithstanding the fact that this absurd triviality has long been refuted by the most competent observers.   One of the most illustrious of modern British scientists, Professor Bain of Aberdeen, treated of this question at length more than twenty years ago, and proved that the study of these languages does nothing but exercise the memory.   In conclusion he proposed that the teaching of Greek and Latin should be limited to one hour a week for two years.   This would indeed be the best solution to adopt in order not too greatly to offend the prejudices of worthy middle-class folk who imagine that a classical education confers a kind of aristocratic superiority on their offspring."

"Our language is Latin," wrote recently one of the most remarkable ministers our University has ever had at its head, M. Léon Bourgeois—"our language is Latin, but to make the Latin heritage the sole treasure of our race—would that not be indeed to stultify it ? "

The only serious argument that the professors of the University can invoke in defence of classical education is that it permits them to make a living, and that apart from their duties of instruction they are absolutely good for nothing ; they could not even serve as translators.   M. Jules Lemaître having declared that the professors of the University of France had a very imperfect knowledge of the Greek they taught, a certain professor came to the rescue of his colleagues, and wrote the following lines, which throw a strange light on the value of the methods of our University :—

"The professors are fully competent if they have enough Greek to decipher patiently, at home, with the aid of the lexicon and standard annoted editions, the complete sense of their text, which they then help their pupils to elucidate in class."

A German or an Englishman reading these lines would be confounded. In England or Germany a person who should propose to teach a foreign language while admitting that he could only "decipher it patiently with the aid of a lexicon" would be ignominiously shown the door of the establishment at which he should present himself.[1]

The Anglo-Saxon peoples succeeded long ago in ridding themselves of our odious educational system, and it is in part because they have done so that they are now in the front rank of civilisation, and have left the Latin nations so far behind them.

Few persons, above all among professors, are yet able to understand wherein the Anglo-Saxon conception of education differs from the corresponding conception among the Latins. It will therefore be useful to consider, in some detail, the fundamental principles which

---

[1] We shall not be too greatly astonished at the inability of our University to teach any tongue whatever, whether ancient or modern, when we consider the amazing manner in which it sets to work. If its avowed object were the total befogging of the unfortunates confided to it, it would scarcely need to change its tactics. M. Fouillée himself, one of the latest partisans of the teaching of Latin, is obliged to recognise this fact in reproducing the following extract from an "elementary" work which was invested with the approbation of the highest university authorities : "The author wishes to state that he has intentionally suppressed all such terms and questions as might alarm the inexperience of children. This is why he speaks to them at length of the pentrametric cæsura which is sometimes replaced by a heptametric cæsura, usually accompanied by a trimetric cæsura. He initiates them into the mysteries of synalexis, apocopis, and apheresis, warning them that he has adopted scansion by anacrusis, and has suppressed the choriamb in logadaic verses. He also reveals to them the mysteries of quaternary hypermetre, of hypercatalectic dimeter, and even of aeneasyllabic alcaics. What are we to say of hexametric dactylic verses, of catalexis in dissylabum, of proceleusmatic catalectic tetrameter, of docmiad dimeter, of the trochaic hipponactæan strophe, of the trochaic hipponactæan distich ? "

form the basis of education and instruction in the two races.

The principles of Anglo-Saxon education are as different from those of the Latin system of education as the principles which form the bases of instruction. A few lines will make this evident.

Civilised man cannot live without discipline. This discipline may be internal—that is to say, in the man himself. It may be external, or outside the man himself; and in that case, necessarily, enforced by others. The Anglo-Saxon, having, amongst his hereditary characteristics, which are confirmed by his education, this internal discipline, is able to direct and control himself, and has no need of the direction of the State. The man of Latin race, having, through his heredity and his education, very little internal discipline, requires an external discipline. This is imposed on him by the State, and it is for this reason that he is imprisoned in a network of regulations, which are innumerable, because they have to direct him in all the circumstances of his life.

The principle of Anglo-Saxon education is this: the child goes through his school life not to be disciplined by others, but to learn to make use of his own independence. He has to discipline himself, and by this means acquire self-control, from which self-government is derived. The young Englishman may possibly leave college knowing little of Greek, Latin, or theoretical science; but he leaves it a man, able to guide himself in life, and to rely on himself alone. The methods which help him to this result are wonderfully simple. They will be found explained in detail in all the works dealing with education written by Englishmen.

The Latin system of education has a precisely contrary object. Its dream is to crush the initiative, independence, and will of the pupil by severe and minute regulations.

His only duty is to learn, to recite, to obey. His least acts are foreordained. The employment of his time is regulated minute by minute. After seven or eight years of this galley discipline all traces of initiative and will-power are eradicated. Then, when the young man is left to himself, how will he be able to do what he has never learnt to do—to conduct himself? Can we be astonished that the Latin peoples understand so ill how to govern themselves, and show themselves so incapable in the commercial and industrial struggles that the modern development of the world has engendered? Is it not natural that Socialism, which will merely multiply the fetters with which the State envelopes them, should be cordially welcomed by all those who have been so well prepared for servitude by their college training?

Are we to hold our professors responsible for the lamentable results of our education? Certainly not. Our college professors, equally with their pupils, are hampered by a perfect network of regulations, which they must obey to the letter under the penalty of being promptly cast aside. They are subordinates, timid and needy, exposed to a thousand indignities from their superiors, and always sensible of the weight of the bureaucratic and pedagogic yoke. Their one dream is of being able to give up what all consider a horrible trade. They do not declare themselves disciples of Socialism, but there are very few among them who do not, in their hearts, long for the triumph of the new doctrines. In this case they might perhaps better their lot, and in any case they could not make their yoke heavier or bitterer than it is to-day.

Now, having considered the respective principles of Anglo-Saxon and Latin education, we will consider those of instruction. The discussions recently raised on the teaching of Greek and Latin, apropos of the remarks of the author I last quoted, show how general and how intense is the incomprehension of this subject.

Indeed, the arguments exchanged by the two sides prove to what an extent the fundamental side of the question is misunderstood in France. No one seems to understand that it is not what is taught, but the manner of teaching it, that must be changed from top to bottom. Above all must we change this dreadful system of *concours* and examinations, which, as a writer recently remarked, "forms the most powerful means of compression ever used by any European nation for the purpose of confining the energies of youth, and its natural impulse towards life." Instruction has, or at least should have for its aim, the development of judgment, initiative, and reflection, and these qualities are developed only by teaching (no matter what is taught) in a certain fashion.

Whether it be a question of teaching a language, a science, or the general knowledge necessary to a profession, there are two methods of instruction which are totally different, and which create equally different methods of thought, reason, and conduct in the mind of the pupil.

The one, which is purely theoretical, consists in teaching orally or from books ; the other first of all puts the pupil in contact with the realities and only exposes the theory of these realities afterwards.

The consequences of these two methods may be judged by the results they produce. Our bachelors, licentiates, or engineers are good for nothing but theoretical demonstrations. A few years after the termination of their education they have completely forgotten all their useless science. Unless the State finds them appointments they are outcasts. If they fall back upon industry they will not be accepted in any but the lowest capacities until they have found time to educate themselves all over again, which they scarcely ever succeed in doing. If they take to writing books their books will be nothing but feeble echoes of their college manuals, equally deficient in originality of form and thought.

So whether we do or do not suppress the teaching of Latin in our colleges, or whether we substitute the teaching of science, or of any other subject, does not matter ; the final result will always be the same, for the methods will not have changed. We shall still be creating nothing but outcasts, stuffed with useless and soon-forgotten formulæ, incapable of judgment, reason, or self-guidance. Are we to believe that a method of instruction can become practical simply because it is called so ? Does no one see that our professors cannot change their natures and teach what they do not know ?

Any one who does not see how thoroughly detestable our methods of instruction are has only to consider the results given by the most practical of our colleges. He will find that under their deceptive label they preserve the same exclusively bookish and theoretical character.

Let us take as example a branch of instruction which at first sight would certainly seem the most practical of all—that of agriculture. A report by M. Méline, recently inserted in the *Officiel*, contains some very interesting inquiries into the results obtained, which show how completely our general methods of instruction are based on the same principles.

Without counting the *Institut agronomic* established in Paris, France possesses eighty-two so-called schools of agriculture, which cost more than £160,000 annually. They count 659 professors and 2,850 pupils, which gives just over four pupils per professor. Thus each pupil costs the State rather more than £56 per annum. " In many establishments there are scarcely any but holders of bursaries, and without them it would almost be necessary to close the school."

It is often difficult to render instruction practical when that instruction has to be given to a large number of pupils.   This is no longer the case when a professor has an average of four pupils.   We might hope, accordingly, that the agricultural training of these numerous schools would be of a really useful character, and that the young agriculturists so expensively trained might be of some service.   They have not been so, alas ! and a psychologist knowing a little of our methods of instruction might have foreseen the fact.   The education of these pupils has remained so theoretical that not a single cultivator is able to make use of them, not even in the simple capacity ˙of farmer's boy.   Being absolutely good for nothing, these pupils who were to have regenerated our agriculture almost always apply for State appointments, above all as professors.   There are more than 500 of these applications for 50 annual vacancies.

" Is it not grotesque ? " concludes *le Temps*, in summing up M. Méline's report.   " This scientific education, this grand orchestra of abstract formulæ, results in abstracting energies from agriculture instead of contributing them !   These schools have only one end in view : to prepare not practical men, but examinees crammed with formulæ and superfluities of scientific appearance, the better to succeed in the examinations of the *concours*, and to obtain administrative situations. Here, as elsewhere, every one is a mandarin."

What has just been said of the teaching of agriculture may be applied to all our schools, even to those which, in the minds of their founders, were intended only to form workmen.   The principles being the same, and the professors having much the same origin, the results, from top to bottom of the scale, cannot but be identical. Here, evidently, we have a racial vice, rendered ineradicable by centuries of education. As a typical example we may cite the case of the *École Boulle*, founded in Paris twelve years ago at the expense of the city, with the object of supplanting the apprenticeship of the workshop and of turning out simple workmen exclusively. The results obtained are given in a report presented to the municipal council. They are lamentable. Out of 387 pupils 45 per cent.—and they were the wisest—relinquished, at the end of a year, a course of instruction of which they had perceived the total inutility. Of the pupils who followed the course of four years only thirteen were able to find situations, and then only on the condition of their becoming apprenticed after leaving the school. To arrive at this miserable result the city expended an enormous sum. Each graduate has cost it more than £280.

We are now not considering Greek and Latin merely. I have cited examples which clearly show the principles underlying our methods of instruction, and why no amount of regulations can change them. It is the ideas of the teachers that we must change, and consequently their entire education, and to some extent their nature. How are we to make them understand that theory is useful when it follows practice, but never when it precedes it ; that it is by practical exercise, and by no other means, that the judgment, initiative, and reason can be developed, and that this development should be the principal aim of education ?

One sees how difficult it would be to-day to modify our Latin system of education. This difficulty appears more than sufficiently proved by the complete futility of all that has been written and repeated on this subject during the last twenty-five years. What has been the result of so many carefully studied reports, so many ingenious dissertations ? Have we modified ever so little our programmes and our systems of competitive examinations, except perhaps to make them more burdensome ? Have the seas of ink poured out in asserting the immense superiority of the English system of education had any results other than the most insignificant reforms —such, for example, as the introduction of football in our schools ?[1] Our university is too old to change, or even to understand that it should change. It will remain, in despite of all attacks on it, an immense factory of the unclassed, and therefore of Socialists. None of our institutions has ever exercised such a lamentable influence over the Latin mind.

---

[1] I have often spoken in this work of the necessity of reforming our Latin system of education from top to bottom, but without entering into any detail, knowing perfectly that all one can say on the subject is absolutely useless. However, since the occasion presents itself, I will say in a few words that the only indispensable reform would consist in suppressing nine-tenths of the subjects taught to our scholars, and replacing them by manual work followed by examinations admitting the successful to State appointments. This would be done not at all with the utilitarian object— which, however, is not to be despised—of affording the pupil a means of livelihood which a reverse of fortune might render extremely useful, but simply to exercise his intelligence and his judgment. Manual work compels the worker to reflect, combine, and reason infinitely better than recitations from text-books and all the various exercises of theme and translation. I should consider such an education perfectly complete, if, by very simple methods, in explaining which I will not waste my time, the pupil were imbued with the habits of observation, reflection, and conduct which his present education does not by any means produce. I should by no means forget in this programme those literary and artistic ideas which are the ornament of life, on the condition that they were taught quite otherwise than to-day. I will not further insist on these principles, which I believe to be absolutely incomprehensible to all teachers and to nearly all parents. This I can understand when I reflect what I should have thought if any one had expressed such ideas to me when I was twenty-five.

2. THE LATIN CONCEPTION OF RELIGION.

Their religious concept, after having played its useful part, has ended by becoming as noxious to the Latin peoples as their concepts of the State and of education, and for the same reason—that it has not progressed, has not evolved.

Without suddenly breaking with the beliefs of the past, the Anglo-Saxons have been able to create a broader religion, able to adapt itself to every modern necessity. All too inconvenient dogmas have been softened down, have taken a symbolic character, a mythological value. Religion has thus been able to exist on good terms with science ; at most it is not a declared enemy which has to be contended with. The Catholic dogma of the Latins, on the other hand, has preserved its rigid, absolute, intolerant form, which was useful, perhaps, of old, but which to-day is extremely pernicious. It remains what it was five hundred years ago. Without it is no salvation. It attempts to impose the most ridiculous historical absurdities on its faithful. No conciliation is possible ; one must submit to it or fight it.

Before the rebellion of reason the least advanced Latin Governments have been forced to renounce the idea of sustaining beliefs so profoundly incompatible with the evolution of ideas, and they have generally ended by abstaining from all interference in the domain of religion.

But thereupon two consequences have ensued. The old dogmas have resumed all their empire over feeble minds, and sway them by exhausted faiths which have no reference to modern requirements. Others, happy at their escape from a heavy and plainly irrational yoke, have rejected the ancient dogmas ; but as they were told in youth that the whole of morality reposed on these dogmas, and could not exist without them, they have imagined that with their disappearance the morality based on them must also disappear. Their morality was in consequence considerably relaxed, and very soon they knew no other rules of conduct than those which are registered in the codes and enforced by the hand of the gendarme.

Thus we see that three conceptions—those of religion, politics, and education—have contributed to the formation of the Latin mind, and have produced its present state. Every nation, at a certain phase of civilisation, has become subject to these conceptions, and none could avoid the subjection, for when the nations are weak, ignorant, and undeveloped, it is plainly advantageous for them, as it is for a child, that superior minds should impose their beliefs and ideas on them, should act and think for them. But in the progress of evolution the moment arrives when the nations are no longer children, but must guide themselves. Those who have not been able to acquire the ability to do so find themselves by this fact alone far in the rear of those who do possess it.

The Latin peoples have not yet succeeded in acquiring this ability. Because they have not learned to think and act for themselves they are to-day defenceless in the industrial, commercial, and colonial struggle ensuing on the conditions of modern existence, in which the Anglo-Saxons have so quickly triumphed. Victims of their hereditary conceptions, the Latin nations turn towards Socialism, which promises to think and act for them, but in coming under its rule they will only be submitting to new masters, and will thus still further retard the acquisition of the qualities they lack.

To be a little more explicit, I should have to follow,

in the various branches of civilisation—literature, art, industry, &c.—the consequences, beneficial or noxious, according to their period, of those fundamental conceptions whose functions I have just very briefly delineated. Such a vast enterprise cannot be undertaken here. It is enough to show how the present progress of Socialism among the Latin peoples is the consequence of their conceptions, and to determine the formation of these conceptions. We shall perceive their influence in every page of this book, and notably when we have occasion to consider the commercial and industrial struggles to which all the nations are condemned by the modern developments of economics. The reader who will apply my principles to any element whatever of civilisation, will be struck with the light they throw on history. Of course they are not sufficient to explain everything, but they give significance to many facts inexplicable without them. Above all, they explain that need of guidance which leaves the Latin races so disconcerted and timid before responsibilities, and which prevents them from succeeding in any enterprise in which they are not firmly conducted by their leaders ; it explains, too, their present leaning towards Socialism. When they have great statesmen, great generals, great diplomatists, great thinkers, great artists at their head, they show themselves capable of the greatest efforts. But leaders of genius are not always to be found, and in default of such the Latin peoples are insecure. With Napoleon they dominated the world. Later, commanded by incapable generals, they were the victims of the most lamentable catastrophes, and were powerless to resist those they had formerly so easily vanquished.[1] It is not without reason that these

[1] When we study in detail the history of our last war, we perceive, incessantly, the gross incapacity not only of the generals placed at the head of our armies, but of the officers of every rank without

nations are so ready to throw the responsibility of their reverses on their chiefs. They are worth what their masters are worth, and they know it. But it is always a misfortune for a nation to depend on a few personalities.

The Latin races must learn to walk alone. For the battle-fields of to-day, whether military or industrial, are so vast that no handful of men, however eminent, can direct all the combatants. In the present phase of the world the influence of men of great capacity is not indeed vanishing, but is becoming less and less a directing force. Authority is so dispersed that it must vanish. The modern man must no longer rely on any guardianship whatever, still less on that of Socialism than on any other. He must learn to count on no one but himself. It is for this fundamental necessity that education should prepare him, and it is for this reason that this education must be changed in entirety.

exception. The latter never dared to undertake the least responsibility, such as seizing an unoccupied bridge, attacking a troublesome battery, &c. Their principal care was to await orders which could not arrive. Like those diplomatists of whom I have elsewhere spoken, they had no doctrines which might indicate the decision to be made in an unforeseen case, and in the absence of their chiefs. The strength of the Germans consisted in the fact that they did possess such a doctrine. Orders were useless to them ; moreover, with the exception of *directions*, according to the expression of Von Moltke, they received very few. Each officer knew what he had to do in the various cases that might present themselves, and he did it instinctively, thanks to a long-continued technical education. An education is complete only when acts which were at first conscious, and demanded painful efforts, have become unconscious. They are then executed instinctively, without reflection ; but this result is never attained by the study of books. Our general staff is beginning, after twenty-five years of reflection, to suspect the importance of these principles ; but the education which our officers received at the *École de Guerre* is still thoroughly Latin, that is to say, deplorably bookish and theoretical.

CHAPTER VI

THE FORMATION OF SOCIALISM AMONG THE LATIN PEOPLES

1. *Absorption by the State :*—Modern Socialism is, among the Latins, the necessary consequence of their old conception of the Government—Progressive extension of the functions of the State—How the exigencies of the public necessitate this extension—The State is obliged more and more to direct important undertakings, and to subsidise those it does not direct—Various examples showing the necessity of the intervention of the State, even though unwilling, in matters of regulation and protection. 2. *The consequences of the extension of the functions of the State :*—All sentiments of responsibility and enterprise in the citizen disappear—Regulations follow regulations —Difficulties experienced by the State in directing everything—Enormous expenditure necessitated by its constant intervention—Inevitable increase of officialism and red-tape in the Latin nations—Decay of the power of the State—Incessant demand of the public for increased regulations—Enormous cost of making of all that is manufactured by the State—Fatal complications of its administration—Various examples furnished by the war and by the navy—Cost of making in private industry—Latin colonial administration—Identical consequences of Latin administration in Italy and in France. 3. *The Collectivist State :*—The Latin peoples need only go a little further to arrive at pure Collectivism—They have for a long time been in the Collectivist phase—Examination of the propositions of the Collectivists, and what of them have already been carried into effect.

1. ABSORPTION BY THE STATE.

THE preceding chapters have sufficiently shown that Socialism, under the form of State Socialism, very nearly akin to Collectivism, is in France the culmination of a long past, the ultimate consequence of institutions already very old. Far from deserving to be considered revolutionary, modern Collectivism should be regarded as a highly retrograde doctrine, and its disciples as timid reactionaries, limiting themselves to developing the most ancient and least elevated of the Latin traditions. They announce uproariously, every day, the approaching triumph of their Utopias. But we were the victims of them long before they were born.

State Socialism, or the centralisation of all the elements of a nation's life in the hands of the Government, is perhaps the most characteristic, the most fundamental, and the most obstinate of all conceptions of Latin societies. Far from having entered into a state of decline, State absorption is only increasing every day. For a long time limited to political functions, it was able to extend itself to the region of industry only at a time when industry scarcely existed. When the latter became preponderant, political authority intervened in every branch of industry. The State finds itself obliged, in the matter of railways, harbours, canals, buildings, &c., to supply the enterprise which the citizen lacks. The most important enterprises it directs itself, exclusively, and retains the monopoly of numerous undertakings—such as instruction, telegraphs, telephones, tobacco, matches, &c.—which it has successively absorbed. Those over which it does not actually preside it is obliged to support lest they should be endangered. Without its subsidies most of them would promptly become insolvent. In this manner it pays to the railway companies enormous subsidies under the title of " guarantees of interest."

It throws the sum of £3,740,000 annually to their shareholders, to which we must add the £1,920,000 of the annual deficit on the lines it itself exploits.

The private enterprises—maritime, commercial, or agricultural—which it is forced to subsidise in various ways, are numerous ; subsidies for the shipbuilders, subsidies for sugar-makers, subsidies for silkspinners, for cultivators—the latter alone, in 1895, had risen to £360,000. There is hardly an industry to-day that does not claim the financial protection of the State. The most hostile political parties are perfectly at one on this point, and unhappily on this point alone. Considered responsible for everything, and obliged to direct everything, the State seems to possess an immense treasure which every one can spend. Should a department require the necessary sum to pay a director destined to ameliorate an absolutely local industry, which brings it in a large revenue, it applies to the State — as in the case of the Chamber of Commerce of X., cited by the *Temps*—and not to the persons interested in the progress of the industry. Another department wishes to build a railway of purely local importance ; it applies to the State. A seaport wishes for improvements by which it alone would profit : always the State. Nowhere do we find the least trace of private enterprise or private association to undertake or support any work whatever.

M. P. Bourde has reported a very typical example of this state of mind. It is the story, absolutely incomprehensible and unreal to an Englishman or American, of the inhabitants of the little town of X. One of their water conduits having been broken, it suddenly received the filth of a neighbouring sewer. To send for a workman and have the accident repaired was an idea too little Latin to recommend itself to the municipal council which met to discuss the accident. Evidently they must address themselves to the Government. Four large newspaper columns were scarcely sufficient to relate the steps taken. Thanks to the intervention of a considerable number of ministers, senators, deputies, prefects, engineers, &c., the application made only twenty pauses in the various administrative departments, and the final decision took only two years to reach the commune. The townsfolk, in the meantime, continued, with resignation, to drink sewage, without once dreaming of remedying the accident themselves. The examples given by Tocqueville show that matters passed in exactly the same fashion under the *ancien régime*.

We have here a special state of mind, which is evidently a racial characteristic. The State is obliged to intervene incessantly, in matters of regulation and protection ; but if it were to lend an ear to all complaints it would intervene far more frequently still. Last year, in the Senate, an honourable senator made himself the organ of the claims of a syndicate of pork butchers, who wished to induce the Government to substitute salt pork for beef in the diet of the army, under the pretext of protecting the raising of little pigs. To the mind of these brave fellows, as the natural function of the State is to protect industry, it would necessarily guarantee the sale of their merchandise by making salt pork obligatory by decree.

It is very unjust to reproach the Collectivists with wishing to place all monopolies, all industries, all public services in the hands of the Government. The dream is not special to them ; it is that of every party ; it is the dream of the race.

Assailed on every hand, the State defends itself as it may; but under the unanimous pressure of the public it is obliged, despite itself, to protect and to regulate. Its intervention is demanded on every hand, and always in the same sense ; that is to say, in the sense of the restriction of initiative and the liberty of the citizen, and of the preponderant action of officials.

The laws of this kind, which are proposed every day, are innumerable : laws to determine the purchase of railways and their administration by the State, laws to monopolise alcohol, laws to engross the administration of the Bank of France, laws to regulate the hours of labour in factories, laws to prevent the competition of foreign produce, laws to give a retiring pension to all aged workmen, laws to force the contractors for public works to employ only certain classes of workmen, laws to regulate the price of bread, laws to tax celibates, so as to oblige them to marry, laws to overwhelm the large shops with taxes for the benefit of the smaller, &c., &c.

Such are the facts; we will now examine their consequences.

2. The Consequences of the Extension of the Functions of the State.

The consequences of this absorption of all functions by the State, and its constant intervention—an absorption and intervention demanded by all parties without exception—are altogether disastrous to the nation that suffers them, or, rather, enforces them. This perpetual intervention is ending by entirely destroying in the breast of the citizen those sentiments of initiative and responsibility of which he already possessed so little. It obliges the State to direct, at great expense, owing to the complexity of its mechanism, such undertakings as private persons, with the motive power of personal interest, might successfully manage at far less expense, as they do in other countries.

These results have long been verified by economists.

"The concentration of economic power in the hands of the State," writes M. Leroy-Beaulieu, "is leading, in the new France, to the ruin of private initiative, and the degeneration of individual will and energy. It must end in a kind of bureaucratic servitude or parliamentary Cæsarism, which will at once enervate and demoralise an impoverished country."

Never were the economists more visibly right; yet

never have their words been more wasted on the desert air. No one contests their assertions, yet none the less we continue to advance further and further along a road which will lead the nations that tread it to the last degree of decadence and servitude.

The truth is that by the very fact that they have entered on this road they are forced to tread it to the end. Only by means of an immense and ever-increasing army of agents is the State able to succeed in directing everything, in administrating everything, in centralising everything. The annual cost of these agents, twenty-five years ago, was scarcely £12,000,000 ; it is now £20,000,000, and their number must inevitably increase in immense proportions. The instruction given by the State is no longer of much use but to create functionaries for the State. Half the pupils of our *lycées* are destined for public service. Only the failures enter commerce, agriculture, or industry ; the exact contrary takes place in England and America.

The Government defends itself as well as it can against this invasion of *diplomés*, whom their hereditary aptitudes and their debasing education have not endowed with the amount of initiative necessary to create independent situations for themselves. They have application only for learning the largest text-books by heart ; in this matter nothing disheartens them. The State is incessantly complicating the subjects of its examinations, and making its text-books thicker and thicker; nothing discourages the candidates. With one quarter of the patience necessary to learn sickening trivialities by heart the greater number of them would make their fortunes in industry ; but they do not even dream of such a thing. It has been said with reason that our century is the century of examinations. It is precisely the Chinese system ; and, as Renan has observed, it has produced, in that nation of mandarins, an incurable senility.

It is, in fact, the bureaucracy that governs France to-day, and will necessarily govern her more and more. The power of the State is scattered among innumerable hands. The irresistible need of the Latins to be governed is accompanied by a not less irresistible need of exercising authority; hence all the agents who represent the State govern one another according to a rigid and trivially detailed hierarchy, which descends by successive degrees from the minister to the humblest *cantonnier*. Each official possesses only the most narrowly limited functions, and therefore cannot perform the most trivial act without having recourse to a whole hierarchy above him. He is imprisoned inextricably in a network of regulations and complications, the weight of which necessarily falls on all those who have occasion to apply to him.

This network of regulations extends itself every day, in proportion as the initiative of the citizen becomes feebler. As Léon Say observed : " The cry becomes always louder and louder for more and more microscopic regulations."

Harassed by the incessant appeals of a public greedy of tutelage, the State legislates and regulates without pause. Obliged to direct everything, to foresee everything, it enters into the most trifling details. A man is run over by a carriage ; a clock is stolen from a *mairie ;* immediately a commission is nominated and charged with the elaboration of a regulation, and this regulation always occupies a whole volume. According to a well-informed journal, the new regulation drawn up in respect of the circulation of cabs and other means of transport in Paris by a commission entrusted with the task of simplifying the existing state of things will comprise no fewer than 425 articles !

This prodigious need of regulation does not appear to be new in history. It has already appeared among many peoples, and notably among the Romans and the Byzantines, at their periods of lowest decadence, and it must have contributed greatly to hasten the final dissolution. M. Gaston Boissier remarks that at the end of the Roman Empire, "never had administrative triviality been carried so far. This period was before all things a scribbling age. An imperial functionary never stirred without his secretaries and stenographers."

From these complicated hierarchies and this narrow regulation it results, first of all, that everything the State produces is produced in a very slow and costly way. Not for nothing can the citizens of a country refuse to direct their own affairs, and confide all to the hands of the State. The latter makes them pay dearly for its intervention. As a very typical example of this, I may cite the various railroads which the departments have forced the State to construct.

In obedience to the pressure of the public, the Government has successively constructed, and directly administered, nearly 1,700 miles of lines, which cost, according to the report of the Budget Commission of 1895, the enormous sum of £51,000,000, including the annual deficit capitalised. The annual profits are £360,000, and the expenses £2,280,000 ; the annual deficit, therefore, is about £1,920,000. This deficit is partly accounted for by the enormous expenses of working. While the working expenses of great companies such, for example, as the Paris-Lyon and the Orléans, amount to 50 per cent., little interested in economy though these companies be—since the State guarantees them a minimum of interest—the working expenses of the State railways reach the incredible figure of 77 per cent. !

"It is impossible," writes M. Leroy-Beaulieu, "adequately to express to what a decay of private initiative the conduct of public works in France is leading. Habituated to rely on the subventions of the commune, department, or central power, the divers agglomerations of inhabitants, and above all in the country, are no longer capable of undertaking any matter whatever by themselves, nor of agreeing upon any point. I have known villages of 200 or 300 inhabitants, belonging to a large and scattered commune, to wait for years and humbly to solicit aid in the matter of a well which was indispensable to them, and which £8 or £12, or a contribution of ten-pence apiece, would have sufficed to put in good repair. I have seen other villages having only one road by which to despatch their commodities, and incapable of taking concerted action when, by means of a prime expense of £80, and an annual sum of £8 or £12, they could easily have rendered the road sound and durable. I am speaking, however, of districts relatively wealthy, far more so at least than the generality of the communes of France.

" We need have no hesitation in saying that of all the wealthy and long civilised nations France is one of the worst off as regards the possession and inexpensiveness of objects of collective use. Gas is dearer than anywhere else ; electricity has but hardly begun to light a few streets of a few towns ; the state of urban transport is barbarous ; tramways are rare, and almost unknown save in cities of the first rank and a few only of the second, and the tramway companies, with perhaps two or three exceptions in the whole of France, have failed ; capitalists, alarmed at these failures, feel no inclination to endow our cities with networks of perfected urban communications. The telephone is twice or thrice as dear in Paris as in London, Berlin, Brussels, Amsterdam, or New York. Thus, in the nineteenth century, we have a great country profiting only in the very slightest degree by the numerous recent developments which have been transforming urban existence for the last fifty years. Is it that the State does not intervene sufficiently ? No, it is because it intervenes too much ! The municipalities, which represent the State, use to excess their double power of restraint : the administrative and legal restraint, which multiplies injunctions or prohibitions, and often, without any restriction, subjects companies to the variable judgment of the municipal councils ; and the fiscal restraint, which is anxious to make of every society of capitalists an inexhaustible milch-cow for the municipality. To these forms of restraint must be added the narrow sentiment of envy which regards all property of private companies as a reflection on the public powers."

The complication of procedure, the routine, and also the necessity which the employés experience, in order to safeguard their responsibility, of subjecting themselves to the most minute formalities, result in the enormous expense which is evident in everything administered by the State.[1] The reports given in the name of the Commission of the Budget, by M. Cavaignac on the War Budget, and by M. Pelletan on the Naval Budget, show that the complexities of our administrations surpass the imaginable. In M. Cavaignac's report we find, among a number of analogous cases, the incredible yet veracious tale of the *chef de bataillon* who, having received permission to have made, at the Invalides, a pair of non-regimental boots, found himself a debtor to the State for the sum of 7 fr. 80, which sum he was perfectly willing to pay. To render this payment regular there

[1] I may cite, as an example of the special state of mind created by bureaucratic necessities, the case, brought to the notice of Parliament by a minister, M. Delcassé, of a long controversy which took place in the offices of a department with the end of discovering whether the expenditure for seventy-seven kilos of iron should figure in the budget of the department as 3 fr. 46 or 3 fr. 47. To decide this question the prolonged deliberation of half-a-dozen chiefs of department was necessary, and finally the intervention of the minister himself.

were necessary three letters from the Minister of War, one from the Minister of Finances, and fifteen letters, decisions, or reports from generals, directors, chiefs of departments, &c., at the head of the various administrative services !

In the report of the Commission on the Naval Budget we find far greater complications. The monthly pay of a simple lieutenant comprises a collection of sixty-five different items, " all provided with long tails of decimals." To obtain, in a seaport, a "sail-maker's palm," a piece of leather worth a penny, it is necessary to make out a special form, for which one must explore every corner of the port in search of six different signatures. When once the scrap of leather is obtained, new signatures and inscriptions are necessary in other registers. As a receipt for certain articles pieces of accountant's work demanding fourteen days' labour are necessary. The number of reports docketed by certain departments is reckoned at 100,000.

There is not less complexity on board ship ; the bureaucratic provisions are prodigious. " We have found there, together with thirty-three volumes of regulations, intended to determine the details of administrative life on board, a list of 230 different types of registers, ledgers, memoranda, weekly and monthly reports, certificates, receipt forms, journals, fly-leaves, &c." The unhappy employés very quickly lose their heads in this labyrinth of ciphers. Crushed by their terrible labour, they end by working entirely at hazard. " Hundreds of employés are occupied exclusively at calculating, transcribing, copying into innumerable registers, reproducing on countless fly-leaves, dividing, totalising, or despatching to the minister, figures that have no reality, that correspond to nothing in the region of facts, which would probably be nearer the truth if they were one and all invented."

It is thus impossible to arrive at any precise information with regard to munitions, for each category thereof is appropriated to a whole series of bureaux, each of which is autonomous. A few verifications, undertaken at random by the writer of the report on the Budget, yielded him the most extravagant figures.

For instance, while essential objects were absolutely lacking—for example, the 23,000 spoons and forks mentioned in his report, which, on sale for one penny retail in the streets of Toulon, were bought by the Administration at the rate of fivepence apiece—we find that of other articles a stock was laid in which would last for thirty years, and in some cases for sixty-eight years. As for the bargains of the Administration, the figures unearthed were truly marvellous. In the extreme East—the place of production—it paid for rice 60 per cent. more than the price at Toulon. The prices paid for all articles are in general double the price that would be paid by a private individual, simply because the Administration is unable to pay for them before innumerable pieces of accountant's work have been passed and filed, and is obliged to apply to intermediaries, who make advances which are often not reimbursed for a very long time, on account of the frightful complication of the necessary documents. All this terrible and unnecessary waste represents millions of pounds as truly thrown away as though cast into the sea. A business man who should conduct his affairs in such a manner would not wait long for bankruptcy.

M. Pelletan had the curiosity to investigate the routine of private industry, and to consider how to avoid these thousands of registers and employés, and this accountant's work which ends, by reason of the perfect impossibility of fathoming it, in the most serious disorder. Nothing could be more interesting than this comparison, which contrasts State Socialism as dreamed of by the

Collectivists with private initiative as understood by the English and Americans. He expresses himself as follows :—

"In order to obtain a point of comparison, we inquired into the procedure of a large private industrial concern which is connected with one of our arsenals, and, like the latter, is devoted to ship-building. We shall form some idea of the importance of this establishment if we consider that there are on the slips, at the present moment, one of our large cruisers of the first class, two Brazilian armoured vessels, a twenty-three knot cruiser, a packet-boat, and five sailing vessels ; in short, a flotilla of 68,000 tons French. We must agree that for such an establishment magazines of a certain importance are necessary.

"One large book suffices for the accounts of each of these magazines. Over the place where each sort of article is stored is a ticket indicating the nature of the object, the corresponding folio of the large book, and above, in three columns, the entered, removed, and remaining stock. Thus a glance of the eye will discover the state of the stock of the article in question. If a foreman wishes to draw from the stock he presents a signed and dated ticket, indicating the nature of the article applied for, and the number thereof. The storekeeper writes on the back the name, weight, price per article, and and the total price. The tickets are transcribed into a ledger, and then into the great book. Nothing could be simpler, nor, apparently, more complete."

It is interesting to compare the cost of production in the case of private firms, who are obliged to make money, with that in the case of the State, which is not so obliged. The comparison has been made long ago ; articles that the State makes for itself cost it, in general, 25 to 50 per cent. more than the same articles made by private firms. In the case of armoured vessels, the total cost of which is about £800,000, the difference of the costs of production in England and France is about 25 per cent., according to a report drawn up by M. de Kerjegu.[1]

This excessive cost of all that is manufactured by the State is the result of many factors. It is sufficient to investigate the fact, without searching into all the causes. We shall limit ourselves to observing that some of these causes reside not merely in the complication of regulations and formalities, but in an essential psychological factor ; the indifference which one naturally brings to all affairs in which there is no question of personal interest. It is for this important reason that we so often see the failure of industrial enterprises which are managed by

---

[1] The comparison between the cost of production by private concerns and by the State establishments is extremely difficult, for the reason that those interested take good care to forget to include, in the cost of production, such considerable expenses as rents, salaries, &c., which are charged to other budgets. Thus it has been proved to the Chamber of Deputies, by a special inquiry made by the Budget Commission, that the *Imprimerie Nationale*, which pretended to make a profit, actually presents an annual deficit of £25,600. This deficit, however, is not brought about by the cheapness of its publications.

The inquiry proved that the costs of production of the publications of this establishment, which is supported by the State, which gives it, indirectly, a subsidy of £35,000 a year, are from 25 to 30 per cent. in excess of the cost of production by private industry. The difference is sometimes greater. Among the examples given before the Chamber we may mention that of a special work which the Minister of the Navy wished to publish. The *Imprimerie Nationale*, a subsidised establishment, demanded £2,400. A private publisher, not subsidised, demanded £800. It is true that in the *Imprimerie Nationale*—which we may regard as a type of the establishments of the future collectivist society—everything passes with the most punctilious regularity. One of the commission, M. Hervieu, says : "It is necessary to obtain a piece of paper authorising one to enter, another authorising one to make the desired purchase, another authorising one to carry away what one has bought, and finally another authorising one to leave the establishment."

intermediaries, and not by any one personally interested.[1]

From these different conditions there necessarily ensue very dissimilar methods of administration. I have recently met with an example, which I here reproduce, as being highly typical and because it clearly illustrates my idea.

A foreign firm had established in France, at its own expense, a tramway line uniting two great industrial centres, which it administered itself. The enterprise succeeded admirably. The annual receipts reached £44,000, and the working expenses did not exceed 47 per cent. The local authorities having observed to the company that it was annoying to see a foreigner at its head, the company consented to replace him by a French engineer. The experiment was highly instructive. The engineer began first of all by reorganising the offices and adorning them with numerous officials—sub-director, accountant-in-chief, advocate-in-chief, cashier, &c.; he then naturally elaborated a long and very complex scheme of regulations, in which all the ingenuity of his Latin mind unfolded itself.

The results were not slow to appear. In less than a year the working expenses had almost doubled. They reached, in fact, the sum of 82 per cent., and the company found ruin staring it in the face.

[1] A large Belgian manufacturer, who has business relations with many countries, and whom for that reason I consulted, writes to me on this subject as follows :—

"An evident proof of your theory—that enterprises superintended by intermediaries are unsuccessful—may be found in the numerous list of businesses quoted on the Bourse, which, after yielding excellent returns, have dwindled almost to nothing as soon as they have been transformed into anonymous companies.

"We have business concerns here which, when they belonged to a handful of persons directly interested, gave dividends of 12 to 15 per cent.; they have been turned into anonymous companies, and the dividends have fallen to an average of 3 per cent.; some no longer yield any dividend whatever."

It took a heroic resolve. The director went to the authorities, placed the results before their eyes, and then offered to allow the engineer to retain his title and emoluments, on the express condition that he should never, under any pretext, set foot in the offices. The proposition was accepted, the old order of things re-established, and the expenses of working quickly fell to their normal figure of 47 per cent. This experiment in Latin administration cost the company nearly £20,000.

Applied to the Colonies our system of administration has engendered the most disastrous results. It has ended in the gradual ruin of all our possessions. While the English Colonies cost the exchequer next to nothing, we spend £3,200,000 a year in support of ours. In exchange for these £3,200,000 we do business with them to the extent of about £3,600,000, which hardly yields £600,000 profit. We have then £600,000 of receipts in exchange for £3,200,000 expenditure, which leaves an annual deficit of £2,600,000. This deficit is far more than a mere loss, for this sum of £2,600,000 really serves to develop the commerce of our competitors, from whom above all our colonies draw their imports, our compatriots being incapable of producing them at the same prices: The exports to our colonies from foreign countries exceed the French exports by £1,840,000, which could hardly be otherwise in respect of the administrative hindrances with which we embarrass our commerce in our colonies. In order to administer the two million inhabitants of Cochin China we employ more officials than the English to administer 250 millions of Hindoos. A journal stated recently that in the times of the kings of Dahomey our traders preferred to establish themselves on their soil rather than submit to the amazing administrative complications which they had to encounter in our colony. The severest tyrant is far less severe than the anony-

mous bureaucratic tyranny to which, in default of knowing how to conduct ourselves, we are absolutely forced to
submit.

Naturally, the Latin administrative methods necessitate
an enormous budget; from £72,000,000 in 1869 it has
gradually increased to £140,000,000, a sum which must
be increased to £200,000,000 if we add the communal
budgets to that of the State. Such a budget can exist
only by crushing taxation.[1] The State, obedient to the
general state of mind, which opposes all undertakings
due to private enterprise, hampers industry by sometimes
extravagant taxes. The Omnibus Company in its last
report, published in 1898, stated that for a dividend of 65
francs per share paid to each shareholder it paid to the
State or the city 149 francs in taxes, or a duty of more
than 200 per cent. In the case of the *Compagnie générale
des voitures* the State and the City levied 2 francs 44 centimes of the daily receipts of each vehicle, so that the
shareholders received only 11 centimes. And so forth.
All these enterprises are consequently approaching ruin,
and they also are destined, sooner or later, inevitably to
pass into the hands of the State.

The preceding figures allow us to foresee what State
Socialism will bring us to when its evolution shall be
complete; the speedy and absolute ruin of every
industry of the countries in which it shall triumph.

It is almost superfluous to add that the effects of
centralisation and absorption by the State which we perceive in France are equally perceptible in the other Latin
countries, and in a far greater degree. Things have
arrived at such a crisis in Italy that on February 21,

---

[1] For products of general use, such as sugar, the duty is double
the value of the product ; the duty on alcohol is five times the value
of the product. Salt, tobacco, and petroleum are taxed in a similar
manner. The most essential products, such as bread and meat, are
often doubled in price by taxation.

1894, the Government laid a Bill before Parliament by means of which the King should be invested, for one year, with dictatorial powers, in order to attempt the reorganisation of the administrations of the State. It is a matter for regret that the Bill did not pass ; for its application would clearly have demonstrated the vanity of all attempts at the reform of institutions when they are the consequences of a racial state of mind.

We may gain some idea of the development of State Socialism in Italy, and of the restraint it produces, from the following extracts from an article by the Italian deputy Bonasi, published in the *Political and Parliamentary Review* for October, 1895.

"The administrative officials in the provinces are not only allowed no initiative ; they are not even allowed the modest latitude of interpretation and application which is nevertheless inseparable from the exercise of an administrative function. Outside of the attributes which are expressly conferred on them by laws, regulations, circulars, and ministerial instructions, they dare not budge an inch without previous authorisation, and the final approbation of the minister on whom they are dependent. . . . The prefects, the commissioners of finance, the presidents of the courts, the rectors of universities, are unable to authorise the smallest expenditure or the least important or most urgent repair, unless their decision has received the benediction of the ministerial *placet*. . . .

"If a commune, or a benevolent society, wish to acquire real estate, though it be a matter only of a square yard of earth, or the acceptance of a legacy made in its favour, even of a few shillings, there must be a deliberation of the communal council, or of the committee of the society ; and more, there is necessary in each case the vote of the administrative provincial commission ; a request made to the King for the supreme authorisation ; a report from the prefect accompanying the application to the minister, with a summing-up and particulars ; a report from the minister to the Council of State ; an advice from the Council, and finally a royal decree, and its registration in the Court of Accounts."

The inevitable consequences of this state of things have been an extremely rapid increase of the number of Italian functionaries, and consequently of the Budget.

Identical facts are to be observed in all the Latin nations, and are clearly the result of the mental constitution of their race. The proof is yet more authentic where we oppose these facts to what I have said in another chapter of the results of private initiative in the Anglo-Saxon race.

It is especially important to keep in mind the proof that it is entirely to ourselves, and not to the Government, that we owe the gradual extension of the *rôle* of the State and its consequences. Let the government be what we will — republic, dictatorship, commune, or monarchy ; let it have at its head Heliogabalus, Louis Quatorze, Robespierre, or a victorious general—the part played by the State among the Latin peoples cannot change. It is the consequence of a racial necessity. The State, in reality, is ourselves, and we can blame none but ourselves for its organisation. By reason of this mental characteristic, which Cæsar in his days perceived and pointed out, we always hold the Government responsible for our own faults, and we are still persuaded that by changing our institutions or our rulers everything will be transformed. No amount of reasoning can cure us of the error. We can, however, foresee it, in considering that when the hazards of politics have placed at the heads of departments such deputies as have the

most searchingly criticised the services they find them
selves called to direct, there has never been an example
of their being able to modify, however slightly, that
which they considered, with reason, to be an intolerable
abuse. These abuses are vices of race, and therefore
incurable. We have only to cite the example of the
Minister of the Navy to more than justify these remarks.

3. The Collectivist State.

We have just been considering the progress of State
Socialism and its consequences. It remains to me to
show how little divides us from complete Collectivism,
as dreamed of by the high priests of the doctrine.

The dangers of Collectivism have not escaped the eyes
of such statesmen as have been endowed with a certain
perspicacity ; but they do not appear to have seen very
clearly that we have long ago entered into the Collectivist
phase. Ensuing are the remarks on this subject of one of
the most distinguished of them, M. Bourdeau, sometime
president of the Chamber of Deputies :—

" The danger to be feared is not that Collectivism is
triumphing, establishing itself, modelling society to its
liking. The danger is that it continues to insinuate
itself into the popular mind, and into our institutions ;
to throw scorn on capital and its use, and on the institutions derived from it (banks and so forth) ; on private
initiative, which is incessantly vilified, to the profit of
State monopolies ; on thrift, on personal property, on
inheritance, on salaries proportioned to the merits and
utility of the returns offered ; on the means which to-day
serve to elevate the lowest, or at least their descendants,
to the highest positions ; on the support given to society
by the millions of initative efforts excited by personal
interest.

"The result of all this is enormously to increase the *rôle* of the State ; to make it responsible for railroads, mines, and banks, and perhaps for navigation, assurance, and stores ; to crush large or medium fortunes and inheritances by duties, together with all that stimulates man to invention, or to adventurous and long-sustained enterprises ; all that makes him a creature of foresight, considerate of future generations ; all that makes him a worker for posterity ; to disgust the worker with difficult tasks, with economy, with the hope of success ; in short, to reduce the individual to mediocrity of desires, ambitions, energy, and talent, under the guardianship of an all-absorbing State ; to replace, more and more, the man animated by personal interest, by a quasi-official."

The conclusions of this statesman are patent to every mind a little familiar with the economic and psychologic necessities which rule a people. He has clearly perceived that the latent triumph of Socialism is still more assured and still more dangerous than its nominal triumph.

The society of the future, dreamed of by the Collectivists, has for some time been gradually realising itself among the Latin nations. State Socialism is, in fact, as I have shown, the necessary conclusion of the past of these nations, the final step towards the decadence which no civilisation has as yet been able to avoid. For centuries subjected systematically to hierarchies, brought to a dead level by a university education and a system of examinations which run all into one mould ; greedy of equality, but little eager for liberty ; accustomed to every kind of administrative tyranny, military, religious, or moral ; having lost all initiative, all power of will ; gradually habituated to have recourse in all things to the State ;—they are doomed by the fatality of their race to suffer the State Socialism which the Collectivists are preaching to-day. I have already said that they have actually been subjected to it for a considerable time. To convince himself, the reader has only to consider what it is that the Collectivists are proposing, and therein to perceive the simple development of the already existent state of things. These Collectivists truly believe themselves to be innovators, but their doctrine is only precipitating a natural phase of evolution whose preparation and advent is none of their work. A brief examination of their fundamental propositions will readily prove this.

One of the principal ends of Collectivism is the State monopoly of all industries and enterprises. Now all that in England, and especially in America, is founded and fostered by private initiative, is, to-day, among the Latin peoples, more or less in the hands of the Government. And the Government is for ever taking over fresh industries—telephones and matches to-day—alcohol, mines, and means of transport to-morrow. When this absorption is complete an important fraction of the Collectivist dream will be realised.

The Collectivists wish to place the public wealth in the hands of the State by various means ; notably by the progressive increase of the death duties. With us these death duties are increasing every day ; a new Bill has just brought them up to 15 per cent. A few successive increases will realise the Collectivist ideal.

The Collectivist State will give every citizen an identical, gratuitous, and obligatory education. Our University, with its terrible bed of Procrustes, has realised this ideal long ago.

The Collectivist State will control everything by means of an immense army of functionaries who will regulate the least acts of the citizen's life. There are already

great battalions of these functionaries ; they are to-day
the true masters in the State. Their number is always
on the increase, by the sole fact that the laws and
regulations which are progressively limiting the initiative
and liberty of the citizen are on the increase. Already,
under various pretexts, they supervise the work of manu-
factories, and of the smallest private undertakings. They
have only to increase their number and their attributes
a little, and the Collectivist dream will be realised on
this point also.

While it hopes to arrive at the absorption of private
fortunes to the profit of the State by increasing the death
duties, Collectivism is also persecuting capital in every
imaginable manner. The State has led the way in this
matter. Every day all private undertakings find themselves crushed by heavier and heavier duties, which are
more and more reducing their returns and their chances
of prosperity. There are, as I have already shown, certain
industries, such as the Omnibus Company in Paris, which
for 65 francs of dividend to the shareholder pay 149 francs
in various taxes. Other sources of revenue are being
extinguished, one after another, by increasing duties.
We are beginning to think of attacking rent. In Italy,
where this stage has long been reached, the duty on rent
has gradually been raised to 20 per cent. A few successive increases of the duty will suffice to arrive at the
complete absorption of revenue, and consequently of
capital, for the profit of the State.

Finally, according to the Collectivists, the proletariat
should deprive the present directing classes of their
political rights. This has not been effected as yet, but
we are nearing it rapidly. The popular classes are the
masters of society by virtue of the universal suffrage, and
they are beginning to send an increasing number of
Socialists to Parliament. When the majority is a Socialist

majority the list of demands will be completely granted. Every fantasy will be possible; and finally, to bring them to an end, will definitely open that period of Cæsars, and then of invasions, which has always marked the final hour of decadence of nations already too aged.

CHAPTER VII

THE PRESENT STATE OF THE LATIN PEOPLES

1. *Weaknesses of the Latin nations :*—The result of the conceptions already treated of—The dangers with which the development of Socialism threatens them—The Latin nations can no longer make experiments or venture on revolutions save under penalty of disappearing—Modern necessities. 2. *The Latin Republics of America. Spain and Portugal :*—Present condition of the Spanish-American republics—They represent the lowest level of Latin civilisation—Their destiny—Spain and Portugal—Their state of decadence—Colonial government of the Spaniards—Why they have lost their colonies—The Spanish-American war considered from a psychological point of view—Influence of the character of the two opposing races—Incidents of the war. 3. *Italy and France :*—Present condition of Italy—Disorganised state of her administration, army, and finances—The revolutions which threaten her—Near triumph of Socialism—Why the triumph of Socialism threatens Italy far more than France—General lowering of morality among the Latin nations—Present condition of France—Symptoms of fatigue and indifference. 4. *The results of the adoption of the Latin concepts by peoples of different race :*—The modern Greeks, since the time of the Independence, have adopted the conceptions of the Latin nations *en bloc*, and notably the Latin conception of education—Results produced in fifty years—Complete disorganisation of finances, administration, and army—Progress of Socialism—The Græco-Turkish war—European illusions with regard to Greece. 5. *The future which threatens the Latin nations :*—The present phase of the evolution of the world will not allow the feeble nations to continue their existence—Predictions of Lord Salisbury—The grave dangers of Socialist experiments for the Latin nations.

1. WEAKNESSES OF THE LATIN NATIONS.

WE have already seen the consequences produced among the Latin nations by the gradual extension of their conception of the State : that is to say, of a central power substituting itself for the initiative of the citizen and acting for him. It is of no significance whether this power be a collectivity or a monarchy ; the fundamental conception remains the same under these meaningless external forms.

From a practical point of view, Socialism represents merely the extension of the same conception. What may still remain of initiative and strength of will in the citizen mind will very soon be entirely broken by the regulation of labour, and the perpetual interference of functionaries in all the acts of life.

A large number of persons who dislike conflict seem to be more and more disposed to allow Socialism to develop. Having no second sight by which to pass the horizon that surrounds them, they have no idea of what is beyond. But that which lies beyond is menacing and terrible. If they wish their existence to continue, the Latin nations must risk no more experiments, no more revolutions. New economic conditions are in process of overturning the conditions of national life, and there will very soon be no place for the weaker nations. Now the weakness of the greater number of the Latin nations will very soon have reached that extreme limit below which no recovery is possible. They will not prevent things from being what they are by intoxicating themselves with brilliant phrases, abandoning themselves to futile discussions, or boasting of the exploits of their grandfathers. The age of chivalry, of heroic and superb sentiments, of ingenious dialectic, has long passed away. We are more and more hedged about with implacable realities, and the subtlest arguments, the most sonorous dithyrambics on right and justice, have as much effect on these realities as had the rods of Xerxes on the sea that he had beaten as a punishment for having destroyed his vessels.

To make my argument clearer I shall attempt to present in a general view the present condition of the Latin nations, and some of its consequences.

2. THE LATIN REPUBLICS OF AMERICA. SPAIN AND
PORTUGAL.

Let us first of all consider the nations at the lowest
level of the scale of Latin civilisation : the twenty-two
Latin republics of America. They have often afforded
me an example to demonstrate the small influence of
institutions on national life, and it would be useless to
return to the consideration of their condition in any
detail. All, without a single exception, have reached
that state in which decadence manifests itself by the
completest anarchy, and in which a people can only gain
by being conquered by a nation strong enough to rule it.

Peopled by exhausted races, without energy, without
initiative, without morality, without strength of will, the
twenty-two Latin republics of America, although situated
in the richest countries of the earth, are incapable of
making use of their immense resources. They live on
European loans, which are divided amongst bands of
political pirates, who are associated with other pirates of
European finance, who make it their business to exploit
the ignorance of the public, and are doubly guilty in that
they are too well informed to believe that their loans will
ever be repaid. Pillage is general in these unhappy
republics, and, as every one wishes to take part in it, civil
wars are a permanent institution, and the presidents are
systematically assassinated in order to allow a new party
to arrive in power and enrich itself in turn. This state of
things will doubtless continue until the day when some
talented adventurer shall place himself at the head of a
few thousand well-disciplined men, undertake the easy
conquest of these unhappy countries, and subject them
to an iron rule, the only rule of which nations deprived
of virility and morality, and incapable of governing themselves, are worthy.

All these degenerate countries would long ago have
returned to a state of pure barbarism had there not been
established in the capitals a few foreigners—English and
Germans—attracted by the natural riches of the soil. The
only one of these republics which to some extent maintains itself, the Argentine Republic, has escaped the
general ruin merely because it has been gradually invaded by the English.

Before becoming republics all these provinces were
under the rule of Spain. They succeeded, by revolution,
in shaking off the gloomy government of her monks and
rapacious governors, but it was too late. The bias was
set, the mind was formed, and recovery was impossible ;
besides which the monks had for a long period been
charged with the duty of suppressing all persons mani-
festing any trace of intelligence and independence.

From the Latin republics of America let us pass to the
Latin monarchies of Europe. Their condition is certainly
less melancholy, but very far from brilliant.

We know what is the present condition of Spain and
Portugal ; the least observant traveller can ascertain it by
a short stay in those countries. The few industries that
prosper are in the hands of strangers, or have been
created by strangers. These countries, of old so powerful, are to-day as incapable of governing themselves as of
governing their colonies, which they are losing one by
one. To Spain remained Cuba and the Philippines ; she
subjected them to such rapacious exploitation, to administrators so corrupt and ferocious, as to provoke an
exasperated rising on the part of the natives, and the
intervention of strangers.

Dr. Pinto de Guimaraes, in a book published under the
title *The Spanish Terror in the Philippines,* has recently
furnished details which show what the Spanish domina-

tion was in the Colonies, and how legitimate was the horror it inspired. I cite the following lines from this book :—

"One thing that appears at the first glance is that the intervention of the United States was no less necessary in the Pacific than in the Atlantic. The Spanish rule weighed on the Philippines as heavily as on Cuba, and if the cruelties committed there have remained more secret it is not that the Filipinos are more long-suffering than the Cubans ; it is because of their absolute isolation, far from the civilised world, and because of the pains taken by the local governors to stifle all complaints and intercept all demands. But the truth, which is stronger than all despotisms, end by making itself heard ; and the Filipinos, despite the Spanish gag, have succeeded in crying so loud that the world has heard them.

"It is impossible to imagine what vexations, what shifty formalities, what ruinous inventions can emanate from the brain of a Spanish functionary. All these gentry have but one object : to make, during their three or six years in the Philippines, the largest possible fortune, and to return home in order to escape the concert of the maledictions of the inhabitants. . . . Every governor whose future is not largely assured after two years of office is universally regarded as an imbecile. The celebrated General Weyler was enabled to deposit, as much in the London as in the Parisian banks, a sum which his own compatriots reckoned to be no less than £500,000 or £600,000. How did he conduct himself in order to save £600,000 in three years, with an annual pay of £8,000 ?

"And yet one cannot refrain from pondering over the marvellous resources of these islands, and of the splendid results which they would assuredly have afforded any other power than Spain. Robbed, oppressed, ruined, tortured, the Philippines nevertheless manage to exist. The character of the functionaries and the fiscal jugglers of the country keep away all those who might contribute to the development of its prosperity."

The clergy, together with the officials, constitute one of the most pernicious plagues of the Philippines. They number six thousand, and their greed[1] is equalled only by their ferocity. They have rehabilitated all the tortures of the Inquisition.

Dr. de Guimaraes gives details of the cruelty exercised toward the natives by the Spaniards which make one shiver. There is notably the story of the hundred prisoners who were confined in a dungeon called the "Death Hole," half full of putrid water, and infested with rats and venomous serpents of all kinds ; altogether worthy of the imagination of a romancer. "They passed a terrible night ; they were heard howling in agony and praying that some one would 'finish' them. Next day all were dead."

"In the presence of such facts," concludes Dr. Guimaraes, "no one will be surprised by the joy felt by the insurgents at the American successes. Spain has for centuries, in these unhappy isles, displayed a spectacle of ferocity that the heroism of her defence cannot atone for." I am of the same opinion.

Naturally the Spanish rule in Cuba has been the same as in the Philippines, and there too the people have finally revolted. The insurgents formed only a few ill-equipped bands whose number never exceeded 10,000 men. Against them Spain sent 150,000 men, commanded by numerous generals, and spent in four years to conquer them nearly

---

[1] According to the figures given by Señor Montero of Vidal, the most humble cures yield their incumbents £400 a year, and some yield £1,000 to £3,000. These sums are paid by the natives, whose poverty is nevertheless extreme.

£80,000,000. But all these generals, with their blasting proclamations, could not, after years of conflict, and despite their implacable cruelties, succeed in triumphing over these ill-armed bands of insurgents. The cruelties of the Spaniards and the massacres of inoffensive populations in which they indulged on an extensive scale, gave the United States an excellent reason for intervention. All those who have a care for humanity have loudly acclaimed their success.

The Spanish-American war is full of instruction for him who studies it from a psychological point of view. Never has the part played in the life of the nations by character, and therefore by race, been more clearly manifested. The world had never yet seen such a spectacle as this of an entire fleet, heavily armoured, annihilated in a few minutes without succeeding in doing the slightest harm to the enemy. In two engagements twenty Spanish vessels were destroyed without even having planned a defence. To die like a stoic is a poor excuse for incapacity, and the world has never seen the results of indecision, lack of foresight, carelessness, and want of coolness better than at Manila and in Cuba. At Manila, where the American fleet entered by night, the Spaniards had forgotten to light the beacons which should have signalled its presence, and had also forgotten to defend the channel by means of mines. At Santiago de Cuba they neglected to send for reinforcements, which were not lacking in the island, and would have made the defence an easy matter ; at Porto Rico there were not even any defenders. When the fleet annihilated itself by voluntarily steaming on to the rocks without one of its projectiles having reached the enemy it afforded a lamentable spectacle. By throwing itself at the enemy instead of running away it might assuredly have done some damage, and would at least have saved its honour.

" One might say," very justly writes M. H. Depasse on this subject, " that the two adversaries belong to different civilisations, or rather to different periods of history ; the one master of its means and of itself through education, the other obeying only the impulsive movements of nature." It would be impossible better to denote, in a few lines, one of the principal differences between the Anglo-Saxon and Latin education.[1]

The natives will gain by this war in that they will pass under an infinitely better rule. Spain herself will not lose over-much by it, since her colonies brought nothing to the State, and since her defeat will serve her as a pretext to imitate Portugal and the Spanish-American republics by suppressing the payment of the interest on her National Debt, and on the stock she has disposed of abroad. By one of those fantastic chances so frequent in modern times, it will really be France who will pay the expenses of this war, since she will almost certainly lose the £120,000,000 of Spanish bonds which she holds. Capitalists will therefore discover that a knowledge of the psychology of nations is a science which possesses a highly practical value. I doubt if a single capitalist knowing a little of the psychology of the Spaniards would ever have risked the slightest sum either in Spain or in any dependency of Spain.

[1] The following extract from an interview with Marshal Campos, published in all the journals, very well sums up the impression produced on the world at large by the incredible successes of the army improvised by the United States against a trained and very numerous army, for the Spaniards had 150,000 men in Cuba ; far more than the Americans had : " Never could even the greatest of pessimists have imagined that our misfortunes would have been so numerous. The disaster at Cavité, the destruction of Cervera's squadron, the fall of Santiago, the rapid and unopposed occupation of Porto Rico—no one would ever have believed these possible, even in exaggerating the power of the States and the inferiority of Spain."

3. FRANCE AND ITALY.

Italy, although she has not fallen as low as Spain, is not in a much better condition, and her disorder is betrayed by her finances. She is the victim not only of the Latin conceptions which have shaped her soul, but also of that fatal idea of unity which has sprung up in the minds of her politicians. In uniting, under a central power, populations as profoundly dissimilar as the Piedmontese, the Lombards, the Sicilians, &c., Italy has undertaken the most ruinous and disastrous of experiments. In thirty years she has passed from a very enviable condition to the completest disorganisation of her politics, administration, finances, and military services.

Her finances are not in such a miserable state as those of Spain, but she is already forced to have recourse to a paper currency, and has established a duty on rent which has gradually, by increase after increase, mounted to 20 per cent., and which in rising further will lead her to a failure like that of Portugal. At a distance she gives the illusion of a great people, but her power is only a thin show, incapable of resisting the least of shocks. Despite the millions spent in creating an army permitting her to figure among the great Powers, Italy has for the first time in the world afforded the melancholy spectacle of an army of 20,000 Europeans annihilated in set battle by savage hordes, and of a great civilised country being obliged to pay an indemnity to a petty African king,

[1] In their manner of comprehending the *rôle* of the State the Italians surpass even the French in pushing the Latin concept to an extreme. Nowhere so much as in Italy is developed the absolute faith in the omnipotence of the State, the necessity of its fostering care in all affairs, and notably in commerce and industry, and as their final consequences the development of officialism and the incapacity of the citizen to manage his own business himself without the constant assistance of the Government.

whose capital had been so easily taken a few years before by a small force of Englishmen. She drags herself along at the apron-strings of Germany, and is obliged to submit without a murmur to the disdain which the German papers incessantly pour on her. The wastefulness and carelessness to be observed in Italy are incredible. She erects useless monuments, such as that of Victor Emmanuel, which will cost more than £1,600,000, while at the same time, in Sicily, she has provinces plunged into the blackest misery, whose villages are abandoned by their inhabitants and invaded by brambles.[1] We may judge of the quality of her administration by the banking scandal, or by the lamentable process of Palermo, in which it was proved that all the Government agents, from the director to the least of the employés, had for years lived by the most brazen pillage of the finances of their province. In the face of the proofs of disorganisation and demoralisation which Italy daily presents, and which show her to be on the eve of revolution, one can understand the scathing judgment which one of the most remarkable of Italian scientists, Signor Lombroso, has pronounced, in a recent work, on his own country ; a judgment which we should like to believe too severe.

"We must be ten times blind not to see that with all our love of boasting, we in Italy form the last but one, if not the last, of the European nations ; the last in morality, the last in education, the last in agricultural and industrial activity, the last in integrity of justice, and, above all, the

---

[1] And yet the needs of the Italian peasantry are very small. The wages of those who work by the day rarely exceed fivepence a day. As for the working men, they reckon themselves extremely well off if their wages are as much as nine or ten shillings a week. If the middle and upper classes possessed a tithe of the endurance and energy of the lower classes Italy would rank among the most prosperous of the nations, instead of finding herself almost in the last rank of the civilised nations.

last in respect of the relative comfort of the lower classes."[1]

Italy would appear to be destined to inevitable revolutions, and very soon to see accomplished that fatal cycle of which I have already often spoken : Socialism, Cæsarism, and dissolution.

M. A. Suissy has very well shown in the following lines how weary is Italy already of her parliamentary *régime*, which is yet the only one that can guarantee her liberties.

" The Italian people are losing confidence in the virtue of the parliamentary *régime*. The debates and intrigues to which their representatives are given up appear to them to be more often than not opposed to the general interests of the country. They have some intuition of the dangers which are gathering, and they have no hope of finding in the parliamentary system, as it is practised, any weapon of defence against them.

" In Rome we are beginning to see all the gravity of lassitude on the one side and exasperation on the other. The poor classes, who suffer the most from the crisis, are goaded to revolution. The middle and commercial classes, on the contrary, cry out for a saviour who shall deliver them from the trouble of defending themselves. The state of siege in Milan, Florence, and Naples offers no objection to their minds. The love of liberty is dying in the hearts of those who pretend to belong to the directing classes."

A factor which has created a problem for Italy, of which the solution is not apparent, is the fact that her desire to imitate the wealthy nations has led her into creating for herself a host of needs in the matters of comfort and luxury which her poverty does not allow her to satisfy.

"The majority of Italians," writes Signor Guglielmo

---

[1] *The Anarchists.*

Ferrero, "are on the threshold of a superior civilisation ; they have developed new wants, and aspire to embellish their lives with a certain degree of comfort and culture, but their means are insufficient. . . . Italy cannot regard fine and beautiful things without wishing to enjoy them. What disillusions, what rage, what vexation, must enter into the daily existence of the majority of men living under such conditions ! . . . Reckon what a prodigious sum of irritability is gathering itself up in the whole of society, and you will have little trouble in comprehending the terrible instability of its equilibrium."

It is among individuals whose needs are very great, and who have neither the capacity nor the energy to acquire the means to satisfy them, that Socialism most easily develops. It offers itself as a remedy for all evils, and for this reason Italy would seem fatally destined to suffer the most dangerous Socialistic experiments.

This craving for luxury, enjoyment, and splendour constitutes one of the greatest differences between Italy and Spain. In all that concerns the external aspect of civilisation, Spain is evidently very far below Italy, but the middle and lower strata of the population have very little to complain of, for their requirements have not multiplied, and so continue to be easily satisfied. As the means of communication, and railways in especial, are little developed in Spain, whole provinces are still isolated from the world, and have been able to retain their ancient manner of existence. Life has remained incredibly easy there ; for as their needs are very small, and luxury is unknown to them, the produce grown on the spot is sufficient for the people. If we leave out of account large towns and external luxury—which are, it is true, the only things we know, because they are the only ones that make themselves heard—Spain possesses a degree of civilisation which is doubtless little refined, but entirely suited to her

mental evolution and its requirements. Socialism, therefore, cannot seriously threaten her.

Among the greater number of the Latin peoples few
but the so-called directing classes are becoming more eager
for the expensive refinements of civilisation. This aspiration is quite allowable when one is confident of the
intelligence and energy necessary to procure these refinements. It is far less allowable when the development of
energy and intelligence are very inferior to the development of requirements. When people wish to make a
fortune at any price, and their capacities do not permit
them to satisfy their desire, they have little regard for the
means they employ ; honesty becomes elastic, and
demoralisation very soon becomes general ; as it has,
indeed, in the case of most of the Latin nations. In them,
indeed, we increasingly perceive the disquieting fact that
the morality of the directing classes is often far below
that of the populace. This is one of the most dangerous
symptoms of the decadence that could appear, for if it is
through the upper classes that civilisations advance, it is
also through them that they perish.

This term "morality" is so vague, and embraces such
dissimilar things, that its use necessarily results in serious
confusion. I employ it here in the sense of simple
honesty, the habit of respecting engagements, and the
sentiment of duty, that is to say, in the sense in which
an English author whom I have already quoted employs
it, in the passage in which he shows that it is owing to
these qualities, so modest in appearance, but in reality so
important, that the English have so rapidly revolutionised
the credit of Egypt and rendered the finances of their
colonies so prosperous.

We must not go to criminal statistics, which register
only extreme cases, to determine the degree of morality
of a nation. It is indispensable to enter into details.

The financial bankruptcy of so many of-the Latin peoples is a barometrical sign which indicates nothing less than a final state reached by successive steps. To form an opinion which shall repose on a reliable basis, we must enter into the intimate life of each country ; we must study the administration of financial societies ; we must consider commercial manners, the independence or venality of justice, the probity of lawyers and officials, and many other symptoms which call for direct observation, and are not to be studied in any books. These are subjects on which a few dozen persons at most in Europe are perfectly informed. Would you, however, without too laborious research, gain an exact idea of the morality of the various nations ? Merely consult a few leading men of business—contractors, manufacturers, engineers—who have close relations with the commerce, administration, and legislatures of various countries. A contractor, who builds railways, tramways, gas and electric light works, in many countries, will tell you, if he cares to speak on the subject, which are the countries in which every one may be bought—ministers, magistrates, officials, and all—which are the countries in which few people are to be bought, and which are the countries in which absolutely no one is to be bought ; those in which commerce is honest, and those in which it is not in the least honest. If, however varied your sources of information be, you find them perfectly concordant, you may evidently convince yourself of their exactitude.[1]

[1] It would be useless to enter into the details of this inquiry, which the relations established by my travels have permitted me to make in a number of countries. I will limit myself to saying that I have been very happy to find that among the Latin nations, with the exception of a few politicians, financiers, and journalists, France is the nation in which the greatest probity exists in administration and justice. The magistracy is often extremely narrow, and yields too readily to political pressure, and to questions of preferment, but it has remained honest. But the morality of our industrial and com-

Our rapid examination of the Latin peoples is not complete until we turn to France, whose part in the world was of old so brilliant and preponderant. She still holds out against decadence, but she is badly shaken to-day. In one century she has known all a nation can know; the bloodiest revolutions, glory, disaster, civil war, invasion, and but little repose. That which she most visibly experiences to-day is a fatigue and indifference which seemingly amount to exhaustion.

"Compared with the same class in England and Germany," recently wrote a German pamphleteer quoted by *la France extérieure,* "the French *bourgeoisie* give one the impression of a person well advanced in years. Individual initiative is gradually decaying; the spirit of enterprise appears paralysed; the craving for repose and for sedentary occupations is increasing; the investments in State funds increase; the number of functionaries increases; energy, and the sentiment of authority, justice, and religion are diminishing; the interest in public affairs is diminishing; expenditure is increasing; imports are increasing all along the line; the infiltration of foreigners is increasing."

Presently, in studying the commercial and industrial struggles of the Western peoples, we shall see to what degree these assertions are unhappily justified.

4. THE RESULTS OF THE ADOPTION OF THE LATIN CONCEPTS BY PEOPLES OF DIFFERENT RACE.

Examples of peoples in an inferior state of civilisation adopting suddenly and in entirety the institutions of other

mercial classes is sometimes dubious enough. Yet there are, on the contrary, countries in which the venality of the magistracy and the administration, and the lack of commercial and financial probity have reached the degree in which such vices no longer even seek to dissimilate themselves under appearances.

peoples are rare in modern times. I can cite no such examples except those of Greece and Japan. Greece presents the interesting phenomenon of a nation that has adopted the Latin concepts *en bloc*, and notably that of education. The results produced are extremely striking, and it is all the more important that they should be given here inasmuch as they have not yet attracted the notice of any writer.

The modern Greeks, as we know, have no relationship to the Latins, nor for that matter with the ancient Greeks. Modern anthropology has shown that they are brachycephalous Slavs, while the ancient Greeks were dolichocephalous, which fact is sufficient to establish an absolutely fundamental separation between the modern Greeks and their pretended ancestors.[1]

The inhabitants of Greece, although unrelated to the Latins, present several analogies to the latter in their character. They also possess, with little strength of will, and little constancy, much levity, mobility, and irritability.

[1] In 1851, at the time of her enfranchisement, Greece possessed about one million inhabitants, of whom a quarter were Albanians or Wallachians. The population was a residue of invaders of all peoples, and notably of Slavs. For centuries the Greeks properly so called had disappeared from Greece. From the time of the Roman conquest, Greece was regarded by every adventurer as a nursery of slaves, which every one might have recourse to with impunity. Slave-traders brought as many as ten thousand Greek slaves to Rome at a single venture. Later on the Goths, Heruli, Bulgarians, Wallachians, and so forth, continued to invade the country and to lead its last inhabitants into slavery. Greece was repopulated a little only by the invasions of the Slavs. The language subsisted merely because it was spoken through all the Byzantine East. The present population consists almost entirely of Slavs, the ancient Greek type immortalised in sculpture having totally disappeared. The celebrated Schliemann, whom I met while travelling in Greece, has, however, called my attention to the fact that the ancient Greek type is still to be met with in remarkable purity in many of the islets of the Archipelago, which are inhabited by a few fishers whose isolation and poverty have probably saved them from invasion.

They have the same horror of prolonged effort, the same love of phrases, the same love of speechifying, the same craving for equality, the same habit of confounding dreams with realities.

However, I do not mention them here on account of these analogies, but simply in order to show, by means of an example full of instructiveness, the effects produced on a nation, in less than fifty years, by the adoption of Latin concepts, and notably by that of education.

Scarcely escaped from a long servitude, truly no school for the spirit of initiative or for strength of will, the modern Greeks imagined that they would be able to raise themselves by means of instruction. In a few years the country was sprinkled with three thousand schools and educational establishments of all sorts, in which were carefully applied our disastrous Latin programmes of education. " The French language," writes M. Fouillée, " is taught everywhere in Greece, concurrently with Greek itself ; our national spirit, our literature, our arts, and our education are far more in harmony with the Greek genius than those of any other nation could be."

This theoretical and bookish education being good for nothing but the production of functionaries, professors, and lawyers, naturally produced nothing else : "Athens is a great factory of useless and noxious lawyers." While industry and agriculture have remained in a rudimentary state, *diplomés* without employment are swarming, and, as with men of Latin race subjected to the same education, their sole ambition is to gain a Government berth.

"Every Greek," writes M. Politis, "believes that the chief mission of the Government is to give a berth either to himself or to a member of his family." If he does not obtain it he immediately becomes a reactionary, a Socialist, and raves against the tyranny of capital, although capital is hardly known in Greece. The principal function of the deputies is to find places for graduates of the colleges.

Favouritism, insubordination, and general disorganisation have soon resulted from such a system of education. Two generations of such outclassed persons have sufficed to lead the country to the last degree of moral and material ruin. Cultured Europe, who regarded the little nation across the classic memories of the time of Pericles, only began to lose her illusions when she beheld the perfect cynicism with which the Greek politicians, after having raised loans all over the continent, suppressed their debt with a stroke of the pen by refusing to pay interest and resuming the profits of the monopolies which had been solemnly set aside as guarantees to the creditors, on the very day when they found no more lenders.[1] Europe was completely enlightened as to the demoralisation and disorganisation of all these brave prattlers when she saw the fortunes of the Græco-Turkish war unfolded, and beheld the spectacle of whole armies at the mercy of the wildest panics, the most inordinate, helter-skelter flights, as soon as a mere Turkish detachment was espied at a distance. Without the intervention of Europe the Greeks would once more have disappeared from history, and the world would have been no loser by it. We were shown what things could exist under a deceptive veneer of

---

[1] This process of the suppression of debts, commercially qualified as bankruptcy, has been adopted by Portugal, the Latin republics of America, Turkey, and many other countries. At first sight it appeared a very simple matter to the politicians who made use of it ; but they did not in any way perceive that these bankruptcies must finally cause the countries that practised them to fall under the strict surveillance, and consequently into the power, of other countries. As it was impossible to find among them the few men necessary to administer their finances with integrity, they have been forced, as Egypt and Turkey have been forced, to allow their finances to be administered by foreign agents, placed under the control of their respective governments.

civilisation. Our young university men, so enthusiastic over Greece, must at the same time have acquired a few notions more serious than those to be found in their text-books. Such of them as had escaped from the *Ecole normale* with a few traces of the spirit of observation must have made some melancholy reflections on the results of Latin education, at perceiving to what a depth of abasement the system had sunk a nation in fifty years.

5. THE FUTURE WHICH THREATENS THE LATIN NATIONS.

Such is, without, I trust, too great inaccuracy, the present state of the Latin nations, and those that have adopted the Latin concepts. While waiting till they shall have found some means of raising themselves they must not forget that in the new phase of evolution through which the world is passing, there is room for none but the strong, and that every nation which becomes weakened is quickly destined to become the prey of its neighbours, more especially at a period when the distant markets are closing one by one.

This point of view is absolutely fundamental. It was extremely well presented in a recent and famous speech of Lord Salisbury's, from which I shall reproduce a few extracts, in view of its importance and the authority of the speaker. It points out with great clearness those consequences of a lowered morality of which I have treated further back, and which form an excellent barometer of national decadence. The protests which this speech excited in Spain cannot affect the exactitude of the propositions enounced by this eminent statesman, nor of the conclusions which he draws from them.

"You may roughly divide the nations of the world as the living and the dying. On one side you have great countries of enormous power growing in power every year, growing in wealth, growing in dominion, growing in the perfection of their organisation. Railways have given to them the power to concentrate upon any one point the whole military force of their population and to assemble armies of a magnitude and power never dreamt of in the generations that have gone by. Science has placed in the hands of those armies weapons ever growing in their efficacy of destruction, and, therefore, adding to the power—fearfully to the power—of those who have the opportunity of using them. By the side of these splendid organisations, of which nothing seems to diminish the forces and which present rival claims which the future may only be able by a bloody arbitrament to adjust—by the side of these there are a number of communities which I can only describe as dying, though the epithet applies to them of course in very different degrees and with a very different amount of certain application. They are mainly communities that are not Christian, but I regret to say that is not exclusively the case, and in these States disorganisation and decay are advancing almost as fast as concentration and increasing power are advancing in the living nations that stand beside them. Decade after decade they are weaker, poorer, and less provided with leading men or institutions in which they can trust, apparently drawing nearer and nearer to their fate and yet clinging with strange tenacity to the life which they have got. In them misgovernment is not only not cured but is constantly on the increase. The society, and official society, the Administration, is a mass of corruption, so that there is no firm ground on which any hope of reform or restoration could be based, and in their various degrees they are presenting a terrible picture to the more enlightened portion of the world—a picture which, unfortunately, the increase in the means of our information and communication draws with darker and more conspicuous lineaments in the face of all nations, appealing to their feelings as well as to their interests, calling upon them to bring forward a remedy. How long this state of things is likely to go on of course I do not attempt to prophesy. All I can indicate is that that process is proceeding, that the weak States are becoming weaker and the strong States are becoming stronger. It needs no specialty of prophecy to point out to you what the inevitable result of that combined process must be. For one reason or for another—from the necessities of politics or under the pretence of philanthropy—the living nations will gradually encroach on the territory of the dying, and the seeds and causes of conflict among civilised nations will speedily appear."

Are nations as shaken, as divided, as unprogressive as the Latin nations of to-day to be subjected to Socialism ? Is it not evident that such a fate would merely increase their weakness, and render them a still easier prey to the stronger nations ? Alas ! the politicians do not foresee this, any more than the theologians of the Middle Ages, absorbed, in the depths of their convents, by religious controversies, were aware of the barbarians who were breaking down their walls and preparing to massacre them.

Must we, however, entirely despair of the future of the Latin nations ? I still hope we need not. Necessity is a mighty prince, and is able to change many things. It is possible that, after a series of such profound calamities and upheavals as history has hardly known, the Latin peoples, wiser for experience, and having successfully escaped from the covetousness of the watchful Powers, will attempt the difficult undertaking of acquiring the qualities in which they are now lacking, in order thenceforth to succeed in life. Only one means is in their power : entirely to change their system of education. We cannot too highly praise those few apostles, such as Jules Lemaitre and Bonvalot, that have applied themselves to such a task. And these apostles can perform a great deal ; they succeed in altering public opinion, and public opinion is all-powerful to-day. But it will be no easy task to sweep away the stubborn prejudices of the *universitaires* and the *intellectuels* through which our system of education is maintained in its present state. History shows us that a dozen apostles have often been sufficient to found a religion ; but religions, beliefs, and opinions have failed in propagating themselves for want of being able to reconcile the dozen.

But let us not be too pessimistic. History is so full of unforeseen occurrences, and the world is on the eve of undergoing such profound modifications, that it is impossible to-day to forecast the destinies of the nations. And in any case the duty of the philosopher is performed when he has pointed out to the nations the dangers which threaten them.

BOOK IV

THE CONFLICT BETWEEN ECONOMIC NECESSITIES AND THE ASPIRATIONS OF THE SOCIALISTS

CHAPTER I

THE INDUSTRIAL AND ECONOMIC EVOLUTION OF THE PRESENT AGE

1. *The new factors of Social Evolution which have been created by modern discoveries :*—The present is the age which has seen the greatest changes in the shortest time—Present factors of social evolution—The action of scientific and industrial discoveries—How they have revolutionised all the conditions of existence. 2. *Modern discoveries as affecting the conditions of existence of societies :*—Necessary material changes of life—And the consequent moral and social changes—The effect of machinery on the family, and on the mental evolution of the workers—By reducing distance, machinery has transformed the world into a single market, emancipated from the actions of Governments—Transformations produced to-day by the discoveries of the laboratory in the life of the nations—Possible employment of natural forces in the future—Instability is everywhere succeeding to the stability of centuries—The life of nations and the conditions of their progress are becoming further and further removed from the action of Governments.

1. THE NEW FACTORS OF SOCIAL EVOLUTION WHICH HAVE BEEN CREATED BY MODERN DISCOVERIES.

THE present, perhaps, is the one age in history which has seen the greatest changes in the shortest time. These changes are the consequence of the appearance of factors very different from those which have hitherto dominated society. One of the principal characteristics of the present period is found precisely in the transformation of the determining causes of the evolution of nations. For centuries religious and political factors have exercised a fundamental influence, but to-day this influence has considerably paled. Economic and industrial factors, for a long time very unimportant, are to-day assuming an absolutely preponderating influence. It was a matter of perfect indifference to Cæsar, to Louis Quatorze, to Napoleon, or to any Western sovereign of old, whether China did or did not possess coal. But now the sole fact that she should possess it and utilise it would soon have the most important effect on the progress of European civilisation. Formerly, a Birmingham manufacturer or an English farmer would never have been concerned to know whether India could grow wheat or manufacture cotton. This fact, which for centuries was so insignificant in the eyes of England, must henceforth have for her a far greater importance than an event as significant in appearance as the defeat of the Invincible Armada or the overthrow of Napoleon.

But it is not only the progress of distant nations that has such an important effect on the nations of Europe. The rapid transformations of industry have revolutionised all the conditions of existence. It has justly been remarked that until the beginning of our century the instruments of industry had scarcely changed for thousands of years ; they were, in fact, identical, as regards their essential parts, with the appliances which figure on the interior of Egyptian tombs four thousand years old.[1] But for a hundred years now there has been no comparison possible between the industry of the present and

---

[1] Proof will be afforded by a glance at the plates of my work *Les Premières Civilisations de l'Orient*, in which the industrial implements of ancient Egypt are represented after the sepulchral paintings.

that of the ancient world. Industry has been completely transformed by the utilisation, by means of steam engines, of the solar energy latent in coal. The most modest of manufacturers has in his cellars more than enough coal to execute a far harder task than any the twenty thousand slaves attributed to Crassus could have performed. We have steam-hammers a single blow of which represents the strength of ten thousand men. For the United States alone the power necessary to effect the annual railway traffic, that is to say, the energy extracted from coal, is valued at the equivalent of thirteen million men and fifty-three million horses. Admitting the absurd hypothesis of the possibility of obtaining so many men and animals, the expense of their keep would be £2,200,000,000, instead of the £100,000,000 or so which represent the work executed by mechanical motors.[1]

2. MODERN DISCOVERIES AS AFFECTING THE CONDITIONS OF EXISTENCE OF SOCIETIES.

The mere fact that man has discovered the means to extract from coal the energies which the sun has slowly stored up in it during millions of years has entirely revolutionised the material conditions of life. In creating new resources it has created new needs, and the changes in everyday life have soon brought in their train transformations in the moral and social state of the nations. Having invented machinery, man has become enslaved by it, as he was of old enslaved by the gods created by his imagination. He has had to submit to the economic

[1] M. de Foville has calculated that the transport of one ton French of merchandise per kilometre costs 3 fr. 33 by means of human porters—(a sum which must be increased to 10 fr. in Africa), 0 fr. 87 by beast of burden, 6 centimes by rail in Europe, and 9·5 centimes in America.

laws which it has by itself established. It is machinery which has allowed women and children to enter the factory, and which at the same time has disorganised the family and the home. Whilst making work easy to the worker, and obliging him to specialise himself, it has lessened his intelligence and his power of effort. The artisan of the old state of things has sunk to the rank of common labourer, from which he can only very rarely rise.

The industrial *rôle* of machinery is not limited to the immense multiplication of available power. In transforming the means of transport it has considerably reduced the distances which separate country from country, and has brought nations face to face which were formerly completely separated. In a few weeks, instead of in many months, the West and the East may meet; in a few hours, in a few minutes even, they can exchange thoughts. Thanks to coal again, the products of one country are rapidly distributed among the others, and the whole world has become a vast market emancipated from the actions of Governments. The bloodiest revolutions, the longest wars, have never had results comparable to those of the scientific discoveries of the century—discoveries which portend results even more far-reaching and more fruitful in the future.

It is not only steam and electricity which have transformed the conditions of life for modern humanity. Inventions almost trivial in appearance have contributed, and are incessantly continuing to contribute, to modify these conditions. A simple laboratory experiment completely changes the conditions of prosperity of a province, or even of a country. Thus, for example, the conversion of anthracine into alizarine has killed the madder industry, and at the same stroke has impoverished the departments which lived by it. Lands worth £800

per acre have fallen to less than £40. When the artificial production of alcohol and of sugar have entered
into the regions of practical industry—and the one
has already been effected in the laboratory, while the
other would appear probable shortly—certain countries
will be forced to abandon their sources of wealth, and
reduced to poverty. Beside such catastrophes what were
such events as the Hundred Years' War, the Reformation,
or the Revolution ? We may form some idea of the
far-reaching consequences of such commercial oscillations when we consider what France lost in ten years
by the invasion of a microscopic insect, the phylloxera.
The loss sustained on 2,470,000 acres of vineyards,
from 1877 to 1887, has been reckoned at £280,000,000.
It was almost as great a disaster numerically as the expense of our last war. Spain was temporarily enriched
by this loss, since it was necessary to make up the
deficiency by purchasing wines from her. From an
economic point of view the result was the same as
though we had been conquered by the armies of
Spain, and condemned to pay her an enormous annual
tribute.

We cannot too strongly insist on the importance of
these great industrial oscillations, which are one of the
inevitable conditions of the present age, and which as
yet are only beginning. Their principal result is to
deprive of all fixity those conditions of existence which
of old seemed stable enough to brave the passage of
centuries.

"One may ask oneself," writes the English historian
Maine, "what is the most terrible calamity which
can be conceived as befalling great populations. The
answer might perhaps be—a sanguinary war, a deso-
lating famine, a deadly epidemic disease. Yet none
of these disasters would cause as much and as pro-

longed human suffering as a revolution in fashion under which women should dress, as men practically do, in one material of one colour. There are many flourishing and opulent cities in Europe and America which would be condemned by it to bankruptcy or starvation, and it would be worse there than a famine or pestilence in China, India, or Japan."

The hypothesis has nothing improbable in it, and it is possible that the revolution in female attire caused by the increasingly general use of the bicycle may very soon make it a reality. But the discoveries of science will assuredly produce changes of very different significance. Chemistry, for example, a science which is only beginning to define itself, holds unforeseen things in reserve for us. When we are able to employ with ease temperatures of from 3000 to 4000 Cent., or temperatures neighbouring on the absolute zero, such as we are now beginning to procure, an entire new chemistry will be necessary. Theory tells us already that our "simple bodies" are very probably nothing but the condensations of other elements, of whose properties we are totally ignorant. One day, perhaps, as the chemist Berthelot suggested in a recent speech, science will fabricate all alimentary substances, and then "there will no longer be fields covered with crops, nor vineyards, nor pastures full of cattle. There will no longer be any distinction between fertile and sterile regions."

We can further imagine a future in which the forces of nature will be at the disposition of all our requirements, and will almost entirely replace human labour. There is no longer anything chimerical in supposing that, thanks to electricity, that marvellous agent for the transformation and transport of energy, the power of the winds, the seas, and waterfalls will presently be at the disposal of man. The falls of Niagara, which are already partially utilised, possess a motive power of 17,000,000 horse power, and the time is not distant when this energy, whose employment has scarcely been commenced, will be transported to a distance by means of cable conductors. The heat of the sun and the central heat of the earth are also inexhaustible sources of energy.

But without insisting on the discoveries of the future, and confining ourselves solely to the progress of the last fifty years, we see that our conditions of existence are changing every day, and are changing in such a precipitate fashion that society is called upon to undergo transformations far more rapid than are proper to the mental state created by the long and gradual inheritance of the units composing it. Instability is everywhere succeeding to the stability of centuries.

From the foregoing it results that the present age is at once a destructive and a creative age. It seems as though none of our past ideas, none of our past conditions of life, could survive in the face of the changes determined by science and industry. The difficulty of adapting ourselves to these new necessities consists above all in this : that our habits and our sentiments change slowly, while external circumstances change too quickly and too radically to allow the old conceptions to which we would fain hold to continue for any length of time. No one can say what social state will be born of these unforeseen destructions and creations. But this we see very clearly : that those phenomena which are most important to the life of States, and the very condition of their progress, are more and more subtracted from their will, and are ruled by economic and industrial necessities over which they are powerless. And one thing that we already foresee, and that will appear still more clearly in the following pages, is the fact that the claims of the Socialists will appear more and more contrary to the economic evolution which is preparing itself without them, and far beyond their reach. They will none the less have to comply with it, as with all those natural fatalities to whose laws man has hitherto been subject.

CHAPTER II

THE ECONOMIC STRUGGLES BETWEEN THE EAST AND THE WEST

1. *Economic competition* :—The Socialists ignore the necessities which dominate the modern world—The will of Governments is more and more subject to the exterior economic conditions to which they are obliged to adapt themselves—The world of industrial and economic relations forms nowadays one single world, and the different countries are becoming less and less able to do as they please—Nations tend more and more to be ruled by external necessities, and not by their individual desires—Consequences of the reduction of distances between the East and the West—Results of the economic struggle between nations having very large requirements and those having very small requirements—The value of merchandise on the market is determined by its value on the market in which it can be produced at the least cost—Result of the competition between European goods and the same goods manufactured by the Orientals—Why England is gradually being obliged to give up agriculture—Competition between India and Japan—Future of European commerce—Future of Russia— Eastern competition and Socialism. 2. *Remedies* :—Objections raised by economists with regard to the consequences of the struggle between East and West—Pretended excessive production—Why the arguments of the economists can have no value except for the future —Protectionism—Its artificial and makeshift character—The agricultural nations and the industrial nations—Various remedies sought by the Anglo-Saxons for the competition with the East—Why they are turning to Africa—Difficulties encountered by the Latin nations in the domain of industrial and economic competition.

1. ECONOMIC COMPETITION.

I HAVE just briefly indicated that the economic and industrial evolution of the world has overturned the old conditions of human existence. This fact will appear more clearly when we come to consider some of the problems which present themselves to-day.

In the setting forth of their claims and their dreams
the Socialists have manifested a complete ignorance of
the necessities which dominate the modern world.
They always reason as though the universe were limited
to the country in which they live, as though all that
passed in the rest of the world could have no influence
on the circles in which they propagate their doctrines,
as though the measures they propose would not completely upset the relations of the nation which should
apply them with all the other nations of the world. It
would have been quite possible for a nation thus to
isolate itself a few centuries ago, but to-day matters are
no longer the same. The *rôle* of the governors of each
nation is tending more and more to being conditioned
by economic phenomena of very remote origin, absolutely independent of the doings of statesmen, and to
which they must submit. The art of government consists to-day in adapting oneself as well as may be to
external necessities which our desires are powerless to
affect.

A country, to be sure, is always a country, but the
world of science, industry, and economic relations
nowadays forms one single world, whose laws are the
more rigorous in that they are imposed by necessities,
and not by codes. In the region of industry and
economics no country is to-day free to do as it pleases,
simply because the evolution of industry, agriculture and
commerce have far-reaching effects in all the nations.
Economic and industrial events in distant parts of the
earth may force the nation which is most completely
removed from those parts to transform its agriculture,
its industrial processes, its methods of manufacture, its
commercial customs, and consequently its institutions
and its laws. Nations tend more and more to be ruled
by widespread necessities, and not by individual desires.

The action of Governments is therefore tending to become more and more feeble and uncertain. This is one of the most characteristic phenomena of the present age.

The problem which we are about to consider in this chapter will afford an excellent illustration of the preceding remarks. It will show us once again how superficial and impossible of realisation are the formulæ for universal happiness proposed by the Socialists.

This problem, which I was one of the first to point out at a time already distant, is that of the commercial struggle between the East and the West. The reduction of distances by means of steam and the evolution of industry have resulted in bringing the Orient to our doors, and in transforming its inhabitants into competitors with the West. These competitors, to whom we formerly exported our products, began to make them themselves as soon as they possessed our machines, and instead of buying them of us they now want to sell them to us. They will succeed in so doing all the more readily in that their needs, by long-continued custom, are almost negligible, so that the cost of production is far less than in Europe. The average Oriental workman can live on twopence or threepence a day, while the European workman cannot live on less than three or four shillings a day. As the price of labour always regulates the price of manufactures, and as the value of the latter in any market whatever is determined by their value in which they can be delivered at the lowest price, it follows that our European manufacturers are seeing all their industries threatened by rivals producing the same goods at a twentieth of the cost. India and Japan have already entered on the phase which I long ago predicted, and are progressing rapidly; China will soon be a third competitor. The imports of foreign-made goods into Europe are gradually increasing, and the exports of European-made goods are decreasing. It is not the military invasion of the Orientals that we have to fear, as has been suggested, but that of their products.

For a long time this competition has been confined to the sphere of agricultural produce, and from its results we can judge what will happen when it extends to manufactured articles.

The first results of this competition have been, as M. Méline has recently observed in the Chamber of Deputies, to lower by one-half in twenty years the value of agricultural products—cereals, wool, wines, alcohol, sugar, and so forth. Wool, for example, which in 1882 was worth about ninepence per pound, is worth only half that sum to-day. Tallow has fallen from 36s. to 16s.

Many economists, and myself amongst the number, consider these reductions in price to be advantageous, since the public, that is to say, the greater number, finally profit by them ; but it is easy to realise that there are points of view from which these reductions may be regarded as harmful. The gravest inconvenience resulting therefrom is that of placing agriculture in a precarious condition, so that some countries might be obliged to abandon it, a state of things that at certain moments might have serious consequences.

The hypothesis that some countries may be forced to renounce agriculture is by no means chimerical, for it is being gradually realised in England. Having to compete with both India and America in the matter of cereals, she has gradually given up producing them, and this in spite of the perfection of the English methods, which allow of crops of 30 bushels to the acre. To-day the annual production of corn in England has fallen to 63,000,000 bushels, while the annual consumption is 193,000,000 bushels. England is therefore obliged to buy 130,000,000 abroad. If she were imprisoned in her island, or if she had not the necessary means to procure this surplus, a great part of her inhabitants would be condemned to die of famine.

France, essentially an agricultural country, has been able to prolong the struggle, thanks to protection, a sufficiently temporary and fictitious means. Her interest in the struggle is vital ; but how much longer will she be able to hold out ? She produces annually 275 millions of bushels, a figure which may fall in a bad year to 200, or rise in a good year to 370 millions. Wheat is to-day worth about 7s. 6d. per cwt., and has been steadily falling in price for several years. This price, however, is artificial, since foreign corn is subject to a protective duty of nearly 3s., its actual value being 4s. 6d., the sale price on the foreign markets, in London, for instance, or New York. This price must infallibly suffer a further fall. In the Argentine Republic Italian cultivators are able to produce wheat at 1s. 10d. per bushel.

Will it be possible much longer to correct this progressive fall by equally progressive protective duties, intended to maintain artificially the dearness of a staple food, and consequently to prevent the people from benefiting by the universal cheapness ? As the annual consumption of wheat in France is 120 millions of hectolitres, the present tariff of 7 frs. per hectolitre, which raises the price of bread by at least a third, represents an annual sum of £33,600,000 levied on the whole populace for the benefit of a few large landowners, for the majority of farmers produce only sufficient for their own needs, and have none to sell. All that can be said in favour of such arbitrary proceedings is that they possess a provisional value in the matter of prolonging the existence of agriculture in a country, or allowing it time enough to ameliorate its condition. But soon no Government will be powerful enough to maintain artificially the dearness of a staple of life.

But the East had hardly entered the lists when the decadence of European agriculture began. The origin of this decadence is to be found in the production of cereals in America, where land costs next to nothing, while in Europe it is extremely dear. When America in her turn found herself in competition with countries such as India, where not only does the land cost nothing, as in the United States, but where labour is ten times as cheap, she suffered the same fate as England, and her agriculture is to-day threatened with complete ruin. The agriculturalists of America find themselves to-day in the most precarious situation. M. de Mandat-Grancy makes mention of farms which were formerly worth $300 an acre which to-day cannot find purchasers at $10. No protective tariff can remedy this state of things, since the Americans are concerned in exporting not in buying cereals. No protective tariff can prevent them from finding themselves in competition on the foreign markets with countries which can produce wheat at far lower prices.

Limited at first to raw materials and agricultural products, the struggle between East and West has gradually extended itself to industrial products. In the Farther East, in Japan and India, for example, the wages of factory hands are rarely more than twopence-halfpenny per diem, and their foremen do not receive very much more.

M. de Mandat-Grancy mentions a factory near Calcutta employing more than 1,500 hands, of which the native sub-manager receives a salary of rather less than £10 per annum. With the price of production so low as this it is not surprising that the Indian exports have increased in ten years from £28,500,000 to more than £160,000,000.

But India possesses but little coal, while Japan possesses it in such quantity that she is able to export it at half the price of English coal. The progress of this country has consequently been even more rapid than that of India. Possessing coal, that greatest of the sources of national wealth, she had only to buy and imitate European machines in order to find herself on a perfect footing of equality with Europe as regards productive capacity, and on a greatly superior footing as regards economy of production, on account of the low rate of wages.

To-day Japan has large factories : cotton factories, for example, employing 6,000 workers,[1] and so prosperous that they are able to pay dividends of from 10 per cent. to 20 per cent., while the dividends of equivalent concerns in England are every day growing less, and have fallen to 3 per cent. for the most prosperous. Others are failing, and no longer declare dividends, simply because their exports are every day diminishing on account of Oriental competition.

The Orientals have begun to manufacture, one by one, all European products, and always at such low prices as to render competition useless. Watches, clocks, pottery, paper, perfumery, and even so-called Paris-made goods, are now being made in Japan. European articles are thus being gradually driven from the East. There are some manufactures, matches, for instance, which the English formerly exported at the rate of £24,000 per annum, a sale that has fallen to £400, while the Japanese

[1] The factory of Kanegafuchi in Japan employs nearly 6,000 hands, working night and day in twelve-hour shifts. The wages are about fivepence a day, and are paid in silver, the market price of which is, as we know, half that of gold. The following figures are taken from the statistical report on the Japanese Empire, published in 1897 at Tokio by Mr. Hanabusa, chief of the Statistical Department ; they are the average wages of different classes of workmen :—Agricultural labourers, 1s. 7d. per week ; printers, 7s. per week ; carpenters, 8s. 9d.

production of this article has risen from nothing to a sum which in 1895 amounted to £91,000. In Geio the Japanese exports in umbrellas amounted to £28 ; five years later it had risen to £52,000, and it is the same with every article they have begun to manufacture.

This wealth of production soon led the Japanese to extend their markets, and in order to avoid dependence on the navies of Europe they first began to purchase vessels and then to build them for themselves. They have great liners, built on the latest models, and lit with electric light. One single company, the Nippon Yusen Kaisha, possesses 47, which compete with our Messageries Maritimes, and especially with the Peninsular and Oriental Company. They have established a bi-monthly service between Japan and Bombay, another with Australia, and are preparing to establish one to France and England. The crews of these vessels are paid at the rate of 8s. 4d. per month, and are fed on a few bags of rice.

Although the Chinese, despite their military inferiority, are from many points of view greatly superior to the Japanese, they have not yet entered the industrial movement, but we can see the time approaching when they will do so. We can foresee also that with her immense and frugal population, her colossal coal deposits, she will in a few years be the first commercial centre of the world, and the ruler of all markets, and that the Bourse of Pekin will determine the prices of merchandise in the rest of the world. We may already form some idea of the power of Chinese competition when we consider the fact that the Americans, recognising the impossibility of struggling against them, have been obliged, as their only resource, to expel the Chinese from their territory by force. The hour is not far distant when a cargo of European merchandise will be a rarity on the Eastern seas. What is to be done ?

Nearly all the English and German consuls in the Far East are unanimous in their reports on this question. Even our own agents, despite the little interest they take in commerce—above all, despite the incurable incapacity of the Latin mind to form an independent conception of foreign affairs—are beginning to perceive and to point out what is going on around them.

In this ever-increasing economic struggle everything is in the favour of the East. The depreciation in value of silver in the West has made competition still more difficult for us. Silver, the only currency in the East, has there retained its full value, while in Europe its value has decreased by almost a half. When a Hindoo, Japanese, or Chinese merchant sends to Europe £100 worth of wheat, cotton, or any other merchandise, he receives £100 in gold, which he can exchange for nearly £200 worth of silver, which he then has only to turn into silver money, with which he pays his workmen. These £200 in silver have in his country the same value that they had twenty-five years ago, for the depreciation of silver in Europe has had no parallel in the East, where, moreover, the cost of labour has everywhere remained the same. As the cost of manufacture is no higher than it formerly was, the Oriental manufacturer, merely by selling an article in Europe, disposes of it at double its cost price. Of course he also has to pay double for anything he may buy of us, since he must pay £200 of silver for £100 of gold, so that he has every incentive to sell us more and more and to buy from us less and less. The present rate of exchange accordingly offers the East an immense premium on exportation. No protective tariff short of one absolutely prohibitive can contend with such differences in the cost of production.

Accordingly, European commerce would appear fatally destined to being reduced, in the near future, to the exchange of merchandise costing twenty times as much as it costs in the East, and paid for in gold, against products costing one-twentieth as much and paid for in silver. As no exchange can continue for long under such conditions, and is lingering on awhile merely because the East has not yet completed the organisation of its industrial machinery, it is plainly evident that Europe is fated shortly to lose her *clientèle* in the Far East as she has already lost it in America. Not only will she lose it, but she will very soon be condemned—being unable to produce enough to nourish her inhabitants—to buy of her old clients without being able to sell them anything. The Japanese have no illusions as to this state of things. One of their ministers of foreign affairs, Mr. Okuna, speaking of Europe in a recently published speech, expressed himself in these words : " She exhibits symptoms of decrepitude. The coming century will see her constitutions in fragments and her empires in ruins."

I believe Japan will be ruined long before Europe, for the simple reason that she has superimposed, on her own civilisation, and without being able to fuse the two, another civilisation which has nothing in common with her past, and which will presently lead her into the completest anarchy. But China, by far the superior of Japan in many respects, and notably in the matter of commercial honesty, is destined to have a powerful future. These small-skulled Asiatics, who can effect nothing but servile copies of our inventions, are doubtless barbarians, but history shows that the mightiest empires have always been brought low by barbarians.

Many causes will arise to complicate, for the greater number of the European nations, the difficulties of the commercial struggle with the East. When the Trans-Siberian railway is finished all the commerce between the

East and the West will tend to concentrate itself in the hands of Russia. As we know, this railway will cross part of China and unite Russia with Japan. The 130 millions of Russia will then be in contact with the 400 millions of China, and Russia will become the first commercial power of the world, since the transit between the East and the West will necessarily be in her hands. From London to Hong-Kong is about thirty-six days by sea. By the Trans-Siberian railway it will be about eighteen. The sea-route will doubtless then be as completely abandoned as the Cape route is to-day, and what then will be the use of England's commercial fleets ? France will lose what little trade remains to her. In that day she will perhaps regret the £400,000,000 lent to Russia, a large portion of which will have gone to the making of this disastrous competition. In 1887 we had £80,000,000 in Russian securities : ten years later the amount reached £400,000,000. It is not unreasonable to ask whether we should not have gained much more by devoting this enormous sum to the development of our own industries and our commerce.[1]

[1] When the Trans-Siberian railway, whose importance none of our statesmen seem to understand, is terminated, Russia will be the mistress of China and her 400,000,000 inhabitants ; and as she maintains a system of absolute protectionism, against both her allies and other nations, the East will be closed to Europe. India, and even Siam, for alliances count for nothing in the face of political interests, will infallibly be absorbed into this gigantic empire, which will then be the greatest power in the world. The ports and concessions recently obtained in Manchuria, which contains 120 millions of inhabitants, render Russia the sovereign mistress of this province, from which she will be able to recruit innumerable armies. The Chinese Imperial Court is to-day reduced to seeking another capital, in order to preserve some remnants of independence.

A circumstance which no one could have foreseen, the conquest of the Philippines by the United States, is the only thing that may retard or prevent the absorption of the East by Russia, an absorption which would be ruinous to the West, and which would mark the end of the progress of liberal ideas in Europe. The conquest of the Philippines, so near as they are to China, brings the United States

The struggle between the East and West whose development I have just denoted is only at its commencement, and we can but suspect the issue. The dreamers of perpetual peace, of universal disarmament, imagine wars to be the most disastrous of struggles. They certainly do destroy a large number of individuals, but it appears highly probable that the industrial and commercial struggles which are approaching will be far more murderous and will accumulate more ruin and disaster than ever did the bloodiest wars. Such struggles, so peaceful in appearance, are in reality implacable. Pity is unknown to them; to conquer or to disappear are the only alternatives.

Socialism scarcely glances at such problems. Its conceptions are too narrow, its horizon too limited. Those nations in which it has most firmly taken root will be those for which the commercial struggle with the East will be hardest, and the defeat of the vanquished most rapid. Only those nations which possess a sufficient degree of initiative in industrial matters, sufficient intelligence to perfect their machinery, and to adapt it to new necessities, will be able to defend themselves. It is not Collectivism, with its ideal of slavish equality in work and wages, that will be able to furnish our workers with the means to struggle against the invasion of Eastern produce. Where will it find the money to pay its workers when their wares find no more purchasers, when all the factories

into the midst of the Chinese question, which Spain was too insignificant to affect. The influence of the United States and England will perhaps re-establish the equilibrium of affairs, which has been tending more and more in one direction. We are certainly on the eve of a gigantic struggle, the struggle for the partition of the East, which will undoubtedly fill the coming century. The disarmament which is proposed to us, I imagine not without irony, does not appear to be a thing of the immediate future. Those nations that accepted it would, no doubt, make a few economies, but at the cost of losing their lives, and that very quickly.

have one by one been closed, and when all the capitalists
have departed for countries in which they meet with
hearty welcome and easily earned dividends, in the place
of incessant persecutions ?

2. THE REMEDIES.

I have just shown how the economic competition
between East and West arose and has developed. The
facts I have cited show in what manner the economic
necessities of the present time are contrary to the aspirations of the Socialists, and how ill the latter have chosen
the time for presenting their claims. Now, in examining
the possible remedies for the economic competition which
we see growing before our eyes, we shall once again
discover how incompatible is victory in the struggle with
the Socialist ideal.

I must observe, first of all, that it is easy to attack in
theory the pessimistic conclusions I have drawn from
this state of things. The economists will tell you, with
reason, that hitherto there has never been such a thing as
actual over-production of any article ; that the slightest
excess of production is perforce accompanied by a fall in
price ; and that if as a consequence of competition the
European workman is obliged to content himself with a
salary of a few pence a day, the smallness of his wages
will be without inconvenience when for these pence
he is able to obtain all the articles for which he had
formerly to pay several shillings. The argument is perfectly just, but it is hardly applicable to any but a remote
period, a period, therefore, that does not interest us to-day.
Before this phase of the universal abatement of the value
of things there will elapse a long transitional period
of disorder. This period will be all the more difficult to
live through in that the conflict between East and West
is not merely a struggle between men earning different

wages, but also, and above all, a struggle between men whose needs are different. This is the factor which made competition with the Chinese impossible to the Americans, who were obliged to expel them. The equality of chances could be established only by the Chinese establishing themselves in America and acquiring the tastes and rates of expenditure of the Americans. But they were subject to influences too deeply ancestral to change themselves to that extent. With no further needs beyond a cup of tea and a handful of rice, they were able to content themselves with salaries far inferior to those demanded by American workers.

Whatever the future may be, it is the present that concerns us, and the solutions we have to seek are present solutions ; so that the remedy that the economists await —the remedy of the spontaneous evolution of things—is for the time being worthless. As for the system of protection, it constitutes a provisional solution, and one of easy application, and accordingly we see the nations of Europe and America adopting it one by one. A small and sparsely populated country may, theoretically, surround itself with a high wall, and refrain from troubling itself about what is passing elsewhere ; but where are such countries to be found in the West ? According to all statistics, there is hardly a country in all Europe, on account of the excessive increase of population, which could produce enough to feed its inhabitants for more than six months. Supposing that a country did surround itself with the wall of which I have spoken, at the end of six months it would be obliged, under pain of perishing of hunger, to break through the wall and go forth to buy food ; but with what would it pay for the corn and other produce it required ? Hitherto Europe has acquired the products of the East by means of merchandise ; but very soon the East will have no more need of our mer-

chandise.   For commerce is based on exchange, of which
money is only the conventional symbol.

Apart, then, from scientific discoveries, which are
certainly possible, the future of Europe, and especially
of those countries which live principally by their commerce, would appear to be sufficiently gloomy.

In the coming struggle two categories of nations alone
would seem to be fitted to resist.   First, those nations
whose agriculture is so well developed, and whose
populations are so small, that they are able to suffice
for themselves and almost completely to abandon outside
commerce.   Secondly, those nations whose initiative,
power of will, and industrial capacities are highly
superior to those of the Orientals.

Few European nations to-day find themselves in the
former category ; of those few France, happily for herself,
is one of the foremost.   She produces almost enough to
support her populace, and it is by a very sure instinct
that she takes care not to increase her population, and
disdains the lamentations of the statisticians on that point.
She would only have to increase her agricultural returns
or reduce her population a little in order to produce
enough for her subsistence.   Far from concerning ourselves with industry, in which we are bad, or with commerce, in which we are incapable, it is towards agriculture
that we should direct all our efforts.[1]

The English and the Americans belong to the second
of the categories I have indicated.   But only by means of

[1] From every point of view our agriculture should be developed.
At an agricultural conference held in Lyons a few years ago M. de
la Roque pointed out that the mortality in the provinces is under
20 per thousand, and is more than 27 per thousand in the towns,
and concluded that by the mere fact of emigration into the towns
France had lost 700,000 inhabitants.   "If our crops of wheat or wine
were to fail, the provinces would lose no less than eight to ten
million inhabitants."   This is an interesting example of the far-
reaching effects of economic facts.

extreme activity and constant improvement of machinery will they be able to maintain their superiority. It will be a conflict of superior capacity against mediocre and inferior capacity. It is thus that the Americans have been able, by immense efforts, gradually to decrease the prices of production by means of machinery, despite the high prices of labour. We find in the United States blast-furnaces of which a single one can run 1,000 tons French of metal per day, while ours can found at most 100 or 200 tons; steel works which roll 1,500 tons per day, while ours turn out 150 in the same time; machines which can load 1,000 tons per hour on rail; others which lade a vessel of 4,000 tons in a few hours, and so forth.

To keep on this footing qualities of initiative and capacities are requisite that few nations to-day possess, and which are the most precious of all inheritances, although so antipathetic to the Socialists. With such qualities no difficulties are too great to be surmounted.

If all these efforts do not avail the Anglo-Saxons they will find other remedies; and they have already sought them. Several manufacturers have succeeded in competing with the Orientals on their own ground, by founding factories in the East and employing native workmen. English manufacturers who could only carry on business at a loss in England have settled in India and entered into competition with English manufactures. But this emigration of capital and capacities, if it were to become general, would leave the English workman inevitably without work, and could scarcely have any other result than to point out to the capitalists the road that the claims of the Socialists may one day force them to take. We may well ask ourselves what would become of a State thus deprived of all its capital and all its best brains, and composed entirely of mediocrities in talent and fortune. Then would Socialism be able to develop itself freely, and to impose its iron slavery.

But the English statesmen are seeking other means to avoid the dangers they see approaching. Knowing that the East must soon be closed to their shipping, they are now turning to Africa, and we have seen how England and Germany have in a few years taken possession of the whole continent, leaving the Latin nations only a few strips of worthless territory. The empire which the English have made for themselves, which reaches from Alexandria to the Cape, comprising nearly half of Africa, will very soon be covered with railways and telegraphs, and in a few years will undoubtedly form one of the wealthiest regions of the world.

The hereditary aptitudes of the Latin peoples, their social organisation, and their system of education, forbid them all such ambitious designs. Their aptitudes are in the directions of agriculture and the arts. They succeed very indifferently in industry, in foreign trade, and above all in colonisation, even when their colonies are at their very doors, as Algeria. It is a fact to be regretted, certainly, but not to be denied, and the knowledge of it is at least useful so far as it helps to make us understand in what direction our efforts should or should not be directed.

For the rest, the Latin nations need not, perhaps, too greatly regret that they will not be able to play a very active part in the industrial and economic struggle which appears destined, in the near future, to displace the poles of civilisation. This struggle, painful enough for energetic natures, will be absolutely impossible for others. The work of simple labourers is always hard and ill-paid. Contrary to the dreams of the Socialists, the future will show it still harder and still worse paid. It seems as though our civilisations can prolong themselves only by means of harder and harder servitude on the part of the mass of workers.   Industry and machinery must grow more and more oppressive.   Only at the cost of labour every day more painful, at the cost of a terrible over-pressure that will necessitate veritable hecatombs of human lives, will the industrial and commercial nations of Europe be able without too great hazard of failure to encounter the peoples of the East on economic grounds.   In every case there will be a war far more atrocious, murderous, and desperate than the military slaughters of old, for no illusion, no hope, will hover over it.   The beacon-lights of the old consoling faiths are flickering, and will soon be extinct for ever.   Man, who fought of old for his hearth, his country, or his gods, seems condemned to have no ideal in the struggle of the near future but that of eating his fill, or at least not to die of hunger.

CHAPTER III

THE ECONOMIC STRUGGLES BETWEEN THE WESTERN PEOPLES.

1. *The results of hereditary aptitudes in a nation :*—The variety of the aptitudes which have helped the progress of nations at various periods of civilisation—The qualities which for a long time ensured the supremacy of the Latins—The greater part of these qualities are now without outlet—In the present phase of the evolution of the world industrial and commercial aptitudes take a front rank—Why the slight industrial and commercial capacities of the Latins were sufficient formerly, but are not sufficient now. 2. *The industrial and commercial situation of the Latin peoples :*—The results revealed by statistics—The indications given by our foreign consuls—Characteristic facts revealing the decadence of our industry and commerce—The apathy, indifference, horror of effort, and lack of initiative of our commercial men—Various examples—The invasion of the French market by German goods—The decadent state of our shipping—Our commercial relations with our colonies are established by strangers—The cost of our colonies, and what they bring us—The steady abatement of the quality of our products. 3. *Causes of the industrial and commercial superiority of the Germans :*—Slight influence of their military superiority over their industrial and commercial success—Technical instruction of the Germans—Their skill in taking the tastes of their customers into account—How they inform themselves of the requirements of their customers in various countries—Their sentiments of solidarity and association—The elements of their information.

1. THE RESULTS OF HEREDITARY APTITUDES IN A NATION.

I HAVE just shown how the economic necessities created by new circumstances have given rise to the very formidable competition of the peoples of the East, who from being consumers have become producers.

Gradually expelled from the Eastern markets, the peoples of the West are reduced to quarrelling over the European markets which remain open to them. What are the qualities which will make for success in the struggles which every day become more severe ? Will Socialism give any advantage ? This we now propose to consider.

The aptitudes which have determined the superiority of races have not been the same in all periods of history. It is largely because a nation possesses certain aptitudes, but cannot possess all, that we see, in the course of the centuries, so many nations pass through all the stages of greatness and decadence, according as the conditions of the period render their characteristic qualities detrimental or valuable.

For a long time the progress of civilisation demanded certain special qualities : courage, a warlike spirit, a fine language, literary and artistic tastes, which the Latin nations possess in a high degree, and in consequence of which they were long at the head of civilisation. To-day these qualities have far less value than of old, and it would even seem that some of them will soon have no more scope. Industrial and commercial aptitudes, which were formerly of secondary importance, are taking the first rank with the present phase of the world's evolution. It follows that the industrial and commercial nations are coming to the front. The centres of civilisation are about to be changed.

The consequences of these facts are very important. As a nation is incapable of changing its aptitudes, it must strive thoroughly to realise what they are, so as to utilise them in the best possible manner, and not to undertake futile struggles in regions where failure awaits them. A man who might make an excellent musician, a brilliant artist, will make a sorry man of business, a very incapable manufacturer. For nations, as for individuals, the first condition of success in life is to know clearly of what one is capable, and to undertake no task too great for one's means.

Now the Latin nations, as the result of the hereditary conceptions of which I have pointed out the origin, possess only in a very small degree the aptitudes for commerce, industry, and colonisation which are to-day so necessary. They are warriors, tillers of the land, artists, inventors ; they are not manufacturers, business men, nor, above all, colonists.

Slight though the commercial, industrial, and colonising abilities of the Latin races may be, they were, nevertheless, sufficient at a time when there was little or no competition between the nations. To-day they are not sufficient. People are always speaking of the industrial and commercial decadence of our race. The assertion is not absolutely exact, since our industry and our commerce are far superior to what they were fifty years ago. One ought to say insufficient progress, not decadence. But the word *decadence* is perfectly just if we understand by that expression that the Latin nations, progressing far less rapidly than their rivals, will soon infallibly be supplanted by them.

The symptoms of this falling behind are clearly to be seen in all the Latin peoples, which proves that we are considering a racial phenomenon. Spain seems to have reached the last limit of this increasing inferiority, and it would seem that Italy must soon keep her company. France is still struggling, but the signs of her failure are becoming clearer every day.

2. THE INDUSTRIAL AND COMMERCIAL SITUATION OF THE LATIN PEOPLES.

In the following investigation we shall concern ourselves only with France ; for the other Latin peoples we have only to repeat, with greater emphasis, that which applies to France. She is the least extinct of the Latin nations, but none the less her commercial and industrial situation is very far indeed from brilliant.

The facts which demonstrate our commercial and industrial weakness are to-day too evident to be contested. All the reports of our consuls or deputies who have been charged with the investigation of the question are unanimous, and repeat one another in almost the same words.

This is how M. d'Estournelles expresses himself in a recent publication :—

"M. Charles Roux has given us a *résumé* of all the regrettable things observed in an already long experience, in a report on the decadence of our commerce. He might have written the same things of our navy or of our colonies. France compromises or neglects her resources through apathy, routine, and attachment to rules of thumb, of which a great number date from Colbert or Richelieu. Like all victims of apathy, she is energetic by fits and starts, and becomes heroic ; but she also has fits of madness, of sentimental reform, undertaken without forethought, and often worse than the evil they are destined to cure. When, for instance, she ceases to exploit her colonies, it is to assimilate them to the mother country from one day to the next, to make French departments of them, and to ruin them. Or she will suddenly decide, without a shadow of motive, and in spite of the natural and insurmountable difficulties in the way, that all the native Jews of Algeria shall be French electors, and consequently masters of the Arab population, and of our colonists themselves. Or, again, thanks to our ignorance, she will ingenuously organise in the colonies a parody, a caricature of universal suffrage ; gives the right of voting on our Budget, and on matters of peace and war, to the representatives of natives, Indian or Senegalese, who do not pay our taxes, do not serve in our army, and do not speak our language."

M. Depasse, in a judicious article, gives the causes of this state of things, which are almost identical with those I have already indicated :—

" France was not born a commercial nation ; she is an artist, a warrior, a revolutionary. It is her glory that she has an ideal raised far above the practical details of commerce, but as wars and revolutions are less and less in fashion she becomes less and less able to respond to the ideal of modern nations, and art itself is suffering profound modifications, since it has to address itself to mobs, and not only to an *élite*.

"All that for centuries has made the superiority of France has lost its value ; another civilisation is preparing itself, which will, we may be sure, have its own splendours ; but France would seem all the less disposed to enter into it with all her heart and all her genius, in that she has shone with a greater splendour and received more advantages and profit in the old civilisation of which she was the mistress. France is far advanced in the matter of political liberties; but politics also have lost their value ; she is falling back into the second rank in the estimation of the world and the requirements of the nations. France is lettered and eloquent ; it has been her character for two thousand years. But the eloquence of words is being supplanted by the eloquence of figures. Thus on every hand this phenomenon is presented for our consideration ; everything, or almost everything, that for long centuries made the power, originality, grace, and wealth of France, has lost its value in the world, and seems to have been cast out of the current of the order of things which is bearing modern humanity forward.

This is perhaps a fact not unworthy of the attention of politicians."

"The German peril!" writes M. Schwob, "well, that is just true ; but let us say also the British peril, the Australian peril, the American peril, and even the Russian peril and the Chinese peril. On the battlefield of modern industry and commerce there is neither peace nor alliance. Treaties are passed that are called commercial treaties, but these treaties themselves have for their object war without limit, without pity, more implacable than war at the cannon's mouth, and all the more perilous in that it victimises its millions without noise and without smoke.

"Thus our political alliance with Russia, and our reciprocal and unalterable friendship, do not prohibit commercial conventions which are, for the moment, entirely to the advantage of Germany, and to our hurt. In the regions of economics, in the present state of Europe and the world, there is no such thing as friendship. A heartless war is being waged on every side."

Our consuls, who witness abroad the steady and rapid decline of our commerce, make the same complaints, despite the reserve imposed on them by their official position. All give the same warnings, which, however, are quite futile. They reproach our manufacturers and commercial men for their apathy, their carelessness, their lack of initiative, their helplessness in changing old processes for new, and in adapting the formalities of every kind with which they surround the slightest actions to the new requirements of their customers ; in a word, they reproach them with their want of commercial intelligence.

Innumerable examples could be given. I will confine myself to the following, since they are highly typical :—

"Our manufacturers, and even the largest of them,"

writes the correspondent of the *Temps* in the Transvaal, " are distrustful busybodies, unwilling to exert themselves, and cheerfully exchanging a lengthy correspondence on matters that their English or German competitors would settle in a few days.

" The English and German engineers have on the spot the current prices, in fullest detail, of every sort of machinery used in the mining industry, and when a tender or an estimate is invited they are able to deliver it within the short limit of five or seven days which is usually allowed. Our French engineers, who have not the same data, thanks to the inertia of their employers, have to abstain from competing, as the six weeks necessary for a messenger to reach and return from France render it impossible. . . . The English and Germans have complied with the demands which were made of them."

There are many analogous facts.

" A year ago," we read in the *Journal*, " a merchant of South America wished to export some American lambskins to France and Germany. He was put in communication, for this purpose, thanks to the officious care of our consul and our minister of commerce, with one of our commission agents. The American merchant then despatched a consignment of twenty thousand skins to the French house, and, simultaneously, an equal consignment to a German house in Hamburg, with whom he had an understanding. A year went by ; the two houses sent in the accounts of the sales. The French house had experienced so many difficulties in selling the merchandise, and was obliged to consent to such low prices, that the operation resulted in a loss of 10 per cent. on the part of the exporter. The German house, more active and more competent, had realised on the same goods a profit of 12 per cent. And the characteristic part of the affair is this : *that it was in France precisely that it was able to place the goods.* All commentary would be superfluous."

I have often been able to verify for myself the profound apathy, the horror of effort, and all the rest of the faults denoted by our foreign consuls. These faults, which are every day becoming more accentuated, appear still more striking when, after an interval of ten years, one renews acquaintance with the representatives of a formerly prosperous or semi-prosperous industry.

When I resumed some laboratory experiments with regard to invisible light rays, which I had put aside for several years, I was struck with the deep-rooted decadence both of the *personnel* and the plant of our manufacturers, a decadence of which I had nevertheless been informed from several quarters, and which, moreover, I had predicted in a chapter of my book *Man and Society,* published eighteen years ago. In one week several different firms refused to sell me certain instruments, representing a total value of more than £20, simply because the delivery would have caused a very slight inconvenience to the vendors. In the first case I had ordered an electric lamp. Before buying it I wrote to the maker to ask him if he would first let me see it working. As I did not even obtain a reply, I got one of his friends to inquire the reason of his silence. " It would be too much bother to sell under such conditions," he was told. In the second case I wanted a water-level to be fixed to a metallic part of a large apparatus. The dealer, although the director of one of the largest manufacturing photographic concerns in Paris, had not a single workman capable of executing the job. Thirdly, I wanted two supplementary contacts fitted to a galvanometer, a task which might require half an hour. The maker had the necessary workmen at hand: "but," he told me, "my partner would be displeased if I were to upset the staff for an order amounting to less than £8."

Not such are the methods of the German manufacturers. A short time after the preceding inconveniences, I was in need of a little laminated cobalt, which is not a particularly rare metal. I wrote to the principal manufacturing chemists in Paris. As the order was not an important one they did not even take the trouble to reply. One firm alone wrote to tell me that they could perhaps let me have the cobalt in the course of a few weeks. Having waited for three months, and being in urgent need of the metal, I wrote to a firm in Berlin. Although this time the order was only of a few francs, I received a reply by return of post, and the cobalt, worked up into the required dimensions, was delivered at the end of a week.

It is always the same with German firms. The most insignificant order is received with respect, and all modifications demanded by the purchaser are rapidly executed. The consequence is that German firms are springing up in Paris every day, and the public is obliged to have recourse to them, despite its patriotic reluctance. You go to one for an insignificant purchase, and soon you go nowhere else. I could mention several large official scientific establishments, which, on account of inconveniences such as I myself have experienced, have come to placing their orders almost exclusively in Germany.

The commercial incapacity of the Latins unhappily finds proof in every branch of industry. Compare, for example, the Swiss hotels, so attractive to the foreigner, with the wretched and inconvenient inns which we find in the most picturesque situations in France and Spain. After this comparison, how can we wonder that these

places are so little visited? According to the official
statistics, the receipts of the Swiss hotels amount to
£4,600,000, yielding their proprietors £1,240,000 profit,
a truly enormous sum for a little country whose annual
receipts hardly amount to £3,000,000. For the Swiss
their hotels are veritable gold mines, rivalling the richest
of Africa.

"How much longer will it be," asks M. Georges
Michel, who cites these figures in the *Economiste
Français*, "before our colonies, on which we have
thrown away so many millions, will yield us a hundredth
part of the amount that Switzerland, who has neither
colonies, nor gold mines, nor silver mines, is able to
levy on the stranger?"

Young Frenchmen to-day are always being told to go
as colonists to foreign countries. Would it not be far
wiser and far more productive to counsel them to
attempt, first of all, to colonise their own country?
Since we do not know how to utilise the natural wealth
under our hands, how can we hope to surmount the
far greater difficulties which we should encounter in
foreign countries?

Our manufacturers and men of business are perfectly
aware of all this, but their apathy is too great to permit
of their being affected by it. I have had occasion to
lecture several on the subject. I cannot remember to
have convinced a single one of the necessity of adopting
new methods. The one dream of one and all is to
gain money without exertion, without risk, and without
work.

"The French," writes one of the authors I have just
quoted, "will be lucky henceforth if they are able to make
a little honest and sure profit, without speculation, and if
they end, in good years and in bad years, in making the
two ends meet, like Lafontaine's cobbler. But they will

end by being unable to make them meet, the two ends of their very honest little thread. They must put away a little sum at once; yes at once . . . And when this is put away it comes forth no more; this modest profit must not be risked in new ventures! Above all, they will take good care not to renew their machinery, not to reform their methods of production. Don't speak to me of reforms! They will go on thus as long as they are able, but that will not be for ever; and the most competent of men, and the most moderate in their judgments, tell us that the end has come, or very nearly."

It has, in fact, come. We are living on the shadow of the past, on the shadow of a shadow, and ruin is approaching with a rapidity which amazes all the statisticians. Our exports, which, twenty years ago, were far greater than those of England, are now far less. As has justly been said, our commercial losses are such to-day that we are paying every three or four years the war indemnity which we thought to have paid once for all.

The total ruin of our exterior commerce is saved by our monopoly of certain natural products, such as wines of superior quality, which almost alone of all others we possess, and the export trade in a few articles of luxury, such as fashions, silks, artificial flowers, perfumery, jewellery, and so forth, in respect of which our artistic ability is not yet extinct; but in all else there is a rapid downfall.

Our mercantile marine has naturally partaken of this decadence. It remains where it was, while all the other nations are increasing theirs in enormous proportions. Germany has almost doubled hers in ten years. England has increased hers by a third. We are gradually falling from the first rank to the last. While the tonnage of the port of Hamburg has increased tenfold in twenty-five years, the decadence of the ports of Havre and Marseilles is more evident every year. Strangers are trading for us on our own territory. Of the 16,000,000 tons French which represent our annual maritime commerce with other countries 4,000,000 tons are carried by French vessels, and the rest, that is to say, three-quarters, by foreign vessels. And, nevertheless, these foreign vessels touch none of the £440,000 of subsidies which the Government is obliged to pay annually to our commercial marine to save it from the total ruin which its incapacity and lack of foresight would otherwise render inevitable.

Can we save ourselves by trading with our colonies ? Alas, no ! They refuse to accept ours, preferring English and German products. These colonies of ours, which cost us so many millions to conquer, are good for nothing but markets for the commercial houses of London, Bremen, Hamburg, Berlin, and so forth. Never have our traders understood that an Arab, a Chinese, a Kanaka, or a negro, may have different tastes from a Frenchman. This inability to represent to one-self ideas other than one's own is, as I have already shown, altogether characteristic of the Latins.

We are unable to establish a trade even with those colonies that are at our doors. One of our journals recently published the following reflections on the commercial relations of France and the Régence of Tunis :—

"Sugars come from England, Austria, and Germany ; alcohol from Austria ; spun cotton chiefly from England, and to a smaller extent from Austria ; cotton, flaxen, hempen, and woollen fabrics from England ; silken fabrics from India and from Germany ; shirts from England and Austria ; wood from America ; candles from England and Holland ; papers from England and Austria ; cutlery from England ; glass from Austria ;

bottles from England; clocks and watches from Germany or Switzerland; toys from Germany; chemical products from England; petroleum from Russia . . .

"And from France? From France there come always soldiers and officials."

And, nevertheless, they cost us terribly dear in men and in money, our too useless colonies. In his report on the Budget for 1897, M. Siegfried, a deputy, has justly called attention to the fact that all the English colonies, with their superficies of 15,000,000 square miles and their 393,000,000 inhabitants, cost the metropolis only £2,480,000, while ours, with less than 3,000,000 square miles of superficies and 32,000,000 inhabitants, cost us £2,960,000. Now, although far less populated and far less in extent than the English colonies, they cost more than the latter. Moreover, it is not for the glory of possessing these colonies that the English pay their money. These two and a half millions are merely an advance which is paid over and over again by the commerce of the colonies with the metropolis. The sole products which the Latins have hitherto exported to their colonies are huge battalions of officials, and a small quantity of a few articles of luxury, which are almost exclusively consumed by these officials themselves. The definitive Budget of our colonies is very lucid. They cost us £2,960,000 annually and bring us in about £280,000. Here is an absolutely deplorable operation, which is accomplished to the great stupefaction of the nations which watch us persist in the practice. Supposing that these colonies were ruled by colonising countries such as England or Holland, it is certain that matters would be reversed. They would cost the mother country £280,000, and bring her in £3,000,000; besides which they would quickly be covered, like all the English colonies, with telegraphs and railways due to private enterprise, and costing the metropolis nothing. We know that the network of 30,000 miles of railways with which India is covered has not cost the English Government a penny.

To the many causes of our national decadence we must unhappily add the unscrupulous procedure of many of our commercial houses, procedures that those who have travelled abroad know only too well. I remember that when I was in the East I was struck by seeing on all the bottles of Bordeaux and cognac a little label in English, indicating that the bottle had been filled by a London house, which guaranteed the purity of the product. On inquiry I learned that the great houses of Bordeaux and Cognac had for a long time sold liquors of such inferior quality to the English merchants established abroad that the latter had entirely abandoned the practice of applying to them directly, preferring to obtain their goods through English houses buying the liquors on the spot. This fact will not surprise those who are informed of the value of the articles that our merchants qualify as articles for exportation.

This decline in quality of our products is to be observed not only in those which are destined for exportation, but is more and more affecting those which are sold at home, a fact which explains the crushing success of foreign competition. Let us take a sufficiently definite example ; for instance, photographic objectives, which to-day form a by no means inconsiderable item of commerce. Any photographer will tell you that the English, and especially the German objective, although two or three times as expensive as the French article, has almost entirely driven the latter from the market. And why ? Simply because the foreign lenses of makers of repute are without exception good, and ours are only good exceptionally. The foreign maker, understanding that it is in his interest not to depreciate his name, does not put failures on the market. The French maker has not yet arrived at such a lofty conception. All that he has made, whether good or bad, must be got rid of, until finally he gets rid of nothing at all.[1] The same is true of a host of products ; photographic plates, for example. Take the best French brands, and in every box you will invariably find one or two bad plates, coated with unsuccessful emulsions, which the maker has slipped in among the good batches, being unable to resign himself to rejecting them. There is nothing of the kind with foreign plates. The English or German maker, possibly, is not more honest than the French maker, but he is far more intelligent in understanding what his interests are. The inevitable conclusion is that in a few years, despite all the protective tariffs imaginable, despite all the outcries of our makers, and by the mere force of things, the foreign plate will supplant the French plate just as the foreign objective has supplanted the French objective.

The relaxed honesty of our merchants is a very serious symptom, and one, unhappily, which is to be observed in every industry, and is on the increase. It is quite in vain that measures upon measures are passed to put a check on fraud in all the branches of commerce. In Paris, for example, the police have almost given up seizing fuel sold in sacks which are sealed with a pretended guarantee of weight. Invariably the weight is 25 per cent. less than that indicated, and the courts would not be sufficient to condemn all the offenders. In one

[1] In a catalogue of *articles de voyage* of the Louvre stores published in June, 1898, of the four kinds of photographic objectives offered for sale three are German and only one French, and this only in connection with a cheap outfit. The French objective is almost unsaleable to-day, while thirty years ago it was the German objective that was unsaleable.

case a delivery of 26 tons of coal was over 6 tons short
The *employés* of the large dealer who committed the
fraud must have known that such things were a daily
practice.   In other similar affairs it was proved that the
merchant used to steal a quarter of the coal delivered,
and the carters another quarter.

And, unhappily, such practices are becoming more and
more general, even in the transactions of educated men.
In a report published in the *Officiel* for December 23,
1896, summing up the analyses made by the municipal
laboratory over a period of three years of products
procured from the chemists' shops, the writer says,
"that the proportion of products or preparations above
all reproach amounts hardly to one-fourth."

3. Causes of the Commercial and Industrial Superiority of the Germans.

The industrial and commercial superiority of the
English, and more especially of the Germans, is so
evident to-day that it would be puerile to seek to deny it.
And the Germans know perfectly well what to make of
this point. This is how one of their writers expresses
himself in a recent publication :—

"Nowadays it is we who export to Paris the Parisian
article! How the times are changed! And how our
parts are changed! . . .

"For excavations, for road-work, for hard and ill-
paid callings, France must have Italians. For manufactures, for banking, for commerce in general, she must
have Germans, Belgians, or Swiss. . . .

"The French workmen out of work are to be numbered by tens of thousands; and yet, and this is a very
significant fact, the German who goes to Paris does not
have to keep his hands in his pockets long.   How many

have we not seen set out for France ! and all, without exception, have found work there.

"Among our neighbours to send a son abroad is the height of luxury, which only a few rich families allow themselves. How many French *employés* will you find in Germany, or in England ? How many with no other means of subsistence than their salary ? For Germany the list is soon reckoned up—perhaps there are a dozen.

"Every year France makes way for such and such a nation in the matter of such and such an article. From the third rank she falls back to the fourth, from the fourth to the fifth, without ever regaining her lost ground. The table of the various exports of the whole world for the last ten years presents a striking spectacle ; it is like watching a race in which France, exhausted and ill-mounted, is letting, one by one, all her competitors outstrip her. . . .

"When a growing nation begins to elbow a more sparsely populated nation, which consequently forms a centre of depression, a current of air is set up, which is vulgarly called an invasion, during which phenomenon the civil code is laid aside. . . . The sparsely peopled nations must pull in their elbows."[1]

Referring to this writer M. Arthur Maillet says :—

"This German has written phrases which continually haunt my mind. He has predicted that France will become a species of colony, which will be administered

---

[1] The young *intellectuels* to whom I have alluded in a previous chapter, apropos of a quotation from Lemaître referring to their utter lack of patriotism, would do well to meditate seriously on the last few lines of this quotation. With a little more intellectuality they would eventually understand that they can only conserve the faculty of cultivating in peace the ego that is so dear to them by scorning their country a little less, and respecting the army which alone can defend it a great deal more.

by French functionaries and supported by German manufacturers, merchants, and agriculturists. The first time I read this prediction, some three or four years ago, it seemed to me a mere insult. But on looking into the matter I was able to see that it was already more than three parts realised. If you doubt that it is so, ask those who are experienced in these matters what would become of the French industries and of French commerce if all foreigners were suddenly obliged to leave France. How many new companies are formed of which they are not the promoters, and of which they do not hold all the shares ? "

Let us try to discover the causes which have given the Germans such an industrial and commercial superiority in less than twenty-five years.

We will first of all set aside the reason, so often given, that their commercial success is facilitated by the prestige of their victories. This prestige has absolutely nothing to do with the matter. The fact is that the buyer is interested solely in the merchandise which is delivered to him, and nothing at all about the nationality of the vendor. Commerce is an individual, not a national matter. All nations are equally free to trade with the English colonies, and if the natives and colonists have long preferred English goods it is because they are better, cheaper, and more to their taste. If they are now beginning to prefer German goods it is evidently because the latter appear to have greater advantages. If then German commerce is steadily invading the world, it is not because the Germans have a large army, but simply because buyers prefer German merchandise. Military successes have nothing to do with this preference. The most that can be said of the influence of the German military system is that the young man who has been subjected to it has acquired habits of order, punctuality, duty, and discipline which will be of great value to him later on in commerce.

This first reason being eliminated, we must seek for others.

In the first rank, as always, appear racial characteristics. But before insisting on these we must first of all remark that the power of the Germans consists not only in their own proper strength, but also in our weakness.

When treating of the formative conceptions of the Latin mind, I denoted the causes of this weakness. My readers know how the aptitudes of the Latin peoples have been created by their past, and to what extent these peoples are to-day suffering from the effects of that past. They know what has been the result of our long-continued centralisation, of our progressive State absorption, which destroys all individual enterprise, and leaves the citizen incapable of doing anything for himself when he is deprived of guidance. They are familiar also with the terrible effect of a system of education which despoils the growing mind of the few vestiges of independence and will which have been left it by heredity, casts them into the midst of life without any knowledge other than words, and perverts their judgment for ever.

And to show to what extent the strength of the Germans consists in our own weakness, it will suffice to point out the fact that it is precisely our manufacturers and our merchants and our shopkeepers who are the pioneers of German products in France. This escapes the statistician, but it reveals a state of mind which I believe to be far more serious than the apathy, the suspicious and petty dispositions, and the lack of initiative with which our consuls reproach our commercial men. Not only are they steadily renouncing all effort and all idea of opposition, but they have begun to furnish our rivals with arms, by selling more and more exclusively the products of those rivals.   In many industries we find that our some-time manufacturers have become simple commission agents, confining themselves to selling, at a large profit, articles which they have imported from Germany, and on which they have put their own names.   It is thus that in less than twenty years the industries in which France was formerly in the first rank, such as the manufacture of photographic apparatus, chemical products, instruments of precision, and even *articles de Paris*, have passed almost entirely into the hands of foreigners. To get the simplest scientific instrument made in Paris is to-day a matter of considerable difficulty.   The difficulty will be insurmountable when the few old makers who are still alive have disappeared.

Evidently it appears far simpler to sell a made article than to make it oneself.   It is perhaps a less simple matter to foresee the consequences of this operation. Yet they are sufficiently obvious.

The German maker, who delivers to his Parisian competitor an article which the latter is the reputed maker, and on which he often realises a considerable profit, presently sees that it is to his advantage to sell the same article directly to the Parisian public in his own name. He commences first of all by selling, to several commission agents, the same article, but with his name engraved on it.   This makes it impossible for the Frenchman to sell it under his own name, and at the same time suppresses his profit.   Encouraged by his success, the German maker presently decides to open a shop in Paris, at which his manufactures shall be sold under his own name.[1]

---

[1] And often a factory as well.   There are at present three German houses in Paris selling objectives.   One of them has installed in the heart of Paris a workshop for the manufacture of these objectives,

Unhappily the manufactures of photographic necessities, instruments of precision, and chemical products are not the only ones that have passed into foreign hands. The *articles de Paris* sold by our great tailors and dressmakers are more and more German. Stuffs for men's clothes come in increasing proportions from England and Germany, and are more and more frequently made up by foreign tailors, who are now setting up their shops in every quarter of Paris. Foreigners are setting up in Paris as booksellers, art dealers, jewellers, and so on, and are now beginning to undertake trade in silks and ladies' clothing. If the jury had advised the elimination from the forthcoming Exhibition of 1900 all articles of foreign origin sold under a French name, our part in the Exhibition would have been a very poor one.[1]

It would, perhaps, be unjust to throw too many stones at our manufacturers, and to attribute exclusively to their incapacity and idleness what is in some part the effect of other causes. It is, indeed, very evident that the increasing demands of the workers, which are favoured by the bounty of the public authorities, together with the enormous taxes which are crushing our industries, contribute as much as the imperfection and insufficiency of our tools and the increase in the cost of production to the impossibility of struggling against

which employs 150 men, all of them, naturally, from Germany, and which can hardly keep up with the orders of its French customers. When our men of business and our manufacturers complain of suffering from foreign competition, should they not be told that it is from their incapacity and their apathy that they are really suffering? The Germans will soon regard Paris as the most productive of their colonies.

[1] As a member of the jury of admission for scientific instruments I had thought of proposing this elimination, but I had to abandon the idea, as it would have aroused too much protest on the part of the exhibitors.

our competitors. It is easy to understand that the
manufacturer, harassed and annoyed, should finish by
giving up the manufacture of articles that he can buy
cheaper than he can make. He accordingly closes his
workshop and descends to the *rôle* of simple retailer. If
he had different hereditary aptitudes he would doubtless
do as his English and American brothers, who are also
affected by the demands of their workers and by competition, but who, thanks to their energy, and the daily
increasing perfection of their plant, are able to compete
without too great disadvantage with their German rivals.
Unfortunately for our manufacturers, they have none of
the qualities which make for success in such a conflict.
At the bottom of all our social questions lies always this
dominant question of race, which is indeed the supreme
arbiter of the destinies of nations. All the facts enumerated in this chapter are contemporary, but how remote
are their causes !

The system of centralisation to which the Germans
have been subjected for some time past will one day,
doubtless, as I have elsewhere remarked, conduct them
to the pass in which we find ourselves to-day ; but in the
meantime they are benefiting by qualities created by
their past, qualities which, though not brilliant, are solid,
and are in entire agreement with the new conditions and
new necessities created by the evolution of the sciences,
industry, and commerce.

What has been said in the preceding paragraph of their
industrial and commercial success will already enable us
to foresee the causes of this success. We shall understand them still better by considering their national
qualities, and what they gain by them.

The principal qualities of the Germans are patience,
perseverance, the habits of observation and reflection,
and a great aptitude for co-operation. All these qualities

are very highly developed by a marvellous technical education.[1]

These are the most general and at once the most funda-mental causes of their success. Commercially and in-dustrially they result in the constant perfection of industrial implements and products,[2] the manufacture of goods in accordance with the taste of the customer, and constant modifications according to his requirements, extreme punctuality in delivery, and the sending out into the entire world of intelligent representatives acquainted with the language and the customs of the various countries they visit, and the means and cost of carriage. A number of commercial societies constantly furnish their associates, by means of numerous agents sent to all quarters of the globe, with the most precise infor-mation. The *Export Verein* of Dresden spent between 1885 and 1895 nearly £20,000 in sending out travelling correspondents. The German Colonial Society possesses an annual revenue of £4,800, furnished by the subscrip-tions of its members, and has 1,051 representatives

[1] A manufacturer was recently speaking to me of the astonishment which he had felt on visiting a large electrical shop in Germany at the number of foremen and simple workmen whom he heard addressed as Doctor or Engineer. The Germans do not suffer as we do from a plethora of unemployed graduates, for the reason that, their technical education being extremely thorough, they are easily able to avail themselves of it in industry, while the purely theoretical education of the Latins fits them only to become professors, magis-trates, or officials.

[2] Certain German factories have been cited as possessing as many as twenty-four chemists, of whom several are employed only in theoretical research, which is immediately put into practice by others, who try to extract therefrom a new industrial application. The German manufacturers are up to date in respect of all new inven-tions, and immediately try to perfect them. A few days after the publication of details of wireless telegraphy, a Berlin house was making the complete apparatus, the Morse recorder included, for £10. I had the instrument under my hands, and I can vouch that the extreme difficulties of adjustment had been admirably sur-mounted.

abroad. The union of commercial *employés* which has its headquarters at Hamburg, has 42,000 members, and places a thousand *employés* a year.

Most of the merchandise destined for exportation leaves by the port of Hamburg, whose commerce has increased tenfold since 1871, and which now surpasses Liverpool in the matter of tonnage, while Havre and Marseilles are declining from year to year. In Hamburg there are numbers of export agents who represent the interests of the manufacturers, and put them in relation with buyers. They have in their warehouses samples of every kind of goods, of which the form and nature are incessantly being modified by the makers, in accordance with information received from the most distant quarters of the globe.

The results obtained by these associations are prompt and valuable. In a report for 1894 an American consul, Mr. Monaghan, gave as an example the business done in Bosnia by the Sofia branch of one of the societies I have been speaking of. After taking the trouble to get up a catalogue in Bulgarian, and sending out nearly 200,000 letters or prospectuses, besides spending nearly £4,000 on commercial travellers, it received orders, after the first year, to the amount of £400,000, and at the same time immensely reduced the trade of all its competitors.

Such results cannot be obtained without trouble ; but the German never shrinks from exertion. Unlike the French manufacturer, he studies with the greatest care the tastes, habits, manners, and, in a word, the psychology of his clients, and the information published annually by the societies I have mentioned contains the most precise information on these subjects. M. Delines, reviewing a report of Professor Yanjoul, has shown how minutely the German investigators study the psychology of the nations with whom their merchants are about to do business. Speaking of the Russians, for example, the German indicates their tastes, speaks of the necessity of taking tea with them before discussing business, then mentions the goods it is possible to sell them, and specifies the most useful of these, from a commercial point of view, with the words " sale absolutely good." In the *Export-Hand-Addressbuch*, which is in the hands of every German merchant, we find characteristic notes of the following kind :—

" The Chinese usually prepare their food in very thin iron utensils ; the rice is quickly cooked, but the saucepan is soon burnt and has to be frequently renewed. An English house, wishing to beat all its competitors, sent out a consignment of iron pots which were thicker, more durable, and were sold at a lower price. The Chinese at first took the bait, and the pots began to sell like wildfire. But this did not last long. At the end of a few days the sale suddenly stopped. The reason was a logical one ; fuel is very dear in China, the English saucepans were very thick, the rice cooked very slowly, and, in short, the new pots turned out to be far less economical than the old ones, in which the rice was cooked in no time. The Chinese returned to their accustomed and more economical utensils."

The same publication cites a still more amusing fact :—

" A European merchant had the brilliant idea of exporting to China a consignment of horseshoes bearing for trademark a most effective and irresistible dragon. What was his stupefaction to learn that the Chinese turned from his goods with anger ! He had not reflected that a dragon figures on the national escutcheon of the Celestial Empire, and that the Celestials would consider it sacrilege to allow a horse to defile this august emblem with his hoofs."

There is another story of an English merchant who put some excellent needles on the Chinese market, needles which ought to have defied all competition, and then fell to vainly racking his brains to explain to himself why they did not sell. He did not know that in China black is a symbol of sorrow, and always carries ill-luck ; and these excellent English needles were done up in sheaths of black paper, so that the Chinese preferred inferior needles from other quarters, which were done up in red or green.

If I enter into such details as these it is to show what elements go to the making of the success of a nation to-day. Taken separately, these details seem infinitesimal. It is the sum of them that makes their importance, and that importance is immense. The turn of mind which allows a German seriously to preoccupy himself with the way in which a Chinaman cooks his rice may seem very contemptible to a Frenchman, whose mind is taken up with such high matters as the revision of the constitution, the separation of Church and State, the utility of learning Greek, and so forth ; but nevertheless the Latins have got to understand that their part in the world will soon be terminated, and that they will utterly disappear from history, if they do not become resigned to abandon their useless theoretical discussions, their futile and sentimental phraseology, in order to busy themselves about these petty practical questions on which the lives of nations to-day depend. No Government can give them what they lack. They must seek help in themselves, not from outside.

Is it to be thought that the application of Socialistic doctrines would remedy the state of things set forth in this chapter ? Would a Socialist society, even more formalistic than ours, be the one to develop that spirit of enterprise and that energy which are so necessary to-day, and which the Latins lack so greatly ? When the Collectivist State directs everything, makes everything, will products be better and less costly, their exportation easier, and foreign competition less to be feared ? To believe it one would have to ignore the universal laws of industry and commerce. If decadence is far advanced among the Latin nations, it is precisely because State Socialism has for a long time been making immense progress among them, and because they are incapable of undertaking anything whatever without continual assistance from the Government. We have only to make the Socialist conquest more complete still further to accentuate this decadence.

CHAPTER IV

ECONOMIC NECESSITIES AND THE GROWTH OF POPULATIONS

1. *The present development of the population of the various nations and its causes :*—Real complexity and apparent simplicity of social problems —The population problem—The advantages and disadvantages of an increasing population, according to the country in which such increase occurs—Psychological errors of the statisticians—The more largely populated nations are more dangerous on account of their industries and their commerce than on account of their cannon—Cause of the decrease in population of certain countries—Why this diminution tends to become general in all countries—The influence of comfort and fore-sight. 2. *The consequences of the increase or decrease of the population in various countries :*—The small part played by numbers in history ancient and modern—The sources of a country's strength are agri-culture, industry, and commerce, not in the number of its soldiers— The dangers to France of an increased population—Why the excessive population of England and Germany is not inconvenient to those countries—The conditions which make emigration advantageous to a nation—The conditions under which it is harmful—The disasters pro-duced in certain countries by the increase of population—The instance of India—The difficulties which the modern development of economics will presently create in too thickly populated nations—The small population of France will very soon be advantageous to her.

1. THE PRESENT DEVELOPMENT OF THE POPULATION OF THE VARIOUS NATIONS AND ITS CAUSES.

SOCIAL phenomena are always deceptive; they always appear very simple, and are in reality of an excessive complexity. The remedies for all the ills we suffer seem to be extremely easy of application, but when we seek to apply them we immediately discover that the invisible necessities which hedge us round very narrowly limit the sphere of our action. The collective life of a people is formed of innumerable particles; if we touch one of them the action set up is speedily communicated to all the the others. It is only by taking separately, one by one, all the little problems which go to make up the great social problem, that we come to comprehend the formidable complexity of the latter, and to see how chimerical are the remedies which simple-minded people are proposing every day.

We shall find fresh proof of the complexity of social problems if we examine a question which is more than others narrowly connected with the progress of Socialism. I mean the question of the relations which exist between the development of the population and the economic necessities which we see growing up every day.

I have tried in the last chapters to present two fundamental points : the first, that the industrial and economic evolution of the world is assuming a character which is entirely different from that it assumed in bygone centuries ; the second, that peoples in possession of certain special aptitudes, which may in the past have been useless enough, must, when these aptitudes become applicable, rise to a high rank.

Now this economic evolution of the world, of which we now perceive but the dawning, has coincided with various circumstances which have in the greater number of the nations provoked a rapid increase of their population.

In the presence of modern economic necessities are we to say that this increase of population presents advantages or inconveniences ? The reply must vary according to the state of the peoples in whom the phenomenon is observed.

When a country possesses a great extent of territory

which is sparsely populated, such as Russia, the United States, or England with her colonies, the increase of her population presents evident advantages, or at least for a certain time. Is it the same with countries which are sufficiently populated, possess no colonies, or have no reason to send their inhabitants to those that they have, which are well off in the matter of agriculture, and very badly off in matters of industries and external commerce ? I think not ; on the contrary, it seems to me that such a country will do very wisely in not seeking to increase its population. Given the phase of economic evolution which I have described, such abstention is its only means of avoiding the deepest misery.

Such is not, as we know, the opinion of the statisticians. Having discovered that the population of most of the European countries is progressing very rapidly, while that of France remains stationary, and even tends to decrease, so that the births were 33 per thousand in 1800, 27 in 1840, 25 in 1880, and 20 in 1895, we find them filling the journals with their lamentations, and complaining no less at the meetings of the learned societies. The State— always the State—must, according to them, intervene at once. There are no extravagant measures—such as a tax on all celibates and bounties to the fathers of large families—that they will not propose, to remedy what they regard as a disaster, and what we should—being given the present state of our country—consider as a blessing, and in any case as a necessity resulting from causes beside which all the measures proposed are patently puerile and ineffective.

For the rest, the only inconvenience that the statisticians have been able to discover in this stationary condition of our population is that the Germans, having far more children, will very soon have more conscripts, and will then be able to invade France with ease. Even if we consider the matter only from this restricted point of view, we need not hesitate to say that the danger which is supposed to be hanging over our heads is slight enough. The Germans threaten us far more with their industries and their commerce than with their rifles, and we must not forget that on the day when they shall be sufficiently numerous to make a successful attempt at invasion, they will be threatened in their turn by the 130,000,000 of Russia at their backs, since the statisticians admit by hypothesis that the most numerous peoples must invade the less numerous.

It is very probable that by the time the Germans are able to gather together such multitudes as will enable them to invade a nation whose warlike aptitudes history will not allow us to miscalculate, Europe will have recovered from the illusion that the strength of armies depends on their numbers. Experience will by then have proved, conformably with the judicious predictions of the German general, Von der Goltz, that the hordes of half-disciplined men, without real military education, and without any possible power of resistance, of which the armies of to-day are composed, will be quickly destroyed by a small army of veteran professional soldiers, as of old the millions of Xerxes and Darius were annihilated by a handful of Greeks, disciplined and inured to all exercises and all fatigues.

When we examine the causes of this progressive diminution of our population we see that it is partly the consequence, almost universal in all ages, of the increased sense of prudence which is born of comfort. Only those that have possessions think of preserving them, and of assuring resources to their descendants, whose number they intentionally limit.

To this determining cause, the effects of which have been observed at every period, and notably at the apogee

of the Roman civilisation, we must add causes that are
special to the present day, of which the chief ones are
the evolution of industry, which, on account of the perfection of machinery, is reducing the number of utilisable
workers, and the absence of the colonising spirit, which
restricts the extent of our outlets, and would leave us
overburdened by a surplus of population.

These data are not particular to France, but are to be
observed in countries inhabited by very different races.
The United States may assuredly be ranked with the most
prosperous of countries, and yet the statisticians, not without stupefaction, have observed in them the same decreasing increase of population as they deplore in France. The
present birth-rate for the States is 26 per thousand, hardly
higher than ours. In ten counties of the States it is even
lower than our own, since it varies from 16 to 22 per
thousand. There one can blame neither the obligatory
military service, which does not exist; nor the sale of
alcohol, which is interdicted; nor the law, for the testator
enjoys the completest liberty; that is to say, the father
has only to restrict the number of his children in order
to avoid the too great division of his fortune.

A similar depression of the birth-rate is to be observed
in Australia, where it has fallen from 40 per thousand to
20 in the last twenty years. All these facts clearly demonstrate the weakness of the arguments of the statisticians in
explaining what they call the danger of our depopulation.

The same decreasing increase of population is to be
seen almost everywhere, even in countries where the birth-
rate has been momentarily highest.

In Germany the birth rate was 42 in 1875, and had
fallen to 36 twenty years later. In England it fell from
36 to 29 in the same time. These losses are greater than
those of France, since in the latter country the rate has
only fallen from 26 to 23 in the same time. The two

nations are thus gradually losing their advance of us, and they will very probably end by losing it altogether.

2. THE CONSEQUENCES OF THE INCREASE OR DECREASE OF THE POPULATION IN VARIOUS COUNTRIES.

We see by the preceding that an abatement in the increase of the population is tending to manifest itself in all countries, and that our rivals will not in the future threaten us by the mere fact of their numbers.

Let us suppose, however, that they will not lose their present advantage over us, and consider whether the increase of their population may prove to be a serious danger for us.

It would certainly appear, to hear the lamentations of the statisticians, whom the *Economiste français* justly qualifies as "harebrained," and whose minds, in truth, seem singularly limited, that the superiority of a nation is made by its numbers. Now a rapid bird's-eye view of history will show us, for example, in the persons of the Egyptians, Greeks, and Romans, that numbers played a very small part in ancient times. Must it be repeated that it was with 100,000 well-trained men that the Greeks triumphed over the 3,000,000 of Xerxes, and that the Romans never had more than 400,000 soldiers scattered over an empire which, from the Ocean to the Euphrates, was 3,000 miles long and 1,500 broad?

And without referring to these remote epochs, can we say that number has played any larger a part in modern times than it did in antiquity? Nothing authorises us to think so. Without speaking of the Chinese, who do not, despite their 400 millions of men, seem to be very formidable from a military point of view, we know that the English are able to keep 250 millions of Hindoos under the yoke with an army of 65,000 men, and that Holland rules her 40 millions of Asiatic subjects with a far smaller army.   Does Germany consider herself to be seriously threatened because she has at her doors an immense civilised empire with a population three times greater than her own ?

Let us leave these puerile fears aside, then, and re-member that what does in reality menace us is not the number of our rivals, but their industrial and commercial capacity and enterprise.   The three real sources of national strength are agriculture, industry, and com-merce ; not armies.

It is, happily, not to be supposed that all the lamenta-tions of the statisticians have resulted in increasing by a single individual the number of the inhabitants of our country.   Let us congratulate ourselves on the complete futility of their discourses.   For suppose that an offended Deity wished to heap upon France the most horrible of calamities, of what would He make His choice ?   War, plague, or. cholera ?   None of these, for these are but ephemeral ills.   He would only have to double the figure of our population.   This, given the present economic conditions of the world, and the needs and psychology of the French people, would be an irremediable disaster. After a brief delay we should witness bloody revolution, hopeless misery, the assured triumph of Socialism, fol-lowed by permanent unending wars and no less incessant invasions.

But why has not the excess of population such incon-venience in other countries, such as England and Germany ?   Simply, on the one hand, because these countries possess colonies into which their surplus population is poured ; and, on the other hand, because emigration, so completely antipathetic to the French, is with them regarded as a highly desirable thing, even when it does not constitute an absolute necessity.

It is the taste for emigration, and the possibility of satisfying it, that allows a nation to increase the figure of its population to any considerable extent. A consequence at first of excessive population, the tendency to emigrate becomes a cause in its turn, and contributes yet more to increase this excess. The celebrated explorer Stanley has presented this point very well in a letter recently published by a journal in reply to a question which had been addressed to him. He called attention to the fact that emigration begins only when the population begins to exceed a certain number to the square mile. Great Britain had 130 inhabitants to the square mile in 1801 ; as soon as this figure rose to 224, which was in 1841, a movement of emigration began which rapidly increased. When the population of Germany attained the same density of 224 to the square mile, she in turn was obliged to look about for colonies.[1] Italy, on account of the extreme sobriety of her inhabitants, was able to wait a little longer, but when finally her population reached the figure of 253 to the square mile, she, too, had to submit to the common law, and seek for outlets. She has succeeded but ill in the attempt (always so difficult to the Latin races), and has expended £8,000,000 in Africa, only to end in humiliating defeat. But on pain of inevitable ruin, towards which she is rapidly marching, she will have to recommence her attempts. The real danger that menaces Italy, and threatens her with approaching revolution and Socialism, is that she is far too densely populated ; with her, as everywhere, misery has been too fruitful.[2]

France, says Stanley, is far less densely populated, and

---

[1] The present figures are : For England, 300; for Italy, 282 ; for Germany, 254 ; for France, 187 ; for Spain, 92.

[2] Poverty is always fruitful, because it is always careless. Are we really to have a high opinion of the morality of persons who create more children than they can nourish; and are we to have much sympathy for them ?

has no need of emigration, and it is deplorable that she should spend the strength of her young men in Tonkin, Madagascar, and Dahomey—to which places no one ever emigrates, save some very expensive officials; above all when she has Algeria and Tunis at her doors, and yet is unable to populate them. These countries, indeed, have only 25 inhabitants to the square mile, and only a very small proportion of those are French.

Stanley is perfectly right, and has very clearly pointed out the very essence of the problem. His conclusions are analogous to those which were formerly indicated by one of his compatriots, Malthus. The latter clearly demonstrated that there is a close relation between the population of a country and the means of subsistence, and that, when the equilibrium is deranged, famine, war, and all kinds of pestilence fall upon the overcrowded country, and so set up a mortality which promptly re-establishes the equilibrium.

The English have had occasion to verify the justice of this law. When, after numerous wars, and murderous ones for the vanquished, they had terminated the conquest of the great empire of India, and brought 250 millions of human beings under their laws, they made further struggles between the various sovereigns impossible, and established a profound peace throughout the Peninsula. The results were not long in showing themselves. The population increased in enormous proportions—at the rate of 33 millions in the last twenty years—and very soon was no longer in equilibrium with the means of subsistence. Being unable to reduce itself by means of wars, since these wars are forbidden, it tends to reduce itself, according to the old law of Malthus, by periodic famines, in which many millions of men die of hunger, and by epidemics almost as disastrous. The English, being unable to cope with the laws of Nature, look on with philosophy at these gigantic hecatombs, each of which destroys as many men as all the wars of Napoleon put together. As it is a question of Orientals, Europe remains indifferent to this spectacle. Yet it does at least merit her attention as a demonstration while waiting for that which Italy will furnish very soon. The statisticians might draw from it this lesson, that they are wrong in preaching the gospel of multiplication to certain nations, and that if their phrases were to have the result they look for, it would be to launch these nations on a path of disasters. The Socialists might learn another lesson from it, that which I enunciated at the beginning of this chapter, that under their apparent simplicity the social problems present a very great complexity, and that the measures by which we essay to remedy apparent ills have often remote consequences which are far more distressing than the ills they were intended to cure.

Can we suppose that with the forthcoming economic evolution which I have described the over-populated nations will in the future derive from their excess of population advantages that they are to-day at a loss to find? It is, on the contrary, plain to see that this excess will be calamitous to them, and that in the future the happiest lot will be reserved to those countries which are more scantily populated; that is to say, those countries in which the population does not exceed the number of human beings that can be nourished on the produce of the country itself. We saw, in the chapter devoted to the economic struggle between East and West, that the greater number of the countries of Europe, on account of the exaggerated development of their population, are no longer able to nourish their inhabitants, and are reduced to sending to the East for their enormous annual alimentary deficit. This deficit they have hitherto paid for by means of merchandise manufactured expressly for the Orientals, but as these Orientals have begun to produce the same goods at a twentieth of the European cost of production, the commerce between the East and West is every day tending to decrease.

The nations which live only by their commerce and industry, not by their agriculture, will presently be the most seriously threatened. Those which, like France, are agriculturists, and produce nearly enough for the consumption of their inhabitants, and could, if the worst came to the worst, dispense with external commerce, will be in an infinitely better position, and will suffer far less from the crisis which is more and more threatening Europe, and which the triumph of the Socialists would quickly precipitate.

BOOK V

THE CONFLICT BETWEEN THE LAWS OF EVOLUTION, THE DEMOCRATIC IDEAL, AND THE ASPIRATIONS OF THE SOCIALISTS

CHAPTER I

THE LAWS OF EVOLUTION, THE DEMOCRATIC IDEAL, AND THE ASPIRATIONS OF THE SOCIALISTS

1. *The relations between living things and their surroundings:*—The existence of all living creatures is conditioned by their environment— The importance of the changes produced by environment, and the slowness of these changes—Why species appear to be immutable— The social environment—The sudden changes produced in these environments by modern discoveries, and the difficulty with which man is able to adapt himself to them. 2. *The conflict between the natural laws of evolution and the conception of the democrats:*—The increasing opposition between our theoretical conception of the world and the realities presented by science—It is with difficulty that the democratic ideas can place themselves in agreement with the new scientific ideas— How the conflict resolves itself in practice—Democracies are finally led to favour all kinds of superiority—The formation of castes in the democratic *régime*—The dangers and advantages of democracies—The financial morals of the American democracy—Why the venality of American politicians is attended with only slight social inconveniences —Democratic ideas and the sentiments of the crowd—The instincts of crowds are not democratic. 3. *The conflict between the democratic ideal and the aspirations of the Socialists:*—The fundamental opposition between the fundamental principles of democracy and Socialism —The fate of the weak in democracies—Why they will gain nothing by the triumph of the Socialistic ideas—The hatred of Socialists for liberty and free competition—Socialism is really the most redoubtable enemy of democracy.

1. THE RELATIONS BETWEEN LIVING THINGS AND THEIR SURROUNDINGS.

THE naturalists have proved long ago that the existence of all living things is rigorously conditioned by the environment in which they live, and that a very slight modification of this environment suffices, on the simple condition that it be prolonged, entirely to transform its inhabitants. The procedure of these transformations is to-day perfectly well known. Embryology, which repeats the series of ancestral phases, shows us the profound changes which have been undergone during the succession of geologic ages.

For these transformations to be produced, it is not necessary that the variations of environment should have been very great, but they must have been very prolonged. If too rapid they would lead to death and not to change. An increase or decrease of temperature to the extent of a few degrees, if continued during a great number of generations, suffices, by slow adaptations, entirely to transform the fauna or flora of a country.

M. Quinton, in a recent work, gives a very interesting example of the changes produced by simple variations of temperature.

"Organised beings, to compensate in themselves for the cooling of the globe, tend artificially to maintain in their tissues the high exterior temperature of primeval times. The importance of this tendency is very great. We know that it already determines, in the branch of vertebrates, the evolution of the reproductive organs, and correlatively that of the osseous processes. It also causes the modification of all the other organic processes, and consequently that of evolution itself.

"This follows plainly, from a simple _à priori_ consideration. Let us imagine an organism of primitive type. The globe begins to cool ; the life of the organism tends to maintain itself at its former high temperature. It can do so only by the production of heat in the tissues, that is to say, by combustion. All combustion demands combustible material and oxygen, and here to satisfy the demands of combustion, are determined the development of the digestive and respiratory processes.   The necessity of carrying these materials and this oxygen into the tissues, a necessity which increases as the combustion increases, demands the evolution of the circulatory system. From the progress of these three systems, to which the reproductive system attaches itself, there necessarily results the progress of the nervous system.   Finally, it is not enough to produce heat ; it must be conserved, and hence is determined the evolution of the integument.   But as the cooling of the earth progresses the thermal difference to be maintained between the two systems, animate and inanimate, increases, so that a quicker combustion and a more perfect organism are incessantly called for.   We thus see how by reason of the cooling of the globe, the very natural effort which life makes to maintain the first conditions of its chemical phenomena incessantly determines the evolution of all the organic processes, and imposes on them *à priori*, a perfection proportionate to their recency.   To confirm this theoretical view we have only to consider the various groups of animals in the order of their appearance on the globe, and to observe the effective advance of all their organic processes in that order."

What is true of physical environments is also true of the moral environments, and notably of social environments.   Living beings always tend to adapt themselves, but, on account of the power of heredity which struggles against the tendency to change, they adapt themselves only with extreme slowness, and the factor of time intervenes.   It is this fact that makes species seem invariable when we consider only the short duration of historical ages.   It is invariable to all seeming, but only as the individual we regard for a moment is invariable. He has not varied visibly, but none the less the slow process which conducts him from youth to decrepitude and death did not cease during that instant, but accomplished its work although we did not see it.

All creatures, then, are conditioned by their physical or moral environments. If they are subjected to environments which change slowly—and such is generally the case with continents and climates as well as with civilisations—they have time to adapt themselves to them. Let any particular circumstance arise which shall violently modify the environment, and adaptation becomes impossible ; the creature is doomed to disappear. If, by a geological upheaval, the temperature of the pole or of the equator were to be established in France, in three or four generations she would lose the greater number of her inhabitants, and her civilisation could not continue in its present state.

But these sudden cataclysms are unknown to geology, and we know to-day that the greater number of the transformations which have come to pass on the surface of the globe have been effected very slowly.

Hitherto it has been the same with social environments. Except in cases of destruction by conquest, civilisations have always changed gradually. Many an institution has perished, many a god has fallen into dust, but gods and institutions alike have been replaced only after a long period of old age. Great empires have vanished, but only after a lengthy period of decadence, which neither societies nor living creatures can escape. The power of Rome finally withered before the invasions of the Barbarians, but it was only very gradually, after many centuries of decomposition, that she finally gave place to them, and it is in reality by the most imperceptible transitions, contrary to what the general run of books tell us, that the ancient world is connected with the modern world.

But by a phenomenon hitherto unique in the annals of the world, the modern scientific and industrial discoveries have in less than a century created far greater changes in the conditions of existence than all that history has recorded from the epoch when man sowed the seeds of his first civilisations on the banks of the Nile and the plains of Chaldea. Old-established societies, established on bases they believed eternal, have seen these bases shattered. The environment has changed too suddenly to allow time for man to adapt himself to it, and the result is a grave confusion of spirit, an intense uneasiness, and a general opposition between the sentiments fixed by hereditary and the conditions of existence and ideas created by modern necessities. Everywhere the conflict is breaking out between the old ideas and the new ideas born of the new requirements.

We do not know yet what will result from all these conflicts ; we can only state their existence. In considering here those which are related to the questions to which this book is dedicated we shall see that some of them are very profound.

2. THE CONFLICT BETWEEN THE NATURAL LAWS OF EVOLUTION AND THE CONCEPTIONS OF THE DEMOCRATS.

Among the conflicts which the near future is preparing for us, and which we already see beginning, perhaps one of the most conspicuous will be the increasing opposition already existing between the theoretical conceptions of the world which were created of old by our imaginations, and the realities which science has finally put before us.

It is not only between the religious conceptions on which our civilisation is still based and the scientific conceptions due to modern discoveries that there is evident contradiction. This discrepancy is no longer militant ; time has rubbed down the corners. The chief antagonists

are the new scientific doctrines and the political conceptions upon which the modern nations base their institutions.

When the men of the Revolution, guided by the dreams
of their philosophers, saw the triumph of their humanitarian ideals, and inscribed the words Equality, Liberty,
and Fraternity, which were the synthesis of those dreams,
on the pediments of the public buildings, the modern
sciences were not born. So that then they could invoke
the state of nature, the original goodness of man, and his
perversion by societies, and no one could formulate a
contradiction ; and then they could act as though societies
were artificial things which they could re-fashion at their
will.

But the new sciences have sprung up to make evident
the vanity of such conceptions. The doctrine of evolution above all has utterly refuted them, by showing all
through nature an incessant struggle, resulting always in
the extinction of the weakest ; a cruel law, no doubt, but
the origin of all progress, without which humanity would
never have emerged from its primitive savagery, and
would never have given birth to a civilisation.

That these scientific principles should ever have seemed
democratic, and that democracy should have assimilated
them without seeing how utterly they were opposed to it,
is one of those phenomena which can only be understood
by those who have studied the history of religions, and
who know how readily the believer will draw from a
sacred text, the most improbable deductions, and the
most completely opposed to the text itself. As a matter
of fact, nothing could be more aristocratic than the laws
of nature. "Aristocracy," as some one has justly said,
"is the law of human societies, as it is, under the name
of selection, the law of species." We have as much
trouble to-day in reconciling the new data of science

with our democratic illusions as had the theologians a short time back in reconciling the Bible with the discoveries of geology. We manage to conceal these divergencies to a certain extent as yet by means of a certain amount of manœuvring, but as they are every day growing greater they must presently be apparent to every eye.

Although very real this conflict is far from being as grave as might be supposed. I doubt even if it will ever be of such importance as to emerge from the region of philosophic discussion. To tell the truth, the disagreement is purely theoretical. In the facts there is no discrepancy. How could there be, when these facts are the consequences of natural laws which are superior to our desires, and of which we cannot, therefore, escape the effects ?

When we come to consider what is the true nature of a democracy we shall see if it does not in reality favour superiority of all kinds, including that of birth, and whether it must not be as necessarily aristocratic, that is to say, as favourable to the formation of a superior class, as the forms of government that have preceded it. If this be so its contradiction of the laws of evolution is only apparent.

For this purpose let us put on one side the words by which people define democracies and consider what their spirit is. I find it admirably presented in the following lines of Paul Bourget's :—

"If you try to define to yourself what is really meant by these two terms, aristocracy and democracy, you will find that the first designates a system of manners which aims at the production of a small number of superior individuals. It is the application of the adage, *humanum paucis vivit genus*. The second, on the contrary, designates a system of manners which aims at the well-being and culture of the greatest possible number of individuals.

The point of excellence of an aristocratic society, its consummation, is the exceptional personage, the supreme result and flower of thousands of destinies occupied in sustaining this one rare being. The point of excellence of a democratic society is a community in which work and enjoyment are distributed in indefinite fractions among a great number. We do not require great powers of observation to perceive that the modern world, and in particular our French world, is tending altogether toward this second form of life. That which constitutes the novelty of modern society is the substitution of the organised mass for personal initiative, the advent of crowds, and the disappearance, or at least the diminution, of the power of the superior class."

Such are undoubtedly the theoretical tendencies of democracies. Let us see if the realities agree with them.

Democracy proposes as its fundamental principle the equality of the rights of all men and free competition. But who will triumph in this competition, if not the most capable,—that is to say, those who possess certain aptitudes more or less due to heredity, and always favoured by fortune ? We reject the rights of birth to-day, and we have reason in rejecting them in order not to exaggerate them by adding social privileges thereto. In practice they always preserve all their power, and even a greater power than they possessed formerly, for free competition, coming to add itself to the intellectual gifts bestowed by birth, can only be yet further in favour of hereditary selection. Democratic institutions are always advantageous to aristocracies of every sort, for which reason these aristocracies must always defend them and prefer them to any other.

Can we deny that democracies give rise to castes having powers very nearly analogous to those of the old aristocratic castes ? This is what M. Tarde has to say on the subject :—

" In every democracy like our own, we may be certain to find a social hierarchy, either established or establishing itself, of persons of recognised superiority, either hereditary or selective. It is not difficult to see by whom the old nobility has been replaced in France. Firstly, the administrative hierarchy has been growing more and more complex, has been growing upwards by increasing the number of its degrees, and outwards by increasing the number of its functionaries ; the military hierarchy has been doing the same, by reason of the causes which constrain the modern European states to universal armament. Secondly, the prelates and princes of the blood, the monks and gentlemen, the monasteries and chateaux, have been suppressed only to the immense profit of journalists and financiers, artists and politicians, theatres, banks, ministries, great shops, huge barracks, and other monuments all gathered together in one quarter of the same capital. All the celebrities foregather ; and what are these various species of notoriety and glory, in all their unequal degrees, if not a hierarchy of brilliant positions, occupied or to let, of which the public alone disposes, or thinks it disposes ? Now, far from simplifying or abating itself, this aristocracy of self-gratifying situations, this daïs of shining thrones, is incessantly growing more grandiose by the very fact of the transformations of democracy."

So we must fully recognise that democracies give rise to castes just as aristocracies do. The only difference is this : in a democracy these castes do not seem to be closed ; every one can enter them, or thinks he can. But he can enter them only if he possess certain intellectual aptitudes which birth alone can give, and which give those who possess them a crushing superiority over their less fortunate rivals. From this it results that superior classes are favoured by democratic institutions, and they may congratulate themselves that these institutions are becoming so prevalent. The time is still distant when the masses will turn away from them. It will come eventually, for reasons I shall presently give. But in the meantime democracy is exposed to other dangers, which arise from its essential nature, and which we must now consider.

The first of these inconveniences is that democracies are very expensive. It is already a long time since Léon Say pointed out that democracy is destined to become the most costly of all systems of government. One of our journals has recently published the following very well-reasoned remarks on this subject :—

" Formerly indignation was justly excited by the prodigalities of the monarchical power, and by the courtiers, who incited the prince to magnificences which returned on them in a rain of favours and pensions. But have the courtiers disappeared now that the people is king ? On the contrary, has not their number grown with the fantasies of the multiple and irresponsible master they have to serve ? No longer are the courtiers at Versailles, where their gilded persons were gathered all together. They swarm in our towns, in the country, in the humblest chief towns of our arrondissements or cantons, wherever universal suffrage bestows a writ, and can confer a morsel of power. They carry their pledges with them ; pledges of ruinous bounties, the creation of superfluous employments, the unconsidered development of public works and services, all the means of facile popularity, and all the electoral dodges. In Parliament they dispense the promised largess, occupying themselves by benefiting their electorate at the expense of the budget ; it is the triumph of close local competition over the interest of the State, the victory of the arrondissement over France."

The exactions of the elector are sometimes singularly excessive ; none the less the legislator who wishes to be re-elected must respect them. Too often he has to obey the orders of wine-merchants, or of dunder-headed petty merchants who compose his chief electoral agents. The elector demands the impossible, and it has to be promised. Hence these premature reforms, undertaken with never a suspicion of their indirect effects. A party that wishes to arrive in power knows that it can do so only by out-doing the promises of its rivals.

"Under every party we see another party rise up, which stings, insults, and denounces the former. In the time of the Convention there was la Montagne, under the Convention, threatening to spring ; and la Montagne on his side feared the Commune, and the Commune was afraid of seeming too lukewarm towards the bishops. Down to the very depths of demagogy this law reigns and makes itself known. But we find, however, in this exploration of the 'extremes' a troubled and ambiguous region where we can no longer very clearly distinguish one party from another ; it is there we find the most ardent souls, the most 'pure,' the most bloody— such as were Fouché, Tallien, Barras—fit to be purveyors to the guillotine, fit valets for a Cæsar. This also, this confusion of parties at their extreme limits, is a constant political law. We have just emerged from an experience which was very conclusive on that point."

This intervention of crowds in democratic governments constitutes a serious danger, not merely by reason of the exaggerated expenses which result therefrom, but more especially on account of this redoubtable popular delusion—that all ills can be remedied by laws. The Chambers are thus condemned to enact an immense

number of laws and regulations of which nobody foresees the consequences, and which have scarcely any
other result than to surround the liberty of the citizen
with a thousand fetters, and to increase the ills they
should remedy.

"The institutions of the State," writes an eminent
Italian economist, Signor Luzzati, " cannot change our
poor human nature, nor imbue our souls with virtues
they lack, nor raise the rate of wages so that we can save
more, because we are dependent on the universal and
inexorable conditions of national economy."

This will seem a very elementary proposition to the
philosopher, but there is no chance of its being understood by the public till after a century of wars, and
bloody revolution, and wasted millions. But then the
greater number of elementary truths have been established in the world only by these means.

Another consequence of democratic institutions is a
very great ministerial instability ; but in this there are
advantages that often balance its inconveniences.   It
places the real power in the hands of the administrations
of which every minister has need, and of which he has
no time to change the old organisation and traditions
which make their strength.   Besides which, every
minister, knowing that his existence will be ephemeral,
and desirous of leaving something behind him, is accessible to a great number of liberal propositions.   Without
these frequent changes of ministers many a desirable
undertaking would have been impossible in France.

It must also be remembered that this facility of change,
one of the consequences of democratic institutions,
renders revolutions useless, and consequently very rare.
To the Latin peoples this should count as no small
advantage.

A more serious inconvenience of democracies is the

increasing mediocrity of the men who govern them. These need little but one essential quality : they must be ready to speak at a moment's notice on any subject whatever, and to find immediate arguments, plausible, or at least blustering, with which to reply to their adversaries. Such superior minds as would reflect before delivering themselves, were they Pascals or Newtons, would cut a sorry figure in Parliament. This necessity of speaking without reflecting eliminates a number of men of solid worth and impartial judgment from Parliament.

Such men are kept out of Parliament by other considerations, and notably by this—that democracies cannot put up with superiority in those that govern them. Those elected, in direct contact with the crowd, can only please it by flattering its least elevated passions and cravings, and by making it the most unlikely promises. By that very natural instinct which forever bids men to seek after their likes, the crowd runs after the men of chimerical or mediocre mind, and more and more does it plant them in the very heart of democratic governments. I quote from a recent *Revue politique et parlementaire* :—

"The masses naturally prefer men of vulgar mind to men of cultured mind, and give their allegiance to the agitated and the voluble rather than to the tranquil and the thinkers. And they make it difficult for the latter to be heard or be elected, by dint of making it disagreeable. The standard is thus being almost continuously lowered of the preoccupations which arise in politics, of the considerations which determine them, of the affairs undertaken, of the *personnel* of those elected, and of the motives that move them. This is what we see at present, and unless we wish to fall into a still lower and more unhappy state we must look into the matter.[1] We have

[1] Our author forgets to tell us how we are to "look into the matter." As it would be impossible to make use of regulations,

arrived at such a point that to curry favour with the crowd even our men of letters and men of talent find it best to hold before it, as an end, the suppression of acquired fortune, and one hardly dares to rebuke it."

And what would seem to show that this vice is inherent in all democracies, and is not merely a racial defect, is that this phenomenon which we observe in France is also to be observed, and even in a far higher degree, in the United States. The decline of the intellectual and moral level of the specially qualified class of politicians is becoming more evident every day, at a rate which bodes ill for the future of the Great Republic.   Again, as political functions are utterly disdained by capable men, they are exercised only by the *déclassés* of all parties. The inconvenience is not so great as it would be in Europe, for as the *rôle* of the Government is very small the quality of the political *personnel* does not matter so much.

It is in America also that we find one of the greatest dangers of democracies—venality.   Nowhere has it reached such a development as in the United States. There corruption exists in every degree of the public services, and there is hardly an election, a concession, a privilege, which cannot be obtained for money. According to a recent article in the *Contemporary Review* a presidental election costs £8,000,000, which is advanced by the American plutocracy. The party which gets in is repaid besides this largely. The first thing done is to discharge all the functionaries and officials at one blow, and their place are given to the electors of the new party. The numerous partisans whom the party is unable to place receive pensions, which are

since such regulations would be the very negation of the fundamental propositions and principles of democracy, it is very evident that his proposition is entirely chimerical.

charged to the fund for pensions for those who took part in the war of secession, although the greater number of the survivors of that war have long ago disappeared. These electoral pensions now reach the annual figure of nearly £32,000,000.

As for the party chiefs, their appetites are much greater. The large speculators especially, who figure prominently in every election, feather their nests royally. Twenty years ago, at the end of an election, it was decreed that they might change metallic silver for gold, on the old basis of exchange, at the Treasury. This meant simply that on depositing in the Treasury a weight of silver bought in the market for £12 they received gold to the value of £20. This measure was so ruinous to the State that it soon became necessary to limit the present which the Government made to a privileged few to the sum of £10,000,000 per annum. When the Treasury was almost exhausted, and bankruptcy threatened, the execution of the Bill was suspended. This colossial piracy had poured such fortunes into the laps of these speculators that they did not trouble to protest very much. We made a tremendous uproar in France over the Panama affair, and the desperate imbecility of a few certain magistrates did all that could be done to dishonour us in the eyes of the world, all on account of a few thousand-franc bills accepted by a few needy deputies. The Americans could not by any means understand the matter, for there was not a politician of theirs that had not done the same thing, with the sole difference that none of them would have been satisfied with such an insignificant recompense. Compared with the American houses, our Parliament rejoices in a Catonian virtue. It is all the more meritorious in that the salaries of our legislators are hardly enough to meet the demands of their position. Moreover, in supporting the Panama scheme, for which they were so bitterly reproached, they did no more than obey the unanimous demands of their electors. The Suez Canal, which made its creator a demigod, was not made in a different way to the Panama Canal, and could not have been made otherwise. The purses of financiers were never filled by proceedings of austere virtue.

There is plainly no possible excuse for the financial manners of the United States. They are a disgrace to the country. However, since the Americans accommodate themselves to them very well and do not find them in the least dishonouring, it must be because they correspond to a certain ideal, which we must try to comprehend. The love of wealth is at least as widespread in Europe as in America, but we have preserved certain ancient traditions, so that even though our shady pro- motors and slippery financiers are envied when they succeed, they are none the less despised, and regarded much in the light of fortunate pirates. They are tolerated, but we should never think of comparing them with our scientists, artists, soldiers, and sailors—with men, that is, who lead careers that are often ill-paid, but that demand a certain elevation of thought or sentiment of which the greater number of financiers are com- pletely destitute.

In a country such as America, a country without traditions, almost exclusively devoted to commerce and industry, in which a perfect equality reigns, and in which no social hierarchy exists, since all employments of any importance, including those of the magistracy, are filled by holders who are incessantly being renewed, and, for the rest, enjoy no more distinction than the smallest of shopkeepers; in such a country, I say, only one distinction can exist—that of fortune. The worth of an individual, his power, and his social position are con-

sequently measured solely by the number of dollars he
possesses. The pursuit of dollars, accordingly, becomes
the ideal which is constantly kept in sight, and all means
are good means to realise it. The importance of a career
is measured only by what it brings in. Politics are
regarded as a simple trade which ought largely to remunerate those who engage in it. Although this conception is plainly very dangerous and very base, the
public accepts it in entirety, since it does not scruple
to give its voice to politicians who are most notorious
for their habits of pillage.

Politics considered as a matter of commerce implies
the formation of syndicates to exploit it. Only thus
can we conceive of the power, so mysterious at first
to Europeans, of associations such as the famous
Tammany Hall of New York, which has been exploiting
the finances of that city on a large scale for more than
fifty years. It is a sort of freemasonry, which nominates
the servants of the municipality, the magistrates, the
police agents, the contractors, and, in short, the whole
staff of the municipality. This staff is devoted to it
body and soul, and obeys blindly the orders of the
supreme head of the association. Once only, in 1894,
the association failed to keep itself in power. The inquiry
then held on its doings revealed the most incredible
depredations. Under one of its chiefs only, the famous
William Tweed, the total sum stolen and divided between
the associates, according to the commission of inquiry,
amounted to £32,000,000. After a short eclipse the
syndicate regained all its power. It is said that at the
last elections it spent £1,400,000 to nominate its candidate
mayor of New York. This sum will easily be paid back
to the associates, since the mayor disposes of an annual
budget of £16,000,000.

Any other nation than the Americans would be quickly

disorganised by such a state of morals. We know what has been their result in the Latin republics of America. But the population of the United States possesses that sovereign quality, energy, which triumphs over all obstacles. As the danger of allowing the intervention of financiers in public affairs has not yet become too conspicuous, the public does not trouble about the matter. When this danger does appear, which will probably happen before very long, the Americans will employ their usual energy in remedying the evil. In such matters their proceedings are abrupt but efficient. We know how they rid themselves of Chinese and negroes who embarrass them. When their financiers and prevaricators embarrass them too much they will have no scruples in lynching a few dozen of them in order to make the others reflect on the utility of virtue.

The demoralisation we have just been considering has hitherto affected only the special class of American politicians, and has but slightly touched the commercial and industrial classes. And I repeat that the effects of this state of things are also narrowly limited by the fact that in the United States, as in all Anglo-Saxon countries, the intervention of the Government in business of all kinds is very slight, instead of being almost universal, as with the Latin nations.

This is a very important point, and explains the vitality of the American democracy compared to the feeble vitality of the Latin democracies. Democratic institutions cannot prosper except among nations having sufficient initiative and force of will to enable them to conduct their affairs without the constant intervention of the Government. The corruption of the State has but few evil consequences when the influence of the public powers is extremely limited. On the contrary, when this influence is great, the corruption spreads everywhere, and disorganisation is imminent. We have the terrible example of the Latin republics of America to show us the fate which lies in wait for democracy in nations without either strength of will, morality, or energy. The love of authority, intolerance, contempt of the law, and ignorance of practical questions rapidly develop themselves, along with an inveterate taste for pillage. Then anarchy quickly follows, and to anarchy always succeeds dictatorship.

Such has been the end that has always threatened democratic governments. Much more would it threaten an entirely popular government based on Socialism.

But in addition to the dangers we have just considered, which arise from the condition of morals, democracies have still other difficulties to contend with, which arise from the state of mind of the popular classes, who do all they can to increase them.

The real ,adversaries of democracy are by no means to be found where people insist on looking for them. It is threatened not by the aristocracy, but by the popular classes. As soon as the crowd suffers from the discord and the anarchy of its governors, it immediately begins to think of a dictator. It was always so at the troubled periods of history among those nations that had not, or had no longer, the qualities necessary to support free institutions. After Sylla, Marius, and the civil wars, came Cæsar, Tiberius, and Nero. After the Convention, Bonaparte ; after the '48, Napoleon III. And all these despots, sons of the universal suffrage of all ages, were always adored by the crowd. How could they have kept in power if the heart of the people had not been with them ?

"Let us have the courage to say it, and to repeat it," wrote one of the firmest defenders of democracy, M. Scherer, "we are condemned absolutely to misunderstand the most characteristic instincts of universal suffrage, at any rate in France, if we refuse to take into account the four plebiscites which raised Louis-Napoleon to the Presidency of the Republic, ratified the outrage of the 2nd of December, created the Empire, and, in 1870, renewed the pact of the nation with the lamentable adventurer."

Only a few years have elapsed since the time when the same pact was to be renewed with another adventurer, who had not even the authority of a name, and had no prestige but that of his general's plume. The judges who have arraigned kings are many; very few are those who have dared to arraign the people.

3. The Conflict between the Democratic Idea and the Aspirations of the Socialists.

Such are the advantages and the inconveniences of democratic institutions. They suit admirably strong and energetic races, of which the individual is accustomed to rely only on his own efforts. They have not in themselves the power to establish any kind of progress, but they constitute an atmosphere admirably adapted to all sorts of efforts. From this point of view nothing equals them, and nothing could replace them. No other system gives the most capable such liberty of development, or gives them such chances to succeed in life. Thanks to the liberty they permit to every individual, and the equality which they proclaim, they favour the development of superiority of every kind, and above all that of intelligence; that is to say, the superiority of which all important progress is born.

But do this equality, and this liberty, in a struggle in which the competitors are unequally endowed, place those who are favoured by an intellectual heredity, and the host of mediocre persons whose mental aptitudes are but little developed, on the same footing ? Do they leave these ill-equipped competitors much chance, not of triumphing over their rivals, but merely of not being too far crushed by them ? In a word, can the weak, without energy and without courage, find in free institutions the support they are incapable of finding in themselves ? It seems plain that the answer is a negative, and it seems evident also that the more we have of equality and liberty the more complete is the servitude of the incapable, or even of the half-capable. To remedy this servitude is perhaps the most difficult problem of modern times. If we set no limit to liberty, the situation of the disinherited can only grow worse every day ; if we limit it—and evidently the State alone can undertake such a task—we arrive at State Socialism, the consequences of which are worse than the ills they pretend to heal. The only means remaining is to appeal to the altruistic sentiments of the stronger ; but hitherto religions alone, and then only at periods of faith, have been able to awaken such sentiments, which even then have constituted very fragile bases of society.

We must thoroughly realise that the lot of feeble and ill-adapted individuals is certainly far harder in a country of perfect liberty and equality, such as the United States, than in countries whose constitutions are aristocratic. Speaking of the United States in his work on popular government, the English historian, Maine, expresses himself thus :—

"There has hardly ever before been a community in which the weak have been pushed so pitilessly to the wall, in which those who have succeeded have been so uniformly the strong, and in which in so short a time there has arisen so great an inequality of private fortune and domestic luxury."

These are, evidently, the necessary inconveniences of any *régime* having liberty as its base, and they are nevertheless the inevitable conditions of progress. The only question we can ask ourselves is this : Are we to sacrifice the necessary elements of progress, are we to consider only the immediate and visible interest of the multitudes, and are we to combat, incessantly, and with all manner of arbitrary means, the consequences of the inequality which Nature continues to repeat in every generation ?

"Which is right," says M. Fouquier, "aristocratic individualism or democratic solidarity ? Which is most favourable to the progress of humanity ? Which is worth the most, a Molière or two hundred worthy schoolteachers ? Which renders the greater service, a Fulton or a Watt, or a hundred mutual aid societies ? Evidently individualism raises and democracy lowers ; evidently the human flower grows from a human dunghill. Only these useless, mediocre creatures, with low instincts, often with envious hearts, with minds empty and conceited, often dangerous, and always stupid, are still human beings !"

We may theoretically admit the inversion of the laws of nature, and sacrifice the strong, who are in the minority, to the weak, who constitute the majority. Such, when rid of empty formulæ, is the ideal pursued by the Socialists.

Let us for a moment admit the realisation of such an ideal ; let us suppose the individual to be imprisoned in the close network of limits and regulations proposed by the Socialists. Suppress capital, intelligence, and competition. In order to satisfy the theory of equality, let us place a nation in such a state of weakness that it would be at the mercy of the first invasion. Would the masses gain anything by it, even for a moment ?

Alas, no ! They would gain nothing, even at the

beginning, and very soon they would lose everything. The progress which enriches the workers is effected only by superior minds, and only such minds can direct the complicated machinery of civilisation. Without superior minds a country would soon become a body without a soul. The workshop could not keep running long without the engineer who builds it and directs it. It would soon be what a ship is deprived of its officers ; a wreck at the mercy of the waves, which will founder on the first rock it approaches. Without the great and the strong the future of the mediocre would apparently be more miserable than it has ever been yet.

Such are the conclusions clearly pointed out by reason. But the proof is not accessible to every mind, because the matter has not been put to the test of experience. The disciples of the Socialist faith are not to be convinced by arguments.

Democracy, by its very principles, favours the liberty and competition which of necessity lead to the triumph of the most capable, while Socialism, on the contrary, aims at the suppression of competition, the disappearance of liberty, and a general equalisation, so that there is evidently an insuperable opposition between the principles of Socialism and those of democracy.

Modern Socialists have finally become aware of this fact, at least instinctively ; for they cannot, with their pretensions that all men have equal capacities, openly recognise the opposition. Of this instinct, most often confused and unconscious, but nevertheless very real, is born the hatred of the Socialists for the democratic system, a hatred far more intense than was felt by the men of the Revolution for the *ancien régime*. Nothing could be less democratic than their desire to destroy the effects of liberty and natural inequality by an absolutely despotic *régime*, which would suppress all competition, give the same salary to the capable and the incapable, and incessantly destroy, by means of administrative measures, the social inequalities which arise from natural inequalities.

There is to-day no lack of flatterers ready to persuade the masses that the realisation of such an ideal is easy. These dangerous prophets know they will live long enough to reap the fruits of their popularity, but not long enough for events to expose them as impostors, so that they have nothing to lose.

This conflict between the democratic idea and the aspirations of the Socialists is so far invisible to superficial minds, and most people consider Socialism only as the necessary development and foreseen consequence of the democratic idea. In reality no two political conceptions are separated by deeper gulfs than Socialism and democracy. A pure atheist is in many respects far more nearly related to a devotee than is a Socialist to a democrat faithful to the principles of the Revolution. The divergency between the two doctrines is as yet hardly beginning to show itself, but it will soon be glaring, and then there will be a violent disruption.

It is not between democracy and science that there is and will be a real conflict, but between Socialism and democracy. Democracy has indirectly given rise to Socialism, and by Socialism, perhaps, it will perish.

We must not dream, as some have done, of allowing Socialism to attempt its object in order to prove its weakness, for Socialism would immediately give birth to Cæsarism, which would promptly suppress all the institutions of democracy. To-day, and not the future, is the time for the democrats to encounter with their formidable enemy Socialism. It constitutes a danger against which all parties without exception must league themselves, and with which none, and least of all the republican party, must ever ally itself. We may contest the theoretical value of the institutions which govern us, we may wish that the march of events had been other-wise, but such avowals must remain platonic. Before the common enemy all parties, whatever be their aspira-tions, must unite. They would have none but the slightest .chances of gaining anything by a change of *régime*, and they would expose themselves to the risk of losing all.

It is true that the democratic ideas have not, from a theoretical point of view, a base any more solid than that of religious ideas, but this defect, which formerly had no sort of influence over the fate of the latter, will no more be able to hinder the destiny of the former. The taste for democracy is to-day universal throughout all the nations, whatever be the form of their governments. We are, then, in the presence of one of those great social movements to seek to stem which would be futile. The principal enemy of democracy at the present time, and the only one which could possibly overthrow it, is Socialism.

CHAPTER II

THE SOURCES AND DIVISION OF WEALTH: INTELLI-GENCE, CAPITAL, AND LABOUR

1. *Intelligence :*—The immense part played by intelligence in the modern evolution of the world—It is the principal source of the wealth by which every worker benefits—The work of the labourer is of profit to himself alone ; the work of the inventor is of profit to all workers—The capacities of a small aristocracy of intelligence produce more wealth than the labour of all the rest of the population—The hatred of the Socialists for intelligence—The foundation, from their point of view, of this hatred. 2. *Capital :*—Definition of capital—The part played by capital—The services rendered by the capitalist to the workers by lowering the cost price of merchandise—The present diffusion of capital in a large number of hands—Progressive sub-division of the public fortune—What would be the result of the equal partition of the public fortune among all the workers—The pro-gressive reduction of the part played by the shareholders in all industrial undertakings, and the constant enlargement of that of the workers—The revenue of the shareholder is gradually tending to disappear—Future consequences—The present condition of real fortune—Why it also is tending to disappear—Great property is no longer a source of wealth, and is steadily tending to become sub-divided—The same phenomena are to be observed in France and in England. 3. *Labour :*—The present relations of capital and labour —The situation of the workers has never been so prosperous as to-day —Constant rise of the wages of the workers—These wages are often greater than the salaries earned in the liberal professions—The working class is the only class whose condition is steadily bettering. 4. *The relations of capital and labour :*—Employers and men—The increasing hostility of the working classes against capital—The total lack of comprehension to be observed in the relations of employers and men—The employer in modern industry—Employers and workers form to-day two always inimical classes.

FROM the generalities of the preceding chapters we shall now proceed to details, inquire into the sources of wealth, and see if it could be produced and distributed conformably with the aspirations of the Socialists.

Practically the Socialists recognise but two sources of wealth—capital and labour, and all their demands are directed against the part, according to them too great, which is assumed by capital. Being unable to deny the necessity of capital in modern industry, they dream of the suppression of the capitalists.

But besides capital and labour there is a third source of wealth—intelligence, which the Socialists usually consider to be of but little value. None the less its action is predominating, and for this reason we shall commence our investigation with a consideration of its functions.

1. INTELLIGENCE.

In the dawn of civilisation intellectual capacity played a part scarcely superior to that of manual labour, but with the progress of industry and the sciences its part finally became so preponderant that its importance cannot now be exaggerated. The toil of the obscure labourer is of profit only to himself, while the works of intelligence enrich the whole of humanity. A Socialist recently assured the Chamber of Deputies that "there are no such men as are in human reality the human equivalent of a hundred thousand men." It is easy to reply to him that in less than a century we can cite, from Stephenson to Pasteur, a whole aristocracy of inventors, each one of which is worth far more than a hundred thousand men, not only by the theoretical value of his discoveries, but by reason of the wealth which his inventions have poured into the world, and the benefits which every worker has derived from them. If on the last Day of Judgment the works of men are weighed at their true worth, how immense will prove the weight of the works of these mighty geniuses! It is to them, thanks to their discoveries, that is due the greater part of the capital existing in the world. The English economist Mallock has reckoned that one-third of the present revenue of England may be imputed to the capacity of a small *élite*, which by itself produces far more than all the rest of the population.

The Socialists of every school are loth to admit the importance of intellectual superiority. Their high priest Marx understands by the term work nothing but manual labour, and relegates the spirit of invention, capacity, and direction, which has nevertheless transformed the world, to a second place.

This hatred of intelligence on the part of the Socialists is well founded, for it is precisely this intelligence that will prove the eternal obstacle on which all their ideas of equality will shatter themselves. Let us suppose that by a measure analogous to the Edict of Nantes—a measure which the Socialists, were they the masters, would very soon be driven to enforce—all the intellectual superiority of Europe—all the scientists, artists, great manufacturers, inventors, skilled workmen, and so forth, were expelled from civilised countries, and obliged to take refuge in a narrow territory at present almost uninhabited—Iceland, for example. Let us further suppose that they departed without a halfpenny of capital. It is nevertheless impossible to doubt that this country, barren as it is supposed to be, would soon quickly become the first country in the world for civilisation and wealth. This wealth would soon be such that the exiles would be able to maintain a powerful army of mercenaries, and would have nothing to fear from any side. I do not think that such a hypothesis is altogether impossible of realisation in the future.

2. CAPITAL.

Capital comprises all objects—merchandise, tools, plant, houses, lands, and so forth—having any negotiable value whatever. Money is only the representative symbol, the commercial unit, which serves to evaluate and exchange objects of various kinds.

For the Socialists, work is the only source and measure of value. Capital would be merely a portion of unpaid work stolen from the worker.

It would be very foolish to waste time to-day in discussing assertions which have been so often refuted. Capital is work, either material or intellectual, accumulated. It is capital that has freed man from the slavery of the Middle Ages, and above all from the slavery of nature, and which constitutes to-day the fundamental basis of all civilisation. To persecute capital would be to oblige it to vanish or to conceal itself, and at the same blow to kill industry, which it would no longer be able to support, and also to suppress wages. These are banalities that really require no demonstration.

The utility of capital in industry is so evident that although all the Socialists speak of suppressing the capitalist they seldom speak nowadays of suppressing capital. Nevertheless, the great capitalist renders immense services to the public by reducing the cost of production and the sale price of general merchandise. A large manufacturer, importer, or tradesman can content himself with a profit of 5 per cent. or 6 per cent., and can consequently sell his wares at far lower prices than those charged by the small dealer or manufacturer, who in order to cover his expenses is obliged to make a gross profit on his goods of 40 per cent. to 50 per cent.[1]

[1] And sometimes a still higher profit. According to a document which has appeared in several papers the price of necessaries is

The following figures, taken from a paper read to the Society of Statistics, and published in the *Officiel* of June 27, 1896, give some information which is very interesting and seems to be exact, at least if taken in general, as is the case with most of the figures of the statisticians. They show at the same time the increase of wealth and that of the number of the participators in this wealth.

The nominal capital of French incomes from property, which was £28,520,000 in 1800, was £177,040,000 in 1830 ; in 1852 it was £220,640,000, and in 1896 it was £1,040,000,000.

The number of annuitants, which in 1830 was 195,000, was 5,000,000 in 1895. The number of annuitants would be twenty-five times as great as in 1814.[1]

The increase in the number of participators in industrial enterprises is also tending to increase. In 1888 there were 22,000 shareholders in the *Crédit foncier*, and there are now 40,000.

We find the same increase in the number of holders of railway shares and bonds : there are now 2,900,000.

We shall see presently that it is the same with property. Nearly two-thirds of France are in the hands of 6,000,000

often quadrupled by small retailers. To give only one example : a consignment of salad is sold to the public in Paris for about 45 francs ; of this the grower receives rather less than 10 francs. "We may say," says the writer of the article, "that in the provision market of the Halles de Paris the Parisian consumer pays 5 francs for what the provincial producer sells at 1 franc." It is easy to see how much the public would gain if large capitalists would undertake the sale of provisions as they have already undertaken the sale of clothing.

[1] But we must not forget that as the same person may have several titles to property, these figures have no absolute value. According to information received from the Minister of Finance, the number of entries, nominative or *au porteur*, were, at the end of 1896, 4,522,449, and not 5,000,000 as in the report I have been quoting. Of course, we do not know among how many these entries really represent, despite the conclusions of the statistician in question.

proprietors. M. Leroy-Beaulieu arrives finally at the conclusion that "three-quarters of the accumulated fortune
of France and probably nearly four-fifths of the national
revenue are in the hands of workmen, peasants, people of
the lower middle classes, and small proprietors." Large
fortunes are becoming more and more rare. The
statistics give the number of families possessing an
income of £300 at 2 per cent. at most. Of 500,000
inherited incomes only 2,600 exceed the sum of £800 in
capital.

Capital is thus tending more and more to diffuse itself
into a large number of hands, and it is so diffusing itself
because it is constantly increasing. The laws of
economics are here acting in the direction desired by
the Socialists, but by very different means to those in
favour with the Socialists, since the effect produced is the
consequence of the abundance of capital, and not its
suppression.

We may, however, inquire what the equal partition
between all of the general fortune of a country would
produce, and if the workers would gain by it. It is easy
to reply to this question.

Let us suppose that, in accordance with the wish of
certain Socialists, the £8,800,000,000 which represent
the fortune of France were divided equally among its
38,000,000 inhabitants. Let us also suppose that this
fortune could be realised in money, a plainly impossible
thing, since we have only about £300,000,000 in money,
the rest being represented by houses, factories, land, and
all kinds of objects. Let us suppose again that at the
announcement of this partition the value of all property
but real estate did not vanish in twenty-four hours.
Admitting all these impossibilities, each individual would
have a capital of about £220. One must know very
little of human nature not to be certain that incapacity

and waste on the one hand, and capacity, thrift, and energy on the other, would soon do their work. The inequality of wealth would be promptly re-established. If, in order to avoid a general partition, we limited ourselves to dividing only the large fortunes ; if, for example, we were to confiscate all incomes over £1,000 to divide them among the poorer citizens, the incomes of the latter would be increased by only 4½ per cent. A man in receipt of an income of £40 would then receive £41 16s. 8d. In exchange for this insignificant increase of 4½ per cent. all commerce, and numerous industries, which provide millions with the means of subsistence, would be totally ruined.[1]   Indeed, the working classes generally would be ruined, and their lot would be far worse than it is to-day.

Concurrently with the observed diffusion of capital, which all sincere Socialists must bless, we also find that the interest from capital sunk in industrial enterprises is

---

[1] This, it is true, is only the material side of the question, and there is also a psychological side which we must not neglect. What constitutes the scandal of great fortunes, and provokes so many recriminations, is firstly their origin, which is only too often to be found in veritable financial depredations ; secondly, the enormous power which they give to their possessors, allowing them to buy anything and everything, down to the title of member of the most learned academies ; thirdly, the scandalous life led by the heirs of those who have founded these fortunes.

It is evident that a manufacturer who enriches himself by selling cheaply a commodity which was formerly dear, or by creating a new industry, such as the transformation of steel in the furnace, a new method of heating, &c., renders a service to the public in enriching himself.   It is quite otherwise with the financiers of foreign extraction whose fortunes are made by lending the public money in a whole series of loans to rotten countries, or in placing on the market shares of dubious companies, from which operations they often derive a profit of 25 per cent.   Their colossal fortunes are practically composed of the adding up of unpunished thefts, and every State must sooner or later find some means or other, whether it be by enormous death duties or by crushing taxation, to protect the public fortune from their thefts, and to prevent them from founding a State within the State.   This necessity has already preoccupied several eminent philosophers.

growing less, whilst, on the contrary, the gains of the workers are increasing.

M. Harzé, Inspector of Mines in Belgium, has shown that in the last thirty years, while the working expenses of the mines have oscillated round the figure of 38 per cent., the profits of the shareholders have steadily fallen to less than half, while the profits of the workers have considerably increased.

It has been calculated that if the revenue of certain enterprises were turned over to the workers, each work-man would gain, on an average, £3 6s. 8d. per annum. But they would not do so for long. The enterprise would necessarily, in this hypothesis, be conducted by the workers, would soon be in straits, and the workers would finally gain far less than in the present state of affairs.

The same phenomenon of the increase of wages at the expense of the remuneration of capital is to be observed everywhere. According to M. Daniel Zolla, while the returns of landed capital fell 25 per cent. the salaries of agricultural labourers rose 11 per cent. According to M. Lavollée, the income of the working classes in England has risen 59 per cent., and the income of the leisured classes has fallen 30 per cent.

The wages of the working man will doubtless continue to rise in this manner until there is left only the minimum amount necessary to the remuneration, not of the capital sunk in an enterprise, but merely of the administrators necessary to the enterprise. This, at least, is the way matters are taking at present ; it may not be the same in the future. The capital sunk in long-established enter-prises cannot escape from the disappearance that threatens it, but in future capital may better know how to defend itself.

The worker of the present day finds himself in a phase

he will not see again, a phase in which he can dictate his own laws and bleed with impunity the goose that lays the golden eggs.   It is certain that the trades-unions will finally arrive at demanding the whole of the profits of all railways, transport and omnibus companies, all factories, workshops, mines, &c., and will stop only at the precise moment at which the dividend of the shareholder will be reduced to zero, but while there will yet remain just enough to pay the directors and administrators. We have learned, by innumerable examples, with what admirable patience the shareholder puts up with first of all the reduction and then the total suppression of his profits on the part of States or private companies. Sheep do not stretch their necks to the butcher with greater docility.

This phenomenon of the gradual reduction, tending to total disappearance, of the profits of the shareholder, is to be observed to-day on a great scale. Through the indifference and weakness of the administrators of our large companies, all the demands of the unions are immediately satisfied ; it is hardly necessary to say that the money to satisfy them must come out of the share-holder's pocket. The demands of the union are naturally promptly repeated, and naturally, again, the adminis-trators, who have nothing to lose, continue to satisfy them, which once more reduces the dividend, and con-sequently the value of the share.   On account of this method of ingenious spoliation many of our large indus-trial enterprises will bring in absolutely nothing in a few years' time. The real proprietors of the enterprise will have been gradually and totally eliminated, which is the dream of the Collectivists. It is difficult to see how it will then be possible to find shareholders to found fresh enterprises. Already we see a judicious distrust forming itself, and a tendency to export capital to the countries in which it runs fewer risks. The exodus of capital, and of capacity too, will be the first result of the complete triumph of the Socialists.

The double phenomenon that we have just been considering as affecting capital—the division of wealth among a larger and larger number, and the reduction of the profits of capital on account of the steady increase of the profits of the workers—will be found to exist as affecting landed property also. According to M. E. Tisserand's report on the last decennial inquiry, there are in France 122,000,000 acres under cultivation. They are divided into 5,672,000 holdings, of which only 2½ per cent. are given over to "*la grande culture*," that is, are of more than 100 acres in extent. But this 2½ per cent. of the holdings comprises in extent 45 per cent. of the soil ; so that if there is a great preponderance in number of the small holdings, it is also the fact that nearly half the soil is comprised by 2½ per cent. only of the number of holdings. Thus nearly half the soil of France is in the hands of large proprietors, but it is evident that this is a state of things that cannot long continue, simply on account of the decreasing part which is left to capital in enterprises of whatever kind. It is easy to show that large properties will very soon be a thing of the past.

The agriculture of France is exercised by about 7,000,000 individuals, or 11,000,000 counting their families and servants. Of this number nearly one-half are the proprietors of the soil they cultivate ; the others work for wages. Now if we compare the agricultural statistics for 1856 with those for 1886, the last published, we see that in 1856 there were 52 agriculturists for every 100 inhabitants, and only 47 in 1886. But this decrease, which the economists find so disquieting, is simply the result of the steady increase of small holdings. This will appear from the results of the two great decennial inquiries of 1862 and 1882. We find that although the number of day labourers and farm servants has fallen from 4,098,000 to 3,434,000, a decrease of 664,000, and the number of farmers from 1,435,000 to 1,309,000, a decrease of 126,000, the number of proprietor-cultivators, on the contrary, has risen from 1,812,000 to 2,150,000, an increase of 338,000. There is, therefore, a very sensible increase in the number of proprietor-cultivators.

This increase in the number of proprietors is a phenomenon exactly parallel with the increase in the number of capitalists. If the number of persons cultivating the soil on their own account increases, it is evident that the number of farmers and farm servants must diminish ; and more especially the number of farm servants, since the costly labourer is being steadily replaced by agricultural machines. Again, the extent of pasture-lands has increased by one-quarter since 1862, and this increase, as pasture demands but few hands, has also contributed to the decrease in the number of labourers and servants. If the country districts have been slightly depopulated— very slightly, as we have seen—it is merely because they require fewer hands ; but they have never had too few. There are plenty of hands ; it is the heads that are a little scarce.

Small holdings, evidently, are not very productive, but at least they feed those who cultivate them. The latter, it is true, earn less than if they were working for others ; but to work for oneself is a very different thing from working for a master.

The situation of the large proprietors is most precarious in France as well as in England, and this, as I have said above, is why they are tending to disappear. Their lands are condemned to subdivision in the near future. Unable to cultivate them themselves, seeing them bring in less and less, on account of foreign competition, while at the same time the demands of their labourers are increasing, they are gradually obliged to give up exploiting them, for the expenses of cultivation are often greater than the returns,[1] so that they or their heirs will be forced to sell their lands at low prices, and in fragments, to small proprietors who will cultivate them themselves. The latter have practically no expenses, neither have they capital to remunerate, taking into account the low price of their purchases. Large property will soon be only an object of useless luxury. Already it is no longer a source, but a sign of wealth.

The facts we have just been considering are to be observed on every hand, and more especially in countries where there are many large properties, as in England. They result, as I have said, from the increasing demands of the working population, together with the fall in the value of the products of the soil, due to the competition of counrties in which the land is without value, as America, or in which labour is without value, as the Indies. This competition has in a few years brought down the price of wheat in France to 75 per cent. of its former value, in spite of a protective tariff of 2s. per bushel, a tariff which is of course paid by all the consumers of bread.

In England, the land of liberty, where there are no protective duties against foreign competition, the crisis is to be observed in all its intensity. The English ports are full of foreign corn, as well as foreign meats. Refrigerator vessels are continually making the passage between Sydney, Melbourne, and London. They carry beef and mutton ready for the shops at a penny or three halfpence a pound, to say nothing of butter, of which

---

[1] In Aisne, a district of large farms, it is said that a few years ago there were 900 important farms deserted ; but we never hear of a single small property being abandoned by its proprietor.

certain of these boats bring over as many as 600 tons in a single voyage. Although the proprietors have reduced their rents by more than 30 per cent. they make next to nothing from their property, for their tenants profit by their embarrassments to pay less and less or nothing at all. M. de Mandat-Grancy, in his remarkable work on the subject, mentions proprietors whose books he has examined, whose property brought in from £20,000 to £30,000 a few years ago, and now brings in no more than £400 or £500; and this on account of the non-payment of tenants. It was impossible to evict the farmers who did not pay, for the simple reason that none could be found who would be able to pay, and that even if they did not pay, they did at least perform the service of keeping the land in condition, and preventing it from going out of cultivation. The proprietors will be obliged to split up their properties and to sell them at very low prices to small cultivators, who will work on them directly, and at a profit, since the price of purchase will be insignificant.

It is perhaps a matter for regret that the large proprietors should everywhere be destined to become, in the near future, the victims of the evolution of economic laws ; but as a matter of fact I think it will be very considerably in the interests of the societies of the future that landed property should be divided to such an extent that every one should possess only as much as he could cultivate. The result of such a State of things would be a very great political stability, and in such a society Socialism would have no chance of success.

In conclusion : what we have said of the repartition of capital is also true of the repartition of the soil. Large properties are doomed to disappear by the action of economic laws. Before the Socialists have finished discussing the matter the object of their discussions will have vanished, by reason of the imperturbable progress of those natural laws that work now according to our doctrines and now in a contrary sense, but always unheeding them.

3. LABOUR.

The figures I have given show the progressive increase of the profits of labour, and the no less progressive decrease of the profits of capital. For a long time capital, on account of its incontestable necessity, has been able to enforce its demands on the workers ; but to-day their respective *rôles* have changed. The relations of capital and labour, which were at first those of master and servant, are to-day like to become inverted. Now it is capital that is descending to the rank of a servant. The progress of humanitarian ideas, the increasing indifference on the part of directors and administrators for the interests of shareholders whom they do not know, and above all the enormous extension of trades-unions, have little by little brought about this effacement of capital.

Despite the noisy demands of the Socialists, it is evident that the situation of the working classes has never been as prosperous as it is at present, and, taking into consideration the economic necessities which rule the world, it is very probable that the workers are passing through a golden age that they will never see again. Never has such justice been done to their claims as to-day, and never has capital been as little oppressive and at the same time so little exacting.

As Mr. Mallock has justly remarked, the income of the modern working classes is far greater than the income of all classes taken together sixty years ago. They possess, in fact, at present, far more than they would have possessed if the whole of the public fortune had then passed into their hands, according to the dreams of certain Socialists.

Since 1813, according to M. de Foville, salaries in France have more than doubled, while money has only lost a third of its value.

In Paris, nearly 60 per cent. of working men earn a daily wage of 4s. 2d. to 6s. 8d., and according to the figures published by the *Office du travail*, the salaries of the better class of workmen are very much higher. The daily wage of a fitter varies from 6s. 3d. to 7s. 1d., and that of a turner from 7s. 6d. to 8s. 4d. Fine stone-cutters can earn as much as 12s. 6d. a day ; electricians from 5s. to 8s. 4d. ; brassfounders, from 7s. 1d. to 10s. 5d. ; sheet-iron workers, from 7s. 6d. to 9s. ; an ordinary foreman earns 8s. 4d. a day, and a really capable one as much as £380 per annum. These are such salaries as an officer, a magistrate, an engineer, or a Government clerk will often serve for years and years to obtain, if he does attain them at all. We may say with M. Leroy-Beaulieu : "The manual worker is the great beneficiary of our civilisation.[1] All situations around him are falling, and his is rising."

4. The Relations between Capital and Labour : Employers and Men.

Notwithstanding the very satisfying position of the

[1] One would gather from reading the speeches delivered in Parliament that the working class is the only class in society to be considered. It is certainly considered more than any other. The peasants, at once more numerous, and, I should imagine, quite as interesting, attract little enough attention. Pensions, banks, aid and assurance societies, economic dwellings, co-operative societies, abatements of taxes, and so forth, are all intended to benefit the working man, and both public and private authorities are always excusing themselves for not doing enough for him. The great manufacturers follow suit, and the workman is to-day surrounded with all kinds of solicitude.

modern workman, we may say that the relations between masters and men, that is to say, between capital and labour, have never been more strained. The workman is becoming more and more exacting in proportion as his desires are more fully satisfied. The more he obtains from his employer the greater grows his hostility towards him. He accustoms himself to see in his master only an enemy, and the master, not unnaturally, tends to regard his men as adversaries, whom it is his duty to mistrust, and finally he no longer dissimulates his antipathy for them.

But although we admit the wants and the evident wrongs of the workers, we must not deny those of the masters. The direction of a staff of working men is a matter of subtle and delicate psychology, demanding a conscientious study of men. The modern employer, who controls an anonymous crowd from a distance, knows nothing or next to nothing about his men. With a little skill he could often succeed in re-establishing an understanding with them, as is proved by the prosperity of certain co-operative workshops, in which the employers and men form a veritable happy family.

But at present the master does not know his men, and controls them by intermediaries, and yet he is always astonished at meeting with nothing but hostility and antipathy, notwithstanding all the aid societies, savings banks,[1] and so forth, to say nothing of the elevation of wages. The fact is that the personal relations of the past have been replaced by an anonymous and strictly rigid

[1] Ninety-seven per cent. of our mining companies give their men pensions, and, according to M. Leroy-Beaulieu, more than half their earnings are turned over to the miners' aid societies. All our directors of industrial companies are engaged in this course, which is a very easy one for them, for all this generosity is at the expense of the shareholders, who, as every one knows, may be taxed and imposed upon at will. The Paris-Lyon railway spends £500,000 annually in this manner, and the other railway companies do the same.

discipline. The employer will often make himself feared, but he no longer makes himself liked or respected, and he has lost all his prestige. Mistrustful of his men, he allows them no initiative, and is always wanting to interfere in their affairs (of course I am speaking for the Latin nations). He will found co-operative societies or providential societies, but he will never suffer them to be managed by the men themselves, so that the latter regard them as speculations, or instruments of bondage, or at the best as a disdainful charity. They imagine they are being exploited or humiliated, and the result is irritation. For the rest, it argues a poor understanding of the psychology of crowds to believe that benefits of a collective kind are received with gratitude. More often than not they merely provoke irritation, ingratitude, and contempt for the weakness of those who yield so readily to all their exactions.[1] In this case the manner of giving is truly of greater importance than the gift. The trades-

---

[1] This was curiously exemplified by the celebrated strike at Carmaux. The director found by experience what excessive benevolence and want of firmness may cost. He used to pay his men far more than they would have received elsewhere, and organised stores at which everything necessary for the consumption of the men was retailed to them at wholesale prices. Here is an extract from an interview with this director published in the *Journal* of August 13, 1895 : "The Carmaux glassworks have always paid higher wages than any others. I paid such high wages because I wanted to make sure of tranquillity. Every year, in fact, I have paid the men £400 more than they would have earned in another glassworks. And what has been the result of this enormous sacrifice ? To create the very troubles I wished at all costs to avoid." With a somewhat clearer knowledge of psychology the director would have foreseen that such concessions must necessarily provoke fresh demands. All primitive beings have always despised weakness and good-nature. The man who possesses these qualities has no prestige in their eyes ; power is the only thing they venerate. Those tyrants who have been noted for their prestige were seldom noted for their benevolence. It was sufficient if they coloured their tyranny with a somewhat remote and haughty benevolence to be adored.

unions, which, on account of their anonymity are able to exercise, and do exercise, a tyranny far more severe than that of the most inflexible employer, are religiously respected. They have prestige, and the workman always obeys them, even when he loses his wages by his obedience.

Again, the employer himself, in our great modern concerns, is tending steadily to become a mere subaltern in the pay of a company, and consequently has no motive in interesting himself in his staff. He does not know how to speak to a workman. A small employer who has himself been a workman will very often be a much harder master, but he will understand perfectly how to manage his men, rate them at their true worth, and save their *amour-propre*. At the present time the managers of workshops are more often than not young engineers from one of our great colleges, with any amount of theoretical instruction, and a profound ignorance of life and of men. They could not possibly know less than they do about their profession, and they will not admit that any customs of men or things can be superior to their abstract science. They are all the more unsuited to their duties in that they profess the deepest scorn for the class from which the greater number of them are sprung.[1]

[1] The candidates for our great Government colleges (l'École polytechnique, l'École centrale, &c.) are to-day recruited principally from the lowest classes of society. The entrance and final examinations demand efforts of memory and an amount of work almost impossible save for those who are spurred on by poverty. Although the fees of the École polytechnique are very low, the families of more than half of the pupils are unable to pay them. They are the sons of small tradesmen, domestic servants, workmen, or small clerks, and have for the most part already obtained a bursary from their lycée. According to an article by M. Cheysson in the *Annales des Ponts et Chausées*, for November, 1882, the number of bursars at the École polytechnique was about 30 per cent. in 1850, and over 50 per cent. in 1880. Since then the proportion has been increasing. According to a personal inquiry of my own, there were in 1897 249 pupils out of 447 who paid no fees.

No one despises the peasant like the son of a peasant, nor the workman like the son of a workman, when he has succeeded in raising himself a little above his caste. Here again is one of those psychological verities which, like the greater number of psychological verities, for that matter, are disagreeable to state, but which must none the less be submitted to. Far more instructed than truly intelligent, the young engineer is totally unable to represent to himself—for that matter he does not try—the ideas and trains of reasoning of the men he is called upon to direct. Moreover, he does not preoccupy himself with the true means of influencing them. These matters are not taught in the schools, and therefore do not exist for him. His entire knowledge of psychology is confined to two or three ready-made ideas, which he has heard repeated by those about him, concerning the grossness and drunkenness of the artisan, and the necessity of keeping a tight rein on him, and so on. He catches only distorted glimpses of the ideas and conceptions of the workman. He will touch the delicate wheels of the human machine wrongly and clumsily. He will be weak or unreasonably despotic, according to his temperament, but in any case he will have no prestige and no real authority.

More than all else it is the insurmountable lack of comprehension which exists between the masters and the men that renders their present relations so strained.

The conceptions which the masters and men form respectively of their respective ideas and sentiments possess one thing in common. Each party being unable to assimilate the thoughts, cravings, and tastes of the other party, they interpret what they know nothing about according to their respective mentalities. The idea that the proletariat has of the *bourgeois*, that is to say, of the man who does not work with

his hands, is simple in the extreme ; he is a hard and
rapacious being who makes the workman work only to
get money out of him, who eats and drinks a great deal,
and amuses himself with all kinds of excesses. His
luxuries—however modest they may be, though they consist only of decent clothes and a fairly tidy house—are
only a monstrous waste. His literary or scientific labours
are sheer foolery, the whims of an idler. He has so much
money that he does not know what to do with it, while
the workman has none. Nothing would be easier than
to remedy this injustice, since a few wholesome laws
would suffice to reconstitute society between nightfall
and sunrise. Förce the rich to give the people what
belongs to them ; it would merely be to repair a crying
injustice. If the proletariat were able to doubt his own
logic there would be no lack of orators, more servile
before him than the courtiers of an Oriental despot before
their master, ready to remind him incessantly of his
imaginary rights. Unless, as I have already shown,
certain notions had been firmly implanted in the popular
subconsciousness by heredity, the Socialists must have
triumphed long ago.

The conception which the *bourgeois* forms of the working man is quite as inexact. For the master, the man is a
rude, drunken boor. Incapable of thrift, he squanders his
wages, without counting them, at the wineshop, instead of
spending the evening soberly in his room. Ought he not
to be thankful for his lot, and does he not earn far more
than he deserves ? He is given libraries, he is allowed
conferences, and cheap dwellings are built for him. What
more can he want ? Is he not incapable of looking after
his own affairs ? He must be controlled by a grip of
iron, and if anything is done for his benefit it must always
be done without his interference ; he must be treated
somewhat as a dog to which one throws a bone from

time to time when it growls a little too loudly. Can we attempt to perfect such an imperfectible being ? Besides, has not the world long ago assumed its final form, as regards political economy, morality, and even religion ? What is the use of all this hankering after change ?

To sum up : among the Latin peoples at least, masters and men form to-day two absolutely inimical classes, and as both classes feel themselves to be absolutely incapable of overcoming the difficulties of their daily relations by themselves, they invariably appeal to the State, thus once again to prove the irresistible need of the French people to be governed, and its inability to conceive of society otherwise than as a hierarchy of castes under the all-powerful control of a master. Free competition, spontaneous association, and personal initiative are conceptions which are inaccessible to our national spirit. Its ideal is always the salaried functionary in his every manifestation, under the laws of a chief. This ideal no doubt reduces the cost of the individual to the lowest level, but it also demands a minimum of character and action. The workman who cries out against his master could not do without him. "Where should we get our bread then ?" one of them asked me one day. And thus we return once more to this fundamental fact—that the destinies of a nation are controlled by its character, not by its institutions.

CHAPTER III

THE CONFLICT OF PEOPLES AND CLASSES

1. THE NATURAL CONFLICT OF INDIVIDUALS AND OF SPECIES.

THE only process that Nature has been able to discover for the amelioration of species is to bring into the world far more creatures than she is able to nourish, and to establish between them a perpetual struggle in which only the strongest and the best adapted

323

can survive. This conflict takes place not only between the different species, but also between the individuals of the same species, and it is often between the latter that it is most violent.

By this process of selection all creatures have been slowly perfected since the beginning of the world; by this process man has been evolved from the primitive types of the geological periods and our savage ancestors have slowly raised themselves to civilisation. From a sentimental point of view this struggle for existence with the survival of the fittest may appear to be extremely barbarous. But we must remember that were it not for this conflict we should still be miserably disputing an uncertain prey with all the animals we have finally subjected.

The struggle that Nature enforces on her creatures is universal and constant. Wherever there is no conflict there is not only no progress, but a tendency towards rapid degeneration.

After showing us the conflict prevailing among all living creatures, the naturalists have shown us that the same conflict prevails in our own bodies.

"Far from lending themselves to a mutual harmony," writes M. J. Kunstler, "the different parts of the bodies of living creatures seem, on the contrary, to be in perpetual conflict with one another. Any development of one part has, as its correlative consequence, a diminution of the importance of the other parts. In other words, any part that increases itself does so at the expense of other parts.

"Geoffroy Saint-Hilaire has already given a rough sketch of this phenomenon in establishing his 'principle of the equilibrium of the organs.' The modern theory of phagocytosis does not add very much to this principle, but it determines with greater clearness the process by which the phenomenon is produced.

" Not only do the organs struggle with one another, but all the parts of the body, no matter what they may be. For example, this conflict is to be observed in the tissues, between the various elements of the same tissue. The evolution of the weaker elements is diminished or arrested, it may be ruthlessly sacrificed for the benefit of the stronger elements, which thereby become more flourishing.

" Events would seem to denote that living organisms have only a determined quantity of evolutive power to expend. If, by means of any artifice or accident, this evolutionary force is directed to any one organ or process, the other organs are rendered more or less stationary, or may even recede. These facts, taken together, naturally lead one to compare them with the observed results of the law of primogeniture. When one of the children of a family is favoured in the division of the paternal goods, the share of the other children is by that fact diminished."

Nature exhibits an absolute intolerance for weakness. All that is weak is promptly doomed to perish. She respects only physical or intellectual strength. As intelligence is in strict relation to the amount of cerebral matter the individual possesses, we see that the rights of a living creature, in the eyes of Nature, are in close relation to the capacity of its skull. By this alone has man been able to arrogate to himself the right to kill the lower animals. If the latter could be consulted they would doubtless remark that the laws of Nature are very afflicting. The only consolation to be offered them is that Nature is full of other fatalities quite as afflicting. With a more highly-developed nervous system the edible animals would perhaps form a sort of trades-union, in order to escape the butcher's knife ; but they would not gain much by that. Left to themselves, no longer able to rely on the interested and even very attentive cares of their breeders, what would be their fate ? In countries still virgin they might pick up a miserable livelihood in the prairies, but there they would encounter the teeth of the carnivora, and if they escaped them it would be only for a slow death by hunger as soon as they became too old to seek out and dispute their food with their fellows.

To the weak, however, Nature has given a certain means of perpetuating themselves through the ages, in spite of all their enemies, by endowing them with a fecundity capable of tiring the appetite of all these enemies. For instance, a female herring deposits more than 60,000 eggs every year, so that a sufficient number of herring always escape to assure the continuation of the species. It would even appear that Nature has brought as much vigilance to bear to assure the perpetuity of the lowest species, the most obscure parasites, as to assure the existence of the highest organisms. The life of the greatest genius is not of more importance to her than the existence of the most miserable microbe. Nature is neither cruel nor kind. She thinks only of the species, and remains indifferent—formidably indifferent— to the individual. Our ideas of justice are unknown to her. We may protest against her laws, but we have to put up with her.

2. THE CONFLICT OF PEOPLES.

Has man succeeded in evading for his own part the hard laws of nature to which all creatures must submit ? Have the relations between one people and another been a little softened by civilisation ? Has the struggle become less bitter in the midst of humanity than between the species ?

History teaches us the contrary. It tells us that the nations have always been struggling, have always continued to struggle, and that since the beginning of the world the right of the strongest has always been the arbiter of their destinies.

This was the law of the past, and it is the law of the present. Nothing denotes that it will not be the law of the future also.

Not that there is to-day any lack of theologians and philanthropists to protest against it. To them we owe the numberless volumes in which they appeal, in eloquent phrases, to right and to justice, a kind of sovereign divinities who direct the world from the depths of the skies. But the facts have always given the lie to their vain phraseology. These facts tell us that right exists only when it possesses the necessary strength to make itself respected. We cannot say that might is greater than right, for might and right are identical. No right can enforce itself without might. No one, I imagine, will doubt that a country which should confide in right and justice, and disband its army, would be immediately invaded, pillaged, and enslaved by its neighbours. If weak states such as Turkey, Greece, Portugal, Spain, and China are still able to subsist, it is only on account of the rivalry of the stronger states that wish to take possession of them. Obliged to consider the sensibilities of states as strong as themselves, the powerful states can despoil the weaker only with prudence, and can assimilate their provinces only by fragments. In this manner have Bosnia, Malta, Cyprus, and Egypt been stolen one by one from the peoples who possessed them. As for those countries that are practically without defence, the powerful states have no scruples in invading their territory.

No nation must forget to-day that its rights are exactly limited by the forces at its disposal to defend those rights. The sole acknowledged right of the sheep is to deliver up its cutlets to beings possessing a greater skull than its own. The sole recognised right of the negroes is to see their country invaded and pillaged by the whites, and to be shot down if they resist. If they do not resist they are merely lightened of all their possessions, and then made to work under the lash in order to enrich the invaders. Such was the history of the natives of America. Such is to-day the story of the inhabitants of Africa. The negroes are now learning the penalty of being weak. To please the philanthropists who write books, a number of amiable orations on the unhappy lot of these native populations are let loose before the shooting begins. This benevolence is even extended to the sending of missionaries, whose pockets are bulging with bibles and bottles of alcohol, in order to initiate them into the benefits of civilisation. The negroes, whose heads are thick, are not very ready to perceive the greatness of these benefits. It is, however, incontestable that even though we do rob them and shoot them down without scruple, we at least save them from the prospect of being eaten by their own countrymen. I imagine, however, that if their flesh had been more than indifferent to the white man, they would not escape this fate now any more than in the past. Then the destiny of the negro would doubtless have been that of the ox, when that pacific animal begins to fail at the plough. When he became unable to work any longer he would be sent to the slaughter-house after a previous fattening. There would have been no lack of profound theologians to thank the Creator that, after evidently having created the ox to furnish men with beefsteaks, He took the trouble to add the negro.

Leaving these foolish babblings of the theologians and philanthropists on one side, we must recognise, as a matter of daily observation, that human laws have been utterly powerless to modify the laws of nature, and that the latter continue to determine the relations of one people with another. All theories of right and justice are futile. International relations are to-day what they have been since the beginning of the world, when different interests are in question, or when it is merely a matter of a nation wishing to enlarge itself. Right and justice have never played any part in the relations of nations of unequal strength. Be conqueror or conquered, hunter or chased : such has always been the law. The phrases of diplomatists and the sermons of orators remind one of the civilities uttered by men of the world when they have resumed their coats. The man of the world will efface himself to let you pass, and will ask with affectionate sympathy after your most distant relations. But let any circumstance arise in which his interests are concerned, and you behold these superficial sentiments vanish on the instant. Then it is a matter of each for himself, though he have to crush the women and children who embarrass him under his heel, or stun them with a cudgel, as at the *Charité* Bazaar or at the wreck of the *Bourgogne*. There are certainly exceptions, brave men who are ready to sacrifice themselves for their fellows, but they are so rare that they are regarded as heroes, and their names are handed down to posterity.

We have very little reason to believe that the conflict of people with people will be less violent in the future than it has been in the past. On the other hand, there are very good reasons for believing that it will be far more violent. When nation was severed from nation by distances that science had not learned to bridge over, the causes of conflict were rare. To-day they are becoming more and more frequent. Formerly international struggles were provoked by dynastic interests or the whims of conquerors. In the future the principal motives of international conflict will be those great economic interests on which the very lives of the nations depend, the importance of which we have already seen. The approaching struggles of the nations will be struggles for very life, and will hardly be terminated but by the utter annihilation of one of the combatants.

These are essential truths which it is in no one's interest to conceal, and which it is very dangerous to wish to conceal. I think it will be admitted as sufficiently evident that one might have rendered the Spaniards a great service in teaching them thoroughly, twenty-five years ago, that as soon as they should be sufficiently weakened by their interminable intestine quarrels any nation could profit by the first pretext to seize on their colonies, and would succeed without difficulty, in spite of the prayers of the monks and the protection of madonnas. Then, perhaps, they would have understood the utility of having fewer revolutions, delivering fewer speeches, and organising their defences in such a fashion as to prohibit the idea of attacking them. A small nation can defend itself very well if sufficiently energetic. Many nations are to-day devoting a third of their Budgets to military expenses, and this price of assurance against the aggressions of their neighbours would certainly be less heavy if it were well employed.

3. THE STRUGGLE OF THE CLASSES.

The Collectivists attribute to their high priest Karl Marx the statement of the fact that history is dominated by the struggles of the different classes over matters of economic interests, and also the assertion that this struggle must disappear on account of the absorption of all classes in one single class—the working class.

The first point, the struggle of the classes, is a banality as old as the world. By the mere fact of the unequal partition of wealth and power, caused by natural inequalities, or merely by social necessities, men have always been divided into classes, of which the interests were necessarily more or less exposed, and consequently at war. But the idea that this struggle might cease is one of those chimerical conceptions that are completely contradicted by the realities, and its realisation is very far from being a desirable thing. Without the conflict of individuals, races, and classes—in a word, without universal conflict, man would never have emerged from savagery, would never have attained to civilisation.

The tendency to conflict, which, as we have seen, dominates the relations of the animal species and of men, is also predominant in the relations of individuals and of classes.

" We have only to look around us in the world in which we live," writes Mr. Kidd, " to see that this rivalry which man maintains with his fellows has become the leading and dominant feature of our civilisation. It makes itself felt now throughout the whole fabric of society. If we examine the motives of our daily life, and of the lives of those with whom we come in contact, we shall have to recognise that the first and principal thought in the minds of the vast majority is how to hold our own therein. . . . The implements of industry prove even more effective and deadly weapons than the sword."

And not only is there a struggle between the classes, but between the individuals of the same class, and the struggle between the latter, as in nature, is the most violent.[1] The Socialists themselves, although now and

---

[1] This is very evident, since competition is scarcely possible except between individuals of the same class : and on account of the increasing number of the competitors, the competition is becoming fiercer. The competitors put up with one another because they cannot do otherwise, but the tenderest sentiment they entertain for one another is a ferocious jealousy. The following description of the *salle de garde* of medical students, recently published in a

then united for a common end, the destruction of our present society, are unable to assemble together without the most violent discord.

The struggle to-day is more violent than it has ever been before, and this for many reasons ; amongst others, for this, that we have followed after chimeras of justice and equality which are unknown to Nature. These empty formulæ have done and will do more ill to man than all the ills which destiny has condemned him to suffer.

" There is no social justice," writes M. Bouge very justly, " because Nature herself is not just. Injustice and inequality are with us from the cradle.

" From the cradle to the grave, all through the course of an existence of which she arbitrarily prolongs or curtails the blessing or the burden, the inequality of Nature follows man step by step.

" Inequality under a thousand forms ! Natural inequality, the chances of birth and inheritance, physical advantages or disgrace, intellectual disparities, and the inequalities of destiny. . . ."

Long before Socialism the religions had also dreamed the dream of suppressing the struggle of people with people, class with class, and individual, but what was the result of their endeavour save to make fiercer the very struggles they wished to abolish ? Were not the wars

medical journal, clearly shows the nature of the sentiments that the necessities of civilisation are steadily propagating in all classes :—

" To-day the *salle de garde* has become orderly, but frigid and taciturn. The medical student is no more the jolly companion of old, ready to chum up with everybody ; he is frozen in his own dignity, and imagines that the eyes of the world are on him. Each student keeps guard over himself, and keeps his ideas to himself, when he has any, for fear lest his neighbour should profit by them. Thanks to the formidable prospect of the examinations, he shuts himself jealously within himself. The comrade of to-day will be the rival of to-morrow, and in the race for diplomas friendship must be forgotten."

they provoked the cruellest of all, the most fruitful of political and social disasters ?

Can we hope that with the progress of civilisation the struggle of the classes will diminish ? On the contrary, everything tends to show that it will become far more intense than it has ever been in the past.

There are two reasons for this : the first is the more and more profound division between the classes, the second is the power which the new methods of association give to the various classes to defend their demands.

The first reason can hardly be contested. The differences between the classes of men and masters, proprietors and proletariats, for example, are visibly greater than the old differences of caste, say the difference between the people and the nobility. The distance created by birth, it was then considered, could not be bridged over. It was the result of the Divine will, and was accepted without discussion. Violent abuses might sometimes give rise to revolts, but the people revolted solely against the abuses, and not against the established order of things.

To-day it is quite otherwise. The people revolt not against the abuses, which were never less than at present, but against the whole social system. At present Socialism wishes to destroy the upper classes, simply to take their place and to take possession of their wealth.

"Their end," says M. Boilley, "is soon stated ; they wish, without preamble, to form a popular class which shall expropriate the upper classes. They wish to launch forth the poor man in pursuit of the rich, and the profit account will be closed by the monopolising of the spoils of the vanquished. Timour and Ghengis Khan led their multitudes on the same quest."

These conquerors, it is true, had much the same motives, but those whom they threatened with conquest knew perfectly well that their only chance of salvation was by defending themselves with energy, while to-day the adversaries of the new barbarians think of nothing but parleying with them, and of prolonging their existence a little by a series of concessions which do nothing but encourage those who are gathering for the assault, and provoke their contempt.

The struggles of the future will be aggravated by the fact that they will not be inspired, as were the old wars of conquest, by the desire to pillage an enemy who once conquered became an object of indifference. To-day furious hatred rages between the combatants, a hatred which is gradually tending to assume a religious form, and thus to acquire the special characteristics of ferocity and insubordination which invariably animate a true believer.

We have already perceived one of the chiefest causes of the present war of the classes in the extreme falsity of the ideas which the opposing parties have formed of one another. While studying the foundations of beliefs we saw too clearly to what a degree the relations of being with being are dominated by utter miscomprehension to wonder at the impossibility of eliminating that factor. The fiercest wars, and the religious struggles which have stained the world with blood, and have done most to change the face of civilisations and empires, have very often arisen from some such miscomprehension. Very often it is the very falsity of an idea which constitutes its strength. The most glaring error becomes, for the crowd, a radiant truth, if it be sufficiently repeated. Nothing is easier to sow than error, and when it has taken root it has the omnipotence of the dogmas of religion. It inspires faith, and nothing can stand against faith. In the Middle Ages half of the West hurled itself on the East for the sake of the most erroneous concepts ; by such errors the successors of Mahomet established their gigantic empire ; by such errors Europe was later on deluged with blood and fire. The falsity of the parent ideas of these upheavals is to-day evident to a child. To-day they are merely vague words, of which the centuries have so exhausted the life that we can no longer understand the power they once exercised. None the less was this power irresistible, for there was a time when the clearest reason, the most obvious demonstrations, were powerless to prevail against it. It is time only, and never reason, that has power to slay phantoms.

The magical empire of lying words is not a thing of the past. The soul of the people has changed, but its beliefs are always as false as ever, and the words that sway it are always as deceptive. Error, under new names, preserves its ancient magic.

4. THE FUTURE SOCIALISTIC STRUGGLES.

Made inevitable by the irresistible laws of Nature, aggravated by the new conditions of civilisation, by the miscomprehension which dominates the reciprocal relations of the classes, by the increasing divergency of their interests, the conflict of the classes is destined to become more violent than it has ever been at any period of the world's history. The hour is approaching when the social edifice will suffer the most redoubtable assaults that have ever been made on it.

The new barbarians are threatening not only the possessors of wealth, but our very civilisation, which appears to them merely the guardian of luxury, and a useless complication.

Never have the maledictions of their leaders been so furious; never has any people whose gods and thresholds were threatened by a pitiless enemy given vent to such imprecations. The more pacific of the Socialists confine themselves to demanding the expropriation of the upper classes. The more ardent wish for their utter annihilation. According to a sentiment expressed by one of them at a meeting, and cited by M. Boilley, "the skins of the infamous *bourgeois* will at least do to make gloves of."

As far as they can, these ringleaders suit the action to the word. The list of crimes committed in Europe by the advance-guard of Socialism during the last fifteen years is very significant. Three sovereigns assassinated, one of them an empress, and two others wounded; six prefects of police killed, and a considerable number of deaths caused by explosions in palaces, theatres, dwelling-houses, and railway stations. One of these explosions, that at the Liceo Theatre at Barcelona, had eighty-three victims; that at the Winter Palace at St. Petersburg killed eight persons, and wounded forty-five. The number of journals in Europe that egg on the movement is reckoned at forty. We may judge, from the violence of these skirmishes, what a savage ferocity will animate the struggle when it has become general.

Doubtless the past has seen struggles as violent, but the conditions of the opposing forces were very different, and the defence of society a much easier matter. Then the crowd had no political power. It had not yet learned how to associate itself and thus to form armies which blindly obeyed the orders of absolute chiefs. What association may do we learn from the last strike in Chicago. It ended in the strike of all the railway men in the United States, and had as its further results the burning of the palaces of the Exposition and the immense workshops of the Pulman Company. The Government assumed the upper hand only by suspending civil rights, proclaiming martial law, and delivering veritable battle to the insurgents. The strikers were shot down without pity, and defeated; but we can imagine the hatred that must fill the hearts of the survivors, among both the vanquished workmen and the successful masters, whose ruin the former had provoked by arson, pillage, and massacre.

The United States would seem fated to furnish the Old World with the first examples of the struggles which will take place between intelligence, capacity, capital, and the terrible army of the unfit of which I shall presently speak, the social sediment which has been so greatly increased by the modern development of industry.

The issue of the struggle in the United States will doubtless be their division into a number of rival republics. Their fate does not concern us ; it interests us only as an example. This example will perhaps save Europe from the complete triumph of Socialism ; that is to say, from a return to the most shameful barbarism.

The social question will be singularly complicated in the United States by the fact that the great republic is divided into regions whose interests are very different, and consequently conflicting. M. de Varigny has very well presented this fact in the following lines :—

"Washington continues to be the neutral ground on which political questions are decided, but it is not the place in which these questions arise and affect American life. The life of the nation is to be found elsewhere ; its unity is not established, and it has no homogeneity. Under the apparent union of a great people—and union is not unity—there are profound divergencies, diverse interests, and conflicting tendencies. They are only emphasised by time ; they grow more evident as history unrolls itself ; and they assert themselves in such facts as the War of Secession, which brought the Union within an inch of destruction.

"If we examine closely this vast republic, which Russia and China alone surpass in extent of territory, and which already ranks fifth in the world in respect of population, we shall first of all be struck by this fact—that the United States are divided into three sections by a geographical and commercial grouping; the Southern States, those of the North and West, and those of the Pacific; and already there are germs of division between the North and the West. The various interests of these groups result in incompatible demands, and for fifteen years the politicians have been seeking, without discovering, the means of making industries live and prosper under a common tariff which in reality call for a special *régime*. The South produces raw material, such as sugar and cotton, the North is manufacturing, the West agricultural, and the Pacific agricultural and mining. The system of protection now in vogue is ruining the South, embarrassing the West, and making the fortune of the North, to which free trade would deliver a terrible blow."

But we must not too closely forecast the fate of any nation on a few general indications. Our destiny is still concealed by the impenetrable mists of the future. It is often possible to foresee the direction of the forces which lead us, but it is futile to seek to define their effects or discern their course. All that we can say is, that the defence of the old societies will become very difficult. The evolution of things has sapped the foundation of the edifice of the past ages. The army, the last pillar of the edifice, the only one that might yet sustain it, has entered on a process of disintegration, and its worst enemies are now to be found in the educated classes. Our ignorance of certain incontestable evidences of psychology, an ignorance which will strike the historians of the future with amazement, has led the greater number of the European states almost entirely to renounce their means of defence, by replacing the professional army, such as England so rightly contents herself with, and with which she dominates the world, by undisciplined crowds, who are supposed to learn one of the most difficult of professions in a few months. You have not made soldiers of millions of men simply because you have taught them drill. You have merely produced mobs without discipline, resistance, or courage, more dangerous for those who try to handle them than to their enemies.[1]

The danger of these multitudes, from the point of view of social defence, resides not only in their military insufficiency, but in the spirit which animates them. The professional armies formed a special caste, with sentiments apart, strangers to everything that did not interest them directly, and having nothing to look for from outside. But these crowds who only pass sufficient time in the army to suffer the tediousness of military life, and to regard it with horror, what sentiments of caste are they likely to have? Taken from the workshop, the factory, the dockyard, where they will promptly return, of what value will they be in the defence of a social order that they disdain, and incessantly hear attacked? This is the danger that the Governments do not yet see, and on which it would consequently be quite useless to insist. I doubt, however, if a single European State can exist long without a permanent army, relying only on universal compulsory service. Doubtless the latter

---

[1] I hope one day to enter more fully into these questions, in a study of the psychology of war. It is plain that we cannot, for reasons of a purely moral order, suppress the universal compulsory service, which has the advantage of giving a little discipline to men who are all but destitute of that quality; but we might arrive at a very simple compromise : reduce compulsory service to one year, and maintain a permanent army of 200,000 to 300,000 men, formed as in England of enlisted volunteers, who would make a military career their profession.

satisfies our eager craving for a low equality, but is it really admissible that the satisfaction of such a craving should endanger the very existence of a race ?

The future will inform both nations and Governments on this point. Experience is the only book that nations can learn from. Unfortunately the reading of this book has always cost them terribly dear.

CHAPTER IV

THE SOCIAL SOLIDARITY

1. *Social solidarity and charity :*—The fundamental difference between the two—Charity is an anti-social and harmful sentiment—The most useful works of solidarity have neither charity nor altruism as their base—They are based on the association of similar interests—The movement towards solidarity is one of the most important tendencies of modern social evolution—The profundity of its causes—Association replaces individual egoism, which is powerless, by a powerful collective egoism, by which every one profits—Solidarity is at present the best arm of the weak. 2. *The modern forms of solidarity :*—It is possible only between individuals having similar immediate interests—Co-operative societies—Their development among the Anglo-Saxons—Why they are unsuccessful among the Latins—Public companies—Their power and utility—They must be made to penetrate into the popular classes—Co-operative societies and their drawbacks—How the workers might become proprietors of their workshops—Unions—Their utility, their power, and their inconveniences—They are the necessary consequence of modern evolution—Disappearance of the old familiar relations between masters and men.

1. Social Solidarity and Charity.

THE struggle which, as we have just seen, is taking place in the heart of society, brings together adversaries who are very unequally endowed. We shall see how the weaker have been able, by associating their forces, to render the warfare less unequal.

For many people the term "social solidarity" always recalls, to some extent, the idea of charity. Its true sense, however, is very different. The societies of the present day are approaching solidarity of interests and relinquishing charity. It is even very probable that the societies of the future will regard charity as a low and barbarous conception, altruistic in nothing but appearance, thoroughly egoistic in essence, and generally noxious.

The term solidarity signifies merely association, and by no means charity or altruism. Charity is a noxious and anti-social sentiment ; altruism is an artificial and impotent sentiment. When we examine the most useful works of solidarity—insurance and mutual aid societies, societies for granting pensions, co-operative societies, &c. —we find that they are never based on charity or altruism, but simply on the combined interests of a number of people who more often than not have never seen one another. Having paid a certain annual subscription, the subscriber receives a pension in proportion to this subscription in the event of sickness or age. It is a matter of privilege without benevolence, just as the man who insures his property against fire has a right, in case of fire, to the amount for which he has insured it. Of course he profits by the collective subscriptions, since the sum he receives is far greater than the sum he has paid, but all the members of the collectivity may profit in the same way, and he owes nothing to any man. He profits by a privilege which he has bought, not by a favour, and it is important to mark clearly the profound difference between associations of interests which are based on financial combinations guided by the calculation of probabilities and the works of charity which are based on the hypothetical good wishes and uncertain altruism of a small number of individuals. Works of charity have no real social value, and are very justly rejected by a large number of Socialists, who on this point are at one with the most eminent thinkers. That there are such institutions as hospitals and assistance bureaux, conducted by the State at the public expense, we can only be thankful ; but charity on the whole is more harmful in practice than useful. In default of an impossible amount of supervision it serves more often than not to support a whole class of individuals who merely exploit pity in order to live in idleness. The obvious result is to prevent a number of destitute people from working, as they find the resources of charity more convenient and even more productive, and to increase professional mendicity to an enormous extent. The countless charitable associations for the assistance of the unemployed, or young consumptives, or widows without resources, or deserted Chinese infants, &c., &c., are at most only of use to afford occupation for unemployed old ladies, or to idle men of the world, who wish to obtain salvation at a cheap rate, and are glad to occupy their leisure by becoming presidents, secretaries, committee members, treasurers, &c., of something or other. Thus they procure the illusion that they have been of some use here below. And herein they are very greatly mistaken.[1]

The movement in favour of solidarity, that is to say, the association of similar interests, which is so generally

[1] Wishing to gain practical information on the possible utility of these works of charity, and thus to be in a position to confirm by experience what I had heard, I informed myself which was the most important of them ; that which would theoretically appear to be the most useful, since it is able, to all accounts, to procure immediate employment to individuals out of work, which is already a great advance on mere charity. Having paid my subscription as a member, I took the simplest cases imaginable, and attempted to obtain work for certain valid individuals who were temporarily unemployed, and who were ready to content themselves with the lowest salaries. Not one of them obtained a place, and I did not even receive a reply. I then sent the same persons to the ordinary employment bureaux, which make no philanthropic pretensions, have no great names on their lists, and have no other motives than personal interest. In a few days my candidates obtained the modest situations they desired. Private interest was thus far more effectual than noisy and decorated philanthropy. I did not regret the small sum thus expended in once more confirming a very elementary truth.

evident, is perhaps the most definite of the new social tendencies, and is probably one of those that will have the greatest effect on our evolution. To-day the word solidarity is heard far oftener than the old shibboleths of equality and fraternity, and is tending to supplant them. It is by no means synonymous. As the final object of the association of interests is to struggle against other interests, it is evident that solidarity is only a particular form of the universal conflict of classes and individuals. Understood as it is to-day, solidarity reduces our old dreams of fraternity to the very closely circumscribed limits of associations.

This tendency towards solidarity in the shape of associations, a tendency which we see extending itself every day, has various causes. The most important of these is the abatement of individual will and initiative, and the frequent uselessness of these qualities under the conditions which have arisen from the modern developments of economics. The need of isolated action is becoming rarer and rarer. It is almost impossible for individual efforts to exert themselves to-day except through the agency of associations, that is to say, by the aid of collectivities.

A still profounder cause is impelling the modern man to association. He has lost his gods, he sees his home threatened, he no longer has faith in the future, and he feels more and more the need of something to lean on. Association replaces the impotent egoism of the individual by a collective and powerful and collective egoism by which every one profits. In default of classification by the ties of religion, the ties of blood, the ties of politics, and all the different ties which are every day growing weaker, the solidarity of interests is able to unite men with sufficient strength.

This kind of solidarity is almost the only means remaining to the weak, that is to say, to the greater number, by which they may struggle against the powerful, and be not too greatly oppressed by them.

In the universal struggle whose laws we have already traced the weaker are always defenceless before the stronger, and the stronger do not hesitate to crush them. Lords, feudal, financial, or industrial, have hitherto never troubled much about those whom circumstances have placed below them.

To this universal oppression, that neither religions nor laws have hitherto been able to combat with stronger weapons than empty words, the modern man has hitherto found nothing to oppose but the principle of association, which consolidates all the individuals of the same group. Solidarity is the best arm that the weak possess in order to efface to some extent the consequences of social inequalities, and to render them a little less hard. Far from being contradicted by natural laws, it has the merit of being based on them. Science knows nothing of liberty, or at least does not accept it in her own domain, since she discovers everywhere phenomena ruled by an inflexible determinism. Still less does she believe in equality, for modern biology sees in the inequalities of creatures the fundamental condition of their progress. Neither will she accept fraternity, since merciless war has been a constant phenomenon since the remotest geologic periods. Solidarity, on the contrary, is not contradicted by any known fact. Certain animals, and above all the weakest, are only able to exist by a rigid solidarity, which alone makes it possible for them to defend themselves against their enemies.

The association of the similar interests of the various members of human societies is assuredly very ancient, since it is to be found in our earliest records of history, but in all ages it was always more or less hampered and limited. It was barely possible on the narrow region of economic and religious interests. The Revolution thought to do a useful work in suppressing the corporations. No measure could have been more disastrous to the democratic cause that the men of the Revolution thought they were defending. To-day these abolished corporations are everywhere reappearing under new names and new forms. In the modern developments of industry, which have considerably increased the division of labour, this renaissance was inevitable.

2. THE MODERN FORMS OF SOLIDARITY.

Now that we have clearly marked the difference between those solidarities which are based on combined interests and those which repose on charity, let us take a rapid glance at the various forms of modern solidarity.

It is at once evident that a solidarity between individuals does not exist simply because they are engaged in a common work, the success of which depends on the association of their efforts ; indeed, we very often find the contrary. The director of a factory, his men, and his shareholders, have theoretically a common interest in working for the success of the concern on which their existence or fortune depends. In reality this far-fetched solidarity only covers very conflicting interests, and the parties in contact are by no means actuated by reciprocal sentiments of benevolence. The workman wants his salary to be raised, which can be done only by reducing the shareholders' profits. The shareholders, on the contrary, represented by the director, have every reason to reduce the profits of the workmen in order to increase their own ; so that the solidarity which theoretically ought to exist between workmen, directors, and shareholders has no real existence.

True solidarity is possible only between persons who

have the same immediate interests. Such are the interests
that have called into being the modern institution of the
trades-union, which we shall presently examine.

There are, however, certain forms of association which
are able to consolidate interests that are naturally
conflicting. They associate the contrary interests of
producers and consumers by offering them reciprocal
advantages. The producer voluntarily contents himself
with a reduced profit on each article sold if the sale of
a large number of articles is assured to him, and this sale
is rendered certain by the association of a considerable
number of purchasers.

In the great English co-operative societies there are
only identical interests associated, as the consumer is at
the same time the producer, these societies producing
almost everything that they consume, and even owning
farms producing wheat, sheep and cattle, milk, vegetables,
and so forth. They present this very great advantage :
that the weaker and less capable members benefit by the
intelligence of the most capable, who are placed at the
head of these enterprises, which could not prosper without
them. The Latin countries have not arrived at this yet.

I have elsewhere shown that it is by themselves administrating their various associations, and notably their co-
operative societies, that the Anglo-Saxon workers have
learned to manage their own affairs. The French workman is too deeply imbued with the Latin concepts of his
race to permit of his possession of the initiative necessary
to found and administer societies which would allow him
to ameliorate his lot. If, thanks to a few intelligent
leaders, he does sometimes found such a society, he
immediately confides its administration to second-rate
men of business, whom he treats with suspicion, and the
affair soon comes to grief.

These Latin societies, which are administered by

intermediaries indifferent to their success, are conducted with the meticulous and complicated procedure
peculiar to our national temperament, and vegetate
miserably. An additional cause of their ill success is
that the Latin workman, having little foresight, will buy
his provisions from day to day at retail, from small shopkeepers, with whom he gossips, and who very willingly
give him credit, for which he has to pay dearly, rather
than of the large stores at which he must pay ready
money, and where he cannot talk half the day over a
purchase. It would, however, be greatly to his interest
to rid himself of intermediaries by means of co-operative
societies. The sum paid in one year in France to the
middlemen, who separate the producer from the consumer, has been reckoned at more than £280,000,000, or
twice the amount we pay in taxes. The exactions of the
middleman are far more severe than those of the capitalist,
but the workman does not see them, and in consequence
supports them without a murmur.

The most widespread of modern forms of association,
and at the same time most anonymous, is the public
company. As M. Leroy-Beaulieu says very truly, it is
"the ruling trait of the economic organisation of the
modern world. . . . Industry, finance, commerce, and
even agriculture, and colonial enterprises—it extends to
everything. It is already in almost every nation the
habitual instrument of the mechanical production and
the exploitation of the forces of nature. . . . The anonymous company seems to be called on to become the
ruler of the world; it is the true heir of the old feudal
system and the fallen aristocracy. It will be the emperor
of the world; for the hour is approaching when the world
will be issued in shares." It is, as our author says further,
a product not of wealth, but of the democracy, and the
dissemination of capital in many hands.

Exploitation by shares is, in fact, the only form of association possible to small capitalists. It constitutes Collectivism in appearance, but only in appearance, for it is a Collectivism which one may enter freely, and leave freely, and the profit is strictly proportioned to the effort, that is to say, to the sum of little economies which each individual brings to it. On the day when the workman becomes the proprietor, anonymous but interested, of the shop in which he works, by means of the system of shares, an immense advance will have been accomplished. It is perhaps only by this method that the economic emancipation of the workman will ever take place—if it ever does take place—and by which the natural and social inequalities of man may be to some extent effaced.

Hitherto the public company has not penetrated so far as the popular classes. The only mode of association approaching to the public company (though in reality very unlike it) known to the people, is the system of profit-sharing. Many societies founded on this principle have succeeded very well. If there are not very many such societies it is because the proper organisation of such enterprises demands very superior and therefore always rare capacities.

I may mention as the oldest and most remarkable of these associations the association of painters founded in 1829 by Leclaire, and continued by Redouly et Cie of Paris; the factory of Guise in Aisne; that of Laecken in Belgium, &c. The first divides 25 per cent. of the profits among its members, who are all workmen, and after a certain number of years gives them a pension of £60. There are now 920 of these pensions.

The Guise factory is a kind of community, in which the association of capital and labour have produced excellent results. In 1894 it did business to the extent of more than £200,000, and made a profit of nearly £30,000.

There are now more than 300 establishments of this kind in France and abroad.

The most celebrated of these societies in England is that of the Equitable Pioneers of Rochdale, which was founded in 1844 by an association of twenty-eight work-men who possessed a little capital. In 1891 it counted 12,000 associates and a capital of £360,000. It does business to the extent of about £300,000, and yields an annual profit of £52,000.

Associations of this kind have had as great a success in Belgium; notably the Woruit at Ghent. There are also many very prosperous concerns of the same kind in Germany. A certain number have been founded in northern Italy in the last few years, but there, as in France, they will perish for want of proper management. Their organisation is altogether Latin in character, which means that their fate will depend entirely on the indi-viduals placed at their head, as the members have neither the capacity nor, so far as that goes, the intention to administer them themselves as the Anglo-Saxon work-men do.

The great danger of these societies is that the sharing of profits necessarily implies the sharing of losses, which are and must be frequent in industry. As long as there is a profit the associates are perfectly at one, but as soon as there is a loss the harmony, as a general thing, is quickly broken. America has recently furnished us with a very striking proof of this. The destruction by fire of the gigantic establishment of the Pulman Company, and the acts of savage vandalism and pillage which followed, shows us plainly what becomes of these great enterprises when they are no longer attended with success.

The Pulman Company had built enormous factories occupying 6,000 men, and a charming town for the latter and their families. This town counted 13,000 inhabitants, and was provided with every modern comfort, a large park, theatre, library, &c. The houses could be acquired only by the workmen, who became proprietors by paying a small annual sum.

As long as affairs were in full swing peace and abundance reigned. The men had deposited nearly £160,000 in the savings banks in a few years.

But the orders lessened on account of the reduced profits of the railway companies, the customers of the company, so that the latter, in order not to work at a loss by employing all their men, were obliged to cut down their wages from 9s. 2d. a day to 6s. 3d. A veritable revolution followed. The workshops were pillaged and burnt, and the workers determined on a strike which spread to the railways and led to such scenes of violence that President Cleveland was obliged to proclaim martial law. The revolt was finally brought to an end by firing . on the strikers.

I have little faith in these profit-sharing societies, which place the man too much at the mercy of his master, and bind him to that master for too long a time. The master has no real interest in sharing his profits with the men, since it is certain that they will always refuse to share in the losses also, and will revolt as soon difficulties appear. Moreover, it is only out of sheer philanthropy that a master consents to share his profits with his men. Nothing can force him to do so. It is possible to found a durable institution on interest, which is a solid and unchanging sentiment, but not on philanthropy, which is a fluctuating and always ephemeral sentiment. Philanthropy, too, is too like pity to inspire any gratitude in its objects. I imagine that Mr. Pulman, before his burning factories, must have acquired those valuable ideas of the value of philanthropy which are not to be learned from books, and yet the ignorance of which often costs so dear.

The only possible form of profit-sharing which absolutely respects the interests of both master and man, and
which makes them independent of one another, is profit-
sharing by means of shares, which implies participation
in the losses as well as in the gains, and is the only equitable and therefore acceptable arrangement.   The £1
share is within the reach of every purse, and I am
amazed that no factories have yet been started in which
the shareholders will be solely workmen.   When once
the workman shall be thus transformed into a capitalist
interested in the success of his business, his present
demands will have no *raison d'être*, since he will be
working solely for himself.   The workman who should
wish for any reason to change his workshop would
merely sell his shares like any other shareholder in
order to regain his liberty.   The only difficulty would
arise in finding the men capable of directing the factory,
but experience would soon teach the workers the value of
these capable men, and the necessity of securing them by
paying them at a suitable rate.

I gave a few hints on this subject a long time ago in
one of my books.   This book recently falling into the
hands of a Belgian engineer, M. Bourson, who is occupied
in industrial matters, he was struck with the practical
utility of my idea, and wrote to me that he was going to
attempt to realise it.   I sincerely hope he will succeed.
The great difficulty, evidently, resides in the subscription
of the necessary capital, which cannot be demanded from
men without any money.   The only method that I can
see is to sell in part or in totality an already existing
factory to the workmen employed in it, as it might be
sold to ordinary shareholders, but so that the workmen
might acquire it gradually.   Let us, for example, suppose
that the proprietor of a factory wished to convert his
business into a company, as many do nowadays. Hitherto,

we will say, he has always paid his men 5s. 6d. a day. He will now pay them only 4s. 9d. or 4s. 6d. a day, and the deficit will be entered to the account of each hand until the total of the amounts held back amounts to £1, the price of a share. This share will be registered in the name of the workman, who may draw the dividend at will, but is not permitted to sell before the lapse of a certain number of years, so as to preserve him from the temptation of parting with it. In this manner the workman will soon become the holder of a more or less considerable number of shares, of which the dividends will soon repay him for the reduction of his salary, and will afford him an income in his old age. He will thus have become a proprietor without any intervention on the part of the State. The moral effect thus obtained would be of even greater value than the material advantages of such a system. The workman would properly regard the factory as a personal property, and would be interested in its success. By attending the meetings of shareholders he would learn first to understand and then to take a part in the discussion of matters of business. He would soon understand the part played by capital, and the interplay of economic necessities. Having become a capitalist he would no longer be a mere labourer. Finally, he would emerge from his narrow sphere, his limited horizon. The present antagonism of capital and labour would gradually be replaced by alliance. The interests at present in conflict would be fused. The man of action and brains who should preach by example and be the first to realise this idea might be regarded as one of the benefactors of humanity.

There is yet one more form of association to be examined, a form born of the necessities of the period, already possessed of great power, and destined to obtain yet more. I am speaking of leagues or unions, which group together, in a momentary or permanent fashion, individuals having the same interests or following the same profession.

This form of association, which is new to the Latin peoples, is already long familiar to such peoples as the Anglo-Saxons, peoples who have long rejoiced in liberty, and who know how to depend on themselves and to help themselves.

"Here," said Taine, speaking of England, "if a man has a good idea he communicates it to his friends. It appears good to many of them. They subscribe money, publish the idea, and summon around them sympathies and subscriptions. The sympathy and the subscriptions arrive ; the publicity of the idea increases. The snowball begins to grow; it strikes against the doors of Parliament, and opens them, or melts away. This is the English mechanism of reforms ; this is how the English manage their own affairs ; and you must understand that all over the soil of England there are little snowballs in process of growth."

It is by associations of this kind, such as the Corn League of Cobden, that the English have obtained their most useful reforms. They enforce their desires on Parliament so soon as it becomes evident that they are the expression of a popular desire.

It is evident that no isolated individual, however influential, can obtain as much as can be obtained by an association representing numerous collective interests. M. Bonvallot has shown what may be obtained by a league of individuals with collective interests.

"The Touring Club, which counts more than 70,000 members, at the present time, is a power. Not only has the Touring Club provided cyclists with road maps, itineraries, reduced hotel tariffs, and assistance depôts, but it has also awakened the terrible administration of the Bridges and Roads department, and has provided roads on which it is possible to cycle. It has made the redoubtable railway companies capitulate ; it has turned the crusty customs officials into obliging fellows, and has made the crossing of the frontier a pleasure."

The Touring Club was founded without any difficulty, since each member, by paying his very modest subscription, obtained the protection of a powerful association, of which he felt the need every day, and which would repay his subscription a hundred times over in the services it would render him. But I doubt if any analogous association could have in France, as in England, for its end, an important reform of general interest—an educational reform, for instance. If my worthy friend Bonvallot could succeed in organising a league for the reform of education which should number only a tenth of the members of the Touring Club, he would be able to boast of having rendered an enormous service to his country.

We must recognise that hitherto the working classes have profited most intelligently by such associations, and we cannot too greatly admire the results of their efforts. They have obtained their present power not by the universal suffrage, but by their trades-unions. These unions have become the arm of the weak and obscure, who are thereby able to meet the greatest princes of industry and finance on an equal footing. Thanks to these unions the relations between the employers and the employed are tending to be completely transformed. The employer is no longer the vaguely paternal autocrat, administrating all questions of labour without discussion, governing whole populations of workers at will, and regulating the conditions of labour, questions of sanitation and hygiene, &c. His will, his whims, his weaknesses and his errors are to-day confronted by the trades-union,

which by number and unanimity represents a power
almost equal to his own : a despotic power, no doubt,
to its members, but a power which on ceasing to be
despotic would cease to be.

Trades-unions would seem to be a very necessary consequence of modern evolution, to judge by their rapid
propagation.   To-day there is not a single calling, from
the school-teacher's to the charcoal-burner's and the
scavenger's, which has not its union.   The employers
are naturally forming defensive unions in turn, but while
in France there are 1,400 employers' unions, with 114,000
members, there are 2,000 trades-unions with more than
400,000 members.   There are unions, such as the railway-
employés' union, which count more than 80,000 members.
These are all-powerful armies, obeying the voice of their
chiefs without discussion, with which it is absolutely
necessary to come to terms.   They constitute a power
which is often blind, but always formidable, and which
in every case is of immense service to the workers, be
it only by raising their moral standard by transforming
them from timid mercenaries into men who must be
respected and encountered on an equal footing.

The Latin peoples, unfortunately, have highly autocratic
tendencies, so that their unions are often as despotic as
ever their masters could have been.   The lot of the latter
is at present far from enviable.   The following lines, from
a speech of a some-time minister, M. Barthou, gives one
some idea of their state :—

"Threatened incessantly by the laws which uphold the
liberty of union, exposed to legal brutalities and to imprisonment, having no effective authority over their men,
overburdened with the expenses of maintaining the funds
to provide for enforced idleness, accident, sickness, and
old age, which he no longer dares to charge to the wages
sheet on account of their very hugeness, which would

provoke a popular rising, hampered still more by the steadily increasing taxation of the fortune gained in spite of all these difficulties and humiliations, no longer masters in anything but in name, and gaining nothing thereby but misfortune and a hundred risks, the masters, the industrial leaders, will renounce their position, will abdicate, or at most will continue to struggle without spirit and without courage, and will fail at their task like the tax-gatherers of the last centuries of the Roman Empire."

Doubtless the relations between men and masters, so strained and embittered as they are to-day, will finally be ameliorated by a force stronger than all institutions— necessity. The Latin workman, who at present treats his master as an enemy, will finally comprehend, with the Anglo-Saxon workman of whom I have spoken else- where, that the interests of the men and the masters are of the same order, and that both are subject to the same master, the public, the sole arbiter of wages.

At all events, the old relations, whether familiar or autocratic, between employers and employed, masters and servants, are to-day done with. We may regret them, but only as we regret the dead, knowing well that we shall never behold them again. In the future evolu- tion of the world the mind will be ruled by interests, not by sentiments. Pity, charity, and altruism are the sur- vivors, without prestige and without influence, of the past that is dying before our eyes. The future will no longer know them.

CHAPTER V

THE FUNDAMENTAL PROBLEM OF SOCIALISM : THE
UNADAPTED

1. *The multiplication of the unadapted :*—Definition of the unadapted—The conditions which are now making for their multiplication—The unadapted of art, science, and industry—The danger of their presence in society—How the present evolution of industry is every day increasing their number—Competition among the unadapted—The consequence of this competition is the lowering of wages in the easy trades—It is practically impossible to find a remedy for this—The gradual elimination of the incapable from all industries—Various examples. 2. *The unadapted through degeneracy :*—The fecundity of degenerates—The present and future dangers of degeneracy—The importance of the problem raised by their presence in society—Degenerates are certain recruits for Socialism. 3. *The artificial production of the unadapted :* —The artificially produced unadapted through incapacity—They are produced largely by our Latin system of education—Education, which was intended to be a universal panacea, has ended in creating an immense host of *déclassés*—Impossibility of utilising the army of unemployed bachelors and licentiates—Anti-democratic sentiments of the university—The illusions regarding the instruction it affords—The considerable part played by the university in the social upheavals that are preparing.

1. THE MULTIPLICATION OF THE UNADAPTED.

AMONG the most important characteristics of our age we must mention the presence, in the midst of society, of a number of individuals who, for one reason or another, have been unable to adapt themselves to the necessities of modern civilisation, and are unable to find a place therein. They form a superfluity which cannot be utilised. They are the unadapted.

All societies have always possessed a certain number of these individuals, but never was their number so great as it is to-day. Unadapted to industry, science, the trades, and the arts, they form an ever-increasing army. Notwithstanding their diversity of origin, they are united by one common sentiment—the hatred of the civilisation in which they can find no place. Every revolution, no matter what end it pursue, is certain to find them hasting to join it at the first signal. It is among them that Socialism recruits its most ardent soldiers.

Their immense numbers, and their presence in every strata of society, renders them more dangerous to modern society than were the Barbarians to the Roman Empire. Rome was for a long time able to defend herself against the invaders from without ; but the modern barbarians are within our walls. The Barbarians of antiquity envied the power of Rome, but they respected it. They might dream of setting themselves up in her place, of speaking in her name, but down to her last days the great city possessed the same prestige in their eyes. Clovis was prouder of his title of Roman Consul than of his title of King of the Franks.

The nations who disputed the succession of the Roman Empire were one and all anxious to maintain it to their own profit. Our new barbarians, on the contrary, will have nothing less than the destruction of the civilisation of which they believe themselves to be the victims. They aspire to its destruction, and not to a conquest, of which they would not know how to avail themselves. If they did not burn Paris completely at the time of the Commune it was only because their means were at fault.

We need not inquire how this residue of the unadapted comes to be formed at every degree of the social scale. It will suffice to show that the evolution of industry has contributed to a rapid increase in their number. The statistics given in a previous chapter denoted the steady rise of the wages of the working classes, and the increasing distribution of wealth among the lower classes, but this amelioration is general only in the middle class of workers. What of those whose natural incapacities place them below this average level ? From the brilliant picture of general amelioration we have just been considering we must turn to one that is very gloomy indeed.

Under the old system of corporations the trades were subjected to regulations which limited the number of workers and prevented competition. The inconveniences of inferiority were not too pronounced. The member of a corporation did not rise very high, but neither did he sink very low. He was not an outcast, a nomad. The corporation was his family ; he was never at any time alone in life. His situation might not be very brilliant, but at least he was sure of finding a place for himself, a cell in the social hive.

With the economic necessities which dominate the modern world, and competition, the present law of production, things have suffered a profound change. As M. Cheysson very justly observes : " The ancient cements which held society together being dissolved, the grains of sand of which it is composed go to-day each its own way. Any man who develops, in the struggle for life, any superiority over his surroundings, will rise as a balloon filled with a light gas rises in the air when there is no rope to check its ascent ; and every man who is morally or materially deficient will inevitably fall headlong if no parachute govern his descent. It is the triumph of individualism, freed from servitude, but destitute of guidance."

In the present period of transition, those who are unadapted through incapacity can hardly manage to live, however miserably. It would seem as though their misery, already so profound, were inevitably bound to increase. Let us consider why.

To-day, in every branch of industry or of art, the most capable advance very quickly. The less capable, finding the best places taken, and being able, by their very incapacity, to produce only inferior work, are obliged to offer this work, of very easy execution, at very low prices. But in the region of incapacity competition is far keener than in the region of capacity, since the first is far more populous than the second, and since easy work finds more to execute it than difficult work. The consequence is that the unadapted person is reduced, in order to gain preference over his rivals, still further to lower the price he demands for what he can perform. The employer, on his side, who pays for these indifferent productions, which are destined for a numerous but by no means difficult *clientèle*, naturally tends to pay as little as possible, in order to sell his wares cheaply, and so still further to increase the number of his customers. The price of the worker thus descends to that extreme limit below which, the victim at once of his own insufficiencies and of economic necessities, he would die of starvation.

This system of competition among the unadapted engaged in easy work is what the English represent by a just and forcible phrase—the "sweating system."

"The sweating system," says M. des Rouziers, "has matters all its own way, wherever individuals without sufficient capacity are producing on their own account ordinary articles of inferior quality.

"The sweating system takes a multitude of forms; the tailor who, instead of executing his orders in his own establishment, gives them out at low prices, is practising sweating, and so is the large shop which gives sewing to poor women who are kept in their own homes by the cares of their households and children."

All the ordinary articles sold in the dressmaking, outfit, and furniture departments are to-day produced at miserable prices by the sweating system. Corset makers, waistcoat hands, shoemakers, shirtmakers, &c., often earn no more than 1s. to 1s. 3d. a day, and furniture hands can scarcely make 2s. 6d. a day. Nothing could be sadder than such a fate, but nothing could be heavier than the chain of necessities which make it inevitable. Are we to blame the employer who pays these wretched wages ? By no means, for the employer is under the thumb of a sovereign master, on whom he is utterly dependent—his *clientèle*. If he pays higher wages he must immediately increase by a few halfpence the price of the shirt which he sells at two shillings, the pair of shoes which he sells at four shillings, and immediately his customers will leave him to go to a neighbour who sells his wares at the lower price. Shall we suppose that all the employers unite to raise the rate of wages ? But then the market will be at once inundatèd with the wares of foreigners who are still working at low wages, which would make the lot of the unadapted more unhappy than before.

The victims of these fatalities thought to find a simple remedy for their ills in establishing, by means of their trades-unions, a fixed rate of wages below which no employer could go without finding himself deserted by all his workers. They were helped in their claims by the minimum rates fixed by the municipalities of the large towns, at which the undertakers of public works are forbidden to employ their workers.

These fixed rates of wages and municipal tariffs have hitherto been more hurtful than useful to those they were intended to protect, and have been of little value save in showing the powerlessness of legislation in the face of economic necessities. In a few old-established industries which demanded complicated or costly implements or very skilful workers, the employers agreed to the terms of the unions. In the case of the other industries, which demanded neither complicated plant nor such skilled labour, the difficulty was soon surmounted, and entirely in the favour of the employer. I will take the case of the furniture industry in Paris, chosen from innumerable analogous cases. Formerly the employers used to employ their hands in their own workshops. As soon as the unions made known their demands the masters dismissed three-quarters of their men, only retaining the most capable for urgent jobs or repairs. The workman was obliged to work at home, and as he had no customer but his employer, he was obliged to offer what furniture he made to him. But now it was the employer's turn to dictate conditions. On account of French and foreign competition the prices of furniture had fallen by one-half, and the workman of average capacity who was formerly able to earn 6s. or 7s. in a day in the workshop, is now with difficulty able to earn 2s. 6d. or 3s. 6d. a day by working at home. The employer has thereby learned how to evade the Socialistic demands. The public has gained thereby in being able to buy furniture—of inferior quality, it is true—at very low prices. The workman, in exchange for his ruin, has been able at least to acquire this notion, that the economic necessities which rule the world are not modified either by legislation or by trades-unions.

As for the contractors who are obliged to accept the tariffs imposed by the municipalities, they have got out of the difficulty in a similar fashion, by employing none but the most capable workmen, that is to say, precisely those who have no need of any protection, since their capacity insures their receiving the highest salaries everywhere. The obligatory tariffs have merely compelled the contractors to eliminate the mediocre workers, whom they formerly employed in work of secondary importance, ill-paid, no doubt, but still paid. In short, the very measures which were designed to protect those workers who by reason of their inferior capacities required protection have turned against them, and have had the sole result of rendering their situation far more difficult than before.

The great lesson to be learnt from all this is that which is indicated by M. des Rouziers in his remarks on the sweating system: "No one can dispense with the workman of intrinsic value."

This, in fact, is the clearest result of the competition set up by the modern economic necessities. Everywhere it makes the most capable triumph, and eliminates the less capable. This formula is precisely the law of selection, whence derives the perfection of species in the whole series of living creatures, and from which man has as yet been unable to escape.

The capable have everything to gain from this competition; the incapable can only lose by it. We can thus readily imagine that the Socialists wish for its suppression; but even supposing that they could destroy it in the countries in which they had gained the mastery, how could they destroy it in the countries where they had no influence, the countries whose products, despite all protective duties, would immediately invade the market?

We saw, while considering the commercial struggles between the East and the West, and between the Western nations themselves, that competition is an inevitable law of the present age. It exists absolutely everywhere, and all the checks that one attempts to impose on it only make matters worse for its victims. It enforces itself whenever there is a question of ameliorating any branch of labour whatever, whether scientific or industrial, whether of private or public interest. The following example, which occurred under my own eyes, shows at once the necessity of competition and the results.

A friend of mine, an engineer, was appointed to the head of an important enterprise, supported by the Government, which consisted in remaking, with great precision, the map of a country. He was left perfectly free to choose his *employés*, and to pay them what he willed, on the sole condition that he was not to exceed the annual sum which was allowed him for that purpose. The sum being little enough, and the *employés* many, the engineer started by dividing the sum equally between them. Finding that the work was being done slowly and indifferently, he decided to pay his *employés* solely by the piece, by devising means of automatic control which allowed him to verify the value of the work executed. Each capable *employé* soon began to do three or four times as much work as the work of three or four ordinary *employés*, and earned more than twice his previous salary. The incapable or semi-capable *employés*, being unable to make enough to live on, eliminated themselves, and in less than two years the allowance made by the State, which at first was hardly sufficient, exceed the expenses by 30 per cent. Thus the State, by this operation, obtained better work at a less expense, and the capable *employés* saw their salaries doubled. Every one was satisfied, except of course the incapable workers who had been eliminated by their incapacity. This result, which was a very happy one both for the progress of the work and for the public finances, was evidently a very unhappy one for the inefficient *employés*. However great may be our sympathy for the latter, can we say that the general interest should have been sacrificed to them ?

The reader who enters into this question will quickly perceive the difficulty of one of the most important social problems, and the impotence of the means proposed by the Socialists to solve it.

2. THE UNADAPTED THROUGH DEGENERACY.

To the class of outcasts produced by competition we must add the hosts of degenerates of all kinds—alcoholic, tuberculous, &c.—who are preserved by modern medical science. It is precisely these individuals that form almost the only class that abandons itself without check to the most disturbing fecundity, confirming the law I have expounded, that in the present period societies perpetuate themselves above all by their lowest elements.

We are aware of the progress of alcoholism through all Europe. Drink-shops are rapidly multiplying themselves everywhere, as much in France as in other countries.[1] I can by no means interest myself in the lamentations of the doctors and statisticians on this point : firstly, because their lamentations are evidently useless; and, secondly, because the public-house is absolutely the only distraction of millions and millions of poor devils ; it is their sole means of illusion, and the only centre of sociability at which many and many a gloomy life is illumined for a moment. They have been forbidden the church ; what would be left them if they were deprived of the public-house ? The consumption of alcohol is first of all an effect ; then it becomes a cause. And it is only in excess that alcohol is hurtful. If the mischief caused by the excessive drinking of alcohol is serious, it is because it compromises the future by the hereditary degeneracy which it causes.

The danger of all these degenerates—rickety, epileptic, insane, &c.—lies in the fact that they multiply in excess,

[1] There were 350,000 in 1850, 364,000 in 1870, 372,000 in 1881, 430,000 in 1891, of which 31,000 were in Paris.

and produce a crowd of individuals who are too inferior to adapt themselves to civilisation, and who are consequently its inevitable enemies.

"We give life to-day," writes M. Schera, "to a host of creatures that Nature has condemned; sickly, lingering, half-dying infants; and we regard it as a great victory that we have thus been able to prolong their days, and this altogether modern preoccupation of society on the subject we regard as a great progress. . . . But this is the irony of the matter. These devoted and ingenious cares which give so many human beings to society do not present them to society sane, healthy, and vigorous, but infected with vices of blood which they contracted at birth; and as neither our customs nor our laws can prevent these people from marrying, they still inevitably transmit the poison. Hence there must evidently arise an alteration of the general health, a contamination of the race."

Dr. Salomon has cited a very striking example of the kind of case that is met with every day. It is that of the offspring of the union of a drunkard with an epileptic. There were twelve children, every one of them either consumptive or epileptic.

"What is to be done with such lamentable creatures?" asks Dr. Salomon, "and would it not have been a thousand times better if none of them had ever seen the light? And what an expense such families are to society, to the budget of public assistance, and even the budget of the criminal courts! Hospital inmate or gaol-bird: the child of the drunkard can hardly aspire to be anything else. Multiply the hospitals and the police; this, it seems, must be the future of civilised societies, which will finally perish through this state of things, if fecundity becomes the special characteristic of those for whom sterility is an absolute duty."

Many other writers, and among them the most eminent, have been preoccupied with this difficult problem. This is what Darwin has to say on the subject:—

"With savages the weak in body or mind are soon eliminated; and those that survive commonly exhibit a vigorous state of health. We civilised men, on the other hand, do our utmost to check the process of elimination; we build asylums for the imbecile, the maimed, and the sick; we institute poor-laws, and our medical men exert their utmost skill to save the life of every one to the last moment. There is reason to believe that vaccination has preserved thousands, who from a weak constitution would formerly have succumbed to small-pox. Thus the weak members of civilised societies propagate their kind. No one who has attended to the breeding of domestic animals will doubt that this must be highly injurious to the race of men. It is surprising how soon a want of care, or care wrongly directed, leads to the degeneration of a domestic race; but excepting in the case of man himself, hardly any one is so ignorant as to allow his worst animals to breed."

We cannot deny that if a benevolent deity were to suppress in every generation the increasing army of the degenerates which we so carefully protect he would be rendering an immense service to civilisation and to the degenerates themselves; but since our humanitarian sentiments demand that we should preserve them and favour their reproduction we can but suffer the consequences of these sentiments. At all events we know that all these degenerates, as John Fiske justly remarks, constitute an element of inferior vitality, comparable to a cancer implanted in healthy tissues, and all their efforts tend to abolish a civilisation which inevitably results in their own misery. They are, in fact, certain recruits for Socialism. As we advance in our study of the question we see of what varied and dangerous elements the multitude of the disciples of the new faith is composed.

3. THE ARTIFICIAL PRODUCTION OF THE UNADAPTED.

To the host of the unfit created by competition and degeneration must be added, as regards the Latin nations, the degenerates produced by artificial incapacity. These artificial failures are made at great expense by our colleges and universities. The host of graduates, licentiates, instructors, and professors without employment will one day, perhaps, constitute one of the most serious dangers against which society will have to defend itself.

This class of artificial outcasts is of quite modern formation. Its origin is psychological ; it is the consequence of the modern ideas.

The men of each period live by a certain number of political, religious, or social ideas, which are regarded as indisputable dogmas, of which they must necessarily suffer the effects. One of the most powerful of such ideas to-day is that of the superiority to be derived from the theoretical instruction given in our colleges. The schoolmaster and the university professor, rather looked down upon of old, have suddenly become the great modern fetiches. It is they who are to remedy the inequalities of nature, efface the distinctions of class, and win our battles for us.

Instruction thus becoming the universal panacea, it was indispensable to stuff the heads of the young citizens with Greek, Latin, history, and scientific formulæ. No sacrifice, no expense, was too great. The fabrication of schoolmasters, bachelors, and licentiates became the most important of the Latin industries. It is almost the only one, in fact, that remains prosperous.

When studying, in another chapter, the Latin conception of education, we saw the results produced by the

French method of instruction. We saw that it permanently warps the judgment, stuffs the brain with phrases and formulæ which are quickly forgotten, in no way prepares the pupil for the necessities of modern life, and, in short, only creates an immense army of men who are incapable, useless, and, consequently, rebels.

But how is it that our system of education, instead of merely being useless, as of old, is to-day manufacturing outcasts and rebels ?

The reason is very clear. Our theoretical education, instilled from our text-books, prepares the pupil for absolutely nothing but public functions, and makes the pupil absolutely unfitted for any other career, so that he is obliged, in order to live, to make a furious rush toward the State-paid employments. But as the number of candidates is immense, and the number of places very small, the great majority fail, and find themselves without any means of existence—outcasts, in fact, and naturally insurgents.

The figures on which these remarks of mine are based will show the extent of this evil.

The University of France creates about 1,200 graduates every year, and has 200 professional chairs at her disposal. It thus leaves a thousand on the pavement. They naturally turn to other professions. But everywhere they find the dense army of graduates of every faculty, seeking for every kind of employment, even the most indifferent. For 40 situations as copyist open every year at the Prefecture of the Seine there are 2,000 or 3,000 candidates. For 150 situations as schoolmasters in the schools of Paris there are 15,000 candidates. Those who fail gradually lower their pretensions, and are often glad enough to take refuge in addressing envelopes, by which means they can earn 1s. 8d. a day by working twelve hours without ceasing. It is not very difficult to divine the sentiments that fill the hearts of these wretched labourers.

As for the successful candidates, it must not be supposed that their lot is very enviable. As Government clerks at £60, magistrates at £72, engineers of the École Centrale at £50—as draughtsmen in a railway office or chemists in a factory, they are not nearly so well off as a working man of average capacity, and are also far less independent.

But why this obstinate pursuit of official employment ? Why do not the army of unemployed graduates fall back on industry, agriculture, commerce, or the manual trades ?

For two reasons. Firstly, because they are totally incapable, on account of their theoretical education, of performing any but the easy duties of bureaucrats, magistrates, or professors. But even then they might recommence their education by apprenticing themselves. They do not do so—and this is the second reason—on account of the insurmountable prejudice against manual labour, industry, and agriculture, which is to be met with in all the Latin nations and nowhere else.

The Latin nations, in fact, in spite of deceptive appearances, possess a temperament so little democratic that manual labour, which is very highly esteemed by the English aristocracy, is by them regarded as humiliating or even dishonourable. The humblest Government clerk, the smallest professor, the humblest of copyists, regards himself as a personage by the side of a mechanic, a foreman, a fitter, a farmer, who none the less will often bring infinitely more intelligence, reason, and initiative to bear in his calling than does the clerk or the professor in his. I have never been able to discover, and I am certain that no one will ever discover, in what a Latin master, a clerk, a professor of grammar or of history could be considered the intellectual superior of a good cabinet-maker, a capable fitter, or an intelligent foreman. If after comparing them from an intellectual point of view we do the same from a utilitarian point of view we shall quickly admit that the clerk and the professor are greatly inferior to the good working man, and it is for this reason that the latter is as a general thing far better paid.

The only visible superiority that one can recognise in the former is the fact that they usually wear a "redingote"—as a rule threadbare enough, but still preserving the appearance of a "redingote"—while the foreman and the artisan work in a blouse, an article of wear which is a little in disfavour with the fashionable public. If we could analyse the psychologic influence exercised in France by these two garments we should find that it is absolutely enormous—certainly far greater than the influence of all the constitutions fabricated in the last hundred years by the host of unemployed lawyers. If, by means of any magic ring, we could be brought to believe that the blouse was as seemly and becoming as the "redingote," all our conditions of existence would be transformed in a single day. We should see a revolution in manners and thoughts of which the effects would be far greater than all those of the past. But we have not advanced so far yet, and the Latin races will suffer the weight of their prejudices and errors for a long time yet.

The consequences of the Latin disdain of manual work will be still graver in the future. It is on account of this sentiment that we see the immense army of the unadapted created by our system of education increasing more and more. Observing the lack of consideration from which manual labour suffers, feeling that they are despised by the middle class and the university, the peasant and the workman finally get it into their heads that they belong to an inferior caste, from which they must at any price escape. Then their one dream is to thrust their sons, by dint of privation, into the caste of graduates. They succeed only in making outcasts of their sons ; incapable of rising to the ranks of the *bourgeois* through lack of money, and incapable on account of their education of following the trade of their father. These outcasts will all their lives bear the weight of the lamentable errors of which their parents have made them the victims. They will be certain recruits for the Socialists.

Not only by reason of the instruction it affords, but also on account of its highly undemocratic spirit, the present university will have played the most disastrous part in France. In affixing its contempt to all manual work, and all that is not theory, words, or phrases, and in making its pupils believe that their diplomas confer on them a kind of intellectual nobility, which will place them in a superior caste, and give them access to wealth, or at least to comfort, the university has played a lamentable part. After long and costly studies the graduate is forced to recognise that he has acquired no elevation of mind, that he has by no means escaped from his caste, and that his life is to begin again. In the face of the time lost, of their faculties blunted for all useful work, of the perspective of the humiliating poverty which awaits them, how should they not become insurgents ? [1]

Of course our university authorities see nothing of all this. Their work inspires them—like all the apostles—with the keenest enthusiasm, and they lose no occasion to intone a chant of triumph.

[1] One may form some idea of the increasing progress of Socialism among the French university youth by reading the manifesto, full of hatred and fury against society, recently published by the "Collectivist Students."

"One must read," writes M. H. Bérenger, "the books of MM. Liard and Lavisse, the two architects-in-chief of our secondary education, in order to comprehend the kind of enthusiasm that has seized them before the result of their works. Do they hear the low but formidable murmur of all those that have been deceived by the university, who have been raised only to fall into greater misery, who are everywhere beginning to be known as the intellectual proletariat ?"

Alas ! no, they do not hear it ; and if they did they would hardly understand. They have performed a bad work—a work far worse than that of Marat and Robespierre, who at least were not guilty of corrupting the mind ; but can we say that the work is truly theirs ? When the minds of men are possessed by certain powerful illusions, how can we blame the obscure agents, the blind puppets, who have merely obeyed the general tendencies of their times !

The hour has yet to sound when our terrible illusions on the worth of the Latin system of education shall have vanished. At present they are making themselves felt more than ever. Every day a laborious youth, more and more numerous, goes up to the university to demand of it the realisation of its dreams and hopes. The number of students, which was 10,900 in 1878, and 17,600 in 1888, is now 27,000. What an army of outcasts, of rebels, of partisans for the Socialism of the future !

And as though the number of these future outcasts were not yet great enough, there are those who would demand of the State the means to increase their number. A few clear-sighted people see the danger, and point it out. In vain ; their voices sound idly, unechoed in a desert.

"The millions that these bursaries cost the Budget," said M. Bouge recently, before the Chamber of Deputies, "are a small matter beside the social problem of preventing them from becoming a means of turning out outcasts. Too many such are being formed already, without the State assisting the process by the distribution of bursaries." [1]

[1] As our superior classical instruction is a matter of luxury, which can be of use only to those that possess a certain amount of leisure, there is not a single serious reason for giving it gratuitously. This is perfectly understood by the Americans. A young man who should feel the need of it, and who should manifest an aptitude for it, should first of all find some means of earning his living, and this would be an excellent preparation for life. This is what the students —poor students—do in a truly democratic country, such as America. In an article on the University of Chicago, which he has visited, one of the most illustrious French savants, M. Moissan, expresses himself as follows:—

"In most of the American universities you will find young men without means, who, in order to pay the fees, which at Chicago amount to about £7 a term, undertake some manual labour out of college hours. One student will be a lamp-lighter; another will offer his services at an hotel in the evening. Another will earn his living by becoming cook or major-domo to his comrades. Another will have saved money out of a modest salary for several years in order to come up to the university and take his degree."

We may be sure that young men possessed of sufficient energy to make such efforts as these will never be outcasts, and will succeed in any career.

CHAPTER VI

THE STRUGGLE WITH THE UNADAPTED

1. *The future attack of the unadapted :*—Hatred of the unadapted for the society in which they can find no place—The unadapted in the United States—Their miserable condition and their number—The violent struggles that will have to be maintained against them. 2. *The utilisation of the unadapted :*—The utilisation of the unadapted constitutes one of the most difficult problems of the present time—Solutions proposed and attempted—Inability of the State to nourish the army of the unadapted—Public or private charity merely increases their number—The right to work—Disastrous results of the experiments hitherto attempted—Vanity of the promises of Socialism.

1. THE FUTURE ATTACK OF THE UNADAPTED.

WE have just seen how the special conditions of the age have immensely multiplied the crowd of the unadapted. This multitude of incapable, disinherited, or degenerate persons is a grave danger to civilisation. United in a common hatred of the society in which they can find no place, they demand nothing but to fight against it. They form an army ready for all revolutions, having nothing to lose and everything to gain—at least, in appearance. Above all, this army is ready for all works of destruction. Nothing is more natural than the sentiment of hatred which these outcasts entertain for a civilisation that is too complicated for them, and to which they are perfectly sensible that they can never

adapt themselves.   They only wait for the occasion to
rise to the assault.

The dangers which threaten Europe threaten the
United States still more immediately.   The War of Secession was the prelude to the bloody conflict which will
presently take place between the various classes living on
American soil.   All the unadapted of the universe direct
themselves to the New World.   Despite these invasions,
the danger of which no American statesman has hitherto
understood, the English race is still in the majority in
the United States ; but the other races—Irish, Slavs,
Germans, Italians, negroes, and so forth—are for ever
increasing.   For example, there are now 7,600,000 negroes
in the United States.   An annual immigration of 400,000
strangers is always increasing this dangerous population.
These foreigners form veritable colonies, perfectly indifferent, and more often than not hostile to their country
of adoption.   Unconnected with her by ties of blood,
tradition, or language, they care nothing for her general
interests.   They only seek to live on her.

But their existence is all the harder, their misery all the
more profound, in that they are in competition with the
most energetic race in the world.   They are scarcely able
to exist save on condition of contenting themselves with
the lowest and most degraded tasks, and therefore the
worst paid.

These strangers form at present only about 15 per cent.
of the total population of the United States, but in certain districts they are very nearly in the majority.   The
state of North Dakotah already counts 44 per cent. of
foreigners.   Nine-tenths of the negroes are concentrated
in the fifteen Southern States, where they form a third of
the population.   In South Carolina they are now in the
majority, the proportion of negroes being 60 per cent.
They equal the whites in number in Louisiana.

We know how the negroes are treated on American soil, where their liberation from slavery is generally regarded as a stupendous error. Theoretically they enjoy all the rights known to the other citizens, but in practice they are shot or hung without any formality at the first offence. Treated everywhere as pariahs, as a species of animal intermediate between the apes and man, they will be perfectly ready to join the first army that shall undertake to attack the great Republic.

"The whites of the North," writes M. de Mandat-Grancy, "spent many millions of dollars and many lives of men, thirty years ago, to break the chains of the worthy negroes of the South. And now these worthy negroes, whom they have enfranchised, and made electors, have reached the number of 8,000,000, for they breed like rabbits. They are already in the majority in several States, and as soon as they form the majority in any State life is no longer tolerable there. The negro's idea of civilisation is that which existed recently in Dahomey, or that which the blacks have established in San Domingo, where nobody works and everybody lives on the exchequer, which is filled by despoiling such whites as are foolish enough to work. This is the ideal order of things, which they hasten to realise as soon as they become the masters ; and they have become the masters in several of the Southern States. The latter are beginning to show signs of anger. . . . Those who are acquainted with the expeditious procedures to which the Americans have recourse when they wish to remedy a state of things that is contrary to their ideas of what should be, would be by no means astonished if some fine day they were to find some means of ridding themselves of the negroes as they have rid themselves of the Chinese."

Very likely ; but 7,500,000 men are too great a host to get rid of easily, and there are too many conflicting interests in question to permit of the re-establishment of slavery. The Americans got rid of the Chinese by forbidding them to enter the country; of the Indians by enclosing them in territories surrounded by vigilant guards armed with repeating rifles, having orders to slaughter them as soon as the pangs of hunger drove them to leave these enclosures. By this summary means they were able to destroy nearly all the Indians in a very few years. But this method would seem difficult of application to the millions of negroes, and quite impossible of application to the immense stock of white foreigners of all kinds scattered through the towns; especially as these whites are electors, able to send their representatives to the Chambers, and to exercise public powers. In the last strike at Chicago the Governor of the State was on the side of the insurgents.

I do not doubt, having regard to the energetic character of the Anglo-Saxons of America, that they will succeed in surmounting the dangers with which they are threatened; but they will do so only at the cost of a more destructive conflict than any history has ever recorded.

But we need not here concern ourselves with the destinies of America. Her intestine dissensions are of little importance to Europe, who has scarcely been treated with tenderness by her rulers. Europe has nothing to lose by the struggle, and many useful lessons to gain.

Our European outcasts are happily neither so numerous nor so dangerous as those of America, but they are none the less very formidable, and the time will come when they will be marshalled under the banner of Socialism, and when we shall have to deliver battle to them. But these acute crises will of necessity be ephemeral. Whatever may be their issue, the problem of the utilisation of the unadapted will present itself for a long period with the same difficulties. The search after the solution of the problem will weigh heavily on the destinies of the peoples of the future, and it is as yet impossible to foresee what means they will find to resolve it. We shall see why.

2. THE UTILISATION OF THE UNADAPTED.

The only methods that have hitherto been proposed for the benefit of the unadapted have been private charity and State aid. But long experience has taught us that these are insufficient methods at the outset, and afterwards highly dangerous. Even supposing that the State or the individuals composing the State were rich enough to support the multitude of the unadapted, this support would merely end in the rapid increase of their number. The true unadapted would promptly be joined by the semi-unadapted, and all those who, preferring idleness to labour, work to-day only because they are driven to work by hunger.

Although relatively limited, charity, whether public or private, has hitherto done little but considerably increase the crowd of the unadapted. As soon as a State-Aid office is opened anywhere the number of poor increases in enormous proportions. I know a little village near the barriers of Paris where more than half the population is entered in the books of the relief office.

Inquiries made on this subject have proved that 95 per cent. of the recipients of relief in France are persons who refuse any species of work. This is the figure given by the inquiries made under the superintendence of M. Monod, director of the Ministry of the Interior. Out of 727 able-bodied mendicants taken at hazard, who all lamented that they had no work, only eighteen consented to undertake an easy employment bringing them in 3s. 4d.

a day. Charity, private or public, merely supports them in their idleness. M. de Wateville wrote, a few years ago, in a report on the state of pauperism in France :—

" During the sixty years of the existence of the *Assistance publique a domicile*, it has never seen an indigent person emerge from his poverty and succeed in supplying his own needs through the assistance of this method of charity. On the contrary, it often causes hereditary pauperism. Thus we see to-day entered in the books of this department the grandsons of the indigents who were given public aid in 1802, while their sons, in 1830, were also in the fatal books."

Herbert Spencer has spoken with great energy on the same subject :—

" Fostering the good-for-nothing at the expense of the good is an extreme cruelty. It is a deliberate storing up of miseries for future generations. There is no greater curse to posterity than that of bequeathing them an increasing population of imbeciles and idlers and criminals. To aid the bad in multiplying is, in effect, the same as maliciously providing for our descendants a larger host of enemies. It may be doubted whether the maudlin philanthropy which, looking only at direct mitigations, ignores indirect mischiefs, does not inflict more misery than the extremest selfishness inflicts. Refusing to consider the remote influences of his incontinent generosity, the thoughtless giver stands but a degree above the drunkard who, absorbed in to-day's pleasure, think not of to-morrow's pain, or the spendthrift who buys immediate delights at the cost of ultimate poverty. In one respect, indeed, he is worse ; since, while getting the present gratification caused by giving gratification, he leaves the future evils to be borne by others—escaping them himself. And calling for still stronger reprobation is that scattering of money prompted

382 THE PSYCHOLOGY OF SOCIALISM

by misinterpretation of the saying that 'charity covers a multitude of sins.' For in the many whom this misinterpretation leads to believe that by large donations they can compound for evil deeds, we may trace an element of positive baseness—an effort to get a good place in another world, no matter at what injury to fellow-creatures."

But in addition to charity properly so called, which is destined merely to aid the necessitous who cannot or will not work, there is another problem. Ought not the State to charge itself, according to the pretensions of the Socialists, with the distribution of labour to those who lack it and demand it? This theory evidently arises from the Latin conception of the State, and we have not to consider it here. Without concerning ourselves with principles, it is enough to inquire merely whether the State is in a position to play the part that is expected of it. As the experiment has often been made—for the right to labour has not been proclaimed for the first time to-day—it is easy to answer the question.

The National Assembly and the Convention, after having in 1791 and 1793 decreased the establishment of a department which should "give work to poor able-bodied men who had been unable to procure it," and having proclaimed that "society owes the means of life to unfortunate citizens," established national workshops. In 1791 these occupied in Paris 31,000 men, who were paid 1s. 8d. a day. These men arrived at the yards at ten o'clock, left at three, and did nothing but drink and play in the interval. As for the inspectors who were charged with overseeing them, when they were questioned they replied simply that they were not in sufficient force to make themselves obeyed, and did not want to risk having their throats cut.

"It was the same thing over again," writes M. Cheysson, "with our national works in 1848, which led to the bloody work of June (when their suppression was attempted).

"It is interesting to discover that, despite the lessons of history, the prejudice of the right to labour has retained its faithful. They have just held, at Erfurt, the sixth Social Evangelical Congress, a sort of Parliament of the Reformed Churches, thoroughly steeped in Socialism, Christian Socialism. According to the report of a distinguished publicist, M. de Masson, the active collaborator with Pastor Badelswing in creating labour colonies, the Congress proclaimed 'that it was the strict duty of a well-regulated State to provide, as far as possible, for the lamentable social scourge of unmerited idleness.' This is the modified formula of the right to labour."

As we see, the problem has long been occupying distinguished minds, and none of them has been able to find even a distant solution. It is evident that if their solution had been discovered the social problem would in great measure have been solved.

And it is because it remains so far unsolved that Socialism, which pretends to resolve the insoluble problem, and which shrinks from no promises, is to-day so formidable. It has in its following all the vanquished and disinherited of the world, and all those unadapted whose formation we have seen. For them it represents the last spark of hope that never dies in the heart of man. But as its promises are necessarily vain, and since the laws of nature that rule our fate cannot be changed, its impotence will be glaring to every eye in the very hour of its triumph, and it will then have as its enemies the very multitudes it had seduced, and who now place all their hope in it. Disabused anew, man will once more take up his eternal task of fashioning such chimera as will for a while charm his mind.

BOOK VI

THE DESTINIES OF SOCIALISM

CHAPTER I

THE LIMITS OF HISTORIC PREVISION

1. *The idea of necessity in the modern conception of social phenomena :*—The change effected by science in our modern conception of the world—The idea of evolution and necessity—Why sociology does not in its present state constitute a science—Its inability to foresee events—Historical foresight would be possible to an intelligence immensely superior to that of man—The utility of the idea of the necessity of phenomena. 2. *The prevision of social phenomena :*—Impossibility of foreseeing social phenomena with any certainty, although they are subject to laws—For previsions are only hypotheses based on analogies, and must limit themselves to the very near future—Our general ignorance of the first causes of all phenomena.

1. THE IDEA OF NECESSITY IN THE MODERN CONCEPTION OF SOCIAL PHENOMENA.

I SHALL very soon have occasion to sum up my predictions on the future of Socialism. In the meantime it will be not without use to inquire within what limits science allows such predictions, and in what degree it is possible to formulate them.

When the progress of science revealed to man the order of the universe, and the ordered sequence of phenomena, his general conceptions of things were transformed. It is not yet so very long ago that a

384

benevolent Providence used to guide the course of events, leading man by the hand, presiding over battles and the destinies of empires. How could its decrees be foreseen ? They were unfathomable. How could they be debated ? They were omnipotent. The nations could but prostrate themselves before it, and seek, by means of humble prayers, to conjure its furies or its caprices.

The new conceptions of the world which have arisen from the discoveries of science have enfranchised man from the power of the gods whom his imagination created of old. The new conceptions have not made him freer, but they have taught him that it is useless to seek to influence by prayer the heavy and imperturbable machinery of the necessities which direct the universe.

After having shown us the hierarchy of these necessities, science has shown us also the general procedure of the transformation of our planet, and the mechanism of evolution which has changed, in the course of time, the humble creatures of the first geological periods to the present forms.

The laws of this evolution having been determined as regards individuals, it was attempted to apply them to human societies. Modern research has proved that societies also have passed through a series of inferior forms before reaching their present level.

Of these researches is born sociology, an order of knowledge which will one day, perhaps, compose itself, but which hitherto has had to limit itself to recording phenomena without being able to predict them.

It is on account of this inability to foresee that sociology cannot be regarded as a science, or even as the beginning of a science. An order of knowledge deserves the name of science only when it allows us to determine he conditions of a phenomena, and, consequently, to reproduce it, or at least to foretell its occurrence. Such sciences are chemistry, physics, astronomy, and even, within certain limits, biology. Sociology is nothing of the kind. All that it can tell us—and it is not sociology, as a matter of fact, that has told us this—is that the moral world, as well as the physical world, is ruled by inflexible laws. What we call chance is merely the infinite concatenation of causes that we are unacquainted with.

But all precise prediction is rendered impossible by the complicated entanglement of these causes. We are able, not to foresee social phenomena, but merely to understand them a little, by studying separately each of the factors which give rise to them, and then seeking to discover the reciprocal action of these factors. Theoretically the method is the same as that of the chemist who analyses a compound body, or of the astronomer who seeks to determine the orbit of a planet. But when the elements acting on one another are too numerous, modern science confesses her inability to discover the definitive effect of so many causes. To determine the relative positions of three bodies, of which the masses and times are different, and which exercise an inter-ethereal attraction on one another, is a problem that for a long time defied the sagacity of the most illustrious mathematicians, and it needed the genius of a Poincaré to resolve it.

And in the matter of social phenomena we have to consider that it is a question not of three bodies, but of millions of elements, of which we have to discover the reciprocal action. How are we to foresee the final result of such a tangle ? To obtain not certitudes, nor even approximations, but simply general and summary indications, it is necessary to act as the astronomer, who, seeking to deduct the position of an unknown planet by the perturbations which it produces in the orbit of a fixed planet, does not attempt to embrace in his formulæ the action of all the bodies in the universe. He neglects the secondary perturbations, which would render the problem insoluble, and contents himself with approximations.[1]

Even in the most exact sciences the best results that our imperfect intelligence can attain are only approximate. But an intelligence like that of which Laplace speaks, " which for a given instant should know all the forces by which Nature is animated, and the respective positions of the particles of which she is composed, granting that it were vast enough to submit all these data to analysis, would then embrace in the same formula the movements of the largest bodies in the universe and those of the lightest atom. Nothing would be uncertain to it, and the future, as the past, would be present to its eyes."

We do not know if among the millions of worlds which pursue their silent ways through the firmament there has ever arisen this intelligence of which Laplace speaks, an intelligence which would have been able to read in the nebula that became the solar system the birth

---

[1] It is only to the smallness of the masses of the planets relatively to that of the sun, to the slightness of the eccentricities and the inclinations of their orbits, to the distance of the nearest stars from the solar system, and finally to the imperfection of the measures of time and space that are accessible to us, that the calculations of the astronomers owe their apparent precision. To the impossibility of more completely establishing these calculations we must add the insufficiency of our methods of observation. What these are we may judge by the fact that for thousands of years generation after generation of astronomers observed Sirius, the most brilliant star in our sky, without ever suspecting that it was moving at the rate of many hundreds of thousands of leagues a day. It was only by indirect method that it was discovered that certain stars are moving through space with a speed fifteen times greater than that of a cannon-ball.

of man, the phases of his history, and the last hours of the last living beings on our frozen earth. Do not let us envy such an intelligence too greatly. If the book of destiny were laid open before our eyes the most powerful motives of human activity would be destroyed. Those whom the Sybil of antiquity instructed in the future paled with terror, and rushed towards the sacred spring whose waters produced oblivion.

The most eminent of thinkers—Kant, Stuart Mill, and quite recently such psychologists as Gumplowicz—affirm that if the psychology of individuals and nations were well known we should be able to foresee their conduct ; but this amounts to enunciating in other terms the hypothesis of Laplace, which supposes known elements too numerous to know, and acting on one another in too complex a fashion for us to submit it to analysis.

We must therefore limit ourselves to the knowledge that the moral world is subject to fixed laws, and must resign ourselves to ignorance of the future consequences of these laws.

The notion of necessity which all the discoveries of modern science increasingly confirm is not a mere vain and useless theory. It teaches us at least tolerance, and permits of our entering upon the study of social phenomena with the coldness of a chemist who analyses a compound or determines the density of a gas. It teaches us to be no more irritated at events which offend our ideas than the scientist at the unforeseen result of an experiment. It is impossible that the indignation of a philosopher should be aroused by phenomena which are subject to inevitable laws ; he must limit himself to studying them, in the persuasion that nothing could have prevented their occurrence.

2. THE PREVISION OF SOCIAL PHENOMENA.

Sociology, then, must limit itself to recording phenomena. Whenever even its most illustrious professors have attempted, as did Auguste Comte, to enter into the region of previsions, they have lamentably erred.

Statesmen even, though they are immersed in the sphere of political events, and are, one would imagine, the best qualified to observe their sequence, are least able of any to foresee them.

"How many times," writes M. Fouillée, "have the prophets been given the lie by events! Napoleon announced that Europe would soon become Cossack. He predicted that Wellington would establish himself in England as a despot 'because he was too great to remain a mere subject.' 'If you accord independence to the United States,' said Lord Shelburne, no less blind from his point of view, 'the sun of England will set, and her glory will be for ever eclipsed.' Burke and Fox were rival false prophets at the time of the Revolution. The former announced that France would shortly be divided like Poland. Thinkers of all sorts, apparently strangers to the affairs of this world, have almost always proved to be more clear-sighted than mere statesmen. A Rousseau and a Goldsmith foretold the French Revolution; Arthur Young foresaw for France, after transitory violence, 'a lasting well-being, resulting from her reforms.' Tocqueville, thirty years before the event, announced that the Southern States of America would attempt secession. Heine told us, years in advance, 'You, you French, have more to fear from a free and united Germany than from the whole Holy Alliance, or all the Cossacks united.' Quinet predicted in 1832 the changes that were to take place in Germany, the *rôle* of Prussia, the threat which would be held over our heads, and the iron hand that would attempt to regain the keys of Alsace. The fact is that as most statesmen are absorbed in the things of the present hour, myopia is their natural state."

We must accordingly be extremely reserved in our predictions, attempting none but indications of a very general character, drawn more especially from the profound study of the characters and histories of races, and for the rest we must confine ourselves to observations.

The optimistic or pessimistic form in which we express these observations merely represents the nuances of language which may facilitate our explanations, but in themselves are of no importance. They depend on our temperaments and frames of mind. The thinker, accustomed to observe the inflexible inevitableness of things, will generally have a pessimistic appreciation of them ; the philosopher, who sees in the world only a curious spectacle, will have a resigned or indifferent appreciation of them. The systematically optimistic conception of them is hardly ever found except in complete imbeciles, who are favoured by fortune and satisfied with their destiny. But if the thinker, the philosopher, and (by chance) the imbecile knew how to observe, their statements of phenonema would be necessarily identical, as identical as the photographs of the same monument taken by different operators.

To make, as the historians do, a statement of past events, and to distribute responsibilities, blame, and praise, is a puerile task that the scholars of the future will justly despise. The train of causes which create events is far stronger than the individuals that have accomplished them. The most memorable events of history —the fall of Babylon or of Athens, the decadence of the Roman Empire, the Revolution, and the recent disasters of the French—are to be attributed not to men, but to generations of men. The marionette who, unconscious of the threads which make him move, should blame or praise the movements of other marionettes, would assuredly be altogether in the wrong. We are influenced by our environment, by circumstances, and by the thoughts of the dead ; that is to say, by those mysterious hereditary forces which survive in us. They determine the greater number of our actions, and are all the more powerful in that we do not see them. Our thoughts, when by rare chance we have any personal thoughts, will have scarcely any influence save on generations that are yet unborn. We can have very little influence on the present, because the present is the outcome of a past which we can do nothing to change. Children of this long past, our actions will have all their consequences only in a future that we shall not see. The present hour is the only one that has any value for us, and yet, in the existence of a race, this short hour is of all but no account. It is even impossible for us to appreciate the true significance of the events which take place under our eyes, because their influence on our own destiny leads us immensely to exaggerate their importance. They might be compared to the ripples which arise and die incessantly on the surface of a river, without disturbing its flow. The insect derelict on the leaf that these ripples rock takes them for mountains, and justly fears their impact. But effect on the flow of the river they have none.

The profound study of social phenomena accordingly leads us to this conclusion : on the one hand, that these phenomena are determined by the interaction of necessities, and are consequently capable of being foreseen by a superior intelligence ; and on the other hand, that such predictions are almost always impossible to limited beings like ourselves.

Nevertheless, man will always seek to raise the curtain which hides the impenetrable future, and the philosophers themselves are unable to escape from this futile curiosity. But at least they know that their predictions are only hypothetical, based more especially upon analogies borrowed from the past, or deduced from the general trend of affairs and the fundamental characteristics of the nations. They know also that even those predictions which are apparently the most assured must limit themselves to the very immediate future, and that even then many unknown causes may give them the lie. A fairly penetrating mind might doubtless have foretold the Revolution a few years before it broke out by studying the general state of mind, but how could it have foretold Bonaparte, the conquest of Europe, and the Empire ?

A scientist, then, cannot give as certain a social prediction relating to a distant date. He sees some nations rising and others falling, and as he knows by the past that the slope of decline does not remount, he is justified in saying that those nations which are on the slope of decadence will continue to descend. He knows that institutions cannot be changed at the will of legislators, and seeing that the Socialists desire entirely to overthrow the institutions on which our civilisations repose, he can readily predict the catastrophes which will follow such events. These are predictions of a very general kind, which have perhaps a little in common with those simple and eternal truths which we call platitudes. The most advanced science is obliged to content itself with such sorry approximations.

And what can we say of the future, we who know next to nothing of the world in which we live, we who hurl ourselves against an impenetrable wall so soon as we seek to discover the cause of phenomena, and the realities which hide themselves under appearances ?

Are things create or uncreate, real or unreal, ephemeral or eternal ? Has the world a reason for being or has it not ? Are the birth and evolution of the universe conditioned by the will of superior beings, or by blind necessities, by the imperious destiny to which both gods and men, according to the ancient conception, must both obey ? And the atom, which seems to form the intimate basis of all things in the world, from the mineral to ourselves—is it anything more than a theoretical conception of our minds ? We find it at the base of all the theories of science. Without it they would crumble to fragments, and nevertheless no human eye has ever seen this mysterious substratum, without beginning and without end, indestructible and eternal.

And our uncertainty is no less in the moral world. Whence do we come ? Whither are we going ? Are our dreams of happiness, justice, and truth anything more than illusions created by a congested state of the brain, and in flagrant disagreement with the murderous laws of the struggle for life ? Let us at least remain in doubt, for doubt is almost hope. We are voyaging blindly on an unknown sea of unknown things, which only become the more mysterious as we seek to discover their essence. Rarely, in this impenetrable chaos, we catch sight of sometimes a few fugitive lights, a few relative truths, which we call laws if they be not too ephemeral. Let us resign ourselves to knowing no more than these uncertainties ; they are fickle guides, no doubt, but they are none the less all that are accessible to us. Science can invoke no others. The gods of barbarism gave us no better. Truly they gave man hopes, but it was not the gods who taught him to utilise to his own profit the forces that surrounded him, and thus to render his existence less painful.

Happily for humanity, it has no need to seek its motives

of action in the cold and inaccessible regions of pure science. It has always demanded illusions to charm it, and dreamers to lead it. They have never been lacking : political chimeras, religious chimeras, military chimeras, social chimeras, they have always exercised a sovereign empire over us. These deceiving phantoms have been and will always be our masters. Since the time, thousands of years ago, when man first emerged from primitive savagery, he has never ceased from creating himself illusions to adore, nor from founding his civilisations upon them. Each has charmed him for a certain period, long or short, but the hour has always sounded when they have ceased to charm him, and then he deposes them with as great efforts as those with which he enthroned them. Once again humanity returns to its eternal task ; without doubt the only one that can make it forget its hardness of its destiny. The theorists of Socialism are only recommencing the heavy task of erecting a new god, destined to replace those of the past, until the time when inevitable evolution condemns it to perish in its turn.

CHAPTER II

THE FUTURE OF SOCIALISM

1. *Summary :*—Summary of the conditions favourable or unfavourable to the development of Socialism—Present power of Socialism. 2. *The elements of success of Socialism :*—Fundamental principles of Socialism —Socialism constitutes a mental state rather than a doctrine — Its danger resides not in the adherence of the crowd, but in that of enlightened minds—Social upheavals begin always from above and not from below—The example of the Revolution—The prevailing state of mind at the time of the Revolution—Its analogy to the present time —The directing classes are to-day losing all faith in the justice of their cause—The promises of Socialism. 3. *What will come of the success of Socialism in the nations in which it triumphs :*—Opinion of eminent modern thinkers—They all arrive at the same conclusions—The immediate destiny of the nations in which Socialism should establish itself — Disorganisation and anarchy will promptly give rise to Cæsarism—Hypothesis of the peaceful and progressive establishment of Socialism. 4. *How the Socialists might seize on the government of a country :*—The modern armies and their mental state—The end of a society becomes inevitable when once its army turns against it—How the Hispano-American republics have fallen into anarchy through the disintegration of their armies. 5. *How Socialism may be fought against :*—The necessity of knowing the secrets of its strength and weakness, as well as the mental states of its disciples—The means of influencing crowds—Why a society must perish when its natural defenders shrink from conflict and exertion—Nations perish through effeminacy of character, not by the decrease of intelligence— How Athens, Rome, and Byzantium perished.

1. SUMMARY.

I HAVE attempted in this book to indicate not the unknown forms towards which the societies of the present day are evolving, but simply the tendencies resulting from the transformed environment produced by the new conditions of modern industry, the progress of the sciences, the connection of nation with nation by means of steam and electricity, and as many more such factors. Man, like all living creatures, cannot live without adapting himself to his surroundings. This he can do only by slow evolution, not by revolution. The determining causes of modern evolution have too recently arisen to permit of our guessing to what they will lead ; so that we can only indicate in the case of each of these causes the general direction of its probable influence.

I have shown on what points the aspirations of the Socialists are in agreement with the course of evolution as we now see it. But such agreement is very rarely to be observed. We have seen, on the contrary, that most of the Socialist aspirations are in direct contradiction with the necessities which rule the modern world, and that their realisation would lead us back to lower phases which society has passed through long ago. For this reason the present position of the nations on the scale of civilisation may be measured with sufficient accuracy by their degree of resistance to Socialistic tendencies.

The association of similar interests—the only practical form of solidarity—and economic competition, are necessities of the modern period. Socialism hardly tolerates the former, and wishes to suppress the latter. The only power it respects is that of popular assemblies. The individual is nothing to Socialism ; but as soon as the individual becomes a crowd it recognises all its rights, and notably that of absolute sovereignty. Psychology, on the contrary, teaches us that as soon as the individual makes part of a crowd he loses the greater part of the mental qualities which constitute his strength.

To suppress competition and association, as the Socialists would propose, would be to paralyse the chiefest levers of the present age. We need not inquire as to whether competition is beneficial or not; we have only to inquire whether it is inevitable, and if we find it to be so we can only try to adapt ourselves to it.

We have seen that economic competition, which would end in crushing the individual worker, has found its natural antidote, formed spontaneously, without any theorising, in the association of similar interests. Associations of workers on the one and of employers on the other hand are able to fight on an equal footing, which the isolated individual could not do. This is doubtless only the substitution of collective for individual autocracy, and we have no reason for calling the first less severe than the second. Indeed, the contrary is sufficiently evident. It is evident also that collective tyrannies have ever been the most patiently supported. The most rapacious tyrant could never have permitted himself such acts of sanguinary despotism as were perpetrated with impunity during the Revolution by obscure anonymous committees acting in the name of the collective interests, real or imaginary.

We have also seen that although Socialism is in contradiction to all the data of modern science it possesses an enormous force by the very fact that it is tending to assume a religious form. Having assumed this form it will be no longer a debatable theory, but a dogma to be obeyed—a dogma whose power over the mind will finish by becoming absolute.

It is precisely for this reason that Socialism constitutes the most formidable of the dangers that have hitherto threatened modern societies. As its complete triumph over at least one society is by no means impossible, it will be as well to indicate its consequences for any nation that may think to assure its happiness by submitting to the prescriptions of the new religion.

2. THE ELEMENTS OF SUCCESS OF SOCIALISM.

Let us first of all recall the principal Socialistic dogmas, and the factors that may end in their adoption.

If we set aside the fantastic portions of the innumerable Socialistic programmes, and consider only those parts which are essential, and which are rendered possible of realisation in certain countries by the natural evolution of things, we shall find that these programmes may be reduced to four principal points :—

1. The suppression of the too great inequality of wealth by progressive taxation, and especially by sufficiently high death duties.

2. The progressive extension of the rights of the State; or of the collectivity which will replace the State, and will differ from it only in name.

3. The resumption of the soil, capital, industries, and enterprise of all sorts by the State ; that is to say, the expropriation of the present proprietors for the profit of the community.

4. Suppression of free competition and equalisation of salaries.

The realisation of the first point is evidently possible, and we may admit in theory that there would be an advantage, or at least a kind of equity, in returning to each generation of the community the surplus of the fortunes accumulated by the preceding generations, and thus to avoid the formation of a financial aristocracy, which is often more oppressive than the old feudal system.

As for the other points, and especially the progressive extension of the rights of the State, whence would result the suppression of open competition, and finally the equalisation of salaries, these could only be realised at the price of national ruin, for such measures are incompatible

with the natural order of things, and would bring the
nation which should submit to them into such a manifest
state of inferiority, compared to its rivals, as would
promptly result in their yielding its place to them. I
do not say that this ideal will never be realised, for I have
shown that certain nations are tending to a greater and
greater extension of the part of the State; but we have
seen that these nations have by that very fact entered on
the downward path of decadence.

The Socialist ideal may therefore still be realised with
regard to these matters, and it may be realised according
to the formula indicated by Mr. Benjamin Kidd :—

"In the era upon which we are entering, the long
uphill effort to secure equality of opportunity, as well as
equality of political rights, will of necessity involve, not
the restriction of the interference of the State, but the
progressive extension of its sphere of action to almost
every department of our social life. The movement in
the direction of the regulation, control, and restriction of
the rights of wealth and capital must be expected to
continue, even to the extent of the State itself assuming
these rights in cases where it is proved that their reten-
tion in private hands must unduly interfere with the
rights and opportunities of the body of the people."

The Socialistic ideal is perfectly formulated in the
preceding lines; an ideal of base equality and humiliating servitude, which would necessarily conduct the
nations which should submit to it to the last degree of
decadence. When we see such a programme proposed
by educated people we perceive at the same moment the
headway and the mischief which the Socialistic ideas
have accomplished.

Herein lies their chief danger. Modern Socialism is
far more of a mental state than a doctrine. What makes
it so threatening is not the as yet very insignificant

changes which it has produced in the popular mind, but the already very great changes which it has caused in the mind of the directing classes. The modern *bourgeoisie* are no longer sure of their rights. Or rather they are not sure of anything, and they do not know how to defend anything. They listen to everything, and they tremble before the most pitiable windbags. They are incapable of the firm will and the severe discipline, of the community of hereditary sentiments, which are the cement of society, and without which no human association has hitherto been able to exist.

They who believe in the revolutionary instincts of crowds are the victims of the most deceptive appearances. The upheavals of the crowd are only the fury of a moment. Returning to their conservative tendencies, they quickly return to the past, and they themselves clamour for the restoration of the very idols which they broke in a moment of violence. This our history repeats on every page for the last century. Scarcely had the Revolution completed its work of destruction, when almost all that it had overthrown—political institutions or religious institutions—was re-established under new names. The river had turned aside for a moment, and had resumed its course.

Social upheavals are commenced always from above, never from below. Was it the people who started our great Revolution ? Not they, indeed ! They had never dreamed of such a thing. It was let loose by the nobility and the controlling classes. This is a fact which, it appears, is still a little novel to many minds ; but it will become a platitude when a less summary psychology than that which contents us to-day shall have made it more clearly understood that material events are always the consequence of certain unconscious states of the mind.

We know very well what was the general state of mind at the moment of the Revolution ; it was the same that we see growing up to-day : an emotional humanitarianism, which began by pastoral poems and the discourses of philosophers, and ended with the guillotine. This apparently so inoffensive sentiment it was that promptly led to the weakening and disorganisation of the directing classes. They no longer had faith in their own cause ; they were even, as Michelet has said, the enemies of their own cause. When on the night of the 4th of August, 1789, the nobility abjured its privileges and its secular rights, the Revolution was accomplished. The populace had merely to follow the hints which were given them, and as usual they carried matters to extremes. They were not long about chopping off the heads of the honest philosophers who thus abandoned their rights. History does not greatly mourn for them ; but they at least deserve the indulgence of the psychologists, who are accustomed to determine the remote causes of our actions. These rights which the nobility renounced so easily—could they, as a matter of fact, have defended them any longer ? They were under the influence of the theories, accumulated theories, and discourses of a century ; how could they have acted otherwise ? The ideas which had gradually taken possession of their minds had finally gained such empire over them that they could no longer discuss them. The forces which our unconscious desires create are always irresistible. Reason does not know them, and if she did know them she could do nothing against them.

But it is nevertheless these obscure but sovereign forces that are the very soul of history. Man has only to bestir himself, and they lead him. They knead him at their will, and will often make him act in contradiction to his most obvious interests. These are the mysterious threads which agitated the brilliant marionettes of history, of which century after century tells us the weaknesses and the exploits. We know no more of the secret causes which made them act as they did than did they themselves.

Here, I repeat, is the danger of the present hour. We are possessed of the same sentiments of sickly humanitarianism which have already given us the Revolution, the most despotic and bloodiest that the world has ever known— Napoleon, the Terror, Napoleon, and the death of three millions of men. What a service would be rendered to humanity by the benevolent divinity which should suppress, to the very last example, the lamentable race of philosophers, and at the same time the no less lamentable race of orators !

The experience of a century ago was not enough ; and it is the renascence of this very vague humanitarianism— a humanitarianism of words, not of sentiments—the disastrous heritage of our old Christian ideas, which has become the most serious element of success of modern Socialism. Under the unconscious but disintegrating influence of this sentiment the directing classes have lost all confidence in the justice of their cause. They surrender more and more to the leaders of the opposing party, who merely despise them in proportion to their concessions ; and the latter will be satisfied only when they have taken everything from their adversaries, their lives as well as their fortunes. The historian who shall know the ruin that our weakness will cause, and the downfall of the civilisations we have so ill defended, will not mourn us, and will decide that we shall have merited our fate.

We can by no means hope that the absurdity of the greater part of the Socialistic theories will hinder their triumph. As a matter of fact, these theories do not contain illusions more ridiculous than the religious beliefs which for so long ruled the minds of the nations. The defect of logic in a doctrine has never hindered its propagation. Now Socialism is far more a religious belief than a theory of reasoning. People submit to it ; they do not discuss it. But it is in every way immensely inferior to the other religions. The latter promised, after death, a happiness of which it was impossible to prove the chimerical side. The Socialist religion, instead of a celestial happiness, of which no one can prove the falsity, promises us a terrestrial happiness, of which we shall all be able easily to prove the non-fulfilment. Experience will promptly teach the disciples of the Socialist illusions the vanity of their dream, and then they will shatter with fury the idol they had adored without knowing.

3. WHAT WILL BE THE CONSEQUENCES OF SOCIALISM FOR THE NATIONS IN WHICH IT TRIUMPHS.

Before the hour of its triumph, which will be quickly followed by that of its fall, Socialism is destined to widen its influence, and no argument drawn from reason will be able to prevail against it.

Yet both the disciples of the new cult and their feeble adversaries will have received no lack of warnings. All the thinkers who have studied the subject of modern Socialism have indicated its dangers and have arrived at identical conclusions with regard to the future it holds in store for us. It would take too long to state all their opinions ; but it will not be uninteresting to quote a few.

We need go back no further than Proudhon. In his time Socialism was not nearly so threatening as it is to-day. He wrote a famous page on the future of Socialism which will doubtless be verified before very long.

"The social revolution could only end in an immense cataclysm, of which the immediate effect would be to lay waste the earth, and to confine society in a strait-waistcoat; and if it were possible that such a state of things should continue only a few weeks, to kill three or four millions of men by an unforeseen famine. When the Government is without resources; when the country is without commerce and without produce; when Paris, starving, blockaded by the provinces, receives from them neither money nor provisions; when the workers, demoralised by the politics of their clubs and the idleness of their shops, seek their subsistence as best they may; when the State requires the jewels and plate of the citizens to send to the Mint; when house-to-house requisitions are the only means of collecting taxes; when the first granary is pillaged, the first house entered, the first church profaned, the first torch kindled, the first blood spilt, the first head fallen—when the abomination of desolation has come upon all France—oh, then you will know what a social revolution is; an unbridled multitude, in arms, drunk with vengeance and with fury, armed with pikes, with hatchets, with naked swords; with cleavers and with hammers; the city mournful and silent; the police at the threshold; opinions suspected, words listened to, tears observed, sighs numbered, silence spied upon; espionage and denunciations; inexorable requisitions, forced and increasing loans, depreciated paper-money; war with neighbours on the frontiers, impitiable pro-consuls, the committee of public safety, a supreme body with a heart of brass; behold the fruits of the democratic and social revolution! With all my heart and soul I repudiate Socialism! It is impotent, immoral, fit only to make dupes and pilferers! This I declare in the face of the subterranean propaganda, the shameless sensualism, the muddy literature, the mendicity,

and the besotted state of heart and mind that are beginning to take hold on a part of the workers. I am free of
the follies of the Socialists !"

M. de Laveleye, despite his indulgence for many
Socialistic ideas, arrives at almost analogous conclusions
when he pictures, at the conclusion of a victorious
Socialist revolution, "our capitals ravaged by dynamite
and petroleum in a more savage, and, above all, a more
systematic, fashion than was Paris in 1871."

Herbert Spencer is no less gloomy. The triumph of
Socialism, he says, would be the greatest disaster the
world has ever known, and the end of it would be
military despotism.

In the last volume of his treatise on Sociology, which
ends the great work which has taken thirty-five years
to write, he has developed the preceding conclusions,
which are those of all modern thinkers. He observes
that collectivism and communism would lead us back
to primitive barbarism, and he fears such a revolution in
the near future. This victorious phase of Socialism
could not last ; but it would produce, he says, fearful
ravages among the nations which suffered from it, and
would end in the utter ruin of many of them.

Such will be, according to the most eminent thinkers,
the inevitable consequences of the near advent of
Socialism ; upheavals such as the times of the Terror and
the Commune give us but a faint idea of ; then the inevitable era of Cæsars, the Cæsars of the decadence,
capable of declaring their horses consuls, or of causing
any one who does not regard them with sufficient respect
to be immediately disembowelled before their eyes ; but
Cæsars whom the populace would put up with, as did the
Romans, when, tired of civil wars and futile discussions,
they threw themselves into the arms of tyrants. The
tyrants were occasionally killed when they became too

despotic, but they were incessantly replaced up to the hour of the final downfall and conquest by the Barbarians. Many European countries also seem fated to end under the yoke of despots, who will possibly be intelligent, but necessarily inaccessible to all pity, and supporting not the faintest appearance of contradiction.

The immediate fate of the nation which shall first see the triumph of Socialism may be traced in a few lines. The people will of course commence by despoiling and then shooting a few thousands of employers, capitalists, and members of the wealthy class; in a word, all the exploiters of labour. Intelligence and ability will be replaced by mediocrity. The equality of servitude will be established everywhere. The dream of the Socialists being accomplished, eternal felicity should reign on the earth, and Paradise descend.

Alas, no! . . . It will be hell, a terrible hell. For what will be the end of it?

The social disorganisation which the new rulers will immediately bring about will succeed horrible anarchy and general ruin. Then in all probability will appear a Marius, a Sylla, a Bonaparte, some or another general, who will re-establish peace with an iron rule, which will be preceded by immense hecatombs, which will not, as history has seen so many times, prevent him from being hailed as a liberator. And justly so, for that matter, for in default of a Cæsar a nation subjected to a Socialist *régime* would be so speedily weakened by this *régime* and by its intestine divisions that it would find itself at the mercy of its neighbours, and incapable of resisting their invasions.

In this brief view of the dangers which Socialism has in store for us, I have not spoken of the rivalry between the various sects of Socialists which would make anarchy still worse. A man is not a Socialist without hating some person or thing. The Socialists detest modern society, but they detest one another more bitterly. Already these inevitable rivalries between the sects of Socialists have led to the fall of the redoubtable *Internationale*, which for many years made the Governments tremble, and is to-day forgotten.

"One fundamental cause," writes M. de Lavelaye, "contributed to the so rapid fall of the *Internationale*. This cause was personal rivalry. As in the Commune of 1871, there were divisions, suspicions, affronts, and finally definite schisms. No authority made itself felt. Understandings became impossible ; association dissolved in anarchy ; yet another warning. What ! you want to abolish the State and suppress the leaders of industry, and you expect that order will naturally issue from the free initiative of the federated corporations ? But if you, who constitute, apparently, the cream of the working classes are utterly unable to understand one another sufficiently to maintain a society which requires no sacrifice of you, and which had only one end, an end desired by all, ' Down with Capital ! ' how will ordinary workmen be able to remain united, when it is a question, a daily question, of regulating interests in perpetual conflict, and making decisions touching the remuneration of each separate individual ? You were unwilling to give in to a general council which imposed nothing at all on you ; how, in the shops, will you obey the orders of the men who will have to determine your task and direct your work ? "

We can imagine, however, the gradual and pacific establishment of Socialism by legal measures, and we have seen that such would appear to be the probable course of events among the Latin nations, who are prepared for it by their past, and who are more and more tending in the direction of State Socialism. But we have seen also that it is precisely because they have entered on this course that they are to-day in the steep downward slope of decadence. The evil would be less extreme in appearance, but it would not be less profound in reality. The State, having successively absorbed all branches of production, "would be obliged," as Signor Molinari remarks, "to subject a portion of the nation to forced labour for the lowest living wage; in a word, to establish slavery," for the cost price of articles produced by the State is necessarily, as we have seen, higher than the cost price of production in private industry. Servitude, misery, and Cæsarism are the fatal precipices to which all the roads of the Socialists lead.

Nevertheless the frightful system would appear to be inevitable. One nation, at least, will have to suffer it for the instruction of the world. It will be one of those practical lessons which alone can enlighten the nations who are bemused with the dreams of happiness displayed before their eyes by the priest of the new faith.

Let us hope that our enemies will be the first to try this experiment. If it take place in Europe everything leads us to suppose that the victim will be a poor, half-ruined country, such as Italy. Many of her statesmen had already a presentiment of the danger when they tried for so many years to turn the storm aside by a war with their neighbours, under the guarantee of the German Alliance.

4. How the Socialists might seize on the Government of a Country.

But by what means could Socialism attain the reins of Government? How will it overturn the wall which constitutes the last support of modern societies, the army ? This would be a difficult matter to-day, but it will soon be less and less difficult, thanks to the disappearance of permanent armies. This we have already seen when considering the struggles of the classes, it will be as well to repeat it.

Hitherto the strength of an army has been determined not by the number of its soldiers, nor the perfection of its armament, but by its soul, and this soul is not formed in a day.

The few nations, such as the English, who have been able to retain a professional army, are almost free from the Socialist danger, and for this reason will, in the future, enjoy a considerable superiority over their rivals. The armies created by universal service are steadily tending to become nothing but an ill-disciplined militia, and history teaches us what they are worth in the hour of danger. Let us remember that our 300,000 Gardes Nationale, at the time of the siege of Paris, found nothing better to do than to create the Commune and burn the city. The famous advocate who passed by the only chance which offered itself of disarming the multitude, was later on obliged publicly to demand "pardon of God and man" for having left them their arms. He might have offered the excuse that he knew nothing of the psychology of the crowd, but what excuse shall we offer, who have not profited by such a lesson ?

On the day when these armed crowds, without real cohesion, and without military instincts, turn themselves, as at the time of the Commune, against the society they are intended to defend, the end of that society will not be far off. Then we shall see capitals in flames ; then will come furious anarchy, then invasion, then the iron glove of the despot liberator, and then the final decadence.

The fate which threatens us is already that of certain

peoples. We need not fly to an unknown future to find nations in which the dissolution of society has been effected by their armies. We know in what a state of miserable anarchy the Latin republics of America live. Permanent revolution, utter dilapidation of the finances, demoralisation of all the citizens, and, above all, of the military element. What goes by the name of the army is nothing but a host of undisciplined mobs, who have no mind but for rapine, and are at the disposal of the first general who is willing to lead them to pillage. And every general who wishes in his turn to seize the reins of government will always find the armed bands necessary to have his rivals assassinated, and to set himself in their place. So frequent are such affairs in all the Latin-American republics that the European papers have almost given up recording them, and are scarcely more concerned with what passes in these lamentable countries than with the affairs of the Laps. The final lot of the southern half of America will be a return to primitive barbarism, at least unless the United States do it the immense service of conquering it.

Brazil alone had to some extent escaped the general fate of which had successively fallen on all the Latin republics of America ; but at last the inevitable era of *pronunciamientos* opened for her also. On the very morrow of the day on which the too benevolent emperor allowed himself to be overthrown, the disorganisation commenced, and it commenced, as always, by the army. To-day the disorganisation is complete, and the country is given over, like the rest of the Latin-American republics, to perpetual military revolutions, and will inevitably return to barbarism, after rapidly passing through all the stages of decadence.

To drag down the richest countries of the earth to the level of the negro republics of San Domingo—this, alas !

is what the Latin race has realised in less than a century for half of the American continent. What a contrast with that which the English have done in North America ! What a contrast—ay, and what a lesson ! And how lamentable to think that such a lesson should be lost !

5. How Socialism may be Opposed.

As the experiment of Socialism must be made in some country or another, since only such an experience can cure the nations of their illusions, all our efforts should be directed to secure the accomplishment of the experiment in any country but our own. It is the duty of the writer, however small his influence may be, to do his best to avert such a disaster in his own country. He must give fight to Socialism, and retard the hour of its triumph—and in such a manner that this triumph may realise itself abroad. For this he must know the secrets of its strength and weakness, and he must also know the psychology of its disciples. Such a study was the object of this work.

The necessary work of defence is not to be undertaken with arguments capable of influencing the scientist or the philosopher. Those who are not blinded by the desire of a loud popularity, or by the illusion, of which every demagogue has been the victim, that they can control at will the monster they have unchained, know very well that man does not re-fashion societies as he pleases, that we must submit to the natural laws which are stronger than we, that a civilisation, at any given moment, is a fragment of a chain to which all the years are joined by invisible links ; that the character of a people determines its institutions and its destinies ; that this character is the work of centuries ; that societies are very certainly undergoing an incessant evolution, and that they cannot be in the future what they are to-day ; but that very certainly this inevitable evolution will not be determined by our fantasies and dreams.

It is not, I repeat, by such arguments that one may influence crowds. Such arguments as are drawn from observation, and limited by reason, are unable to convince them. Little they care for reasoning, and for books ! Neither will they suffer themselves to be seduced by those who flatter them with the most humiliating servility, as is done to-day. They give their support to those that flatter them, but they support them with a just disdain, and immediately raise the level of their demands in proportion as the flatteries become more excessive. To act on the crowd one must know how to work on their sentiments, and especially on their unconscious sentiments ; and one must never appeal to their reason, for they have none. One must accordingly be familiar with their sentiments in order to manipulate them, and to be so familiar one must be incessantly mixing with them, as do the priests of the new religion that is growing under our eyes.

Are they difficult to direct, these crowds ? One must know little of their psychology and their history to think so. Is it necessary to be a founder of religion, such as Mahomet, a hero such as Napoleon, or a visionary such as Peter the Hermit, in order to steal their hearts ? No, no ! No need of these exceptional personalities. It is only a few years since we saw an obscure general, with no greater merits than plenty of audacity, the prestige of his uniform, and the beauty of his horse, reach the very verge of supreme power, a limit which he dared not cross. A Cæsar without laurels and without faith, he recoiled before the Rubicon. Let us remember that history shows us that popular movements are in reality

only the movements of a few leaders ; let us remember
the simplicism of crowds, their immovable conservative
instincts, and, finally, the mechanism of those elements
of persuasion which I attempted to present in a preceding
volume—affirmation, repetition, contagion and prestige.
Let us remember, again, that in spite of all appearances
it is not interest, powerful though it be in the individual,
that leads the crowd. The crowd must have an ideal,
a belief, and before it becomes impassioned by its ideal
or belief it must become impassioned by its apostles.
They, and they only, by their prestige, awaken in the
popular mind those sentiments of admiration which
furnish the most solid basis of faith.

One may direct the crowd at will when one has the
will. The most uncomfortable *régimes*, the most intolerable of despots, are always acclaimed by reason of
the sole fact that they have succeeded in establishing
themselves. In less than a century the crowds have
extended their suffrages to Marat, to Robespierre, to the
Bourbons, to Napoleon, to the Republic, and to every
chance adventurer as readily as to the great men. They
have accepted liberty and servitude with equal resignation.

In order to defend ourselves, not against the crowd, but
against its leaders, we have only to wish to do so. Unhappily the great moral malady of our times, and one that
seems incurable among the Latins, is want of will. This
decay of will, coinciding with the lack of initiative and
the development of indifference, is the great danger which
threatens us.

These, no doubt, are generalities, and it would be easy
to descend from generalities to details. But how could
the march of events be altered by the counsels that a
writer might formulate ? Has he not completed his task
when he has presented the general principles of which
the consequences may easily be deduced ?

Again, it is of less importance to indicate what we ought to do than to indicate what we ought not to do. The social body is a very delicate organism, which should be touched as seldom as possible. There is nothing more lamentable for a State than to be for ever subject to the fickle and unreflecting will of the crowd. If one ought to do a great deal for the crowd, at least one ought to do very little by means of it. It would be an immense progress if we could merely give up our perpetual prospects of reform, and also the idea that we must be always changing our constitutions, our institutions, and our laws. Above all ought we to limit, and not incessantly extend, the intervention of the State, so as to force the citizens to acquire a little of the initiative and the habit of self-government which they are losing by the perpetual tutelage that they cry for.

But once, again, what is the use of expressing such wishes? Is not to wish for their realisation to wish to change our souls and to avert the course of destiny? The most immediately necessary of reforms, perhaps the only one of any real use, would be the reform of our education. But it is also the most difficult of accomplishment, for its realisation would really imply this veritable miracle—the transformation of the national mind.

How can we hope for it? And, on the other hand, how can we resign ourselves to silence, when we foresee the dangers that are approaching, and when, theoretically, it appears easy to avoid them?

If we allow doubt, indifference, the spirit of negation and criticism, and futile barren discussions and rivalries to increase their hold on us—if we continue always to call for the intervention of the State in the least affairs—we shall soon be submerged by the barbarians. We shall be obliged to give place to more vigorous peoples, and disappear from the face of the earth.

Thus perished many civilisations of the past, when their natural defenders gave up struggle and effort. The ruin of nations has never been effected by the lowering of their intelligence, but by the lowering of their character. Thus ended Athens and Rome ; thus ended Byzantium, the heir of the civilisations of antiquity, of all the dreams and all the discoveries of humanity, all the treasures of art and thought that had accumulated since the beginning of the world.

The historians relate that when the Sultan Mahomet appeared before the great city, its inhabitants, occupied in subtle theological discussions and in perpetual rivalry, took little trouble to defend it. Thus the representative of a new faith triumphed easily over such adversaries. When he had entered the famous capital, the last refuge of the lights of the old world, his soldiers promptly deprived the more noisy of these babblers of their heads, and reduced the others to servitude.

Let us strive not to imitate these descendants of too ancient races, and let us beware of their fate. Let us lose no time in barren recriminations and discussions. Let us take care to defend ourselves against the enemies who threaten us within, while yet there is no need to defend ourselves against the enemies without. Do not let us disdain the slightest effort, and let each contribute it in his sphere, however modest it may be. Let us, without ceasing, study the problems with which the sphinx confronts us, and which we must answer under pain of being devoured by her. And when we think, in our secret hearts, that such counsels are perhaps as vain as the vows made to an invalid whose days have been numbered by fate, let us act as if we did not think so.